"America's leading source of self-help legal information." ★★★★
—YAHOO!

P9-DIF-205

LEGAL INFORMATION ONLINE ANYTIME

24 hours a day

www.nolo.com

AT THE NOLO.COM SELF-HELP LAW CENTER, YOU'LL FIND

- Nolo's comprehensive Legal Encyclopedia filled with plain-English information on a variety of legal topics
- Nolo's Law Dictionary—legal terms <u>without</u> the legalese
- Auntie Nolo—if you've got questions, Auntie's got answers
- The Law Store—over 200 self-help legal products including Downloadable Software, Books, Form Kits and eGuides
- Legal and product updates
- Frequently Asked Questions
- NoloBriefs, our free monthly email newsletter
- Legal Research Center, for access to state and federal statutes
- Our ever-popular lawyer jokes

Quality LAW BOOKS & SOFTWARE FOR EVERYONE

Nolo's user-friendly products are consistently first-rate. Here's why:

- A dozen in-house legal editors, working with highly skilled authors, ensure that our products are accurate, up-to-date and easy to use
- We continually update every book and software program to keep up with changes in the law
- Our commitment to a more democratic legal system informs all of our work
- We appreciate & listen to your feedback. Please fill out and return the card at the back of this book.

OUR "NO-HASSLE" GUARANTEE

Return anything you buy directly from Nolo for any reason and we'll cheerfully refund your purchase price. No ifs, ands or buts.

Read This First

The information in this book is as up to date and accurate as we can make it. But it's important to realize that the law changes frequently, as do fees, forms, and procedures. If you handle your own legal matters, it's up to you to be sure that all information you use—including the information in this book—is accurate. Here are some suggestions to help you:

First, make sure you've got the most recent edition of this book. To learn whether a later edition is available, check the edition number on the book's spine and then go to Nolo's online Law Store at www.nolo.com or call Nolo's Customer Service Department at 800-728-3555.

Next, even if you have a current edition, you need to be sure it's fully up to date. The law can change overnight. At www.nolo.com, we post notices of major legal and practical changes that affect the latest edition of a book. To check for updates, find your book in the Law Store on Nolo's website (you can use the "A to Z Product List" and click the book's title). If you see an "Updates" link on the left side of the page, click it. If you don't see a link, that means we haven't posted any updates. (But check back regularly.)

Finally, we believe accurate and current legal information should help you solve many of your own legal problems on a cost-efficient basis. But this text is not a substitute for personalized advice from a knowledgeable lawyer. If you want the help of a trained professional, consult an attorney licensed to practice in your state.

3rd edition

Your Limited Liability Company

An Operating Manual

by Attorney Anthony Mancuso

Third Edition	January 2004
Editor	Peg Healy
Illustrator	Mari Stein
Cover Design	Susan Putney
Book Design	Stephanie Harolde
Book Production	Margaret Livingston
Proofreader	Joe Sadusky
CD-ROM Preparation	André Zivkovich
Indexer	Thérèse Shere
Printer	Delta Printing Solutions, Inc.

Mancuso, Anthony

    Your limited liability company : an operating manual / by Anthony Mancuso. -- 3rd ed.

      p. cm.

    Includes index.

    ISBN 0-87337-999-3 (alk. paper)

    1. Private companies--United States--Popular works.   I. Title.

    KF1380.Z9M3643 2004

    346.73'0668--dc22

2003061003

Copyright © 2000-2004 by Anthony Mancuso

ALL RIGHTS RESERVED.

Printed in the U.S.A.

No part of this publication may be reproduced, stored in a retrieval system, or transmitted in any form or by any means, electronic, mechanical, photocopying, recording, or otherwise without prior written permission. Reproduction prohibitions do not apply to the forms contained in this product when reproduced for personal use.

For information on bulk purchases or corporate premium sales, please contact the Special Sales Department. For academic sales or textbook adoptions, ask for Academic Sales. Call 800-955-4775 or write to Nolo at 950 Parker Street, Berkeley, CA 94710.

Acknowledgments

Many thanks to Beth Laurence and Ilona Bray for their invaluable assistance in organizing and editing the first edition of this book. Thanks also to Jaleh Doane and all of Nolo's Production Department for their great design and layout work and to André Zivkovich in Nolo's Applications Development Department for making all the forms accessible on the CD-ROM. Special thanks to Peg Healy for editing this third edition.

About the Author

Tony Mancuso is a California attorney and the author of Nolo's best-selling corporate law series, including *How to Form Your Own Corporation*, *Form Your Own Limited Liability Company,* and *How to Form Your Own Nonprofit Corporation*. Tony is also the author and programmer of Nolo's *LLC Maker*, a software program that prepares the forms to organize an LLC in each of the 50 states (plus Washington, DC). In addition, he is co-author of *How to Create a Buy-Sell Agreement*, which shows readers how to create an agreement between owners that controls the selling and transferring of shares in a corporation or LLC. Tony's recent titles include *Nolo's Quick LLC*, a book that gives readers a short course in understanding the legal and tax benefits of forming an LLC.

TABLE OF CONTENTS

Introduction

CHAPTER 1

LLC Documents and Laws

CHAPTER 2

When to Use LLC Meetings, Minutes, and Written Consents

CHAPTER 3

Preliminary Steps Before Holding an LLC Meeting

CHAPTER 4

How to Hold an LLC Meeting

CHAPTER 5

How to Prepare Written Minutes of LLC Meetings

INTRODUCTION

This book is designed to help limited liability companies (LLCs) do their own legal house-keeping efficiently and at low cost. To this end, the book shows you step by step how to comply with essential LLC legal formalities:

- hold and document LLC managers' and members' meetings

- document actions taken by managers and members without having met, and

- approve common ongoing LLC legal, tax, and business decisions.

The paperwork you'll use to provide this documentation consists of minutes and written consent forms for members and managers, together with resolution forms that are inserted into the minutes or consent forms to show approval of various types of LLC actions. To help you complete these forms, we have included detailed instructions and samples in each chapter. All of the forms are included in Appendix D and on the CD-ROM accompanying this book.

The information and forms in this book are intended for smaller LLCs. By "smaller," we mean those that are privately owned (membership interests are not offered and sold to the public) and have a manageable number of members (up to about 35) and employees (up to about 50). A typical example is a family-owned LLC or an LLC that is owned by several people. Similarly, this book addresses businesses in which the people who own a majority of the membership interests are actively involved in managing, or at least supervising, the business or have a close personal or preexisting business relationship with those who perform these tasks. LLCs in this category typically have annual sales from $100,000 to $10,000,000.

Put another way, this book is primarily intended for LLC members and managers whose interests and visions for their smaller-sized company are substantially similar. They should also routinely work together and attend to necessary legal procedures and recordkeeping without a great deal of controversy.

MANAGERS AND MEMBERS IN A SMALL LLC

In the text, we refer to managers' and members' meetings and decisions. In practice, most smaller LLCs are member-managed—that is, all members manage the LLC and there are no specifically designated "managers." If that describes your LLC, you do not need to hold separate managers' meetings to approve legal or tax decisions. Just one members' meeting will do. But if your LLC is managed by just some (not all) members, or is managed by one or more nonmembers, then you should hold separate managers' and members' meetings to approve important LLC decisions. After all, you want to make sure that all owners (all members) agree with all important decisions made by the separate management team.

THE REASON FOR THIS BOOK

You've already been through some critical, but probably tedious, LLC start-up tasks: preparing and filing articles of organization (called a "certificate of organization" in some states) and preparing and signing an LLC operating agreement. Typically, after these documents are prepared and the initial membership interests are sold to the founders and initial investors, the owners take a deep breath and get back to doing what they do best—running the day-to-day business. As a result, the owners often put off dealing with the many tasks necessary to properly run their new LLC entity.

It's foolish to neglect the ongoing legal care and feeding of your LLC entity. You can lose crucial tax benefits if you fail to properly document and support important tax decisions and elections. Even worse, the fact that you have ignored the legal technicalities of running your LLC may result in its legal existence being similarly disregarded by the courts, with the risk that you may be held personally liable for LLC debts. And, of course, as time passes and memories fade, the reasons for approval of important LLC decisions, and the extent of each member's or manager's participation in the approval of these decisions, may be forgotten. This often leads to controversy and dissension, even in the ranks of a closely held LLC. The use of written minutes, consent forms, and resolutions, which record all important LLC manager and member decisions and the votes taken to approve them, helps defuse these potential blowups.

With the help of this book, you can do most of this routine paperwork yourself. You will need a lawyer or accountant only when you need help with a complicated legal or tax issue.

And, finally, there is a practical reason for going to the trouble of preparing paperwork to authorize and record ongoing LLC business. The LLC, unlike its famous limited liability counterpart, the corporation, is a new type of legal animal. Banks, creditors, suppliers, escrow and title companies, and other businesses generally are less familiar with the LLC legal entity. You'll undoubtedly find that your business will benefit enormously if you prepare and present these outsiders with written LLC minutes and resolutions that show specific approval of the loan, contract, or real estate transaction at hand.

WHY KEY LLC DECISIONS SHOULD BE RECORDED

The good news is that you don't need to document routine business decisions—only those that require formal manager or membership approval. In other words, it's not required by law or practice that you clutter up your LLC records binder with mundane business records about:

- purchasing supplies or products
- hiring or firing minor employees
- deciding to launch new services or products, or
- other ongoing business decisions.

However, key legal, tax, and financial decisions absolutely should be acted on and recorded by your managers and/or members. These kinds of decisions are considered "key":

- the proceedings of annual meetings of managers and/or members
- the admission of a new member by the LLC
- the buyback of an existing membership interest by the LLC
- the purchase of real estate
- the authorization of a significant loan or substantial line of credit, and
- the making of important federal or state tax elections.

These, and other important decisions, should be made by your managers and/or members and backed with legal paperwork. That way, you'll have solid documentation if key decisions are questioned or reviewed later by managers, members, creditors, the courts, or the IRS.

There's more good news about the task ahead of you. As you'll learn, having your managers and members ratify important LLC decisions doesn't necessarily mean dragging everyone to formal meetings every time. Valid LLC decisions can also be made by other means of communication. Some states allow methods of voting in addition to voting in person or by written consent. (Check your state LLC Act in Appendix B.)

If decisions are made using these less formal methods, there are several easy ways to document them: You can prepare written minutes for a "paper" LLC meeting or written consent forms to be signed by the managers and members. No meeting need be held in these cases. Instead, managers and members sign the minutes or the consent form that records their agreement to a particular transaction or decision.

Why bother to prepare minutes of meetings or written consents for important LLC decisions? Here are a few excellent reasons:

- Annual LLC meetings may be required under your state law. If you fail to pay at least minimal attention to this and other ongoing legal formalities, you may lose the protection of your LLC limited liability status. If this happens, LLC members can be held personally liable for the debts of the LLC.

- Your legal paperwork provides a record of important LLC transactions. This "paper trail" can be important if disputes arise. It will show your managers, members, creditors, and suppliers; the IRS; and the courts that you acted appropriately and in compliance with legal requirements.

- Formally documenting key LLC actions is a fail-safe way to keep all members (managing as well as nonmanaging) informed of major LLC decisions.

- Managers and members of small LLCs commonly approve business transactions in which they have personal, material, or financial interests. Your minutes or consent forms can help prevent legal problems by proving that these "self-interested" decisions were arrived at fairly, after full disclosure to the disinterested managers and members.

- Institutions like banks, trust companies, escrow companies, title companies, and property management companies often ask LLCs to submit a copy of a manager or membership resolution that approves the transaction that is being undertaken, such as taking out a loan or purchasing or renting property.

How to Use This Book

Let's face it—you've got more important and interesting work to do than to spend your days reading a book about LLC forms and formalities. So here are some suggestions on how to most efficiently use this book:

- Begin by reading Chapters 1 and 2. These chapters give you the legal background information on LLCs and LLC decision making. They compare and contrast different ways to get things done in the LLC context. Then, for a particular decision at hand, you can decide whether you'll (1) hold a meeting of your managers and/or members, (2) prepare minutes for a meeting that doesn't actually occur (called a "paper" meeting), or (3) obtain the written consent of your managers and/or members to the action or decision at hand.

- If you decide to hold a real meeting of your managers and/or members, follow the steps covered in Chapters 3 and 4 to prepare for and hold the meeting. Then prepare the appropriate minutes form to document the decisions taken at the meeting, following the step-by-step instructions in Chapter 5.

- If you opt for a "paper" meeting—one that occurs on paper only but reflects the real decisions of your managers and members—follow the instructions for creating minutes for a paper meeting in Chapter 6.

- To document a particular decision by preparing written consent forms to be signed by the managers and/or members, follow the instructions in Chapter 7.

- In addition, if a business deal or transaction needs to be approved and is covered by a resolution included in this book (Chapters 8 through 15), fill in the resolution form following the instructions contained in the appropriate chapter, then place or paste the completed resolution into your minutes or consent form. (See the beginning of Appendix D for a list of resolution forms included with this book, with a cross-reference to the chapter and section of the book that contains instructions for preparing each resolution).

Each chapter has sample forms and line-by-line instructions for all LLC minutes, consents, and resolutions. The forms themselves are provided in two formats: Appendix D at the back of the book contains tear-out versions that you can fill in with a typewriter or pen. The CD-ROM included with this book contains text-only and word-processing versions of each form for use on your computer. (For specific instructions on selecting and using the computer forms, see Appendix A, How to Use the CD-ROM.)

All of this may sound like a lot of work. Don't worry—all of the steps and forms are covered in sequence, and we carefully explain each in detail. As you'll see, there are often several approaches to accomplishing necessary tasks, so you can often skip good-sized chunks of material.

WHEN TO CONSULT A PROFESSIONAL

Small, privately held LLCs routinely hold LLC meetings and prepare standard resolutions and other legal paperwork. But it's a fact of business life that a particular tax or legal formality may present important legal, tax, or financial considerations.

Even professionals feel the need to consult other professionals in areas that are new to them. You should take advantage of this commonsense business precaution. Please see a tax or legal specialist before using the forms in this book if any of the following are true:

- The decision you are facing is complex.

- You anticipate any complications or objections.

- You simply have questions and need more information.

A consultation of this sort will be far more cost-effective than making the wrong decision and having to fix it later. For information on choosing and using a legal or tax professional, see Chapter 16.

NOTES AND ICONS

Throughout the text, we have included special notations and icons to help organize the material and underscore particular points:

 A suggestion to seek the advice of a professional.

 The "Fast track" marker letting you know that you may be able to skip some material that doesn't apply to your situation.

 A caution to slow down and consider potential problems.

 A legal or commonsense tip to help you understand or comply with legal requirements.

 A reminder.

 Instructions or notes about using the files on the CD-ROM.

 A suggestion to consult another book or resource.

LLC Documents and Laws

By the time you finish this book, you'll know how to request and hold LLC meetings for members and managers. You'll know how to conduct votes and record LLC decisions. And, you'll become familiar with a bucketful of new terms and procedures. Mastering this material isn't difficult, but it does require attention to some unfamiliar detail. In this chapter we provide legal and practical background information about basic LLC documents and the state LLC laws on which they are based.

When to skip this material

If you recently formed an LLC and feel you understand the purpose of your articles of organization and ymour operating agreement and the need for LLC records, much of the material in this chapter may seem old hat. If so, skip ahead to Chapter 2 for an overview of the common methods of ongoing LLC decision making. These include holding LLC meetings and preparing written consents of manager and member decisions.

A. ORGANIZE YOUR LLC RECORDS

Anyone who sets up an LLC needs to be able to quickly locate key organizational documents. These are your LLC articles of organization (sometimes called a "certificate of formation" or a "certificate of organization") and operating agreement. Because these are really the constitution of your LLC, you'll refer to them again and again. When using this book to produce LLC minute and consent forms, you'll often be referred to your LLC's organizational documents.

If you have not already done so, set up an LLC records binder that contains all key LLC documents. You can do this on your own with a three-ring binder.

Your LLC records binder should contain:

- articles of organization (see Section A1, below)

- operating agreement (see Section A2, below)

- membership certificates and stubs (if your LLC decides to issue certificates to members—see Section A3, below)

- membership register that lists the names and addresses of your members (see Section A4, below)

- membership transfer ledger, showing the dates of any transfers of membership interests by a member (see Section A5, below), and

- minutes of LLC meetings and written consent forms (see Section A6, below).

If someone helped you form your LLC, such as a lawyer, accountant, paralegal, or financial planner, you probably received copies of these documents. However, some lawyers attempt to hold on to LLC records in the hope that you will have them take care of all ongoing technicalities. If so, you will need to request copies of all the LLC documents in your client file. (In California, you are entitled to the *original* LLC documents, although the lawyer can keep copies, made at the lawyer's expense.) This is your property, so don't take "No" for an answer.

If you can't locate a copy of your articles, write your Secretary of State's LLC filing office and request a certified or file-stamped copy of your articles. (Appendix B lists state LLC filing offices and their addresses and phone numbers.) It's a good idea to call first so that you can also send the correct copying fee, which should be just a few dollars.

LLC RECORDS REQUIRED UNDER STATE LAW

In many states the LLC Act has a provision listing the records required to be maintained by LLCs. These records must be available for inspection by members and managers. Below is a representative statute, taken from Section 9 of the Massachusetts Limited Liability Company Act.

Note that you must keep copies of tax returns and a list of members' capital contributions, either as part of the operating agreement or in a separate statement. This is typical of state LLC records requirements.

a. Each limited liability company shall keep at its records office—usually the principal office—the following:

    1. a current list of the full name and last known address of each member and manager;

    2. a copy of the certificate of organization [this is the Massachusetts name for articles of organization] and all certificates of amendment thereto, together with executed copies of any powers of attorney pursuant to which any certificate has been issued [in case a certificate was signed by an outsider under a power of attorney];

    3. copies of the limited liability company's federal, state, and local income-tax returns and reports, if any, for the three most recent years;

    4. copies of any then effective written operating agreements and of any financial statements of the limited liability company for the three most recent years; and

    5. unless contained in a written operating agreement, a writing setting out:

        i. the amount of cash and a description and statement of the agreed value of the other property or services contributed by each member and which each member has agreed to contribute;

        ii. the times at which or events on the happening of which any additional contributions agreed to be made by each member are to be made;

        iii. any right of a member to receive, or of a manager to make, distributions to a member; and

        iv. any events upon the happening of which the limited liability company is to be dissolved and its affairs wound up.

b. Records kept under this section shall be subject to inspection and copying at the reasonable request and at the expense of any member or manager during ordinary business hours.

1. Articles of Organization

The first key organizing document any LLC must have is its articles of organization (in some states, this document is called a certificate of organization or certificate of formation). An LLC comes into existence when its articles of organization are filed with the state LLC filing office. The articles normally contain fundamental structural information about the company, such as:

- the name of the LLC
- whether the LLC is managed by all of its members or by specially selected managers (most smaller LLCs are member-managed)
- the names and addresses of its members and/or managers and its registered agent, and
- the agent's office address (this is the registered office of the LLC to which legal papers can be sent by the state and by persons serving legal process on the LLC).

For the majority of small LLCs, no additional information is required in this document. However, larger LLCs sometimes add optional articles containing special provisions if they wish to set up a more complex structure for their LLC.

> **EXAMPLE:** The Equity Investors Capital LLC adopts articles that specify a multiclass membership structure for the LLC, consisting of Class A Voting Memberships and Class B Nonvoting Memberships. The reason for this two-class membership structure is that the primary investors (Class A) will be issued voting, managing memberships, while nonmanaging members will receive nonvoting membership interests (Class B).

To prepare and file articles for a new LLC
If you have not yet formed your LLC, Nolo publishes *Form Your Own Limited Liability Company*, also by Anthony Mancuso. This book shows you how to prepare and file articles of organization with your state's LLC filing office. It also takes you through the other LLC formation steps, including the preparation of an LLC operating agreement. This book is good in all states, with state-by-state rules included in Appendix A. In addition, *Nolo's LLC Maker* software creates articles of organization and operating agreements for every state.

AMENDING YOUR ARTICLES: DO YOUR ARTICLES LIMIT THE TERM OF YOUR LLC?

Early state LLC statutes, adopted when the LLC legal form was just gaining ground, required LLCs to limit the duration of the LLC in their articles—for example, to a term of 30 years—and on that date the LLC would automatically dissolve. This state term-limit requirement was tied to old federal tax classification rules that said LLCs needed to limit their term in order to be treated as a partnership for tax purposes (the tax treatment most LLC owners desire for their LLC). Under the current IRS rules, however, an LLC is automatically treated as a partnership for tax purposes, so most states have eliminated this "limited term" requirement in their state LLC Act. (You probably dealt with this requirement when you formed your LLC, so we don't include it in Appendix B of this book, where we provide state laws on many ongoing LLC issues. You can find this information in Appendix A of Nolo's *Form Your Own Limited Liability Company* or by researching your state's laws yourself—see Section C, below.)

If your LLC articles do contain a provision that limits the term of your LLC, and you know your state no longer requires this limitation, you have two choices:

1. File an amendment to your articles that deletes the limitation of the term of your LLC—just retype your articles, omitting the provision that limits the term of your LLC—and file the amended articles with the state LLC filing office.

2. Do nothing for now. You can file the amendment to the articles later, just before the end of the term stated in your articles.

2. LLC Operating Agreement

The LLC operating agreement is an LLC's second-most important document. The operating agreement does not need to be filed with the state—it is an internal document, much like corporate bylaws or a partnership agreement. It lists the capital, profits, and voting interests of current members of the LLC. The operating agreement may specify:

- the frequency of regular meetings of managers and members, and

- the call, notice, quorum, and voting rules for each type of meeting. Or it may be silent on these issues, leaving these details to the LLC managers and members to decide later. Typically, state requirements for approving special matters are also included in the operating agreement. This includes any state-mandated manager and member voting requirements for admitting new members or for approving the sale of a membership interest by a current member to a new member.

⚠️ State LLC voting rules are changing

As part of their LLC statutes, many states originally passed voting rules that required a majority of, or all, LLC members to vote to approve the admission of a new member who was transferred a membership from a prior member. State rules also required a majority of all members to vote to continue the legal existence of the LLC after a member died, withdrew, or otherwise gave up his or her membership interest. These rules were passed by states simply to help LLCs qualify for partnership classification with the IRS. They are no longer necessary (since LLCs are now automatically treated as partnerships for tax purposes by the IRS and most states). Most states have eliminated or are in the process of eliminating these unnecessary voting requirements, but operating agreements still may contain these rules. If yours does, you can keep these rules in your agreement and

follow them, if and when a member transfers an interest to a new member or when a member dies or departs the LLC. After all, it should not be difficult to get all members to approve the admission of a new member or the continuance of the LLC. If you can't obtain approval, chances are there is dissension that you will need to deal with, before getting on with the business of your LLC.

📖 If you haven't prepared an operating agreement

You may have formed your LLC in a hurry, by filing articles of organization as the only organizational formality. If so, you need to take the extra step of preparing a basic operating agreement for your LLC. You can use Nolo's *Form Your Own Limited Liability Company* or *LLC Maker* to prepare your agreement.

3. Membership Certificates and Stubs

It is not legally necessary to issue membership certificates to members. However, some LLC owners like this additional formality.

Typically, there is no state-required format for such membership certificates. Most certificates show the name of the LLC, the name of the member, and the date of issuance of the certificate. Certificates are signed by one or more LLC officers (the LLC president and secretary, typically). A certificate normally does not show the exact capital, profits, or voting interests of an member; instead, it simply recites that the member is entitled to the rights and subject to the responsibilities of membership, as set out in the articles of organization and operating agreement of the LLC. After the certificate is issued to a member, a certificate stub is filled out by the LLC secretary, showing the date of issuance and certificate number. The certificate stubs are kept in the LLC records binder. The stubs usually contain a transfer section that is completed if and when a member transfers the membership back to the LLC or to another person.

4. Membership Register

State law generally requires an LLC to keep an alphabetical list of the names and addresses of all current members. This list can be inspected by any member during regular business hours of the LLC. It should also be made available for inspection to all members at any membership meeting. This list is used by the LLC secretary to prepare and mail notice of meetings to members. If the LLC is managed by specially selected managers, the LLC should have a list of the managers' names and addresses.

5. Membership Transfer Ledger

You should keep a record of the date and details of any transfers of membership in your LLC. Typically, a membership transfer ledger shows:

- the name of the transferring member (the transferor)

- the date of the transfer of membership, and

- the name of the transferee (the person or entity to whom the membership is transferred).

If a membership is redeemed (bought back) by the LLC itself, the transferee is the LLC.

If the transferring member was originally issued a membership certificate, the certificate should be returned to the LLC, marked "canceled" by the LLC secretary, and attached to the transfer ledger. If your LLC issues membership certificates with stubs, and the stubs contain a transfer section for supplying transfer information, the retained certificate stubs can serve as your membership transfer ledger.

6. Minutes of LLC Meetings and Written Consent Forms

If your LLC has been in existence for some time, you may have previously prepared minutes of LLC manager or member meetings or written consent forms. This is especially likely if a lawyer helped you form your LLC. Contact your attorney to get copies of previously prepared minutes and written consents, and place them in your LLC records binder.

If you have not prepared minutes or written consent forms, this book shows you how to prepare them (in Chapter 5 and Chapter 7). You will add these items to your LLC records binder on an ongoing basis.

B. State LLC Filing Offices

Each state has an LLC filing office where you can file paperwork and pay filing fees to:

- create your LLC

- change your LLC structure by filing amendments to your articles of organization, and

- dissolve your LLC by filing LLC dissolution papers.

Typically, the state office that handles LLC filings is the Secretary or Department of State, located in the state capital. But some states have a different name for this office, and some maintain branch offices in satellite cities where LLC filings also can be made. Usually, the Corporations Section or Division within the Secretary or Department of State's office handles LLC filings, but some states set up a special LLC section or division for this purpose. Throughout this book, we refer to the office that accepts LLC filings as the state LLC filing office. A listing of the name, address, telephone number, and Web address (URL) of each state's LLC filing office is provided in Appendix B.

State LLC filing offices are sometimes divided into departments that oversee special areas, such as LLC name availability, LLC fee information, and LLC legal counsel. Regardless of how your state's LLC filing office is organized, you'll normally find that the main phone number for the LLC filing office will lead you through a voice system to the particular LLC department where you want to go.

Contact your state LLC filing office on the Internet

All Secretary of State and other state LLC filing offices have websites. On many of these, you can click a button to go to a page for the Corporations or LLC Section or Division. There you can download LLC statutory forms (articles of organization, reservation of LLC name, amendment of LLC articles, change of LLC registered agent or registered office address, and the like). Many of these sites also contain links to your state's business tax, employer registration, state licensing, and other offices and agencies. To find out the Web address of your state LLC filing office, check your state's listing in Appendix B.

C. STATE LLC LAWS

In addition to the rules and procedures set out in your articles of organization and operating agreement, the organization and the operation of LLCs are regulated by laws adopted by each state. The primary source of laws that apply to your LLC will be found in your state's LLC laws (statutes). It is usually titled as follows: "[Name of your state] Limited Liability Company Act." Legal citations to sections of a state's LLC law are usually given in the following form: "Sec. 21.2 of the [name of state] LLC Act" or "Article 2-12, LLCA."

You can look up your LLC law yourself. LLC statutes are organized by subject matter and are well indexed and cross-referenced. For the most part, the statutes themselves state fairly simple rules or requirements that, despite the inevitable lawyer jargon, can be comprehended by the average reader. Here are three easy ways to find your state's LLC Act:

- Most states have placed their LLC Act on the Web for viewing and downloading. See the website for your state's LLC office, listed in Appendix B. Follow the instructions in Appendix B for how to link to the LLC Act if available in your state.

- Many state LLC filing offices provide a copy of the state's LLC Act for free or for a small charge. Or, they may refer you to a commercial publisher that sells a volume containing your state's LLC statutes.

- Visit a local law library, a law school library that is open to the public, or a larger public library with a good business collection. Ask the research librarian to show you where the business law material is shelved. (Most LLC Acts are bound along with the state's Business Corporation Act or Corporations Code.) The majority of LLC law volumes are published as annotated codes. These include annotations (references) to court cases that have relied on or discussed sections of the LLC law. They also have cross-references to related code sections, law review articles, and other sources of relevant legal information. Admittedly, we're in the early days of LLC case law, and normally you won't find many references to help you understand an LLC statute, but, on occasion, an annotation will be given.

LLC ACT SIMILARITIES

The basic LLC statutes of many states contain the same, or quite similar, rules for organizing and operating LLCs. The reason for this uniformity is that many states have borrowed from one another in drafting their original LLC laws. More recently, a Model LLC Act and a Uniform LLC Act have been drafted. These acts will help states achieve even greater uniformity as they draw from these sources to adopt changes to existing LLC statutes.

D. OTHER STATE LAWS

In addition to a state's LLC Act, other state laws regulate special areas of LLC activity. These include the following.

Securities Act, or "Blue Sky" laws. These laws contain each state's rules and procedures for offering, issuing or selling securities. In many states, LLC membership interests are considered securities, just like stock interests in a corporation or ownership interests in limited partnerships. Therefore, they must be registered with the state, or must qualify for a state exemption from registration, before being issued to members. In some states, like California, sales of membership interests are exempted from the securities laws if all members are active in the LLC business. In other states, streamlined notice procedures can be used to register LLC memberships if they are issued to a limited number of people privately within the state.

Tax or Revenue Code. Each state's Tax or Revenue Code (or similar law) regulates the taxation of business profits. In most states, LLC profits pass through to the members and are reported on their individual state income tax return (if the state imposes an individual state income tax). In some states, LLCs must pay a separate entity-level income or franchise tax like a corporation. We list the Web address of your state's tax or revenue office in Appendix B. That website should link you to state tax publications and LLC-related tax statutes.

Commercial Code. The state's Commercial Code contains the rules for entering into and enforcing commercial contracts, promissory notes, and other standard commercial documents.

Other state and local laws. Various state laws may affect the activities and operations of all businesses, whether operated as LLCs or otherwise, for example:

- state and local building codes
- professional and vocational licensing laws, and
- zoning and public health laws.

These special state statutes are carried in law and business libraries, and may be posted on your state's website. (For tips on locating state statutes, see Section C, above.) ■

CHAPTER 2

When to Use LLC Meetings, Minutes, and Written Consents

- **Approval of a management decision.** Management decisions, such as approval of a standard sales contract, are just the sort of decisions that fall within the purview of the management team. The managers should meet or sign a written consent to signify their formal approval.

- **Approval of a decision that significantly impacts LLC profitability or involves the personal financial interests of one or more managers.** It is wise to have all members who do not also serve as managers join the managers in approving decisions of this sort. This is easily accomplished by holding a joint meeting of all managers and members. Or, you can have all managers and members sign a written consent to the decision. (As you'll see in the succeeding chapters, our minute and consent forms accommodate attendance and approval by either managers or members or both.) After all, if a course of LLC action will reduce or gamble LLC profits, obtaining the advance approval of all members can help avoid membership complaints later if the LLC loses money on the decision or deal. And if an action may benefit one or more managers personally—such as a hefty pay raise for a manager (who also works as an LLC officer and receives an officer salary) or the lease of property by a manager to the LLC—asking members to approve it is just fair play and common sense. If, after full disclosure, the members approve a deal that benefits a manager personally, it's less likely that a member will complain (or sue) later. (Self-interested transactions are specifically covered in Chapter 15.) The point here is to treat nonmanaging members in a manager-managed LLC just as you would any outside investor in a business: You don't normally need to let them in on basic managerial decisions that are meant to be decided by the managers themselves—in fact, nonmanaging members usually won't want to get involved in these decisions. But you will want to get their advance approval for decisions that may affect their pocketbook or upset them if they're surprised by them later.

How to proceed once you are ready to act
If you are already sure of how you want to conduct most of your official LLC business (that is, how you'll make certain types of decisions)—whether in face-to-face meetings, paper meetings, or written consent forms—you may want to skip the rest of this chapter. If so, here's where to go next:

- **Real meeting with minutes.** Chapters 3 and 4 cover the steps necessary to hold a real LLC meeting of managers and/or members. Chapter 5 shows how to prepare minutes to document the decisions reached at those meetings.

- **Paper meeting with minutes.** Chapter 6 explains how to prepare written minutes for a paper meeting to document a decision as though it were reached at a real meeting.

- **Action by written consent.** Chapter 7 covers the procedure and forms necessary to obtain manager and/or member approval by written consent.

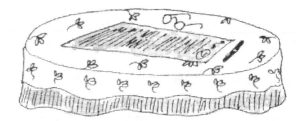

C. QUESTIONS AND ANSWERS ABOUT LLC MEETINGS, MINUTES, AND WRITTEN CONSENTS

The questions and answers below shed light on the advantages and disadvantages of each of the three LLC decision-making formalities. It's important to recognize that there is no one best way for all LLCs to proceed. LLCs, large and small, take advantage of each of these procedures to varying degrees. Which method they use depends on:

- the nature of their business
- the type of decision involved, and
- the amount of time available to make and document a particular decision.

We suggest you read this material and then consider which approach or approaches are best for you.

1. Should You Hold a Real or a Paper Meeting?

A real meeting allows the participants to meet face to face and arrive at decisions that require the give-and-take of conversation, argument, or persuasion. It results in a formal record of the meeting's activity. A paper meeting, like a real meeting, also results in the preparation of formal minutes that document manager or member decisions, but does not require the time and effort involved in getting everyone together for a meeting. The written consent procedure is the quickest and simplest of all, allowing the managers or members to agree to an uncontested item of business with a minimum of formality and paperwork.

Sometimes it will be clear that you really do need to hold a formal meeting. In other situations, it would be a waste of time to do so. You can use whichever method works best under the circumstances.

If you have a one-member LLC that you manage yourself

In practice, member meetings for a one-member LLC and manager meetings for a one-manager LLC are often held on paper only, to formally record decisions that the sole member or manager wishes to document. If you are in this situation, turn to Chapter 6, where we focus on the steps you need to take to prepare minutes for this type of "paper meeting." You may also record decisions by written consents (see Chapter 7) or hold a real one-person meeting (you can talk to yourself if you wish).

2. When Should LLCs Hold Formal Meetings?

LLC operating agreements sometimes require annual meetings of members and, in manager-managed LLCs, annual meetings of managers. In manager-managed LLCs, the annual members' meeting is held first, in order to elect the managers for the upcoming year. After the members' meeting, and usually on the same day, the annual managers' meeting is held. At this meeting, the managers accept their positions for the upcoming year and tend to any business and LLC planning that is appropriate.

All other meetings of the managers or members are special meetings, which may be called (requested) anytime during the year, according to rules contained in the operating agreement. Special meetings may be called to discuss urgent items of business or approve legal or tax formalities that arise from time to time. For example, a special meeting might be called to approve:

- the adoption of a new LLC tax year recommended by the LLC's accountant
- the conditions of an LLC loan made to an officer of the LLC, or
- a bank loan or real estate transaction.

3. Why Bother to Document LLC Decisions With Minutes or Written Consent Forms?

LLC minutes and consent forms serve a dual role. They not only show that important LLC decisions were reached with the proper notice and vote of your managers or members, but they also allow you to set out the reasons for these decisions. This can be crucial later if an LLC decision is examined by the IRS as part of a tax audit or scrutinized by a court as evidence in a lawsuit. In other words, minutes serve to document and substantiate important LLC decisions.

Likewise, your minutes may be used to document LLC strategies or decisions to incur expenses that might give rise to controversy or even lawsuits, (Lawsuits may arise among the members and managers themselves, as well as from creditors making claims against the LLC because of a negligent or wrong-headed LLC decision.) Examples include:

- settling a claim against a disgruntled employee
- setting the buyout price to purchase the membership interest of a departing member, or

• deciding to implement safeguards in a hazardous location or line of LLC activity (for instance, paying for protective measures for pedestrians at a construction site or implementing manufacturing controls in producing a consumer product).

Even if your managers or members don't need to actually meet to reach a decision, it looks good to prepare regular minutes or consent forms. If, for example, you later sell your business, a formal record-keeping system can make your business look even better and more substantial. Minutes and consent forms can be important, in themselves, to show that you respect and are entitled to the benefits that arise from the separate legal status of your LLC.

> **EXAMPLE:** In preparation for a lawsuit against the LLC by an unpaid creditor, the creditor's attorney requests copies of minutes of all annual and special meetings of your members and managers. If your LLC record binder is bare, or contains minutes for just a few meetings over the life of your LLC, the plaintiff will stand a better chance of convincing the judge that the LLC is simply an alter ego of the LLC principals—its members and managers—who should therefore be held personally liable for any money judgment obtained against the LLC.

4. What Paperwork Should an LLC Prepare?

Here's our recommendation for your paper trail: At a minimum, prepare written minutes (for either real or paper meetings) for any annual meetings scheduled in your operating agreement. Typically, this means preparing minutes for an annual members' meeting. Manager-managed LLCs will also prepare minutes for the annual managers' meeting that follows.

Also prepare formal LLC documentation for all important legal, tax, financial, or business decisions reached by the managers or members during the year. This documentation can be in the form of minutes for special meetings—either real or on paper—or written consent forms signed by your managers or members.

By preparing this simple paperwork, you will have prepared a paper trail of important LLC decisions, which should give your LLC records binder enough girth to help satisfy courts, the IRS, and others that you have attended to the necessary legal and tax niceties.

5. When Can Written Consents Be Used Safely?

Legally, written consents work just as well as written minutes of meetings to document manager or member decisions. They are the quickest way to approve and document a formal decision by an LLC's managers or members, since they do not require the time and effort needed to hold a meeting and prepare minutes (or document a paper meeting). Managers or members simply sign consent forms that state the action or business approved. The written consent forms are then placed in the LLC records binder as proof of the decision.

But written consents do have weaknesses. Depending on the situation, you may decide to use written consents anyway, but you should do so after careful consideration of their potential problems. Okay, what's the downside?

For managers or members who not directly work in the business, a request to sign a written consent form may come as a surprise. After all, they may not have any idea about the LLC action or decision at hand, nor the reasons why it should be approved. As explained in Section 7, below, many LLCs decide that a real meeting works best to let outsiders know the reasons for important LLC decisions.

This being said, there is still a role for the written consent procedure in many circumstances:

• **One-person or two-person LLCs.** Written consent forms are particularly useful in one-person, member-managed LLCs where one individual owns and manages the LLC as its only member. The consent form procedure allows the sole LLC manager-member to formally approve LLC decisions without going to the trouble of preparing minutes for a pretend meeting. The same holds true for a member-managed LLC where two people who work closely are the only persons active in the business.

- **In larger LLCs, to document noncontroversial or time-sensitive decisions.** Particularly where time is of the essence and where a face-to-face meeting of managers or members is not necessary, it may make sense to take action by written consent.

EXAMPLE 1: Better Mousetraps, LLC, a member-managed LLC, is advised by its accountant to pass a resolution approving a change in tax year. After discussing this issue briefly, its LLC president asks the LLC secretary to prepare a written consent form for the members to sign that shows their approval of the tax election. They see no need to meet in person to approve the decision or to prepare paper minutes for a fictitious meeting. In this situation, either of these procedures seems like overkill for this simple tax formality.

EXAMPLE 2: The treasurer of Best Business Bureaus, Ltd. Liability Co., a commercial furniture supplier organized as a manager-managed LLC, decides to ask the managers to approve an LLC 401(k) profit-sharing plan for employees. A special meeting of managers is scheduled to discuss whether the LLC will make matching contributions for employees and to hear various LLC personnel, including the chairperson of the Employee Benefits Committee, who wish to present to the managers different opinions on the advisability of adopting a plan and the level of LLC contributions to be made.

At this meeting, comments and feedback are exchanged before the managers reach a decision on options available under the plan. This allows the managers a chance to discuss the financial implications and pros and cons of this important piece of LLC business. Because of the complexity of the issues involved, a real face-to-face meeting is more appropriate here than paper minutes or written consents.

6. What's the Best Way to Hold Meetings for Closely Held LLCs?

A small, "closely held" LLC—that is, one owned and operated by a close-knit group of friends, family, and business associates—has only a few members, who are usually all active in the business. The typical closely held LLC is member-managed by all members.

In a closely held LLC with an annual meeting of members scheduled in the operating agreement, minutes are typically prepared for a paper meeting. These minutes show the approval by members of the prior year's business and approval of plans for undertaking business in the new year. In a small, manager-managed LLC, the paper meeting is a joint managers'/members' meeting. The members re-elect the current managers to another term, and the re-elected managers accept their positions by approving the minutes of a paper meeting.

EXAMPLE: Windows, Drapes, Sofas, and Ottomans, LLC, is a closely held LLC owned by members Saul and Barbara, a married couple. Barbara is the designated manager of the manager-managed LLC (Saul stays in the background as an investor in the spousal LLC). At the end of each LLC fiscal year, Saul and Barbara approve minutes of a paper meeting that show that they both vote to re-elect Barbara as manager, and that Barbara accepts her manager role for another year. (The meeting is a joint managers'/members' meeting.) If any important decisions need to be reached for the upcoming fiscal year, these decisions are also noted in the minutes, along with Barbara's managerial approval.

Special meetings of the managers and members of closely held LLCs follow a similar pattern. If the resolution or business at hand is a tax or legal formality that everyone agrees must be made, special meetings of members and/or managers are often held on paper, not in person. But if the issue that forms the basis of the special meeting requires discussion (such as the approval of competing bids for the remodeling of LLC headquarters), then the members or managers often decide to get together for a real meeting. At the meeting, they discuss the pros and cons of the proposed business, prior to making a decision and preparing minutes.

MANAGER-MANAGEMENT VS. MEMBER-MANAGEMENT
WITH NONVOTING MEMBERS

We've already discussed member-management vs. manager-management above, and mentioned that most member-managed LLCs are managed by all members. But what if your LLC does not want to elect managers, but have member-management by fewer than all members? Since state law allows an LLC to establish differences among memberships, including differences as to voting rights, LLCs can accomplish this by granting voting power (that is, management authority) only to the members who are active in the business. The remaining members, who wish to assume a passive, investor role in the LLC, are issued nonvoting memberships (they are not given specific voting power in the LLC operating agreement).

So, what's the difference between an LLC with member-management by some but not all members and an LLC with manager-management? Not much, really, for practical purposes. But note the following differences:

1. In a manager-managed LLC, management voting authority may be given to a nonmember; in a member-managed LLC, only members are given voting power.

2. In a member-managed LLC with nonvoting members, a nonvoting member may not have a right to vote at all, even on important structural changes such as amendments to articles or the approval of new members (unless state law says otherwise—we cover the voting rules for important LLC decisions in Appendix B). In a manager-managed LLC, all members typically have voting rights (unless the operating agreement says otherwise). They are allowed to participate in decisions brought before the membership for a vote, such as the amendment of articles or the operating agreement, approval of the issuance or transfers of memberships, or a vote to dissolve the LLC.

3. In a member-managed LLC, all members, including any nonvoting members, are normally considered "agents" of the LLC under state law. This means any member can bind the LLC to a contract or transaction (as long as the party dealing with a member does not know that the member has no authority to act for the LLC). In a manager-managed LLC, usually only managers are legally considered agents of the LLC under state law.

It seems sensible to us, and more in line with the way LLCs really operate, to elect manager-management when one or more members will not be active in the LLC. In other words, elect the active members as the LLC managers, and issue the nonmanaging members regular voting memberships—this gives the passive members rights to vote on special matters brought to the membership for a vote.

If all members will be active and will participate in management, then member-management makes sense (with all members getting full voting rights). Of course, your articles and operating agreement will tell you exactly how the organizers of your LLC decided to set up your LLC legal structure. But, if your structure no longer suits you, you can change it by making amendments to these documents.

Preliminary Steps Before Holding an LLC Meeting

If you're planning to hold a real (peopled) LLC meeting, you'll need to handle a few premeeting procedures. These include having someone call (request) the meeting and providing notice for the meeting, according to the rules contained in your LLC operating agreement and in your state's LLC statutes. Even if your operating agreement and state law do not require notice to be given for each meeting, we think it's wise to do so. That way, you'll make sure all potential participants know about the upcoming meeting and the nature of the business to be presented and discussed there.

In this chapter, we explain how to take these recommended steps prior to holding an LLC meeting. We also discuss practical measures to get the most out of the meeting process. These include preparing an agenda, sending participants any necessary background information, arranging for the presentation of reports, and making arrangements to keep good minutes. To help you handle all premeeting formalities, we include forms you can use to:

- create meeting summaries
- call meetings
- draft meeting participant lists
- provide notice of meetings
- acknowledge receipt of notice, and
- grant proxies to other members.

All of these forms are included as tear-outs in Appendix D and on the computer disk that comes with this book. Instructions for filling the forms out are in this chapter.

➡ If you know the steps to take

If you are experienced in holding LLC meetings, you may wish to skip the overview of LLC meetings in Section A below. If so, skip ahead to Section B, below, where we show you how to prepare our premeeting forms.

Other shortcuts: Skip to Chapter 6 if you're planning to hold paper meetings instead of face-to-face meetings. Or skip to Chapter 7 if you want to take action by written consent instead.

➡ If you have a single-member LLC that you manage yourself

The sole member or sole manager of a one-member or one-manager LLC does not need to provide notice of a real meeting, then actually attend the meeting at the scheduled time. A paper meeting or written consent is more practical and a lot more realistic. Go directly to Chapters 6 and 7 to learn how to record your official LLC decisions with a paper meeting or written consents.

However, a single-member or single-manager LLC can hold a real meeting where only the sole member or manager attends. The sole member or manager can also schedule and hold a real meeting, for instance, if you want to invite staff or officers to present reports and discuss plans.

A. OVERVIEW OF LLC MEETINGS

Before you dive into the mechanics of preparing for your LLC meetings, it's helpful to know where you're headed. Here are the typical steps involved in holding an LLC meeting:

- The meeting is called (requested) by someone authorized under the operating agreement or state law to do so. (See Section B, Step 3, below.)

- The LLC gives notice of the time, place, and purpose for the meeting, together with any necessary meeting materials, to all potential meeting participants. (See Section B, Steps 5 and 6, below.)

- The meeting is held—business is discussed and approved or disapproved. (See Chapter 4.)

- Minutes of the meeting are prepared, signed and placed in the LLC records binder. (See Chapter 5.)

We discuss the legal formalities associated with the first two procedures above in Section B, below. We also provide commonsense compliance tips designed to allow you to meet (or exceed) any state law requirements for preparing for meetings (for example, how to prepare meeting summary sheets and meeting participant lists prior to the meeting). Finally, we make a number of practical suggestions for making your meeting a productive one—a goal that's easy to lose sight of if you become too focused on the legal rules.

LLC MEETINGS CAN BE MANAGERS' AND/OR MEMBERS' MEETINGS

In a member-managed LLC, since the members manage the LLC directly (and there are no special "managers" designated in the articles or operating agreement), all meetings are members' meetings. This also goes for LLCs where not all of the members actively manage the LLC.

In a manager-managed LLC (one whose articles or operating agreement designates one or more persons, who may or may not be members, as "managers"):

- **Managers' meetings.** If the LLC has more than one manager, managers' meetings are held to discuss and approve major management decisions. If the LLC has only one manager, the manager may wish to prepare written minutes of a manager meeting to provide a record of the reasons for an important decision, which the members can refer to later if they have any questions about the decision. (Of course, this manager meeting can be held on paper only, as explained in Chapter 6. Or, for less important decisions, the manager may choose to use a written consent form to record his or her decision—see Chapter 7.)

- **Joint managers'/members' meetings.** If a decision is important enough, the managers may invite members to the meeting so that they can listen to reports and join in the discussion, prior to a vote on the matter by the managers.

- **Members' meetings.** If the articles or operating agreement call for the periodic election of managers, regular (annual or semi-annual)

members' meetings are usually scheduled in the operating agreement to elect and re-elect managers. Special members' meetings are also called by the managers or members to make decisions that are reserved to members under state law or by the articles or operating agreement. Examples of these include:

- a vote to approve an amendment to the articles or operating agreement

- the issuance of a new membership

- the admission of a transferee (a person who is sold a membership interest by a departing member)

- the continuance of the LLC, or

- the voluntarily dissolution of the LLC after a membership interest is terminated (for example, on the death or departure of a member).

Often, these votes are required under state law to be made by the full membership.

In this book, we refer to the people who are expected to attend an LLC meeting as the meeting "participants"—that is, the members, for a members' meeting; the managers, for a managers' meeting; and both the members and managers for a joint managers'/members' meeting, plus any other people, such as LLC officers, asked to attend the meeting to present reports or otherwise join in discussions at the meeting.

REGULAR AND SPECIAL LLC MEETINGS

There are two basic types of LLC meetings: *regular* and *special* meetings. Regular meetings are usually scheduled in the LLC's operating agreement to be held at certain intervals. These may be annual members' meetings for the election of managers (in manager-managed LLCs whose managers are elected for a fixed term). Or they may be semi-annual meetings of members, where reports by LLC officers are provided to all members, and members review and plan LLC business operations (in member-managed LLCs).

In a few states, where managers hold office for one year or another specified fixed term, manager-managed LLCs are required to hold regular members' meetings for the election of managers. In most states, however, managers are elected for indefinite terms, so this annual meeting is not normally legally necessary. (See the heading "Manager Election" in Appendix B for your state's rule.) Accordingly, in these states, your operating agreement does not have to provide for annual or other regular meetings. But even if regular (annual or other prescheduled) meetings are not required by state law or your LLC operating agreement, periodic meetings of members are recommended. They help to make sure that all members are kept current on LLC business operations and to provide a paper trail showing that each person received regular reports on LLC operations.

Special meetings are those held at any time when called for by a member, manager, or LLC officer, or anyone else allowed under the operating agreement (or state law) to call an LLC meeting. (See Step 3, below, for who may call special meetings.) Special meetings may be called to discuss urgent items of business or approve legal or tax formalities that arise from time to time. For example, a special meeting might be called to approve:

- the adoption of a new LLC tax year recommended by the LLC's accountant

- the conditions of an LLC loan made to an officer of the LLC, or

- a bank loan or real estate transaction.

State law does not require the holding of special meetings—by definition, these are called as the need arises by the appropriate LLC member, manager, or officer.

One-person or family-run LLCs
LLCs owned and operated by one person or one family normally don't need to pay particular attention to preliminary meeting steps, and can usually forego calling and providing notice for LLC meetings. (Again, skip to Chapter 6 if you want to prepare minutes for a paper meeting.)

HOW TO FIND THE LEGAL RULES FOR HOLDING LLC MEETINGS

The legal rules and procedures for calling, providing notice of and holding formal meetings should be stated in your operating agreement. If your agreement is silent on these rules (or you haven't yet prepared an operating agreement for your LLC), check the heading "Meeting Requirements" for your state in Appendix B; it lists the basic meeting rules that apply under your state's LLC Act.

If you want to go further—perhaps to read the language of the statutory rule yourself or look at related provisions—locate a copy of your state's LLC Act or browse it over the Internet (as explained in Chapter 1, Section C). Then search for the section number given in brackets for each rule listed in Appendix B.

We summarize the most common state rules that apply to LLC meetings in the discussions in the text below. For now, we'll note that most states let you call, provide notice of, and hold LLC meetings of members and managers pretty much as you wish, and provide specific rules for meetings in a very few instances. Moreover, these few rules usually apply only if you do not provide otherwise in your operating agreement. For example, your state LLC Act may require an annual meeting of members "unless otherwise provided in your operating agreement." If your operating agreement says that meetings of members shall be held only when called by one or more members, you have eliminated the necessity of holding annual LLC members' meetings.

B. STEPS TO HOLD A MEETING

In this section, we present and discuss the sequential steps normally taken in preparation for an LLC meeting. If you run your LLC formally, or if your LLC has more than 30 or so members, you will probably want to follow all of the procedures discussed in this section. If not, you may wish to sidestep some of the preliminaries covered below. But glance through these steps at least once. Then use your own judgment in deciding what steps to take.

Step 1. Prepare a Meeting Folder

You may be surprised at the number of forms and other paperwork that even the most routine meeting can generate. To avoid misplacing any of them, we suggest you set aside a blank file folder for each upcoming meeting. Put the date and type of meeting on the tab for the folder (for example, "Annual LLC Meeting, July 6, 2004" or "Special LLC Meeting, March 15, 2004") and keep the folder handy.

As you create each document for your meeting, place it in this file folder. After the meeting takes place and you have prepared and completed the written minutes and any other paperwork, you can transfer the entire contents of the file folder into the minutes section of your LLC records binder.

If you're using a computer to generate documents for your meetings, another way to keep your materials organized is to place all copies of computer files associated with a given meeting in one folder on your hard disk. For example, a computer user may wish to create a folder named "ANNMTG04" on the hard disk to hold all computer files generated for the annual LLC meeting in 2004.

Step 2. Prepare Meeting Summary Sheets

While you are planning and carrying out the many legal and practical details necessary to make your meeting as productive as possible, paperwork and tasks can mount up fast. To help you keep track of key dates and times, including when important notices should be sent, we provide a Meeting Summary Sheet in Appendix D and on the enclosed disk. This form contains spaces for you to enter information that summarizes what you have done or should do to prepare for the meeting and to check off whether you've done it. Use your Meeting Summary Sheet as both a scheduler and a reminder sheet for all LLC meetings. And, if any questions are raised later, it also serves as an excellent record of meetings actually held by your LLC and as documentation that meetings were called, noticed, and held correctly.

You'll need a separate Meeting Summary Sheet for each meeting. Start by having your LLC secretary prepare summary sheets for any annual (or other regular) meetings required in your operating agreement. Note that we include room for the secretary to insert information on the basic call and notice requirements for each meeting—this will help the secretary handle the pre-meeting call and notice requirements in time. The secretary should keep the Meeting Summary Sheets handy and refer to them often enough to:

- keep track of and provide timely notice of upcoming meetings

- make revisions to existing sheets (for example, when meetings are postponed or adjourned), and

- add sheets as necessary.

When a manager, an officer, a member, or another authorized person calls for a special managers' or members' meeting, the secretary should create a new sheet, filling in all relevant information for the meeting.

Meeting Summary Sheets help if you are audited

Meeting Summary Sheets for your LLC can come in handy if you later need to show members, managers, a court, or others, at a glance, that you paid serious attention to LLC formalities. Members and managers sometimes ask to see a record of LLC meetings to track the legal and tax history of the company. Summaries of this sort are also prepared by lawyers prior to a lawsuit, to have a clear record of key LLC decisions—particularly if the suit involves a decision made at an LLC meeting. Preparing your own meeting summary forms in advance may save you time and money later.

Below is a sample of the Meeting Summary Sheet included on the CD-ROM and as a tearout form in Appendix D. (See Appendix A for information on selecting and using the CD-ROM files.) Fill in the form following the special instructions provided below.

MEETING SUMMARY SHEET

Name of LLC:

_____[insert name of LLC]_____

Year of Meeting: _____[insert year]_____

Type of Meeting: ☐ Regular or ☐ Special ❶

Meeting of: ☐ Managers and/or ☐ Members ❷

Date: _____ Time: ____:____ ____.M. ❸

Place: _____ ❹

Meeting Called by: _____ ❺

Purpose: ❻ _____[insert purpose of meeting]_____

_____

Committee or Other Reports or Presentations: ❼ _____

Other Reminders or Notes: ❽ _____

Notice ☐ Written ☐ Verbal ☐ None ❾

Notice Must Be Given by Date: ❿ _____

Notice of Meeting Given to: ⓫

Name	Type of Notice*	Date Notice Given	How and Where Communicated	Date of Acknowledgment

*Types of Notice: Written (mailed, hand-delivered); Verbal (in person, telephone conversation, answering machine, voice mail); Email; Fax.

Special Instructions

❶ Check the type of meeting—whether it is a regularly scheduled meeting (either an annual or other periodic meeting) or a special meeting. If regular, in the blank, show the period for holding the meeting, such as "annual," "semi-annual" (twice a year), "monthly," "biennial" (every two years).

❷ Indicate whether it is a managers' or members' meeting (if both, check both boxes).

❸ If you know the meeting date and time, fill that in. If you expect to hold a special meeting but are not sure of the exact date, make a note anyway of the possible meeting date as a reminder.

❹ Show the location of the meeting. Most meetings will be held at the principal office of the LLC.

LOCATION IF MEETING IS HELD IN CYBERSPACE

Some companies may use technology to help them get together by holding a meeting "in cyberspace." You can do this via a conference telephone call, a video conference hookup, or even a conference on a local Bulletin Board System (BBS) or company intranet. If you use any of these alternate meeting methods, make sure to specify the location and method of holding these high-tech meetings on the Meeting Summary Sheet—for example, "a video conference located at the following video conference sites: [name the sites]." Most state statutes are not high-tech enough to specifically authorize electronic meetings, but the few states that do chime in on this issue say that electronic means can be used to hold meetings as long as each member can hear one another and can simultaneously have his or her voice heard. We'll leave it to you to decide if your electronic meeting satisfies these conditions. Generally, we think it's fine to meet electronically as long as all of the following are true:

- Your participants are technologically savvy and equipped.

- You can verify that each participant is in attendance and is heard from on all decisions.

- You don't expect anyone to object later to your method of holding an electronic meeting ("I didn't have an Internet account," "I couldn't get my modem to work").

- You can keep a complete record of the electronic meeting (a text-file log of a bulletin board or intranet session, a video tape of a video conference, or an audio tape of a conference call) to place in your LLC records binder.

❺ Normally, no one needs to call regular managers' and/or members' meetings, as they are usually already scheduled in the operating agreement. If so, just insert "operating agreement" in this blank. Special meetings of the members or managers are called by those authorized to do so under the operating agreement. (See Step 3. Call the Meeting, below, for more information.)

❻ For all meetings, set forth a brief statement of the purpose of the upcoming meeting. The purpose of a regular members' meeting in a manager-managed LLC will usually include "the election of managers of the LLC for another term." The purpose of other regular LLC meetings is typically "to hear reports from LLC officers, review past LLC business, and to plan upcoming LLC business and the transaction of any other business that may be brought before the meeting." Special meetings are called for a particular purpose, such as:

- "the purchase of real property by the LLC"

- "the admission of a new member"

- "to consider whether members will be required to make an additional capital contribution to the LLC"

- "authorizing a distribution of cash to LLC members"

- "to vote on whether to purchase the membership interest of a departing member and the terms of the purchase," or

- "to vote on the continuance of the LLC, as required by law, following the departure of a member of the LLC."

Resolution forms available to approve particular actions

Chapters 8 through 15 of this book explain and provide resolutions that will handle many of the most common special and recurring items of business that occur during the life of the LLC. (For a list of the titles of these resolutions, see the first page of Appendix D.) You'll be able to use these resolution forms at your special meetings to approve most of the objectives listed above.

❼ Indicate any LLC committee or officer reports you will wish to have presented at the meeting, for example:

- financial report by treasurer

- operations report by president

- report by compensation committee appointed by managers on proposed salary increases to LLC officers, or

- report by building committee on projected cost of site improvements to LLC headquarters.

❽ The LLC secretary should insert any reminders to help make arrangements for the upcoming meeting (for example, "Reserve video conference facility by January 10," "Have John in MIS verify each member's ability to log on to company intranet by February 15").

❾ Check your operating agreement for the type of notice for the meeting that must be provided—written or verbal. If no notice is required—if, for example, your operating agreement specifically dispenses with notice for annual manager meetings—*and* you decide not to send notice anyway (even though we recommend it in Step 5a, below)—check "None."

❿ Enter the date by which you need to send out or personally provide notice to the meeting participants. If notice is not required under your operating agreement, and you do not plan to send out notice, write "no notice given" in the blank.

⓫ After notice is actually given, fill in this portion of the form to show who received notice prior to a meeting. Insert the name of the person who was given notice, the type of notice (written or verbal), and the date the notice was given (mailed or communicated). Next, show how and where the notice was communicated—for example, "first-class mail to LLC address," "faxed to 555-5555," "in person at LLC office," "email to person@place.com," "phone conversation at 555-5555," "phone message left on answering machine at 555-5555," "voice mail left at 555-5555." Finally, if you receive documentation from the participant showing receipt or acknowledgment of notice (see the Acknowledgment of Receipt form in Step 7, below), show the date of the receipt or acknowledgment on the summary sheet. Place the receipt or acknowledgment in the meeting folder or the meetings section of your LLC records binder.

Step 3. Call the Meeting

If a meeting is a regular meeting (one scheduled in your operating agreement, such as an annual meeting of members), technically, no one needs to call it. The LLC secretary is expected to remember when to start making arrangements for this type of prescheduled meeting. This, as mentioned above, is one of the purposes of the Meeting Summary Sheet: to serve as a reminder to the secretary to make arrangements for each upcoming regular meeting scheduled in the operating agreement.

To call a special LLC meeting, someone makes an internal request within the LLC that a meeting be scheduled. Usually this request is made to the LLC secretary. Under your operating agreement or state law, particular individuals may be authorized to call meetings. Typically, LLC operating agreements allow the LLC president, any member (or a specified number or percentage of members), or one or more managers of a manager-managed LLC to call LLC meetings. Check your operating agreement to determine who may call meetings.

Most states let you call managers' and/or members' meetings as you like, but some states have a default rule that applies in the absence of a provision in your operating agreement. Typically, in these instances, the state's LLC Act allows a manager or the LLC president to call a managers' or members' meeting (in a manager-managed LLC), and a specified number or percentage of members, such as 10%, to call members' meetings (in both manager- and member-managed LLCs). For state rules on calling meetings, see "Meeting Requirements" for your state in Appendix B.

a. How and When to Call LLC Meetings

The legal requirements for the manner and timing of calling an LLC meeting are normally not specified under state law or in the operating agreement (but check yours just to be sure). Absent specific requirements, a call for a meeting can be made verbally or in writing, and can be made by any LLC officer (we suggest the LLC secretary). However made, the call should allow enough time for the secretary to:

- provide meeting participants with ample notice of the meeting—usually a minimum of ten days prior to the meeting date, but two to three weeks is generally considered more appropriate, particularly for important LLC meetings (see Step 5, below), and

- prepare any necessary background material and other materials for the meeting—this can, and often does, take more than ten days, particularly if important financial or business reports or presentations are to be made at the meeting.

In smaller LLCs where members (or managers) are in close contact and act with substantial harmony, a simple verbal call a day or two prior to the meeting works fine. However, in larger LLCs, especially those with nonmanaging members (for example, a member-managed LLC where one nonvoting member takes a passive role in management), and for any meeting at which a hot topic will be discussed, a written call of the meeting should be made, at least ten days (or more) prior to the meeting, to create a record of the fact that the meeting was properly called well in advance.

EXAMPLE 1: Pants de Lyon, LLC, a Miami clothing boutique, is a small, member-managed LLC, owned and operated by Stephanie and Claude and their spouses. Stephanie has been working hard to set up a 401(k) retirement plan for the members/employees of the LLC. At long last, she is ready to discuss and approve investment options under the plan, and to put it in place. Stephanie, the president, asks Claude, the secretary, to arrange for a special members' meeting in one week to approve the 401(k) plan. Stephanie and Claude inform their respective spouses of the meeting, and no formal notice is sent out.

EXAMPLE 2: Home Redux Limited Co., a home-remodeling and furnishing company organized as a manager-managed LLC, is owned and run by two manager/employees, Kevin and Gale, who are also members. In addition, five other people hold nonmanaging memberships in the LLC. The operating agreement allows any manager, the LLC president, or members owning at least 10% of the LLC to call a meeting of managers or members.

Gale wants to increase the LLC's line of credit with the local bank. Also, the LLC's accountant suggests that the managers approve a change in the accounting method used by the LLC, an election traditionally within the discretion and authority of the managers. Since Gale's co-manager, Kevin, is in complete agreement, and the manager meetings will be held as a formality to document these managerial decisions, Gale feels that an in-person call and five days' written notice is sufficient—after all, she and Kevin are the only managers. At the meeting, Gale notes for the record that the increased credit line is necessary to meet increased costs of doing business, which she specifies. Kevin reads the accountant's recommendation and reasons for a change in the accounting method used by the LLC. The minutes of the meeting are placed in the LLC records binder, which is open to inspection by any of the nonmanaging members at any time (as required under state law and the LLC's operating agreement), should they wish to later examine Kevin and Gale's managerial track record.

EXAMPLE 3: Grand Plans, Ltd., is a medium-sized building contractor with five managers and seven members (a manager-managed LLC). Two key managers conclude that the business needs more capital and, to get it, an additional membership should be sold. The LLC's operating agreement and its state law require full membership approval for the issuance of a new membership The president prepares a written call for a special joint managers' and members' meeting, where the managers will present a proposal to seek out and admit an additional member and the full membership will vote on it. The president gives the written call of meeting form to the LLC secretary six weeks before the desired date for the meeting. The secretary mails three weeks' written notice of the meeting to all meeting participants.

b. How to Prepare a Call of Meeting Form

A written Call of Meeting form should specify:

- the type of meeting (members' and/or managers')
- the date, time, and place of the meeting
- the purpose of the meeting, and
- how much advance notice participants should be given of the upcoming meeting.

The secretary will use this as a guideline for sending out notice, as explained in the Special Instructions below.

Below is a sample of the Call of Meeting form included on the CD-ROM and as a tear-out form in Appendix D. (See Appendix A for information on using CD-ROM files.) Fill the form out following the special instructions provided below.

CALL OF MEETING

Secretary: _____[insert name of LLC secretary]_____ **❶**

Name of LLC: _____[insert name of LLC]_____

LLC Address: _____[insert address of principal office]_____

The following person(s):

Name	Title	Membership Interest (if any) **❷**
_____	_____	_____
_____	_____	_____
_____	_____	_____

authorized under provisions of the operating agreement of the LLC and/or provisions of state law, hereby make(s) a call and request to hold a meeting of [_"members" and/or "managers"_] **❸** of the LLC for the purpose(s) of: **❹**

_____[describe purpose(s) of meeting]_____

The requested date and time of the meeting is: __[state preferred date and time for holding meeting]__. **❺**

The requested location for the meeting is:___[the principal office of the LLC, or other location]_____ **❻**

_____.

The following LLC officers and other individuals are expected to attend to present reports or otherwise contribute to the meeting, and, in addition to managers and/or members, should be included in those who receive notice of the meeting:

Name	Address
[list any other individuals who will be asked attend] **❼**	_____
_____	_____
_____	_____

The secretary is requested to provide all proper notices as required by the operating agreement of the LLC and state law to all persons entitled or asked to attend the meeting, and to include with the notice any other materials necessary or helpful to the holding of the upcoming meeting. If possible, the secretary is requested to provide at least __[if appropriate, specify requested notice period]__ notice of the meeting to all meeting participants. **❽**

Date: _____ **❾**

Signed:_____

Signed:_____

Special Instructions

❶ Insert the name of the LLC secretary (to whom the call will be given), the name of the LLC, and the LLC address (where the call will be delivered or mailed).

❷ List the name of each person calling the meeting. In the columns to the right of the name, show whether the person is a member, manager, or officer of the LLC and, if a member, the percentage of ownership interest the member currently holds in the LLC. Note: The amount of ownership interest entered here should correspond with the amount of ownership interest required to call the meeting according to your operating agreement (if any). For more information, see "Measuring Membership Interests in the LLC," below

For example, if the operating agreement says that members owning 10% of the total capital interests in the LLC may call a meeting, list each member's percentage of capital ownership (that is, the proportion of the member's current capital account balance in the LLC relative to the total current capital account balance). If the agreement allows members with a specified percentage of profits interests in the LLC to call a meeting, list each member's proportion of profits interests in the LLC. Similarly, if the agreement language speaks in terms of members who own a particular proportion of the capital and profits interests in the LLC, show each member's proportion of current capital and profits interests in the LLC.

If your operating agreement lets any member call a meeting, or allows a specified number of members call a meeting regardless of their percentage of ownership in the LLC—or if it is silent on this issue—you can leave the "Membership Interest" item blank.

MEASURING MEMBERSHIP INTERESTS IN THE LLC

State LLC statutes and operating agreements sometimes tie the right to call meetings of the LLC (as well as other LLC membership rights such as voting rights) to a member's capital, profits, or capital and profits interests in the LLC. Let's look at each.

Capital interests. A member's current capital interest is the percentage of capital contributed to the LLC, relative to total capital contributions made by all members. For example, if two LLC members form an LLC, with one member contributing $10,000 in cash and the second paying $20,000 in property, the first member has a one-third (33%) capital interest in the LLC, and the second a two-thirds (67%) capital interest. These numbers get adjusted from time to time if members make additional contributions (raising the members' capital account balances) or the LLC distributes cash or property to members (reducing members' capital account balances). This is why some statutes speak in terms of a member's current capital account balance with the LLC, rather than each member's initial capital contribution to the LLC.

Profits interests. One of the rights of LLC ownership (membership) is the right to receive a percentage of the profits (and losses) of the LLC. Generally, unless so-called "special allocations" of profits and losses are made to members in the LLC operating agreement, each member is entitled to the same percentage of LLC profits and losses as the member's capital interest. (Check your operating agreement to be sure.) So a member with a 10% capital account balance also will have a 10% profits interest in the LLC. But LLCs sometimes do make special (disproportionate) allocations of profits and losses, perhaps giving a 20% profits interest to a member paying 10% of the capital in cash, in recognition of the extra liquidity the cash-paying member provides (compared to the property contributions made by other members). Your operating agreement should specify the profits interests of all members. Many simply say that profits (and loss) interests follow the capital interests of the members.

Capital and profits interests. Many state statutes specify membership rights in terms of each member's share of the capital *and* profits interests of each member. In other words, you must average each member's share of total capital and total profits interests in the LLC. For example, if Sam has a 10% capital interest and a 20% profits interest in his LLC, he has a 15% capital and profits interest (the average of the two). In most LLCs, profits interests follow capital interests, so capital interest and profits interest will be the same. For example, Jerry has a 10% capital interest and a 10% profits interest, yielding an average capital and profits interest of 10%.

WHAT THE TERM "CAPITAL ACCOUNT" MEANS It is easy to confuse capital account balances with other accounting and tax terms, such as an owner's basis in the owner's interest or the owner's distributive share of profits and losses. The capital accounts of the members show, in bookkeeping terms, the current amount of each member's capital interest. When an LLC member contributes cash or property to a company, his or her capital account is credited with the cash amount or fair market value of the contribution. When profits are allocated to the owner at the end of the tax year of a partnership or LLC, the capital account balance goes up (the business owes the owner this money); as distributions of profits are made, the capital account balance goes down (the business no longer owes this money to the owner).

❸ Fill in the type of meeting being called. In a member-managed LLC, all meetings will be meetings of members. In a manager-managed LLC, meetings can be meetings of managers, meetings of members, or joint meetings of managers and members. (See "LLC Meetings Can Be Managers' and/or Members' Meetings," above.)

❹ In the space provided, briefly state the purpose of the meeting. You can copy this from the Meeting Summary Sheet. If you haven't filled out a Meeting Summary Sheet, refer to Step 2, above (Special Instruction # 6), for a list of common meeting purposes. Here are some suggestions:

- For an annual meeting of members for manager-managed LLCs, where managers have one-year terms: "electing the managers of the LLC."

- For annual (or other regular) meeting of members (in member-managed LLCs) or managers (in manager-managed LLCs): "review of the prior year's business, discussion of LLC operations for the upcoming year, acceptance by the managers of re-election by members for another term of office [if appropriate], and transaction of any other business that may properly come before the meeting."

- For special meetings, state the specific purpose for which the meeting was called, for example, "approval of amendments to the articles of organization and the operating agreement of the LLC."

❺ If an annual or other regular meeting, specify the time and date scheduled for the meeting in the operating agreement. If a special meeting, state the specific date or general time-frame when you wish the meeting to be held, such as "January 15, 2005 at 10:00 a.m.," "latter half of the month of October," or "first Monday in June."

❻ Specify the address where the meeting is to be held. Normally, meetings are held at the main office of the LLC, but you may wish to specify another location if it's convenient for all participants and if your operating agreement allows alternate locations for LLC meetings.

❼ If you know in advance, specify any LLC officers, staff, consultants, or outsiders who will be asked to present reports or otherwise participate in the meeting. By listing their names (include addresses for any outsiders who do not work at the LLC), you make sure they will receive notice of the upcoming meeting.

❽ If the person making the call feels that a minimum period of notice should be given to meeting participants, specify it here. If the caller has no preference for a particular notice period for the meeting, insert "N/A." As long as the period requested meets or exceeds any minimum notice requirements for the meeting set by the operating agreement or state law, the secretary should comply with this notice request. (We generally recommend providing at least ten days' advance notice of all meetings to make sure to comply with any state law requirements—see Step 5, below.)

EXAMPLE: The LLC president calls for a members' meeting to discuss the purchase by the members of the interest of a departing member. Included with the notice are the financial statements, including balance sheets, of the LLC for the past three years. The president feels that members should have at least one month's notice of the meeting to review their personal finances and the LLC's financial statements before attending the meeting to discuss valuing and purchasing the departing member's interest. The president inserts "30 days'" as the requested notice period in this blank on the form. Since the operating agreement requires only 14 days' written notice of meetings of members, the secretary will comply with the one-month notice of meeting request.

❾ Date the form and have each person making the call sign below the date line.

When you've completed the form, give a copy to the LLC secretary, who should make sure to place it in the folder for the upcoming meeting or in the meetings section of the LLC records binder.

Step 4. Prepare a Meeting Participant List

It's important that everyone who is legally entitled to be notified of an upcoming meeting receive such notice. You can also invite others such as an accountant or lawyer. By preparing a Meeting Participant List, you'll organize your records and make sure that no one is overlooked when you mail or otherwise provide notice (as part of Step 5, below). The list also comes in handy when a member or manager wishes to plan for an upcoming meeting and wants to know whom to expect in attendance at the meeting (to assess voting strength and interests, for example). Having this list handy for inspection by a member or manager is one way to help a member or manager satisfy their curiosity.

The Meeting Participant List is normally sorted alphabetically by last name. It lists the name and address of all LLC members and managers, plus the voting interests of each member. It also includes the names and addresses of any other person, such as an LLC officer or consultant, who will be asked to attend the meeting.

If you decide not to produce a participant list for every meeting, perhaps because your LLC is small or the same people are invited to every meeting, or you're just not a "records person," make sure that you do provide free access to a list of all LLC members and managers (required in many states). Use your membership and manager lists from your LLC records binder instead. These records should be maintained by all LLCs and should show the names, addresses, and interests of all LLC members (and for manager-managed LLCs, the names and addresses of all managers).

Below is a sample of the Meeting Participant List included on the CD-ROM and as a tear-out form in Appendix D. (See Appendix A for information on selecting and using CD-ROM files.) Fill the form out following the special instructions provided below.

MEETING PARTICIPANT LIST SHOULD BE AVAILABLE AT THE MEETING

To help members and managers vote at a meeting, particularly for a large meeting with many participants or for meetings where a controversial issue will be proposed, bring along copies of the meeting participant list to the meeting, and let the participants know they can request a copy if they wish. This helps everyone feel that the meeting is being held by the LLC with a maximum of full disclosure and good faith.

If you did not prepare a Meeting Participants List, bring along a copy of the membership and management lists from your LLC records binder. These lists are not specific to a particular meeting (they may list nonvoting members not entitled to vote at a meeting or omit LLC officers or outsiders specifically asked to attend a meeting). But they should satisfy the curiosity of participants who wish to examine a list of the full voting power of the LLC at the meeting.

MEETING PARTICIPANT LIST

Name of LLC:_____[insert name of LLC]_____

Type of Meeting: ☐ Regular (_____) or ☐ Special ❶
Meeting of: ☐ Managers and/or   ☐ Members ❷

Date: _____ Time: _____:_____ ___.M. ❸

Meeting Participants (list names in alphabetical order): ❹

Name:_____

Address: _____

Telephone: _____

☐ Manager _____

☐ Member: Number or Percentage of Voting Power [per capita or according to percentage of capital, profits, or capital and profits interests as specified in operating agreement]:

_____

_____

☐ Officer: Title _____

☐ Other (position and reason for attendance): _____

Name: _____

Address: _____

Telephone: _____

☐ Manager _____

☐ Member: Number or Percentage of Voting Power [per capita or according to percentage of capital, profits, or capital and profits interests as specified in operating agreement]:

_____

_____

☐ Officer: Title _____

☐ Other (position and reason for attendance): _____

Special Instructions

❶ Check the type of meeting, whether it is regular (either an annual or other periodic meeting) or special. If regular, in the blank, show the period for holding the meeting, such as "annual," "semi-annual" (twice a year), "monthly," or "biennial" (every two years).

❷ Indicate whether it is a managers' and/or members' meeting (if both, check both boxes).

❸ Fill in the date and time of the upcoming meeting.

❹ Fill in, in alphabetical order, the names, addresses, and phone numbers of:

- all managers and/or members asked to participate at the upcoming meeting, and

- others who may attend the meeting, such as officers who will present reports at the meeting.

If you need to fill in more names than the form allows, make additional copies of the paragraphs providing information about meeting participants. After each name, check whether the person is an LLC member, a manager, an officer (check all that apply), or an outsider (by checking "other"). Supply any additional information requested (member's voting power, title of officer, and the like). Note that a manager's voting power is not specified since, under most operating agreements, managers are given one vote each on any matter brought before the managers.

How to specify a member's voting power
Specify a member's voting power according to the provisions of your operating agreement. (If your agreement is silent on how members vote, see the "Meeting Requirements" heading for your state in Appendix B for your state's default membership voting rule.) For example, if your operating agreement says that members vote per capita, then each member gets one vote, and you should insert "one vote" as each member's voting power.

If your agreement says that members vote according to their capital interest or current capital account balance, list the members' percentage of capital ownership (that is, the proportion of the member's current capital account balance in the LLC relative to the total current capital account balance). Thus, if an agreement measures voting power according to capital interests or current capital account balance, a member who has contributed 25% of the capital to the LLC will exercise 25% of the voting power. This assumes there have been no adjustments made to the LLC capital accounts due to additions by or distributions to members. In this case, insert 25% as the member's voting power in this blank.

If your agreement establishes membership voting power according to members' profits interests in the LLC, list the member's percentage of profits interest as the member's percentage of voting power.

Finally, if your agreement specifies membership voting power in terms of members' average percentage of both capital and profits interests in the LLC, show this combined percentage as the voting power of the member. For more information, see "Measuring Membership Interests in the LLC" in Step 3b, above.

Here are several guidelines to follow when you fill in your list of participants:

- For a manager meeting (in a manager-managed LLC), list all managers, since managers, by definition and under law, are entitled to vote in management decisions. Rare exception: If your operating agreement sets up an unusually complicated LLC management structure with different classes of managers, with each class managing separate areas of LLC operations, list just the managers from the class entitled to vote on the decisions being brought before the meeting. This is indeed a rare situation. Most manager-managed operating agreements establish one level of management, with managers given equal authority to vote on all areas of LLC management. (Typically, each manager has one vote).

- For a meeting of members, you normally should list all members, unless your articles or your operating agreement establishes one or more nonvoting memberships or special classes of memberships with separate decision-making authority over different areas of LLC operation. Nonvoting memberships are more common than special classes of membership interests in the LLC world, particularly if the LLC is member-managed and one or more members wish to stay in the background as investors only (like passive shareholders in a corporation). For most member-managed LLCs, however, all members are entitled to attend all members' meetings and vote on the matters presented there. Check your articles or operating agreement if you have any doubts about the voting power of memberships issued by your LLC.

- For a joint managers'/members' meeting, the same guidelines apply. All managers and members should participate in the meeting unless your LLC has established separate nonvoting memberships, or classes of membership or management not entitled to vote on the matters to be presented at the meeting. But keep the following point in mind: If you are asking members to attend a meeting not just to vote their interests but to listen to and participate in discussions held at the meeting, you probably will want to invite your entire membership to the meeting. This is true even if some memberships are nonvoting.

EXAMPLE: Dog Days Pet Boutique Franchises, LLC, is a manager-managed LLC with two classes of membership: Class A voting and Class B nonvoting memberships. The Class A members serve as managers of the LLC. They make all management decisions and also attend and vote at members' meetings when a full membership vote (unanimous membership approval) is needed to meet state legal requirements and provisions of the LLC operating agreement .

The operating agreement requires an annual managers'/members' meeting to review the past year's business and discuss future plans, to present year-end financial and business reports, and to provide a forum for discussion by members to assess management performance and review the current value of their investment in the LLC. Since the operating agreement provides for an indefinite term for managers (and a majority membership vote taken at a members' meeting called for that purpose is required to remove a manager), the annual meeting is not called to solicit any particular membership votes. In effect, the annual meeting serves as a red carpet, rolled out yearly to facilitate communication and goodwill between management and the full membership (like a yearly corporate stockholders' meeting, only without the voting of shares). In this situation, it is important that all members—including those who hold nonvoting memberships—are asked to attend the joint managers'/members' meeting.

Also list any additional people who will be asked to attend (to give reports or listen to or participate in discussions). If you prepared a written call of meeting (see Step 3, above), include the additional people listed in the call form.

When you've completed the form, place it in the folder for the upcoming meeting or in your LLC records binder.

Step 5. Prepare Notice of the Meeting

Your next step is to provide all of the possible participants who may attend the upcoming meeting with notice of the time and date, and usually the purpose as well. In doing so, you'll want to meet, at a minimum, any notice requirements set out in your operating agreement. If your operating agreement says nothing, take a look under the heading "Meeting Requirements" for your state in Appendix B to learn of any state default rules for providing notice. (In most states, any notice rules set by the state LLC Act apply in the absence of any contrary provision in your operating agreement.) If neither your state law nor your operating agreement specifies notice requirements, or if you're not sure what they are, we suggest you do two things: First, provide notice of the meeting that gives all participants plenty of time to make arrangements to attend. Second, comply with the most stringent notice requirements required under any state's law.

a. Always Provide Notice

We think it makes sense to give all members and/or managers, as well as anyone else asked to attend an LLC meeting, plenty of advance notice of an upcoming meeting. After all, if an issue or decision is important enough to warrant holding a meeting, it's worth giving everyone a good shot at getting there. And, of course, it's particularly important to provide notice when members or managers are likely to disagree on the matter at hand. The last thing you want is for a member or manager to try and set aside a key LLC decision based on a contention that a meeting was not adequately noticed.

To exceed any state's legal notice requirements, simply follow these rules:

- Provide written notice of all meetings. Your operating agreement may dispense with notice for regular meetings of members or managers—these are the annual or other periodic meetings scheduled in your operating agreement—but we strongly suggest you provide notice even of these meetings. After all, do you really expect members and/or managers to remember exactly when these meetings are to be held?

- Provide notice at least ten, and no more than 50, calendar days prior to all meetings—unless your operating agreement requires a longer notice period for meetings. (In the latter case, follow your operating agreement requirements.) We pick this

requirement because the few states that do specify mandatory notice periods usually pick this range of days as the outside time limits for providing notice.

- Always state the purpose of the meeting in the notice. We suggest this as a practical matter: Some LLC's operating agreements as well as some states' LLC Acts say that only matters stated in the notice of the meeting can be discussed and voted on at the meeting. To be sure to comply with your operating agreement and your state law, we recommend that you always state the purpose of the meeting in the notice. In addition, knowing what the purpose is before the meeting can be very helpful to the participants. After all, how can a member make an informed decision about whether to attend a meeting if she doesn't know the purpose of holding it?

If you follow these suggestions, you should be in compliance with any state's strictest statutory notice of meeting rules, and everyone will be fully informed about your upcoming meeting.

If you need to meet right away
If you don't have time to comply with the meeting call and notice requirements discussed in Steps 3 and 5, you may have other options. If yours is an LLC where all participants agree, you can simply prepare a waiver of notice form and have it signed by each person either before, at, or after the meeting. This should meet your operating agreement or state law's notice requirement. (See Chapter 6, Section B, Step 1, for instructions on preparing this waiver form.) However, this less-buttoned-down approach is definitely not recommended if there is dissension in the ranks of your members and/or managers. The dissidents may simply refuse to sign.

NOTICE REQUIREMENTS IF PRIOR MEETING WAS ADJOURNED WITH UNFINISHED BUSINESS

If a managers' or members' meeting is adjourned to continue business at another time, there is normally no requirement to send out notices for the second, continued meeting if it's held soon after the adjourned meeting. We mention this point in case you need to carry a meeting over to the next day and do not wish to go to the trouble of giving notice of the second meeting.

Otherwise, give notice of all meetings to be continued. It's not hard to do this, and everyone gets reminded that the business will be carried over at the next meeting. Besides, providing a new notice gives any managers or members who happened to miss the first meeting a chance to attend the second.

---

b. Nonvoting Shares May Be Entitled to Notice

As mentioned, LLCs occasionally issue nonvoting memberships to investors and other inactive owners in the LLC. But some states' laws as well as some LLC operating agreements require that all members (voting and nonvoting) be given a chance to approve special matters that may affect their investment. Examples of such decisions include:

- amendments to articles or operating agreement
- the issuance of a new membership
- the approval of a transfer of interest
- a vote to continue the LLC business after a member leaves (state law may require this vote)
- the approval of distributions of cash or property to members
- a vote to require additional contributions from members, and
- a vote to dissolve the LLC.

We cover state law requirements for these matters in Appendix B. If your state law says that unanimous membership approval is required for special decisions, that means voting and nonvoting members must approve the decisions. For now, we want to emphasize that LLCs with a complex membership structure involving nonvoting memberships should take a broad view of who is entitled to receive notice of meetings. Even if a member is not entitled to vote at a meeting (although in many of the instances just given, state law may give even nonvoting members a vote in the decision), we suggest you go the extra step of inviting all interested parties, voting or nonvoting, to attend important LLC meetings. Doing so can curtail complaints made by members later that they were kept in the dark or that major LLC decisions were made behind their back.

c. Manner and Contents of Notice

All notices should be in writing. The notice should state the time, place, and date of the upcoming meeting. The purpose of the meeting should also be placed in the notice. You can hand the notice in person to each participant, or mail (first class, please) the notice to each member, manager, or other meeting participant at their address, which should appear in your LLC records. Other forms of providing notice are possible, such as email, fax, voice mail, and the like, as long as you are sure they are reliable (will be received and read by the participant) and the participant will not object to an alternate form of notice.

d. Fill in Notice of Meeting Form

To give formal notice of a special or annual meeting, you can use the Notice of Meeting form below.

Below is a sample of the Notice of Meeting form included on the CD-ROM and as a tear-out form in Appendix D. (See Appendix A for information on selecting and using the CD-ROM files.) Fill the form out following the special instructions provided below.

NOTICE OF MEETING

Name of LLC: _____ [insert name of LLC] _____ ❶

A meeting of _____ ["members" and/or "managers"] _____ of the LLC will be held at

_____ [location of meeting] _____,

on _____ [date of meeting] _____ at _____ [time of meeting] _____. ❷

The purpose(s) of the meeting is/are as follows:_____

_____ [summarize the purpose(s) of the meeting] _____ ❸

_____, LLC Secretary ❹

Signature of Secretary

Special Instructions

❶ Insert the full name of your LLC.

❷ Indicate if the meeting is of members and/or managers, and insert the place, date, and time of the meeting. LLC meetings are normally held at the principal office of the LLC, although state law and operating agreements usually allow manager and member meetings to be held anywhere. Of course, make sure you schedule the meeting far enough in advance to allow sufficient notice of the meeting.

If you are in a hurry, use waiver of notice forms

If you are sending notice late, or want to hold a meeting in a hurry without giving formal notice (perhaps you want to hold an important meeting after only one or two days' notice), have each member and/or manager sign a written waiver of notice form—see Chapter 6, Section B, Step 1. This procedure helps you avoid legal challenges regarding short or informal notice when you are in a hurry to hold a meeting.

❸ Succinctly state the purpose(s) of the meeting. Here are some suggestions:

- "Annual [or regular] meeting of members for electing the managers of the LLC."

- "Annual [or regular] meeting of members and managers to review the prior year's business, discuss LLC operations for the upcoming year, re-elect managers for a one-year term, allow managers to accept election, and transact any other business that may come before the meeting."

- "Special meeting of members for the purpose of" [state the specific purpose for which the meeting is being called, for example, "approval of cash distribution to LLC members"].

Ready-to-use resolutions for special business

Chapters 8 through 15 contain instructions on approving various types of ongoing LLC business decisions. See the beginning of Appendix D for a list of tear-out and computer disk resolution forms included with this book, along with cross-references to the chapters and sections of the book that contain instructions for preparing each resolution. You may want to skip ahead at this point and review any legal or tax ramifications discussed there for one or more items of special business listed in your notice form.

4 Have the LLC secretary sign the notice form.

If your operating agreement allows proxy voting by members

Some LLC operating agreements allow members who cannot attend a meeting to cast their votes by proxy. That is, members are allowed to sign a proxy form that authorizes another person, typically a spouse or another member, to vote their LLC interest at a meeting. Note: Managers are not normally allowed to act by proxy. After all, if you are specifically selected as an LLC manager, it's a bit irresponsible (and legally risky) to let another manager vote in your place when deciding LLC business. Some states specifically allow proxy voting by members, but most state LLC Acts are silent on this issue. As always, operating agreements may establish rules not otherwise prohibited under state law for the regulation of LLC affairs, including proxy voting by members. If your LLC agreement allows proxy voting by members and the upcoming meeting is a members' meeting, you can insert the following paragraph into the notice form. It tells members that they are allowed to sign proxies to let others vote their membership interests at the upcoming meeting:

If you are an LLC member and cannot attend the meeting, the LLC operating agreement allows you to designate another person in writing to vote your membership on your behalf. If you wish to do this, please deliver a signed proxy form to the secretary of the LLC before the meeting. Contact the secretary if you need help preparing this proxy form.

If you do include this paragraph in your notice, you will probably want to include a blank proxy form with each notice sent out. Refer to Step 8, below, for a sample proxy form and instructions.

Include additional information with notice

You will probably want to send out additional material with your notice to help make your meeting as productive as possible and to help your managers and/or members understand the issues to be discussed at the upcoming meeting. For example, one way to fully inform all potential participants of the business to be proposed at the meeting is to prepare and send out an agenda for the meeting, listing all the items and business that will be discussed or proposed for approval. We discuss the preparation of an agenda as well as other premeeting materials in Step 6, below.

Step 6. Prepare a Premeeting Information Packet

You will probably wish to include materials to help participants prepare for an upcoming meeting when you send out notices. You may wish to provide this material even if you do not send out a formal written notice of the meeting (if you provide verbal notice of a meeting, for example).

To adequately prepare people for a meeting, especially those who are not involved in the day-to-day management of the LLC, it normally makes sense to send out:

- **An agenda for the meeting.** This should include new items as well as any unfinished business carried over from a prior meeting.

- **Copies of reports, presentations, and background material.** Include all information that may help participants familiarize themselves with the issues to be decided at the upcoming meeting. Doing this not only saves time at the meeting, but helps your LLC make better decisions.

- **Copies of proposed LLC resolutions.** If applicable, use one of the ready-made LLC resolutions contained in this book and on the computer disk.

- **Minutes of the last managers' or members' meetings.** One of the first items on your agenda will probably be to approve the minutes from the last meeting. Approval of minutes forms can be sent out to members along with the prior minutes before the meeting to obtain signed approval of those minutes. Using this form can save time and has the added advantage of providing signed consent by all members and/or managers to decisions reached at previous meetings. This may be helpful, for example, if some members or managers did not attend the last meeting but you wish to have their approval on record of any important decisions reached at that meeting. (To prepare a written Approval of LLC Minutes form, see Chapter 6, Section B, Step 3.)

- **Proof of receipt.** (*Optional.*) If you want the participants to acknowledge that they received notice of the meeting, send an Acknowledgment of Receipt of Notice of Meeting form to be signed and returned. (See Step 7, below.)

- **Member proxies.** (*Optional.*) You may wish to enclose a blank proxy form with notice of a members' meeting if you anticipate that a member will wish to send another person to the meeting to vote his or her membership interest. (See Step 8, below.)

Step 7. Prepare Acknowledgment of Receipt Forms (Optional)

If you have an important or controversial meeting coming up, or if you generally run your LLC in a formal manner, you may wish to dot all the i's and cross all the t's for your LLC records. This can include preparing documentation of the fact that all managers, members, and other upcoming meeting participants actually received notice of the meeting. This may be particularly important if you provide informal (verbal or email) notice or if you have some nonmanaging members (for example, two nonvoting members who take a passive role in management in a member-managed LLC, or the nonmanager members in a manager-managed LLC). Distributing Acknowledgment of Receipt forms allows you to create a record that notice was properly received by your managers and/or members.

Below is a sample of the Acknowledgment of Receipt of Notice of Meeting form included on the CD-ROM and as a tear-out form in Appendix D. (See Appendix A for information on selecting and using the CD-ROM files.) Fill the form out following the special instructions provided below. You should fill out a separate form for each person acknowledging notice.

ACKNOWLEDGMENT OF RECEIPT OF NOTICE OF MEETING

LLC Name: _____[insert name of LLC]_____ ❶

(Recipient of Notice: In paragraph 1, please fill in the date on which you received notice of the meeting; in paragraph 2, review for accuracy the type of notice checked, making and initialing corrections as appropriate; in paragraph 3, date and sign your name; and mail or deliver a completed copy to the LLC officer listed in paragraph 4.)

1. I received notice of a meeting of the _____["members" and/or "managers"]_____ of the LLC on _____[leave date blank for recipient]_____. The notice of meeting stated the date, time, place, and purpose of the upcoming _____ meeting ❷

2. The notice of meeting was: ❸

   ☐ received by fax, telephone number _____

   ☐ delivered verbally to me in person at _____

   ☐ delivered verbally to me by phone call, telephone number _____

   ☐ left verbally in a message on an answering machine or on voice mail, telephone number _____

   ☐ delivered by mail to _____

   ☐ delivered via email, email address _____

   ☐ other: _____

3. Date: _____

   Signed: _____

   Printed Name: _____ ❹

4. Please return to: ❺

   Name of LLC Officer: _____

   Name of LLC: _____

   Address: _____

   Phone: _____

   Fax: _____

Special Instructions

❶ Insert the name of your LLC.

❷ Insert the type of meeting (members' and/or managers'), but leave the date line blank—the person acknowledging receipt of notice will insert the date of receipt of notice in this blank.

❸ Check the box to indicate how notice will be (or was) sent to the recipient. Fill in any additional information as requested for a particular type of notice (such as the telephone number used for verbal notice or the recipient's address to be used for mail or email).

❹ Insert the recipient's name on the line just after the signature line in paragraph 3.

❺ If you will send out Notice of Meeting forms by mail, include an Acknowledgment of Receipt form with each notice. Also enclose a self-addressed, stamped envelope (SASE) that shows the LLC officer's name and LLC address. If you gave notice verbally or by email to meeting participants, you may either mail or give an Acknowledgment form to each participant, or you can hand out the forms at the meeting to be signed and dated.

When you receive completed, signed receipts from the recipients, place them in the folder for the upcoming meeting or in your LLC records binder.

Step 8. Prepare Proxies for Members' Meetings (Optional)

A proxy lets a member authorize another person to vote his or her shares at an upcoming members' meeting. Some states specifically authorize member voting by proxy. A few have special restrictions, such as limiting the proxy's duration. Most states are silent on this issue, so your operating agreement can establish its own rules for proxy voting. (See Appendix B for links to your state's LLC Act.) Larger LLCs, or those that have members scattered throughout a wide geographic region, may routinely include blank proxy forms with the notice and other premeeting materials sent to members. For smaller LLCs, there is no practical necessity to send out proxy forms. This is because most of the time there is no conflict among members and no desire on the part of an absent member to authorize someone else to vote in his or her stead. However, in rare instances, you may be asked to provide a proxy to a member prior to an upcoming meeting. (But if your notice form includes a reference to proxy voting—see Step 5d, above—you probably will wish to include a blank proxy form with your mailed notice.)

At a joint managers'/members' meeting, members may be asked to vote on actions proposed by the managers, such as an amendment to the articles or operating agreement of the LLC, so a membership voting proxy is appropriate for this type of meeting, too.

Below is a sample of the Membership Voting Proxy form included on the CD-ROM and as a tear-out in Appendix D. (See Appendix A for information on selecting and using the CD-ROM files.) Fill the form out following the special instructions provided below.

MEMBERSHIP VOTING PROXY

(Member: Insert name of proxyholder—the person you are authorizing to vote in your place—in first paragraph, then date, sign, and return by the date indicated to LLC officer at address listed below.)

The undersigned member of _____ [insert name of LLC] _____, a limited liability company, authorizes __[recipient inserts proxyholder name]__ to act as his or her proxy and to represent and vote his/her LLC membership at a meeting of: ❶

    (Check one or both boxes) ❷

      ☐   managers

      ☐   members

to be held on ___[insert date and time of meeting]___. ❸

This proxy is effective for all items of business brought before the meeting.

Date: _____ [leave blank] _____

Signature of Member: _____ [leave blank] _____

Printed Name of Member: _____ [insert printed name of member] _____ ❹

Please return proxy by __[insert latest date for return of signed proxy]__ to: ❺

Name of LLC Officer: _____

Name of LLC: _____

Address: _____

Phone: _____ Fax: _____

Special Instructions

❶ Insert the full name of the LLC in the first blank. Leave the second blank empty—the member inserts the name of the proxyholder in this blank.

❷ Check whether the upcoming meeting is a joint managers'/members' or just a members' meeting (for a joint meeting, check both boxes; for a members' meeting, check the second box). Remember, at a joint meeting, members may be able to vote on business proposed by the managers, such as an amendment to the articles or operating agreement of the LLC, so a membership voting proxy is appropriate for this type of meeting, too.

❸ Insert the date and time of the upcoming meeting.

❹ Type or print the name of the member after the signature line, but leave the date and signature lines blank—the member making out the proxy will date and sign the form in these two blanks.

❺ Insert the date by which the proxy must be returned (mailed or delivered) to the LLC, and the name and address to which the proxy must be sent (normally, the LLC secretary at the LLC office). Normally, your LLC will specify a date close to—or even on the same date as—the meeting, but if you want more notice (or if your operating agreement requires more notice) of the member's vote by proxy, specify an earlier date here.

If a member mails or delivers a completed proxy form to your LLC for use at an upcoming meeting, place it in the meeting folder or your LLC records binder.

Using proxies for multiple meetings

In the few states that specifically deal with proxy voting by members in their LLC Act, the legal effectiveness of a written proxy may be limited to a particular period. For example, Section 322B.363 of the Minnesota LLC Act says that a written proxy is only valid for 11 months unless the proxy says otherwise. (This is a typical provision for the few states that address proxies in their LLC Act.) If you use proxies at all, we expect you to have them signed by members no more than a few weeks prior to a meeting, and to limit their use to one meeting only. If you wish to have your members sign proxies to be effective for longer durations (to be able to use one proxy for additional future meetings), check your state's LLC Act first to see if additional language needs to be added to the proxies to make them effective for this.

Step 9. Distribute Notice Forms and Information Packet

Have the secretary of your LLC deliver (by mail or personally or electronically) the Notice of Meeting form to the meeting participants, together with any premeeting information you have prepared, as explained above. If the information is mailed to a member or manager, use the exact address as shown in your LLC records. On the Meeting Summary Sheet (see Step 2, above), have the secretary complete the lines at the bottom of the form indicating how and when each manager or member was given the notice form. Place the notated Meeting Summary Sheet in your folder for the meeting or your LLC records binder.

a. When to Use Certified Mail

Normally, using first-class mail for notices of meetings is all that's legally required, and is the usual way to provide written notice. However, if you have a dissident manager or member, or have another good reason to want to prove that a person actually received a mailed notice, send the notice by certified mail with a return receipt requested. Place the certification number or return receipt in your meeting folder or LLC records binder.

OTHER WAYS TO PROVIDE NOTICE

You may occasionally decide to provide notice of LLC meetings verbally: in person or by phone, answering machine, voice mail, or email. This is particularly likely to happen in small, closely held LLCs where a few people who own and run the LLC agree to contact one another by the quickest, most convenient method available. For example, you may decide to fax or email notice of an upcoming meeting instead of mailing it. Although not specifically authorized under most LLC statutes, electronic or other alternative forms of providing notice should work fine if everyone agrees to the method. If you do use a verbal or electronic means of providing notice, it's wise to prepare documentation showing how and when the notice was given and received by the member or manager (or other meeting participant). In Step 7, above, we explain how to prepare a written Acknowledgment of Receipt of Notice for this purpose.

---

b. Certification of Mailing Form (Optional)

If you don't want to take the time to get receipts of notice from each meeting participant (either by sending notice by certified mail, return receipt requested, or by getting each person to sign and submit an Acknowledgment of Receipt of Notice to the LLC secretary), you can prepare an in-house certification of mailing form. In this form, your LLC secretary certifies that notice for an upcoming meeting was mailed to each participant on time.

Below is a sample of the Certification of Mailing of Notice form included on the CD-ROM and as a tear-out form in Appendix D. (See Appendix A for information on selecting and using the CD-ROM files.) Fill the form out following the special instructions provided below.

CERTIFICATION OF MAILING OF NOTICE

I, the undersigned acting secretary of _____[insert name of LLC]_____, a

limited liability company, certify that I caused notice of the meeting of the ____["members" and/or

"managers"]____ of the LLC to be held on __[insert date and time of meeting]__ to be deposited in the

United States mail, postage prepaid, on ____[insert date of mailing]____, addressed to the following

persons at their most recent addresses as shown on the books of this LLC as follows: ❶

____[names and addresses of persons to whom notice was mailed]__ ❷

_____

_____

A true and correct copy of the notice is attached to this certificate.

Date: _____

Signed: _____, Secretary

Printed Name: _____ ❸

Special Instructions

❶ Fill in the full name of the LLC, the word(s) "members" and/or "managers," and the date and time of the upcoming meeting. Have your LLC secretary fill in the date of mailing.

❷ Have the secretary fill in the names and addresses to the participants to whom notice was mailed.

❸ Have the secretary date, sign, and print his or her name on the form. Attach a copy of the previously mailed written notice to the certification form, and place the form in your meeting folder or LLC records binder. ■

How to Hold an LLC Meeting

In this chapter we look at the basic steps necessary to hold a successful LLC meeting. Don't be daunted by the fact that we present a few more premeeting steps below. If you've read Chapter 3, you've already learned what you need to know about premeeting formalities, and we refer you back to these steps to accomplish them quickly. Only a few of the meeting steps are legally required, and you can skip or combine the others as you see fit. Don't worry that you'll miss an important step: The minutes form set out in the next chapter (and in Appendix D) reminds you to take care of all the legally required steps.

➡ If you know how to hold meetings

If you're experienced in holding LLC meetings and wish to get right to the task of preparing your minutes, skip to Chapter 5. Likewise, if you wish to document a managers' or members' decision without holding a real meeting, skip to Chapter 6 to prepare minutes for a paper meeting or to Chapter 7 to take action by written consent.

➡ If you have a one-member LLC that you manage yourself

In practice, member meetings for a one-member LLC and manager meetings for a one-manager LLC are often held on paper only, to formally record decisions that the sole member or manager wishes to document. If you are in this situation, turn to Chapter 6, where we focus on the steps you need to take to prepare minutes for this type of "paper meeting." You may also record decisions by written consents. (See Chapter 7.) However, a sole LLC member can also hold a real one-person meeting (you can talk to yourself if you wish) or hold a real meeting where you invite others (staff, officers, advisors, lawyers), for instance, to present reports and discuss proposals.

💡 If you neglect to hold or document a meeting

Preparing paper minutes is a good way to document past decisions. Obviously, if you failed to hold an annual meeting last year, it's too late to hold a real meeting. This can be a problem if you wish your LLC records to include past managers' and members' meetings that were not properly documented. The

best way to catch up on LLC paperwork is to follow the paper meeting approach, which allows you to quickly document decisions after the fact. (See Chapter 6.)

Step 1. Call and Provide Notice of the Meeting

Before holding your meeting, it's standard procedure to call and provide notice of the meeting, according to the legal requirements contained in your operating agreement. The steps you'll take to accomplish these tasks are fully described in Chapter 3.

➡ To bypass normal notice requirements

If you wish to sidestep all legal requirements for calling and noticing your meeting, your managers or members (or both, if it's a joint meeting) can sign a waiver of notice form. Dispensing with notice of an upcoming meeting is particularly appropriate for small LLCs whose managers or members are all involved in the business and maintain regular contact. (See Chapter 6, Section B, Step 1 for instructions on preparing waiver of notice forms.)

Step 2. Prepare an Agenda for the Meeting

Especially for larger meetings, the person in charge of the meeting (whom we refer to as the "chairperson" throughout the remainder of this chapter and this book) will have an easier time if he or she has a written agenda that lists the order of business for the meeting. (See Chapter 3, Section B, Step 6, for a discussion of preparing a premeeting agenda.) An agenda can help the chairperson keep an eye on the clock, making sure that all proposed items are covered within the time allotted for the meeting.

Step 3. Prepare Meeting Resolutions in Advance

As a practical matter, it is usually best to prepare ahead of time drafts of resolutions to be introduced at a meeting. Drafting suitable resolutions for approval at meetings involves understanding the issues involved and using language that clearly states the business or matter to be approved by the managers and/or members at the meeting.

You don't need to use fancy or legal language for your resolution. Just describe as specifically as you can the transaction or matter approved in a short, concise statement. Normally, resolutions start with a preamble of the following sort: "The (members and/or managers) resolved that …", but this is not required.

Following are some examples of resolutions:

EXAMPLE 1 (Bank Loan): "The managers resolved that the treasurer be authorized to obtain a loan from _____ [insert name of bank] _____ for the amount of $_____ on terms he/she considers commercially reasonable."

EXAMPLE 2 (LLC Hiring): "The members approved the hiring of [insert name of new employee], hired in the position of __[insert job title]__ at an annual salary of $_____ and in accordance with the terms of the LLC's standard employment contract."

EXAMPLE 3 (Tax Year): "The members decided that the LLC shall adopt a tax year with an ending date of 3/31."

EXAMPLE 4 (Amendment of Articles): "The members resolved that the following new article be added to the LLC's articles of organization: _____ [language of new article] _____."

Resolutions covered in Chapters 8 through 15

Each of the above matters is covered in a specific resolution included with this book and explained in Chapters 8 through 15. We offer the language above just to show you how to go about preparing your own resolution if you can't find one of our resolutions to handle the upcoming business planned for your meeting.

Step 4. Get Together to Hold the Meeting

Your next step is to have the meeting participants (members and/or managers, as well as any additional people called to the meeting to present reports or otherwise participate in the meeting) meet at the time and place specified in your notice of the meeting. Most LLC operating agreements select the principal office of the LLC as the place where meetings are held, but they usually allow meetings to be held at any location inside or outside the state as designated by the members or managers. (For a discussion of several state-of-the-art ways to hold a meeting over phone lines, on a company intranet, or via video conference hook-ups, see Step 5, just below.)

Step 5. Hold a Meeting in Cyberspace If You Have the Equipment and Know-How

When to skip this material

This section is not really a separate, consecutive step in the LLC meeting process—rather, it is a discussion of alternative ways of convening LLC meetings intended to supplement the rest of this chapter. If you plan to meet in person, you can safely skip this "step" and proceed to Step 6. If you're interested in setting up a meeting without the need to get everyone together at the same physical location, we hope this step gives useful suggestions for using technology to help streamline the LLC meeting process. In any event, you'll have to make these arrangements in advance, and make sure everyone can use the technology.

Telecommunications advances now allow a number of people to simultaneously communicate over phone lines using telephone, video, and computer conference hookups. Technological refinements should soon allow us to communicate completely unplugged, using cellular and other wireless technologies to project our voices and video images over the air. In short, the fast-widening horizons of what many call "cyberspace"—that virtual meeting area of voice and image located somewhere over the phone lines and network nodes or in the atmosphere—allows LLC and business meetings to routinely be held by participants in separate locations.

Most existing LLC statutes are worded broadly enough to allow managers and members to meet by using a means of telecommunication that allows each of the participants to hear one another simultaneously. Do the participants in a computer bulletin board conference "hear" each other, even though each person's comments are displayed on a computer screen (assuming the PCs are not equipped with sound cards that actually speak the words shown on the screen)? We think the answer is "yes" and that you should be safe in discussing and concluding business over a computer network this way. However, if you anticipate that any participant may object to a meeting that's not held in person, or if a matter to be resolved at a meeting is controversial, it's best to meet in person.

Here is a short review of some of the most common types of alternative meeting technologies available today.

Telephone conference call. Many modern offices and even some home telephone systems have a built-in capability for one person to call and add additional callers in a conference call conversation. Of course, you'll have to go through a long-distance telephone carrier if you want to link up participants in different states or in widely separated locations. If you don't have conference-call capability, the local phone company can hook up a third party to a two-person call on a one-time basis for a special charge (on top of local and long-distance phone charges). If you need to link additional callers, the conference center of your local phone company can arrange a multiparty telephone conference at an additional charge.

Video conference rooms. If you have substantial amounts of cash handy, you can purchase the fairly sophisticated equipment necessary to set up your own dedicated video conference facility (you'll need at least two—one room for each end of the conference). A less expensive, though by no means cheap, alternative is to rent the use of video conference facilities provided by a private vendor, and have your participants assemble at the leased locations. Video conference companies have offices in most major U.S. cities, as well as many cities abroad. The cost to rent each video conference site typically starts at about $300 per hour. A more recent development involves the use of desktop video conferencing products, which allow personal computer users to set up their own video conference at significantly reduced costs. Expect the computer video and audio channels to be somewhat slow, with slightly delayed or staggered sounds and images, in comparison with their pricier dedicated video conference counterparts.

Computer bulletin board conference. Most large-scale national computer bulletin board systems (BBSs), such as CompuServe, Dialog, or America Online, have the capacity to allow an individual user to invite others to participate in a private conference. The person coordinating the meeting notifies the other participants, each of whom must be a member of the BBS, to sign onto the board or a particular forum on the board at a prearranged time using a password or PIN (personal identification number). As each person signs on, the meeting coordinator, who is already logged onto the board or forum, invites each participant to chat, thereby linking everyone together in one online conversation. Each participant types his or her comments on a computer screen for others to view.

To avoid confusion and overlapping messages, the meeting chairperson should introduce and lead each discussion, asking each of the participants in turn for comments and votes on each matter. The secretary of the meeting can capture all dialogue on the screen by saving it to a file on a computer disk. Once the meeting is concluded and each participant has signed off the board, the secretary can assemble, format, and print the contents of the screen dialogue saved in the computer file, making a copy for each participant to review and approve.

Local computer network meetings. Many companies maintain a network server on the premises that implements a local, company-based email system. If your meeting is local—that is, held in company buildings—participants who work onsite may be able to use a "chat" or similar conferencing feature of your email software to talk to one another simultaneously. Holding a meeting like this usually means all participants need to be seated at their workstations in the same building, and this is only minimally more convenient than having to assemble face-to-face in one room for a real meeting. Still, for some LLCs, letting participants hold a meeting by keying in discussions and votes at their workstations in a live email chat session can be a time-saving alternative. Also, this can be helpful if the company has buildings in different geographical areas attached to the same network. As with the BBS method discussed above, the participants should be able to view each other's responses, and the secretary should generate a printout of the meeting session and save it in the LLC records binder.

Company intranet meeting. One of the advantages of the Internet is the ability to link people situated in different locations into one virtual location. If your LLC maintains a private Internet site for employees and other authorized users (with a built-in "firewall" to prevent unauthorized access to the private website), you may be able to hold a meeting from your "intranet Web page." This approach is more flexible than email since it allows participants to attend the online meeting no matter where they are located, within or outside your company's buildings or network. Of course, your Internet server and each participant's Web browser must have the appropriate conferencing software installed to allow you to set up an intranet conference and let all authenticated participants join the meeting session from your company Web page. Again, make sure to place a record of the intranet meeting session in your LLC records binder.

Step 6. Appoint a Chairperson and Secretary

Before the meeting begins, you'll need to find people to fulfill two important roles at the meeting:

- **Chairperson.** This person, usually the president, directs the activity at the meeting.

- **Secretary.** A person to act as secretary of the meeting—usually the LLC secretary. He or she takes notes of the order and outcome of business discussed and voted on at the meeting. These notes will be used later to fill in the blanks on the minutes form, as explained in the next chapter.

Exactly how a meeting is organized and conducted and how each person does each job at the meeting is up to you. State LLC law generally does not concern itself with parliamentary procedures used at meetings. For a discussion of practical steps to take to introduce, discuss, and vote on proposals at LLC meetings, see Step 12, below.

> ### FORMAL RULES FOR RUNNING A MEETING
>
> You can plan your meeting to be as formal or informal as you wish in terms of raising and making motions, and seconding and voting on items of business. We do not include a guide to the many parliamentary rules and procedures (formal rules for conducting meetings) that can be used to run LLC meetings, because we believe they are usually unnecessary. If your LLC has only a few members and/or managers in attendance at a meeting, a conversational format will probably work best. For slightly larger meetings, we have found that an agreeable, but no-nonsense, chairperson will be the key to keeping meetings on track.
>
> LLCs with more than about ten participants may need to establish more detailed ground rules for meetings. For example, the chairperson may wish to call on members or managers individually to elicit comments and opinions prior to a vote, setting a time limit for remarks to five minutes or so. Or the chairperson may wish to have motions formally proposed, seconded, and discussed before the question is called and a vote taken.
>
> If you need guidance in setting ground rules or the level of formality, you can use formal parliamentary procedures. For a remarkably easy-to-use guide to implementing the most commonly used parliamentary procedures at meetings, see *Parliamentary Law at a Glance*, by Ethel Utter (Contemporary Books, Inc.).

Step 7. Chairperson Calls the Meeting to Order

The chairperson normally calls the meeting to order by announcing that it's time to begin. The chairperson then directs the order in which business will be covered at the meeting. Typically, the chairperson will introduce some items himself (or herself) and call on other meet-ing participants to take the lead for certain items of business. For example, the chairperson may ask the meeting secretary to read a proposal and take the votes after the issue is discussed.

> ### NOTE TAKING AT MEETINGS MADE EASY
>
> The secretary of your meeting does not need to provide a longhand narrative of all the happenings at an LLC meeting. It is normally enough to list who is present, the nature of the proposals raised, and the outcome of votes taken. This information can then be used after the meeting to complete the minutes form discussed in the next chapter. The quickest method of all is for the secretary to fill in the minutes form at the meeting (either on copies of the tear-out forms in Appendix D, or by using a computer to fill out the minutes form provided on the disk included with this book).

Step 8. Secretary Determines Whether a Quorum Is Present

 What about one-manager or one-member LLCs?

If your LLC has one member—or, if it is manager-managed with just one manager—the old adage about seating arrangements for a 500-pound gorilla applies: You can hold member and manager meetings pretty much wherever and whenever you wish. If you, as the sole member or manager, are present, you have a quorum; otherwise, you have an empty room. In reality, member meetings for a one-member LLC and manager meetings for a one-manager LLC are held on paper only, to formally record decisions that the sole member or manager wishes to document. Turn to Chapter 6 if you are in this situation, where we focus on the steps you need to take to prepare minutes for this type of "paper meeting."

The secretary should note those present and absent from the meeting, making sure that the required number (a quorum) of members or managers (or of each for a joint members'/managers' meeting) is present. If your LLC allows proxy voting by members, and you are tallying up the interests of members at a meeting to compute whether a quorum is present, make sure to include any membership interests represented by proxies at the meeting. (For more on proxies, see Chapter 3, Step 8.) If a quorum is not present at the start of a meeting, the chairperson should adjourn the meeting to a new time and date, and start over by providing notice of the new meeting date, time, and purpose to all participants, as discussed in Chapter 3, Step 5.

EXAMPLE: The operating agreement of XYZ LLC states that the LLC must have seven managers and that a majority of the authorized number of managers represents a quorum for managers' meetings. Four managers, therefore, must attend managers' meetings for business to be discussed and approved by them. This is true even if any manager's slot is currently vacant.

If your operating agreement does not state the minimum quorum requirements for a meeting, see the "Meeting Requirements" heading in Appendix B for your state's default quorum rules. Note that many states with quorum rules (many do not have them) set a quorum for manager meetings as a majority of the total number of managers authorized in your LLC and a quorum for members' meetings as a majority of the members (or a majority of all of the members' capital and/or profits interests). Again, check your operating agreement or your state's law in Appendix B to be sure.

Suppose you are holding a members' (or joint members'/managers') meeting, and your operating agreement or state LLC Act sets the minimum quorum requirement for members' meetings as a percentage of capital and/or profits interests held by members. See "Measuring Membership Interests in the LLC" in Step 13, below, to understand how to determine if the required membership percentage is present at your meeting.

EXAMPLE: Dollars to Donuts, LLC, a bakery, is a manager-managed LLC, operated by three member-managers. Four relatives of the three active member-managers also have invested in the LLC as passive members. Because the LLC is closely held by a few people and their close family members, the LLC operating agreement requires the attendance of the three active member-managers, plus no fewer than two of the three passive members, at membership meetings. Super-majority quorum requirements of this sort are common in the LLC world, particularly when the LLC is owned and operated by a close-knit group.

A quorum must be present when action is taken

For the managers or members to take action, the required number of them (a quorum) must be present at the meeting. For example, if a quorum of members is not present at a members' meeting, or a member leaves and the quorum is broken, the meeting must be adjourned until another time when a quorum of members can be obtained for the meeting.

How do you measure quorum in an LLC with special membership classes?

For the great majority of smaller LLCs, all members are issued voting memberships. If the operating agreement does not specifically list the voting rights granted to members, you can assume all members having voting power. But if your operating agreement creates different classes of membership interests (granting voting power to some classes and denying it to others), a quorum of the membership interests with voting power on a matter must be present before a vote is taken on the matter.

EXAMPLE: Green Construction LLC has issued six voting and two nonvoting memberships. The operating agreement defines a quorum for members' meetings as a majority of the members who are entitled to vote. The LLC ignores the two nonvoting memberships in its calculation of a quorum. If four out of the six voting members attend a members' meeting, there is a majority quorum in attendance and the meeting can begin.

Very Rare Exception: State LLC law is flexible, and some LLCs with unusual needs may allow one member to have the exclusive vote on a particular matter. For example, the operating agreement may authorize the issuance of a special membership interest to a bank or financial institution, granting it exclusive voting power to approve or veto the distribution of cash to LLC members. Obviously, the holder of this special type of membership interest must be present at a meeting to vote on a proposed distribution of cash to LLC members, whether or not a quorum of the full voting membership is also present at the meeting.

Voting quorum rules for special business or important structural changes

In special cases, your operating agreement may require a meeting of all members. (See your operating agreement and check Appendix B to see where to locate state law.) This may be required, for example, when the LLC members are voting to:

- amend articles of organization or the operating agreement

- approve a new member

- sell all LLC assets

- voluntarily dissolve the LLC, or

- continue the LLC after the disassociation of a member (which is the loss of membership rights due to the death, disability, expulsion, or bankruptcy of a member).

In such cases you cannot vote on these matters unless all members attend. Note: Not all members have to vote (some may abstain). And the vote need not necessarily be unanimous. Check your state's laws and your operating agreement for details.

Step 9. Secretary Reads Minutes of or Summarizes Business of Last Meeting

After determining that a quorum is present at the meeting, it is customary, but not legally required, for the secretary of the meeting to read or summarize the minutes of the last meeting. After that, the minutes are approved by the participants. This is particularly tradition when the LLC holds regular manager or membership meetings every month or so. It is a polite and efficient way to have everyone agree that the written minutes for the prior meeting properly reflect and summarize the actions taken and decisions reached at that meeting. Often, a member or manager will have a small correction to the minutes. It is up to the president or chairperson to accomplish this without having meeting participants completely rehash the proceedings of the prior meeting.

Save time by sending out minutes in advance

To save the trouble and boredom of reading and discussing minutes of a prior meeting at the current meeting, you can send them out as part of the premeeting packet discussed in Chapter 3, Section B, Step 6. You may also want to send out an "approval of minutes" form in advance instead of waiting for the upcoming meeting to have the participants approve these minutes. Doing this can save time at the meeting, as well as provide a signed document showing that the managers and/or members specifically approved actions taken at a prior meeting. This is an especially good document to have if a manager or member missed a previous meeting. (See Chapter 6, Section B, Step 3, for instructions on preparing the Approval of LLC Minutes form.)

Step 10. Handle Any Unfinished Business

No matter how long meetings last, an item of business is often carried over to the next meeting. If this happened at your last LLC meeting, make sure to tackle any "old business" first before taking care of the new business items on the agenda. Of course, any notice (or waiver of notice) for the current meeting should have included a summary of any unfinished business to be considered at the current meeting.

Step 11. Officers and Committees Present Reports

The next item on the agenda of many meetings, particularly annual membership or manager meetings, is for the chairperson to call on committees, LLC officers, department managers, and outside consultants or advisers to make presentations or hand out reports. Obviously, if all members or managers work in the business and are fully current on its affairs, presenting formal reports may not be necessary. But when members who are not in day-to-day contact with the business are asked to attend, these summaries can be extremely valuable.

Do the dollars first
For annual meetings, it makes sense to review the LLC's profit and loss picture first, as these are usually the figures everyone is most interested in, particularly outside investors. Reports are often made to update those present on past or projected LLC operations (such as upcoming plans for increasing the LLC's market share of sales in a particular area of operation), or on a particular aspect of LLC performance (such as the LLC's net worth reflected on the latest balance sheet). Reports can also provide members or managers with the information necessary to make an informed decision on an issue. For instance, it would be helpful to have a discussion of important options associated with the adoption of a 401(k) profit-sharing plan or a report by the president explaining the reasons for the creation and issuance of a new class of membership.

EXAMPLE 1: At a management meeting, prior to proposing a vote on a resolution to increase the coverage limits of the LLC's product liability insurance, the chief financial officer summarizes current coverage limits and options for increased coverage, based on data obtained from the LLC's insurance broker. Next, the LLC's outside legal advisor gives a report summarizing current trends and outcomes in product liability law cases involving products similar to the LLC's product line.

EXAMPLE 2: At the annual managers'/members' meeting for Yolodyne Ltd. Liability Co., the chairperson calls on the treasurer to report on past and projected balance sheet figures, followed by a report by the president outlining new operations planned for the upcoming year. Providing past and prospective information of this sort to members can be essential to keeping outside investors satisfied with the work goals and performance of the LLC. Following the presentation of reports, managers are nominated for election or re-election, and the membership vote is taken.

Try to avoid presenting completely new material
To save time at meetings, and to avoid surprise, we recommend that reports and background information be mailed to managers, members, and other meeting participants prior to the meeting. (See Chapter 3, Section B, Step 6.) The presenters can then restrict their comments to reviewing the gist of the circulated reports, emphasizing the most important points.

> ### THE LEGAL AND PRACTICAL VALUE OF REPORTS PRESENTED AT MEETINGS
>
> The LLC Acts of many states specifically immunize a manager from personal liability if he or she relied on misleading or false reports when reaching a decision. (The exception is if the member or manager knew, or should have known, that the information submitted in the report was unreliable.) This gives LLC members (in member-managed LLCs) and managers (in manager-managed LLCs) an additional measure of legal protection, and increases their comfort level when discharging their managerial duties
>
> Reports at LLC meetings can have another, broader purpose: They are an excellent way to keep members informed of LLC operations and performance. Such reports not only provide a good jumping-off point for discussion at the meeting, they can also head off objections by members to a course of business taken by the LLC management team. If reports have been distributed before and read at a meeting, the members can't claim that they haven't been kept informed.

Resolutions reminder

This book provides 80-plus resolution forms, ready for use to tackle common types of ongoing business raised at LLC meetings. If you need, or wish, to prepare your own resolution, short and simple language works best. See the examples given in Step 3, above, and in Chapters 8 through 15.

Step 12. Introduce and Discuss Specific Proposals

After any reports or background presentations have been made at the meeting, the chairperson normally will want to formally introduce proposals for discussion and vote by the managers or members (or both). Proposals are best introduced in the form of resolutions that clearly and legally state the item or business or matter to be approved. This allows you to include the exact language of the resolution in your minutes, with no need to reword it later.

The procedures used by LLCs to introduce, discuss, and decide resolutions at meetings take many forms. Typically, the chairperson or another LLC officer follows a prepared agenda to introduce a proposal to be discussed, such as whether or not to increase the liability limits of the LLC's general liability insurance policy. The proposal can be introduced by way of a formal motion that is seconded by another participant and then discussed. Or a proposal can simply be introduced by the chairperson with the assumption that some discussion will occur before a formal motion is made.

Either way, a discussion of the merits and possible parameters of the proposal is likely unless all participants are already fully informed and ready to vote. For example, the president, acting as chairperson, might introduce an agenda item consisting of a resolution to increase LLC insurance coverage. The participants debate whether all that extra insurance coverage is really necessary. Once the general discussion is over, the chairperson can either propose adopting the resolution if one has been introduced, or propose specific language for the resolution.

After a resolution has been introduced and discussed, it's normal to move for a voice vote. However, experienced chairpersons, aware of the desirability of achieving a consensus, will be sensitive to divergent views. The chairperson will normally allow participants to suggest modifications to the resolution prior to calling for a vote, consistent with getting necessary business accomplished. For example, a member may propose a resolution asking for the purchase of $50,000 additional liability coverage by the LLC. Another member may propose that the insurance resolution be made more specific by authorizing the purchase of $50,000 of general liability insurance coverage from the lowest bidder, after getting quotes from the LLC's current insurance carrier and outside companies.

After the language of a resolution is decided, the managers or members (or both) vote to approve or veto it. (See Step 13, below.) When a resolution passes, it is inserted into the minutes for the meeting and becomes the official act of the LLC. If it fails, it normally isn't mentioned in the minutes, unless you want a record stating that the resolution didn't pass.

Introducing resolutions at joint managers'/members' meetings

At joint managers'/members' meetings (in manager-managed LLCs), managers may propose one or more resolutions for membership approval. For example, if management is proposing an amendment to the articles to change the LLC name or to authorize an additional class of membership, the chairperson normally will ask a manager to introduce and discuss the amendment prior to taking a membership vote on it. (For a discussion of the decision-making roles of LLC managers and members, see Chapter 2.) The difference here is that the specific language of the resolution is not normally hammered out at the joint meeting. Instead, the managers will have approved the proposed language in advance of the meeting—typically, at a managers' meeting—then mailed the proposed resolution to members as part of the premeeting materials distributed prior to the meeting. This gives members a chance to understand the measure ahead of time, and to make an informed decision at the meeting after hearing any additional reports or background on the proposal at the meeting.

EXAMPLE: At the annual managers'/members' meeting of the Rackafrax LLC, a manager-managed LLC, the members are asked to ratify an amendment to the operating agreement that requires additional contributions from members whenever the cash reserves of the LLC fall below a threshold amount. The resolution presented for approval at the members' meeting is a copy of a resolution approved earlier by the managers at a managers' meeting. This resolution, together with a written summary of the reasons for the amendment, was sent out to the Rackafrax members as part of the premeeting materials mailed in advance to each participant. (See Chapter 3, Section B, Step 6.)

The chairperson, who is also LLC president and a manager-member of the LLC, introduces the resolution. The managers and members, LLC officers, and staff present at the meeting discuss the resolution. Following the discussion, the chairperson makes a motion for a member vote on the written resolution. After being seconded, the motion carries, and a member vote on the amendment is taken. The only other important item of business raised at the annual managers'/members' Rackafrax meeting is the election of the managers for another term of office. The president (chairperson) moves that all existing managers be re-elected by members. A voice vote of members is taken, and all approve the re-election of the managers for another year.

Step 13. Take the Votes of Managers or Members

After resolutions have been presented in final form at a meeting, the managers or members must vote on them. Most resolutions require the majority vote of those present at a meeting. Remember, a resolution presented at a meeting will be submitted to a vote of members or managers, or both, depending on the type of meeting and the type of resolution, as follows:

- **Members' meetings.** In a member-managed LLC, all meetings are members' meetings. Members vote either per capita (one vote each) or in proportion to their percentage of capital, profits, or capital and profits interests. (We repeat the sidebar from Chapter 3, "Measuring Membership Interests in the LLC," below to help you understand the differences among these measures of voting power.) Typically, a majority of the membership interests represented at a meeting is required to approve a resolution. Your operating agreement should tell you how the voting power of your members is computed, and what membership vote is necessary for members to take action at a meeting. If it doesn't, see the "Meeting Requirements" heading in Appendix B to see if your state's LLC Act has a default member voting rule that applies in the absence of an operating agreement rule. Remember: If your LLC has is-

sued memberships to nonvoting members, normally only members with voting rights are entitled to vote on a resolution presented at a meeting of members (except when a full membership vote is required for very important decisions— see "LLC Articles, Operating Agreement, or State Law May Contain Special Membership Voting Rules," below).

- **Manager's meetings and joint members'/ managers' meetings.** In a manager-managed LLC, the managers vote on most resolutions presented at meetings, asking for membership approval only for important issues that require a membership vote (see "LLC Articles, Operating Agreement or State Law May Contain Special Membership Voting Rules," below). Under standard LLC operating agreements and any state default rule for manager voting, managers get one vote each, with the approval of a majority of managers necessary for the managers to take action at a meeting. Again, check your operating agreement.

If you are confused about who decides what at meetings of manager-managed LLCs, refer back to Chapter 2, Section B, for a more in-depth explanation.

MEASURING MEMBERSHIP INTERESTS IN THE LLC

State LLC statutes and operating agreements tie membership rights such as voting rights to a member's capital, profits, or capital and profits interests in the LLC. Let's look at each:

- **Capital interests.** A member's current capital interest is the percentage of capital contributed to the LLC, relative to total capital contributions made by all members. For example, if two LLC members form an LLC, with one member contributing $10,000 in cash and the second paying $20,000 in property, the first member has a one-third (33%) capital interest in the LLC, and the second a two-thirds (67%) capital interest. These numbers get adjusted from time to time if additional contributions are made by members (raising the members' capital account balances) or distributions of cash or property are made to members (reducing members' capital account balances). This is why some statutes speak in terms of a member's current capital account balance with the LLC, rather than each member's initial capital contribution to the LLC.

- **Profits interests.** One of the rights of LLC ownership (membership) is the right to receive a percentage of the profits (and losses) of the LLC. Generally, unless so-called "special allocations" of profits and losses are made to members in the LLC operating agreement, each member is entitled to the same percentage of

LLC profits and losses as the member's capital interest with the LLC. (Check your operating agreement to be sure.) So a member with a 10% capital account balance also will have a 10% profits interest in the LLC. But LLCs sometimes do make special (disproportionate) allocations of profits and losses, perhaps giving a 20% profits interest to a member paying 10% of the capital in cash, in recognition of the extra liquidity the cash-paying member provides (compared to the property contributions made by other members). Your operating agreement should specify the profits interests of all members. Many simply say that profits (and loss) interests follow the capital interests of the members.

- **Capital and profits interests.** Many state statutes specify membership rights in terms of each member's share of the capital and profits interests of each member. In other words, you must average each member's share of total capital and total profits interests in the LLC. For example, if Sam has a 10% capital interest and a 20% profits interest in his LLC, he has a 15% capital and profits interest (the average of the two). In most LLCs, profits interests follow capital interests, so capital interest and profits interest will be the same. For example, Jerry has a 10% capital interest and a 10% profits interest, yielding an average capital and profits interest of 10%.

EXAMPLE 1: Wirewrap Electronics, LLC, is member-managed, with four members who have each contributed 25% of the capital to fund the LLC. The operating agreement grants voting rights to members in proportion to the current value of each member's capital account. (Under the agreement, capital accounts are adjusted, if necessary, by deducting from the accounts any distributions to members and adding any additional contributions made by members after the formation of the LLC.) At the time of the mem-

bers' meeting, no adjustments to the initial balances of the capital accounts have been made, and each member's account balance equals $15,000 (25% of the total $60,000 capital contributed to the LLC at its formation). The operating agreement requires the approval of at least a majority of the membership voting power present at a members' meeting to pass a resolution. All four members attend the meeting, so the approval of at least three of the four members (representing 75% of the capital interests of the LLC) is necessary to pass a resolution.

EXAMPLE 2: Syncopation Sound Recording, LLC, is manager-managed by five active members. The operating agreement requires the majority per capita vote of all managers present at a manager's meeting to pass a resolution. A quorum of three managers attends an LLC managers' meeting. The affirmative votes of two of the three managers present are necessary to pass a resolution.

Here's a discussion of a few key issues that may arise during the voting process:

- **If a member or manager abstains.** When a member or manager abstains, it often means he or she doesn't agree to a particular action, but simultaneously doesn't want to annoy others by voting "no." In short, a manager may want to duck the issue by having the minutes reflect a neutral position. Here's how it might play out: If five managers or members are present at a meeting (assuming per capita voting and a majority passage rule), you need three "yes" votes to pass a resolution. With two "yes" votes, two "no" votes, and an abstention, the resolution fails.

- **Liability of silent managers.** Some states specify that a manager (in a manager-managed LLC) or a member (in a member-managed LLC) can be held personally accountable for unlawful decisions—such as the approval of a cash distribution that makes the LLC insolvent—if the manager or member voted to approve the decision. Also, courts may hold members or managers personally liable if an LLC decision turns out (perhaps through 20-20 hindsight) to have involved a serious risk of injury to others, and others do, in fact, get injured because of the decision—for example, a decision by LLC managers to go forward with a product line that causes harm to customers. Will an abstention in either of these situations be enough to keep a member or manager protected from personal liability? In some state courts, the answer may be "no." It's safer to vote "no" than to abstain if you want make it clear that you disagree with an LLC man-

agement decision or policy, and you wish your minutes to record your dissociation from the decision.

- **Method of voting.** Typically, LLC statutes are silent on how members or managers should cast their votes. Standard practice is as follows: Unless a specific request for a written vote (ballot) is presented at the meeting, voice votes are normally taken on resolutions brought before (raised at) meetings. By the time a vote occurs, often everyone is ready to say "yes." But this isn't always the case. If there is any opposition, it's usually best to poll the participants (member or managers or both) by asking each member to voice his or her vote individually. Written ballots are normally only requested when the issue at hand is controversial or contested, and members of the board don't wish to announce their decision at the meeting.

- **Proxy voting by members.** Members may sign a proxy form that allows another person to vote their membership interest at a meeting. (See Chapter 3, Section B, Step 8, for a discussion of proxies and instructions on preparing proxy forms for membership voting.)

- **Election of managers.** If members of a manager-managed LLC hold a regular (annual or other periodic) meeting for the election of managers, this is usually done by taking the voice votes of members. The managers who receive the highest number of votes will be elected to the management team—for example, the top three vote-getters out of five nominees are elected to a three-manager team. Some LLC operating agreements contain specific provisions, based on state statutes, that specify special voting procedures to be followed to nominate and elect managers at the members' meeting. For example, some operating agreements provide that any member may request the election of managers to be by written ballot or the use of cumulative voting. The latter is a special type of voting process used primarily to protect minority member interests in larger LLCs (See "Cumulative Voting by Members," below.)

Although you should know that this special election voting procedure exists, it rarely has relevance to small LLCs with roughly proportionate member-ownership. That's because the outcome of a cumulative and a regular election in these smaller LLCs is usually the same.

CUMULATIVE VOTING BY MEMBERS

Cumulative voting by members in the election of managers can help protect minority member interests in larger LLCs. If your operating agreement requires the use of cumulative voting in an election of managers, then each member can cast a total number of votes in the election equal to the number of shares owned, multiplied by the number of persons to be elected to the board. These votes can be cast all for one candidate or split up among the candidates as the member sees fit.

Example: Members A and B own 2,000 shares each, and Member C owns 1,000 shares. At the annual members' meeting, four candidates are nominated for election to a three-person board. Under normal voting rules with one share equal to one vote, C's candidate can always be outvoted by A's or B's choice. With cumulative voting, however, C is given 3,000 votes (A and B have 6,000 votes each). While still outnumbered, if C cumulates all 3,000 votes in favor of one candidate and A and B split their votes among two other candidates, C has a chance of electing his or her nominee to the board.

 Members of small manager-managed LLCs normally re-elect the entire management

Unless there is controversy or ill will among LLC principals, the members of small manager-managed LLCs routinely re-elect all LLC managers to serve another term at each annual meeting of members. Routine re-election of managers is allowed under state law, which does not limit the number of consecutive terms a manager may hold. Just as typically, the operating agreement specifies an unlimited term for managers, who serve until they resign or are removed by a vote of members. In other LLCs, the operating agreement may set up a "classified" manager structure, with a few of the managers elected each year—for example, if the members of a manager-managed LLC elect three out of nine managers each year, each manager serves for a three-year term even though members' meetings for the election of managers are held each year.

LLC ARTICLES, OPERATING AGREEMENT, OR STATE LAW MAY CONTAIN SPECIAL MEMBERSHIP VOTING RULES

As mentioned in Chapters 2 and 3, whether your LLC is manager- or member-managed, your articles or operating agreement may require the vote of all members, or a majority of the total membership interests in your LLC (not just a majority of those present at a meeting, which may be less), for some decisions. Typically, the following decisions require the approval of all or a majority of all membership interests (check your articles, your operating agreement, and your state's law as summarized in Appendix B):

- the amendment of articles of organization or operating agreement

- issuance of a new membership

- admission of a transferee of a departing member as a new member

- distribution of cash or property to members prior to the sale of a membership or dissolution of the LLC

- vote to continue the LLC after a member dies, departs, or otherwise loses a membership interest (in some states, this vote must be taken to avoid a dissolution of the LLC)

- the sale of substantially all LLC assets not in the ordinary course of business

- the voluntary dissolution of the LLC.

Very rarely, the articles or operating agreement give one class of memberships the right to a separate vote on certain proposals. So, if you're making decisions fundamental to the organization or operation of your LLC, check your articles and operating agreement for special provisions (and check your state's law in Appendix B). If you find any, make sure you understand what is required, and check your conclusions with your legal advisor if the decision is important enough.

Step 14.　Adjourn the Meeting

After the managers or members have voted on all resolutions at a meeting, the chairperson should propose adjournment. If no further business is proposed and the motion carries, the meeting is adjourned.

If the secretary didn't prepare minutes at the meeting, your next step is to prepare minutes to place in the LLC records binder. We cover these and related forms in the next chapter. For now, place all papers presented or drafted at the meeting in the folder for the meeting or directly in your LLC records binder.

If a meeting is adjourned with unfinished business

If an LLC meeting is carried over to another time when unfinished business can be concluded, we recommend providing notice to all participants of the continued meeting (even though your operating agreement and state law may require notice only to persons not in attendance at the original meeting). For instructions on providing notice of the continued meeting, see Chapter 3, Section B, Step 5. ■

How to Prepare Written Minutes of LLC Meetings

In this chapter, we show you how to use our LLC minutes form to document actions taken at LLC meetings. You will find a sample minutes form in this chapter, and a ready-to-fill-in form in Appendix D and on the computer disk. Our minutes form is designed to document the most common procedures and actions taken at LLC meetings. It allows you to insert one or more resolutions to show approval of special business at these meetings. Inserting resolutions in your minutes forms is easy, as explained in, "How to Use LLC Resolutions," below.

If you have a one-member LLC that you manage yourself

In practice, member meetings for a one-member LLC and manager meetings for a one-manager LLC are often held on paper only, to formally record decisions that the sole member or manager wishes to document. If you are in this situation, turn to Chapter 6, where we focus on the steps you need to take to prepare minutes for this type of "paper meeting." You may also record decisions by written consents. (See Chapter 7.)

However, a sole LLC member or manager can also hold a real one-person meeting (you can talk to yourself if you wish). Or you can hold a real meeting where you invite others (staff, officers, advisers, lawyers) to present reports and discuss proposals.

HOW TO USE LLC RESOLUTIONS

We've included in the minutes form contained in this chapter the standard language for the approval of business customarily handled at LLC meetings, such as the review of past business of the LLC and the election of LLC managers (for a manager-managed LLC with fixed-manager terms). To take other actions at LLC meetings, you will want to add the language of one or more resolutions to show formal approval of LLC legal, tax, and other business decisions. To help you do this, this book provides more than 80 resolutions that cover standard items of LLC legal, tax, and business transactions. (See Chapters 8 through 15 for instructions on using the various resolutions forms included with this book.) In most cases, you can simply fill in one of these resolutions and insert it into your minutes, as explained in the special instructions in this chapter.

If you need to prepare your own language for a resolution (because you want to approve an item of business at a meeting not covered by one of our resolution forms), it's easy to do. We provide examples of using your own language in the special instructions to filling out the minutes form below.

Most LLC resolutions stand on their own and don't require the preparation of additional documentation. However, some types of resolutions ratify or refer to additional backup agreements or paperwork, and you should attach this supplementary material to your minutes. For example, if members approve a resolution to make a loan to a manager, you can prepare and attach a promissory note to your minutes. We include some backup paperwork (for example, promissory note forms) with the appropriate resolutions included with this book. But finding and adding your own supplemental forms, if necessary, is also easy to do. For example, standard loan, real estate, and other business forms are available from banks, real estate brokers, legal stationers, business law libraries, and other sources.

A. OVERVIEW OF LLC MEETINGS

Before diving into the minutes form, let's review a few key details.

Regular vs. special LLC meetings. A regular LLC meeting is one scheduled in your operating agreement. It may be scheduled annually or at more or less frequent intervals, such as monthly, quarterly, or every second year. A special meeting is one held when called by one or more LLC managers or members to discuss and approve special items of LLC business. Your operating agreement may set special notice requirements for this sort of meeting. (For example, the operating agreement may require an extra two weeks of written notice to participants, in addition to the normal notice required for annual meetings.) Our minutes form below is designed to document decisions made at both regular and special LLC meetings.

Attendance at LLC meetings. The people asked to attend LLC meetings vary according to the type of LLC (member- or manager-managed), type of meeting (regular or special), and nature of the business to be proposed at a meeting. In general, members and/or managers may be asked to attend for one of two reasons:

- The LLC operating agreement or state law requires the members and/or managers to approve a particular type of proposal. (For example, the full membership must approve an amendment to the articles or operating agreement under the terms of most operating agreements as well as state statutes.)

- Even if members and/or managers are not needed to vote on a proposal, their attendance is necessary or desirable for other reasons. (For example, the managers wish to review LLC business operations with the members at the annual LLC meeting.) See "Who Attends LLC Meetings?," below, for attendance scenarios at LLC meetings.

When should minutes be prepared? Minutes should be prepared shortly after the meeting is held (within a few days or so). If you wait longer, you may forget to prepare the minutes, or be unable to follow your notes or recollection as to the proposals made and votes taken. Here are some suggestions:

- **If you hold a real meeting.** If you are preparing minutes for a face-to-face meeting, as described in Chapter 4, the secretary will normally wait until after the meeting to fill in the minutes form, based on his or her notes. Or, the secretary may prepare a draft of the minutes form before the meeting and complete it during or shortly after the meeting. Some secretaries prefer to fill out the entire minutes form during the meeting, either by using a fill-in-the-blanks minutes form (see Appendix D) or by filling in the downloaded form with a computer at the meeting.

- **If you hold a paper meeting.** To prepare minutes for a paper meeting (one that doesn't actually occur), follow our instructions in Chapter 6. The secretary normally prepares the minutes form whenever it's convenient; it need not be on the exact paper meeting date. The secretary then distributes a copy to all members for their approval, as explained in Chapter 6, Section B, Step 5.

WHO ATTENDS LLC MEETINGS?

There are several common scenarios for attendance at LLC meetings, as follows.

Annual meetings (or other regular meetings scheduled periodically in your operating agreement):

- In a member-managed LLC, the entire membership is asked to attend the annual meeting to review the prior year's business and plan upcoming LLC operations. This is a good time to propose any special resolutions that require approval, such as amendments to the articles or operating agreement, or to discuss other important items of LLC business by the membership (the possible admission of new members, approval of a cash distribution to members, and the like).

- In a manager-managed LLC, if the managers are elected at specific, fixed intervals such as yearly or every other year, the members attend an annual (or other regular) members' meeting to vote on the election (or re-election) of the managers of the LLC. Members may also review past business and discuss future operations, and vote on special items of membership business. Managers may be asked to attend the meeting to report to the membership on past and upcoming LLC operations. Following their election or re-election by the members at the annual

members' meeting, the managers will attend the annual managers' meeting to accept their management positions for another term.

- In a manager-managed LLC where the managers hold their positions for an indefinite term (until they resign or are removed by the members), the members will probably not hold annual or other regular meetings. The managers may still hold an annual or other regular meeting to discuss past business and future plans. The members may be asked to attend to hear reports given at the meeting, as well as to vote on any special membership resolutions prepared by the managers.

Special meetings (called for a particular purpose by one or more members or managers):

- In a member-managed LLC, the members are sometimes asked by other members or managers to attend a meeting to approve one or more items of LLC business.

- In a manager-managed LLC, if the matter is a standard item of business, only the managers attend special meetings to approve the action. If the matter to be decided requires membership approval (amendment of articles, admission of a new member), the members are also asked to attend. At the meeting, the managers propose the resolution, and the members vote on it.

B. PREPARING THE MINUTES FORM

This section shows you how to prepare the minutes for an LLC meeting, using the minutes form included with this book.

The LLC minutes form presented in this section is designed to accommodate any meeting scenarios. We provide check boxes and language to handle each of the options for attendance and the approval of regular and special matters.

Below is a sample of the minutes form included on the CD-ROM and as a tear-out form in Appendix D. (See Appendix A for information on selecting and using the CD-ROM files.) Fill the form out following the special instructions provided below.

MINUTES OF LLC MEETING

LLC Name: _____[insert name of LLC]_____

1. A meeting of the ___["members" and/or "managers"]___ of the LLC was held on _____[date of meeting]___ at __[time of meeting]__ at _____[place of meeting]_____, ❶ for the transaction of all business that may properly be brought by participants before the meeting, including any of the special purposes listed below:

    [If applicable, check one or more boxes below, and supply additional information as appropriate.] ❷

    ☐   Election of LLC manager(s) by LLC members

    ☐   Review of past LLC business and discussion of future operations

    ☐   The approval of one or more resolutions as follows:

    [If this box is checked, insert summaries of resolutions.]

2. _____[name of chairperson]_____ acted as chairperson, and _____[name of meeting secretary]_____ acted as secretary of the meeting. ❸

3. The chairperson called the meeting to order.

4. The secretary announced that the meeting was: ❹

    [Check one of the boxes below and supply additional information.]

    ☐   a regular meeting scheduled to be held __[insert period for holding regular LLC meeting]__ under provisions in the LLC operating agreement

    [or]

    ☐   a special meeting called by the following person(s):

    _____   ☐ Manager   ☐ Member   ☐ Other: _____

    _____   ☐ Manager   ☐ Member   ☐ Other: _____

    _____   ☐ Manager   ☐ Member   ☐ Other: _____

5. The secretary announced that the meeting was held pursuant to notice, if required and as required under the operating agreement of this LLC, or that notice had been waived by all participants entitled to receive notice under the operating agreement. Copies of any certificates of mailing of notice prepared by the secretary of the LLC and any written waivers signed by participants entitled to receive notice of this meeting were attached to these minutes by the secretary. ❺

6. ☐ **Members Voting.** [Check if members will vote at the meeting, and supply information below.]

   The secretary announced that an alphabetical list of the names and interests held by all members of the LLC was available and open to inspection by any person in attendance at the meeting. The secretary announced that there were present, in person or by proxy, the following voting power of the members of the LLC, representing a quorum of the members. (The secretary attached written proxy statements, executed by the appropriate members, to these minutes for any membership voting power listed below as held by a proxyholder.) ❻

   Name of Member   Member's Voting Power

   _____   _____

   _____   _____

   _____   _____

   _____   _____

7. ☐ **Managers Voting.** [Check if managers will vote at the meeting, and supply information below.]

   The secretary announced that an alphabetical list of the names of the managers of the LLC was available and open to inspection by any person in attendance at the meeting. The secretary announced that the following managers of the LLC were present, representing a quorum of the managers: ❼

   Name of Manager

   _____

   _____

   _____

   _____

   _____

8. The secretary announced that the following persons were also present at the meeting in the following capacities: ❽

Name   Title

_____   _____

_____   _____

_____   _____

_____   _____

9 ☐ **Previous Meeting Minutes.** (Check if previous meeting minutes will be approved at this meeting, and supply information, checking one or both additional boxes below.)

The secretary announced that the minutes of the LLC meeting held on __[date of prior meeting]__ ❾

☐ had been distributed prior to the meeting, and the secretary was in receipt of any written approval of minutes forms signed and returned by persons who had read and approved the minutes.

☐ were distributed at the meeting, then read by the secretary.

After counting any written approvals, and, if necessary, taking the voice vote of __["members" and/ or "managers"]__ at the meeting, the secretary announced that the minutes as distributed, read, and corrected, as appropriate, were approved. The secretary attached a copy of the approved minutes together with any signed approvals of minutes forms to these minutes.

10. The following reports were presented at the meeting by the following persons: ❿

_____ [describe reports and name of person presenting report(s)] _____

_____

_____

11. ☐ **Election of Managers.** (Check if managers will be elected, and supply information below.)

The chairperson announced that the next item of business was the nomination and election of the managers for another __["one-year" or other period]__ term. The following nominations were made and seconded: ⓫

Names of Manager Nominee(s):

_____

_____

_____

The secretary next took the votes of members entitled to vote for the election of managers at the meeting, and, after counting the votes, announced that the following persons were elected to serve as managers of this LLC:

Names of Elected Manager(s):

_____

_____

_____

_____

☐ **Managers' Acceptance.** [Check if managers accepted positions.]

The above managers, having been elected, accepted their management positions. The secretary announced that the presence of current managers of the LLC at the meeting represented a quorum of managers of the LLC.

12. ☐ **Resolutions.** [Check if resolutions will be passed, and supply information below.]

After discussion, on motion duly made and carried by the affirmative vote of [check one or more boxes and supply any required information]: ⓬

   ☐ a majority of the membership voting power in attendance

   ☐ a majority of the managers in attendance

   ☐ other, as follows:

   _____[insert other member and/or manager approval or list votes of each participant]_____

   _____

   _____

The following resolution(s) was(were) approved at the meeting:

_____ [describe the resolution(s) approved by the above voting procedure] _____

_____

_____

☐ **Additional Resolutions.** (Check if additional resolutions will be passed, and supply information below.)

After discussion, on motion duly made and carried by the affirmative vote of [check one or more boxes and supply any required information]: **12**

    ☐ a majority of the membership voting power in attendance

    ☐ a majority of the managers in attendance

    ☐ other, as follows:

        [insert other member and/or manager approval or list votes of each participant]

_____

_____

The following resolution(s) was(were) approved at the meeting:

_____ [describe the resolution(s) approved by the above voting procedure] _____

_____

_____

There being no further business to come before the meeting, it was adjourned on motion duly made and carried. **13**

The above minutes were completed in final form on the date shown below by the undersigned secretary of the meeting:

Date: _____

Signature: _____

Title: _____

Special Instructions

❶ Insert the type of meeting ("members," "managers," or "members/managers") and the date, time, and place of the meeting. Many operating agreements call for meetings to be held at the principal office of the LLC unless the members or managers have decided to hold the meeting elsewhere.

❷ Use one or more check boxes to show the purpose(s) of the LLC meeting. Note that the preamble states that the meeting was held for the transaction of "any lawful business." This means that if the purpose of the meeting was simply to allow the members and/or managers to get together to discuss and decide any matter of importance, you do not need to check any of the boxes—in this case, you are simply holding a general LLC meeting for the discussion of LLC-related business.

The third box is an important one for special meetings called to discuss and approve one or more special items of LLC business. Check this box if a purpose of calling the meeting was to discuss a specific proposal (other than the election of managers or review and planning of LLC business—these matters are covered by the first and second check boxes). In the space provided, briefly summarize the specific items of business for which the meeting was called—such as "a change of LLC tax year," "approval of a cash distribution to members," "admission of a new member," "purchase of the membership interest of a departing member," and the like.

❸ Insert the name and title of the persons who acted as chairperson and secretary of the meeting. Typically, the LLC president will act as chairperson, but you may decide to designate any other officer or a manager or member of the LLC. Usually, the secretary of the LLC acts as secretary of all LLC meetings. In his or her absence, another officer typically assumes this task.

Note: In the instructions for this form, unless otherwise specified, references to the "secretary" are to the secretary of the LLC meeting. Again, normally this is the person who is secretary of the LLC.

❹ If the meeting is an annual or other regular meeting scheduled in your operating agreement, check the first box, and insert in the blank the period for hold-ing the meeting. For example, if the meeting is an annual meeting, check the first box, then insert "annually" in the blank; if the meeting is a monthly meeting, insert "monthly." Insert another period for regular meetings held at other intervals, such as "the first Monday of each calendar quarter."

If the meeting was not scheduled in your operating agreement, check the second box to show the meeting is a special meeting, then list the person(s) who called the meeting. Next to each name, check whether the person is a member and/or manager of the LLC, or has another title. If you check "other," indicate the person's title, such as "president" or "treasurer." Remember: Your operating agreement may specify who may call LLC meetings—typically a manager, a specified number of members, or an LLC officer. (See Chapter 3, Step 3.)

If your operating agreement is silent on this issue, state law may specify who may call LLC member or manager meetings. (See the "Meeting Requirements" section for your state in Appendix B for any state default rules.)

❺ This paragraph states that *if required by your operating agreement* each meeting participant either 1) was given notice if and as required by your operating agreement or 2) waived notice by signing a written waiver of notice form. Although your operating agreement (or state law if your agreement is silent on providing notice of meetings) may not require the giving of notice for some or all LLC meetings—particularly regular LLC meetings scheduled in your operating agreement—we generally recommend providing written notice prior to each meeting, since this is the best way to make sure each member or manager knows about the meeting well in advance and understands the nature of the proposals to be discussed there. (See Chapter 3, Step 5, for notice of meeting requirements and our recommendations concerning notice.) If you own and run a closely held LLC, you may be able to safely use waiver of notice forms.(See, "Closely held LLCs: Hand out waiver of notice forms at the meeting to save time," below.)

If notice was mailed to members, attach to the minutes any Certificate of Mailing of Notice or Acknowledgment of Receipts. (See Chapter 3, Section B, Steps 7 and 9b.) Attach any written waivers of notice for the meeting that were signed by members. (See Chapter 6, Section B, Step 1, for instructions on preparing waiver of notice forms.)

Closely held LLCs: Hand out waiver of notice forms at the meeting to save time

Small LLCs with only a few members or managers—who are almost guaranteed to attend meetings—sometimes decide to dispense with official premeeting notice formalities entirely, and, instead, the LLC secretary informally notifies all members of the meeting. The secretary of the meeting then hands out written waiver of notice forms for each participant to sign at the start of the meeting. This is perfectly legal and does no practical harm if you are sure each member knows about the meeting and its purpose well in advance, and as long as all members and managers are getting along fairly well.

6 Check this box if members attended and voted at your LLC meeting. This paragraph applies to a meeting of members or a joint meeting of managers and members where members were asked to vote. If only managers attended the meeting, or if members were in attendance to hear or participate in discussions, but not to vote, don't check this box—skip to Special Instruction #7, below.

The first sentence of the paragraph restates a common practice that an alphabetical list of members was made available for inspection during the meeting (to allow the secretary and members to assess the voting interests of other members). You can prepare a Meeting Participant List as explained in Chapter 3, Section B, Step 4, or you can simply make your LLC records binder available for inspection at the meeting, if it includes a membership register with a current listing of your members and their membership interests. The paragraph also states the important fact that a quorum of the membership was in attendance at the meeting. If a quorum is not present, members can attend the meeting but can't vote to approve LLC business.

If you check the box at the start of the paragraph (because members attended and voted at the meeting), list the names of the members present at the meeting. To the right of each name, show the voting power of each member. Remember that how voting power is handled is set out by your operating agreement or, in the absence of a provision in your agreement, by state law. (See Appendix B.) Generally, members vote either 1) per capita (one vote each), 2) according to their capital account balances in the LLC, 3) according to their profits interests (rights to receive profits of the LLC), or 4) according to both their capital and profits interests in the LLC. In cases 2 through 4, a member's voting power will be specified as a percentage of the total voting power in the LLC. (For example, a member whose capital account reflects 10% of the LLC's capital will have 10% of the LLC voting power.) To measure and specify a member's voting power, see "How to specify a member's voting power" in Chapter 3, Section B, Step 4.

The total voting power listed here should be at least equal to a quorum of your membership as defined in your operating agreement or under state law. Typically, a quorum is defined as 1) a majority of the total number of members or 2) members who own a majority of the capital and/or profits interests in your LLC. (For more information on quorum requirements, see Chapter 4, Step 8.)

EXAMPLE: The annual meeting of Raster Graphics, LLC, a manager-managed LLC, was held as scheduled in the LLC operating agreement. Both managers and members were in attendance, with the members voting to approve a resolution proposed by management to seek an additional $2,000 capital contribution from each of the members. (Notice of the proposal was mailed to each member in advance of the meeting.) The LLC managers are the CEO and VP, neither of whom are LLC members. The LLC has four members, with each member voting according to his or her profits interests in the LLC. A majority of the profits interests constitutes a quorum of members under the operating agreement.

Stan, a staff member acting as the LLC and meeting secretary, notes at the meeting that profits interests in the LLC are proportionate to capital contributions. In other words, a member who contributed 10% of the capital to the LLC also gets a 10% profits interest in the LLC and 10% of the LLC voting power. (This is the way most LLC operating agreements set up capital and profits interests.) He also notes by referring to the membership register of the LLC brought to the meeting that the following members, who made the following capital contributions, are present at the meeting: Max Nyquist, $10,000; Carol Starling, $25,000; Rudy Caruthers, $6,000.

Stan also notes that one member, Sarah Schelling, who made a $9,000 capital contribution, is not present. (She called a few days prior to the meeting to say that she would not attend, but was comfortable letting the other members vote to decide on the membership proposal without sending a proxy to represent her membership interest.) Stan computes that members who contributed $41,000 of the LLC's total capital of $50,000 were in attendance, which represented a majority of the capital as well as profits interests of the LLC. A majority of the LLC's voting power was, therefore, in attendance and the members could vote on the additional capital contribution proposal presented by the managers. After the meeting, Stan fills out this portion of the minutes to read as follows:

Name of Member	Member's Voting Power
Max Nyquist	20%
Carol Starling	50%
Rudy Caruthers	12%

What about proxyholders?

If a member was represented by written proxy at a meeting, list the proxyholder's name on the left, followed by the words "proxyholder for" and the name of the member. Show the member's voting power (that has been delegated to the proxyholder) in the column at the right. Attach to the minutes a written proxy statement dated and signed by each member whose voting power is represented by proxy. See Chapter 3, Section B, Step 8, for a discussion of when to use and how to prepare a written proxy for use at members' meetings.

❼ Check this box if managers attended your LLC meeting. This is the case whenever you hold a manager meeting or joint meeting of LLC managers and members. If you check it, list the managers in attendance at the meeting below the paragraph. Of course, a quorum of managers—normally, a majority of the number of managers under most operating agreements and state default rules—must be present for the managers to take action at the meeting.

❽ Specify any LLC officers and others in attendance at the meeting. If a manager or member was also present in the capacity of an LLC officer, a committee chairperson, or a consultant, or in another capacity—for example, as CEO to present a report—list them here again in their nonmember or nonmanager capacity.

❾ For some LLC meetings—particularly a meeting scheduled within a month or so of the past meeting—participants may be asked by the secretary to approve the minutes of the previous LLC meeting. This applies if the last meeting was of the same type as the current meeting—for example, if both meetings were a meeting of members or a joint meeting of managers and members. Mostly, this formality of approving prior minutes is meant to remind everyone of any special business approved at the last meeting, and to allow any objections prior to placing a formal copy of the minutes in the LLC records book. If this item of business was part of the current meeting, check this box, and insert the date of the prior meeting in the first paragraph. Then check one or both of the next two boxes as follows:

Box 1. If you sent copies of the minutes of the last meeting to each participant to read prior to the meeting (as part of the premeeting materials prepared as explained in Chapter 3, Section B, Step 6), check this box. To save time and get approval by all members and/or managers to the prior minutes, the secretary also may have sent out a written approval of minutes forms for signing and returning by people receiving the premeeting materials. (This form is covered in Chapter 6, Section B, Step 3). The text following this box acknowledges that these approval forms may have been sent, signed by participants, and returned to the secretary.

Box 2. If you distributed copies of the minutes at the current meeting, check this box.

Boxes 1 and 2. You can check both boxes 1 and 2 if you combine these procedures to approve the minutes of the last meeting. For example, the secretary may have distributed the minutes prior to the meeting, but not received written approvals back from all of the participants. In this case, the secretary should redistribute copies of the prior meeting's minutes at the current meeting and read them, then take a voice vote to make sure everyone approves the minutes.

Normally, the prior meeting's minutes are routinely approved. But if any member or manager brings up any objections or mistakes, the secretary will need to work these out. This can be done either by making appropriate corrections to the prior minutes and taking a new approval vote, or by obtaining a majority vote to approve the final version of the minutes over the objection of one or more participants.

In the last paragraph of this section, insert whether members and/or managers approved the minutes of the last meeting. Again, we assume the prior and the current meeting are of the same type. Insert "members" if both meetings were members' meetings, "managers" if both were manager meetings, or "members and managers" if both were joint managers'/members' meetings. The secretary should attach the approved minutes of the prior meeting to the minutes of the current meeting, and also attach any written approval of minutes forms signed and returned to the secretary.

❿ Managers, members, or LLC officers may have presented annual or special reports at the meeting. For example, the president may have presented an annual operating report and the treasurer may have summarized the past year's financial profits or losses. List a description of the reports given, such as "treasurer's report of year-end profits and loss," along with the name and title of the presenter. The secretary should attach any written copies of reports to the minutes.

⓫ This box does not apply to member-managed LLCs. For manager-managed LLCs, check this box if the meeting was held for members to elect managers of the LLC. In LLCs where managers are elected to fixed terms, this is a typical item of business for the annual members' (or joint managers'/members') meeting, but also can be an agenda item for a specially called members' meeting held at the end of managers' terms. It also can apply to manager-managed LLCs in which managers serve for indefinite terms. For instance, the members may be asked to attend a meeting to fill a vacancy in management after a manager resigns or is removed. However, LLC operating agreements and default state law rules often allow the remaining managers to fill a temporary manager vacancy themselves.

If you check this box, supply the additional information in this section. In the first sentence, insert the terms of office of managers in the blank. If managers have a fixed term, a one-year term is the most common, but your operating agreement may set a longer term. If managers are elected to serve for indefinite terms, insert "indefinite" in this blank.

Under "Name of Manager Nominee(s)," fill in the names of all nominees who the members may vote for. Many small LLCs simply nominate (and re-elect) the current manager team for another term of office, but members or managers may place other names in nomination. Just as in a small corporation where the directors who are majority shareholders are routinely nominated and re-elected, everyone in an LLC typically nominates and re-elects the current managing members unless they decide it's time for a change.

Does your manager-managed LLC have a classified management structure?

LLC statutes allow manager-managed LLCs to provide for a classified or staggered manager election procedure in their operating agreement. Typically, this means that the management team is broken down—or classified—into two or more sections, with the elections for each section occurring in alternate years.

> **EXAMPLE:** Quark LLC, a manager-managed LLC, has a nine-member manager team, and its operating agreement provides for one-third of the managers to be re-elected every three years. At each annual LLC members' meeting, three of the managers are elected to a three-year term.

In the spaces under the heading "Names of Elected Manager(s)," indicate the persons who were elected by the members to serve as managers for another term (or for an indefinite term). Of course, if your manager-managed LLC has just one manager, only one name will be inserted here.

There are different ways membership votes can be taken and counted. Most LLCs elect managers by voice vote or written ballot, and those nominees who receive the most votes win. Remember, while sometimes each member gets one vote (a per capita voting scheme), under a different operating agreement the voting power of each member may be expressed as a percentage of total membership voting power, since it may be tied to the member's proportionate share of capital and/or profits interests in the LLC. (See Special Instruction #6, above.)

> **EXAMPLE:** Ten members of a manager-managed LLC, each with 10% of the LLC voting power, are voting to elect three of five nominees to a three-person management team. Each member may cast his or her 10% vote in favor of each of three candidates (each may cast a 10% vote three times). The results are as follows:

Candidate	Percent of Vote Received	Result
Nominee 1	100%	Elected (Ten members voted for this candidate)
Nominee 2	100%	Elected (Ten members voted for this candidate)
Nominee 3	50%	Elected (Five members voted for this candidate)
Nominee 4	30%	Not Elected (Three members voted for this candidate)
Nominee 5	20%	Not Elected (Two members voted for this candidate)

Note that a total of 300% of the voting power of the LLC was exercised. This makes sense since the ten members, who hold 100% of the LLC voting power, each get to vote for three candidates. The total voting power percentage cast for each candidate is totaled, and then these candidate totals are compared to find the three candidates who received the three highest percentages of LLC voting power. In the above example, Nominees 1 and 2 received votes from all ten members, while Nominees 3, 4, and 5 received the votes of five, three, and two members, respectively. The three candidates receiving the largest number of votes, Nominees 1, 2, and 3, are elected to the board.

Cumulative voting procedures. There is another way of electing managers—namely, by cumulative voting procedures. Your articles or operating agreement should state whether your members may ask to cumulate their votes to elect managers of the LLC. (Most LLCs do not allow cumulative voting.) Cumulative voting differs from standard voting (called "plurality" voting) in that a member gets to cumulate his or her entire election voting power in favor of any one candidate, or to split it up as she sees fit. In the above example, this means that each member gets to vote 30% of the LLC voting power (the normal 10% voting power possessed by the member times the number of managers who are to be elected) in any way the member see fits.

> **EXAMPLE:** Using the same ten members and five nominees as in the previous example, under cumulative voting rules each member is given a total of 30% to cast for one or more manager nominees. This means that any one member has a better chance of tipping the scales in favor of one candidate, since he or she is no longer limited to casting 10% voting power for a particular candidate. Of course, a member will lose a chance to vote for any other candidates by casting all 30% for one nominee. In fact, this is the purpose of cumulative voting, and a reason why it is used in larger LLCs: It gives minority members a better shot at electing one candidate to the management team, despite the voting power of the majority members. (For a further discussion of cumulative voting rules, see Chapter 4, Step 13.)

At the end of Item 11 is a check box. If the managers were elected at a membership-only meeting, leave this box blank. Check this box only if all of the following are true:

- You held a joint managers'/members' meeting.
- The members elected managers at the meeting.
- A quorum of the newly elected managers were present at the meeting after their election.
- The managers accepted their management positions.

⓬ This section of the minutes allows you to record the passage of one or more resolutions that were discussed and voted on at the LLC meeting. If your meeting was held simply to present reports, hold discussions, and, if appropriate, elect managers of a manager-managed LLC to another term, you can skip this section. (The previous sections of the minutes form cover these areas.) For most LLC meetings, however, this section should be used to show the actual business of the meeting—that is, the discussion and approval of one or more special items of business—by the passage of resolutions by LLC managers and/or members.

If your meeting was held to approve one or more specific resolutions, check the box at the start of this section, then check one or more of the subsequent three boxes to show the type of vote used to approve the resolution. Check the first box if a majority of the membership voting power present at the meeting passed the resolution. This is the normal membership voting rule for most member-managed LLCs or for membership approval of matters brought before the members in a manager-managed LLC.

Check the second box if a majority of managers present at the meeting passed the resolution. This is the normal manager-voting rule for manager-managed LLCs. Check both boxes if both members and managers approved the proposal by a majority vote. If your members and/or managers approved the proposal by a different vote—for example, by the unanimous vote of all members or managers (see "LLC special vote requirements," below)—check the "other" box, then insert the vote of members and/or managers used to pass the resolution. Checking the "other" box is also appropriate if you wish to list "yes" and "no" votes of each member and/or manager to a resolution, regardless of the type of vote required to pass the resolution.

LLC special vote requirements

Your LLC operating agreement or state law may require a special vote for special matters. For example, a common requirement is that all, or a majority of all, members (not just a majority of members present at a meeting) approve amendments to LLC articles or operating agreements or the admission of a new member to the LLC. To review LLC voting requirements for special matters, see the sidebar in Chapter 4 entitled "LLC Articles, Operating Agreement, or State Law May Contain Special Membership Voting Rules."

After checking the appropriate boxes, insert the resolution approved by members and/or managers at the meeting. In many instances, you can insert one of the ready-to-use resolutions included in this book, following the instructions for preparing the resolution from one of the later chapters (Chapters 8 through 15). See the beginning of Appendix D for a list of tear-out and computer disk resolution forms included with this book, with cross-references to the chapters and sections of the book that contain instructions for preparing each resolution.

If you wish to approve business not covered by one of our resolutions, supply your own language for the resolution in this space in your minutes. You don't need to use fancy or legal language for your resolution. Just describe as specifically as you can the transaction or matter approved by your members and/or managers at the meeting in a short, concise statement. Normally, resolutions start with a preamble of the following sort: "The members resolved that ...", but this is not required. Here are a couple examples of resolution language.

EXAMPLE 1 (Amendment of articles): "The members ratified a managers' resolution adding the following new articles to the LLC's articles of organization: [language of new articles] ."

EXAMPLE 2 (Amendment of operating agreement): "The members approved an amendment to the operating agreement of the LLC. The text of the changed operating agreement provision is as follows: [language of amended operating agreement provision] ."

What If More Than One Resolution Is Approved at an LLC Meeting?

If you use the same voting procedure to pass more than one resolution, you can list the other resolutions below the first one in the space provided in Section 12 of the minutes form. But if you use different types of voting procedures for different resolutions, you need to group them together according to the voting procedure used to pass them. An example should help clarify what we mean.

Example. Cake Walk Custom Bakery, L.L.C., is member-managed. At the LLC's annual meeting, three proposals were presented by the secretary for approval by the members. Two were passed by normal voting procedures—that is, by a majority of membership voting power present at the meeting. The third proposal—an amendment to the LLC operating agreement—required the vote of all members. It also passed. After the meeting, the LLC secretary filled in Section 12 in the minutes form as follows:

12. ☒ Resolutions. [Check if resolutions will be passed, and supply information below.]

    After discussion, on motion duly made and carried by the affirmative vote of (check one or more boxes and supply any required information)

    ☒ a majority of the membership voting power in attendance

    ☐ a majority of the managers in attendance

    ☐ other, as follows: _____

    _____.

The following resolution(s) was(were) approved at the meeting:

    <u>The members resolved that the accounting and tax period of this LLC shall end on May 31 of each year.</u>

    <u>The members approved the hiring of Laurence Kernan for the position of Chief Financial Officer.</u>

And on the next page:

☒ **Additional Resolutions.** (Check, if extra resolutions will be passed, and supply information below.)

After discussion, on motion duly made and carried by the affirmative vote of (check one or more boxes and supply any required information)

    ☐ a majority of the membership voting power in attendance

    ☐ a majority of the managers in attendance

    ☒ other, as follows: <u>unanimous vote of all of the members of the LLC.</u>

The following resolution(s) was(were) approved at the meeting:

The members approved an amendment to the operating agreement of the LLC. The text of the changed operating agreement provision is as follows: <u>[language of amended operating agreement provision]</u> .

As you can see, the secretary used the first page of Section 12 of the minutes form to show approval by normal membership voting of the first two resolutions passed at the meeting. The secretary then filled in the "Additional Resolutions" section to show the approval of the operating agreement amendment by all members.

Our tear-out minutes form includes an additional page that duplicates the first page of Section 12 to allow you to do this. If you need to show the separate passage of additional resolutions, just copy this page as many times as you need, then fill them in. If you use the computer forms, just copy and paste the page that follows the first page of Section 12 as many times as you need.

⑬ This concluding adjournment paragraph and signature line are included on a separate page. It should be attached at the very end of your minutes, after your resolution page or pages (see Special Instruction #12, above). The secretary of the meeting should date and sign on the blanks, then type his or her title (usually LLC Secretary or another LLC officer). The date inserted should be the date of completion of the minutes, not the date of the meeting.

Save your minutes

Remember to file the completed minutes in your LLC records binder together with all attachments. If you prepared a separate meeting folder for the meeting (see Chapter 3, Section B, Step 1), now is the time to transfer all forms and attachments related to the meeting from the folder to your LLC records binder. ■

How to Hold a Paper LLC Meeting

In this chapter, we present the few simple steps necessary to document a "paper" meeting of your LLC members and/or managers. With a paper meeting, members or managers don't actually hold a meeting, but instead arrive at decisions informally. To make a clear record of these decisions, minutes are prepared (normally by the LLC president or secretary), and the managers or members approve them by signing them.

A. DECIDE WHETHER TO HOLD A PAPER MEETING

The paper meeting procedure works best for family LLCs or for LLCs with only a few managers or members who work together or know each other well and agree on most LLC decisions. Of course, paper meetings also work well for a one-person LLC, where the sole member really doesn't need to sit down and talk to himself (or if he does, then perhaps it's time for a two-week vacation).

In such small LLCs, the paper meeting procedure allows LLC principals to conduct and document routine LLC business without going through the motions of holding a face-to-face meeting. Legally, preparing and ratifying paperwork for a fictional LLC meeting will not present problems for your LLC as long as every member or manager agrees to the procedure and, of course, approves the decisions reflected in the minutes of the paper meeting.

⚠ Avoid paper meetings if there is conflict or disagreement

We usually recommend paper meetings for small, closely held LLCs with no more than a few members and managers. However, even for small LLCs, we suggest you use this procedure for LLC decisions only when everyone is really in agreement. If there is even a whiff of dissent in the wind, or if the decision requires additional discussion, it is far better to hold a real meeting.

1. Documenting Past Decisions With Paper Meetings

If you failed to properly document past LLC meetings of your managers and/or members, you are not alone. Many, if not most, smaller LLCs that do their own paperwork forget to document important legal and tax decisions as they occur, putting off the task of preparing the paperwork until later. Often, the impetus for preparing this overlooked paperwork is an IRS audit or a request for minutes of a meeting from members or managers, or a bank or other financial institution.

As long as all managers and members mutually agreed to the past actions when they were taken, using the paper meeting approach to re-create LLC records after the fact should work well for your LLC.

EXAMPLE: Small Systems, LLC, is a small, closely held member-managed LLC with six members who work in the business. The LLC has been in operation for five years when the treasurer is notified of an IRS audit of the LLC's informational income tax returns from the last two years. (A multi-member LLC files informational partnership returns unless it has elected corporate tax treatment—see Chapter 9.) For the audit, the treasurer is asked to produce minutes of any LLC meetings for the years in question.

Like many other small LLCs, the daily grind of business has consumed the energies of the co-owners. Procedural niceties, such as annual membership meetings (required to be held under provisions in the LLC operating agreement), have been skipped. The only special items of formal legal or tax paperwork executed during the first five years of the LLC were the signing of a lease by the LLC president and treasurer, as well as the approval by members of a change of accounting period recommended by the LLC tax advisor. These decisions were approved by all members informally.

The members decide it is best to formalize these past decisions by preparing paper minutes for annual membership meetings for the last five years. They also decide to prepare minutes of two special membership meetings to formally document the approval of the LLC lease and the change of accounting period. These minutes of paper meetings are placed in the LLC records binder, and copies of the minutes of meetings for the two years in question are given to the IRS.

2. Comparison of Paper Meetings and Written Consents

As we have mentioned several times, for those who don't want to hold a formal LLC meeting, or for those who missed holding one, there are two alternative procedures:

- preparing minutes of a paper meeting, or
- acting by written consent.

If you prepare minutes for a paper meeting, you are, in essence, approving LLC business by the written consent of your managers and/or members. (We assume all members and/or managers will be listed in your minutes of the paper meeting.) So the two procedures are quite similar. Which one you use depends on your tastes and your reasons for preparing the documentation. If you think minutes look better than a written consent to document the approval of an LLC decision, use the minutes of a paper meeting approach; if it seems simpler to obtain the written consent of members and/or managers to a decision, use written consents instead.

Here is a recap of a few important points if you're still not sure whether paper meetings or written consents best meet your immediate needs.

For standard annual business, minutes of paper meetings are usually preferable over written consents. Minutes of paper meetings summarize the discussion and approval of items of business taken up annually by the members and/or managers. Such business includes the annual review of past and present LLC business by LLC members or managers, as well as the annual election of managers (in a manager-managed LLC). The reason to use minutes of paper meetings for standard decisions is simple: The IRS, courts, financial institutions, and others generally expect

LLC records to contain standard minutes of meeting forms. Written consent forms with no supporting documentation may not be enough to convince others that you paid attention to the ongoing formalities of LLC life, particularly if your LLC operating agreement requires the holding of regular LLC meetings.

Written consents can be used safely to show approval of special items of business. Written consent forms are generally used to document special decisions that would normally be approved at special meetings of members and/or managers. In smaller LLCs, these isolated decisions, approved as needed, are commonly approved and documented with written consent forms rather than the more formal minutes of a paper meeting.

LLC records may contain both minutes and consent forms. It's fine to prepare minutes of paper meetings for some decisions and written consents for others.

> **EXAMPLE:** Bert and Jennifer are a married couple and the two active members of a small manager-managed LLC. They are its only two managers. Their children have been given an investment interest in the business as nonmanaging minority members. Bert and Jennifer routinely re-elect themselves as managers at the end of each year. (The LLC operating agreement gives managers a one-year term.)
>
> After a few years of operation, they realize that they haven't kept up their LLC records. Bert prepares minutes of the annual membership meetings for the past two years, showing the nomination and re-election of each manager for another one-year term. He accompanies these with minutes of annual manager meetings showing the managers' (Bert's and Jennifer's) acceptance of their re-election for another year. Of course, these minutes forms also restate the discussion and approval of standard agenda items and business normally taken up at these meetings, such as reading and approval of past minutes and the review of LLC business operations.

To save time and form preparation, Bert prepares a written consent form showing membership approval of a special decision approved by Bert and Jennifer during the second year of the LLC: the admission of their children as new members of the LLC. Approval of the admission of the children as LLC members could also be documented by preparing minutes of a paper membership meeting attended by Bert and Jennifer (at the time, the only two members of the LLC). But consent forms seem adequate, especially given the fact that the annual meetings are now fully documented.

B. How to Prepare Minutes of Paper LLC Meetings

If you've decided to hold a paper meeting, follow the steps below to prepare the necessary paperwork.

Step 1. Prepare a Waiver of Notice of Meeting Form

If you're going to prepare minutes for an LLC meeting that will never actually occur, you'll obviously want to sidestep (legally) any formal call and notice requirements for holding the meeting. (See Chapter 3, Section B, Steps 3 and 5, for an overview of call and notice requirements contained in operating agreements and state LLC statutes.) The best way to do this is to have each meeting participant entitled to notice—each member and/or manager who will be shown as in attendance at the meeting—sign a written "Waiver of Notice of Meeting" form. The waivers may be dated before, on, or after the meeting date that will be shown in the minutes. State LLC laws allow waivers of meeting notice to be signed at any time, either before or after the date of a meeting.

We strongly advise you to always summarize the purpose(s) of the upcoming meeting in your Waiver of Notice of Meeting form. In some cases, it is legally required. This way you make sure all managers and/or members appreciate the nature of the business to be reflected in your minutes. Plus, state laws sometimes prohibit the transaction of any business not specified either in the notice, or the waiver of notice, for a special LLC meeting.

Other reasons to use a Waiver of Notice of Meeting form

You may use a Waiver of Notice of Meeting form even if you are planning to hold a real meeting. As discussed earlier in Chapters 3 through 5, you should use a waiver of notice form whenever you wish to hold a meeting of your members and/or managers and do not have the time, or choose not to spend the time, to provide everyone with advance verbal or written notice.

Below is a sample of the Waiver of Notice of Meeting form included on the CD-ROM and as a tear-out form in Appendix D. (See Appendix A for information on selecting and using the CD-ROM files.) Fill the form out following the special instructions provided below.

By signing this form, the manager or member waives any meeting notice requirements that are required under state law, as well as any additional or alternative notice rules set out in your operating agreement. You can prepare one Waiver of Notice of Meeting form for multiple managers and/or members to sign, or you can prepare one form for each person.

Pass out all paperwork at once
In Steps 2 through 5, below, we provide instructions on filling out paper minutes and approval forms that you'll send to your managers and/or members. So, to avoid contacting managers or members twice (once to sign the waiver, and a second time to approve the paper minutes), prepare the waiver forms and include them for signing when you pass out all paperwork.

WAIVER OF NOTICE OF MEETING

Name of LLC: _____

The undersigned waive(s) notice of and consent to the holding of the meeting of the LLC held at

_____[location of meeting]_____ on _____[date of meeting]___ at

__[time of meeting]__ . The purposes of the meeting are as follows:

[insert summary of purpose(s) of meeting] ❶

_____

_____

_____

_____

_____

_____

Dated: _____ ❷

Signature   Printed Name

_____   _____

_____   _____

_____   _____

_____   _____

_____   _____

Special Instructions

❶ When preparing a waiver of notice form, whether for a real or paper meeting, it's always important that you state the purpose(s) of the meeting. Be as specific as you can regarding the proposals to be presented at the meeting.

> **EXAMPLE:** A meeting of members is held on paper to approve an amendment of the operating agreement that requires additional capital contributions from members whenever a majority of managers decides additional capital is needed by the LLC. The purpose of the meeting stated in the waiver of notice form reads as follows: "to add a new provision to the LLC operating agreement to allow managers to require additional capital contributions from members."

❷ If more than one person will sign the form, the date inserted here should be the date the first person signs the waiver form.

 Who signs the waiver form?

- If the waiver is for notice of a members' meeting, have all members sign it.

- If the meeting is a managers' meeting, have all managers sign it.

- If it is a joint managers'/members' meeting, all members and managers should sign it.

Step 2. Prepare Minutes of the Paper Meeting

Your next step is to prepare the actual minutes for your paper LLC meeting. Usually, the secretary of the LLC prepares and distributes this paperwork, but the task can be assigned to anyone. Have the designated person follow these steps:

- To prepare minutes, follow the sample LLC minutes form with instructions provided in Chapter 5. Fill out all blanks as if you were holding a real meeting, with all members or managers present. For example, for the date and time, fill in the date and time the minutes were prepared. For location of the meeting, fill in the principal office of the LLC.

- Make copies of the minutes for each manager and/or member (who will review them prior to signing the Approval of LLC Minutes form discussed in the next step).

- Place a copy of the minutes of the paper meeting in your LLC records binder.

Step 3. Prepare an Approval of LLC Minutes Form

After preparing minutes for your paper meeting, we recommend that you have each manager and/or member specifically sign off on the decisions approved in the minutes by signing an approval of minutes form. *This step is essential when you use the paper meeting procedure to document past LLC decision making.* Because a real meeting was not held, you need to be sure everyone agrees to your summary of the decisions reflected in your minutes. (Again, if the meeting is a members' meeting, get the signature of *all* members; if a managers' meeting, obtain the approval of *all* managers. For a joint managers'/members' meeting, have all members and managers sign the approval.)

 When to use an Approval of LLC Minutes form for minutes of a real LLC meeting

The Approval of LLC Minutes form can come in handy to obtain approval of minutes of a real LLC meeting, after the meeting has been held and the minutes have been prepared. For example, as we suggest in Chapter 4, prior to holding a regularly scheduled LLC meeting, you may wish to send the minutes of the previous regular meeting to the participants so they can read them before the new meeting. Instead of waiting for the upcoming meeting to have the participants approve these minutes, you may wish to ask them to sign and mail an approval form beforehand. Doing this can save time at the upcoming meeting, as well as create a signed document showing that the managers and/or members specifically approved actions taken at a prior meeting. If a manager or member missed a previous meeting, it's an especially good idea to get a written record of their signed approval to important decisions that were reached at that earlier meeting.

Below is a sample of the Approval of LLC Minutes form included on the CD-ROM and as a tear-out form in Appendix D. (See Appendix A for information on selecting and using the CD-ROM files.) Fill the form out following the special instructions provided below.

You can prepare one Approval of LLC Minutes form for multiple managers and/or members to sign, or you can prepare one form for each person to sign individually.

APPROVAL OF LLC MINUTES

Name of LLC: _____

The undersigned consent(s) to the minutes of the LLC meeting held at _____ [location of _____ meeting]_____ on _____[date of meeting]_____ at ____[time of meeting]____, and attached to this form, and accept(s) the resolutions passed and the decisions made at such meeting as valid and binding.

Dated: _____ ❶

Signature	Printed Name
_____	_____
_____	_____
_____	_____
_____	_____
_____	_____
_____	_____
_____	_____
_____	_____

Special Instructions

❶ If multiple signatures will be obtained for the approval form, show the date the first person signs.

Step 4. Prepare a Cover Letter to Meeting Participants

You may wish to send along a cover letter to members and or managers when you send the paper minutes and approval form. This letter explains the reasons for asking for approval of paper minutes and can come in handy if the people asked to sign the approval form are not LLC insiders or are unfamiliar with LLC procedures and formalities.

Below is a sample of the cover letter included on the CD-ROM and as a tear-out form in Appendix D. (See Appendix A for information on selecting and using the CD-ROM files.) Fill the form out following the special instructions provided below.

COVER LETTER FOR APPROVAL OF MINUTES OF LLC MEETING

Date: _____

Name: _____

Mailing Address: _____

City, State, Zip: _____

Re: Approval of LLC Minutes

Dear _____:

I am enclosing minutes of a meeting of _____[name of LLC]_____ that show approval of one or more specific resolutions.

Since these items were agreeable to the members and/or managers entitled to vote on them, we did not hold a formal meeting to approve these decisions. We are now finalizing our LLC records and preparing formal minutes that reflect these prior LLC decisions.

To confirm that these minutes accurately reflect past decisions of the LLC and to formally signify your agreement to them, please date and sign the enclosed Approval of LLC Minutes form and mail it to me at the address below. If you have corrections or additions to suggest, please contact me so we can hold a meeting or make other arrangements to finalize and document these changes.

Sincerely,

_____, ⊕

Title: _____

enclosures: Minutes & Approval of LLC Minutes form

Please return to:

Name: _____

LLC: _____

Mailing Address: _____

City, State, Zip: _____

Phone: _____ Fax: _____

Special Instructions

❶ Normally, the Secretary signs the letter, inserting the title of "Secretary" under the signature line. The Secretary's name, and the address and telephone number of the LLC, are inserted on the remaining lines.

Step 5. Get Managers' and Members' Approval

After you've completed the forms (Steps 1-4, above), make copies of all of them. Then distribute the copies of the forms to each manager and/or member. If it's easier, you may send around one copy of the forms to be signed—this is particularly efficient when the members and/or the managers all work at the business.

Remember to include:

- Waiver of Notice of Meeting form

- Minutes, which include resolutions for the approval of special items of business along with any reports or other attachments (see Chapter 5 for instructions on including resolutions in your minutes), and

- Approval of LLC Minutes form.

Remember to place signed copies of these forms in your LLC records binder.

You may want to include other background materials

You can send out additional material with your written minutes and approval forms to help your members and/or managers understand the issues involved in the decision at hand. Such material might include copies of reports and background material that may help your members and/or managers familiarize themselves with the issues. ■

CHAPTER 7

How to Take Action by Written Consent Without an LLC Meeting

State statutes (either explicitly or implicitly) allow the managers and members of an LLC to take action without holding a meeting (real or paper), simply by signing written consent forms. Under the usual procedure allowed by state law, you simply insert into a written consent form the language of the decision or action to be approved. For this purpose, you may use one of the resolutions that are explained in Chapters 8 through 15 of this book or you may write your own. Then, all members and/or all managers sign that piece of paper, legally approving the resolution.

Taking the written consent approach to LLC decision making is often appropriate for small LLCs with only a few members and/or managers. Written consents are sometimes even suitable for slightly larger companies that have a deadline to meet for making a decision and don't have time to assemble the full membership or management at a special meeting.

Action by written consent is most appropriate if the issue at hand is a routine tax or financial formality—for instance, the approval of standard loan terms offered by a bank or the approval of a tax election recommended by the LLC's accountant. It is not appropriate where a decision may cause debate or disagreement among managers or members.

Absent managers and/or members can use written consents to approve decisions

Written consent forms also come in handy when one or more managers and/or members are not able to attend an important LLC meeting. At a meeting where one or more managers or members are absent, even if you obtain a quorum that can approve decisions, it's wise to also get the written consent of any nonattending members or managers, especially if important resolutions were adopted at the meeting. Doing this ensures that all managers and/or members are informed of actions taken at a particular meeting, and it provides clear evidence of their assent to the action taken.

Some states allow less-than-unanimous votes to pass resolutions with written consents

Some states laws specifically allow a majority or other less-than-unanimous percentage of votes to take action by written consent (or allow the LLC's operating agreement to establish its own voting rule for written consents, regardless of what the state statute says). But to be legally safe and avoid controversy within the LLC, we recommend getting the signatures of all members and/or managers on written consent forms.

WHEN TO USE MINUTES OF PAPER MEETINGS INSTEAD OF WRITTEN CONSENTS

You can safely use written consents to show the approval of most special decisions that would otherwise be documented by preparing minutes of a special LLC meeting (one held specifically to approve a particular decision). But for decisions usually made at annual meetings, larger LLCs will want to use minutes to document the annual business of their LLCs. Even small LLCs usually prepare minutes of a real or paper meeting to document the decisions made at annual or other regularly scheduled meetings. Written minutes take a little more time to prepare than written consents, but minutes look more convincing and official in the LLC records binder. As a result, written minutes are better for more important LLC decisions that may someday become the subject of controversy. (For instructions on preparing minutes for real and paper meetings, see Chapters 5 and 6.) For more information on when to use face-to-face meetings, paper meetings, and written consents, see Chapter 2.

If you have a single-member LLC that you manage yourself

You will typically document day-to-day business decisions with written consents or perhaps "paper meetings." (See Chapter 6.) However, a sole LLC member may also call a real meeting (see Chapters 4 and 5) for big decisions such as amending your articles, hiring staff, or admitting a new member—especially if you want to invite your staff, officers, tax adviser, or attorney for input and discussion.

Step 1. Check Your Operating Agreement for Any Written Consent Rules

Start by checking your operating agreement to determine your LLC's rules for taking action by written consent. The most common requirement found in operating agreements is that members (and managers in a manager-managed LLC) can take action without a meeting only by unanimous written consent. But some state LLC Acts, and some operating agreements, allow fewer than all members or all managers to approve decisions by written consent.

 Get unanimous written consent to avoid problems

Don't get too caught up in your operating agreement's language on this issue. If you follow our practical suggestion to have all written consents signed by every member or manager, you should meet the statutory requirements for written consents in your state.

Step 2. Prepare Written Consent Form

Who signs the written consent forms?

The people entitled to vote on the decision at hand sign the consent form. In a member-managed LLC, this means the members. In a manager-managed LLC, this generally means the managers. But the members must also sign for certain important decisions, such as amendments to the articles or operating agreement, the admission of new members, the approval of additions of capital, distributions of cash or property to members, or a vote to dissolve the LLC. (For more information on who makes LLC decisions, see Chapter 2, Section B.)

Below is a sample of the Written Consent to Action Without Meeting form included on the CD-ROM and as a tear-out form in Appendix D. (See Appendix A for information on selecting and using the CD-ROM files.) Fill the form out following the special instructions provided below.

You'll see that it only takes a minute or two to fill out written consent forms, which must then be distributed to your managers and/or members for signing.

WRITTEN CONSENT TO ACTION WITHOUT MEETING

Name of LLC: _____

The undersigned hereby consent(s) as follows:

[insert one or more resolutions] ❶

_____

_____

_____

_____

_____

_____

_____

Dated: _____ ❷

Signature   Printed Name

_____   _____

_____   _____

_____   _____

_____   _____

_____   _____

Special Instructions

❶ Insert a description of the actions or decisions (in the form of resolutions) agreed to by the members and/or managers. Chapters 8 through 15 contain instructions for preparing the ready-to-use resolutions included with this book. (See the beginning of Appendix D for a list of these resolutions with cross-references to the chapters and sections of the book that cover each one.) If you wish to approve a matter not covered by one of our resolutions, insert your own resolution language in the consent form. You don't need to use fancy or legal language for your resolution. Just describe as specifically as you can the transaction or matter approved by your members and/or managers, in a short, concise statement. Normally, resolutions start with a preamble of the following sort: "The [members and/or managers] resolved that...", but this is not required.

The following are examples of the language typically found in resolutions:

EXAMPLE 1 **(bank loan)**: "It is resolved that the LLC treasurer be authorized to obtain a loan from _____[name of bank]_____ for the amount of $_____ on terms he/she considers commercially reasonable."

EXAMPLE 2 **(LLC hiring):** "Managers resolved that ____[name of new employee]____ be hired in the position of _____[job title]_____ at an annual salary of $_____ and in accordance with the terms of the LLC's standard employment contract."

EXAMPLE 3 **(tax year):** "It is resolved that the LLC adopt a tax year with an ending date of _____."

EXAMPLE 4 **(amendment of articles):** "Resolved that the following new article be added to the LLC's articles of organization: _____[language of new article]_____."

If you find after browsing Chapters 8 through 15 that you need to draft your own resolution language and you have trouble doing so, or if the matter has important legal or tax consequences, you may wish to turn to a lawyer or accountant for help. (See Chapter 16.)

❷ Date the consent form and have your members and/or managers sign their names.

As mentioned above, if you have only a few members or managers, it may be easiest to prepare one master consent form to be relayed to each of your members or managers to sign. In this case, date the form as of the date of the first signature by a member or manager. Another method, more appropriate when you have a larger number of members or managers, is to prepare separate consent forms for dating and signing by each person. Either method (or a combination of both methods) will work.

 You may want to include background materials

You want to send out additional material with your written consent forms to help your members and/or managers understand the issues involved in the decision at hand. Such material could include copies of reports and background material that may help your members and/or managers familiarize themselves with the issues.

STEP 3. PLACE SIGNED CONSENT FORMS IN YOUR LLC RECORDS BINDER

After distributing your Written Consent to Action Without Meeting forms and obtaining the signatures of your members and/or managers, make sure to place each completed form in your LLC records binder. It's common to place these papers in the minutes section of the LLC records binder, arranged according to the date of the action by written consent. ■

Standard LLC Business Resolutions

This chapter presents resolutions that allow LLC members and/or managers to authorize standard items of ongoing LLC business, including:

- opening a bank account for the LLC
- adopting a fictitious LLC name
- approving LLC contracts and purchasing, or
- leasing real property.

This chapter also provides forms that can be used to delegate, approve, rescind, or certify LLC decision-making authority. Where appropriate, we provide relevant legal and tax information to help you select and use the resolutions.

If you don't find a resolution you need for a standard item of LLC business in this chapter, scan this book's index or table of contents for Chapters 8 through 15. It's quite possible you'll find it in a later chapter.

A. WHEN TO USE RESOLUTIONS INCLUDED IN THIS CHAPTER

Much of the paperwork covered in this chapter may not be legally or sometimes even practically required to consummate a standard LLC business deal (depending on the importance of an LLC decision or action). In fact, many smaller LLCs forgo passing formal resolutions for all but the most important items of ongoing LLC business, such as the purchase or sale of LLC real estate or the approval of long-term business or financial commitments. But even small LLCs sometimes decide to prepare formal paperwork for less critical business matters when an outsider wants to be sure of full member or manager approval before entering into a business deal with the LLC. For example, perhaps a vendor wants membership approval of a long-term purchase order before agreeing to grant a hefty long-term discount for goods or services.

 The persons managing the LLC should approve resolutions at hand

The LLC resolutions contained in this chapter need to be approved by the person or persons responsible for managing the LLC. In a member-managed LLC, this means the voting members; in a manager-managed LLC, this means the person or persons appointed as managers. For convenience, we refer to the "members" below as the persons who approve standard LLC business resolutions (since most smaller LLCs are member-managed). Just keep in mind that if your LLC is manager-managed, you will want to have these business resolutions approved by your LLC manager (or managers).

Of course, you may choose to have all members (not just voting members) or both members and managers (in a manager-managed LLC) approve or ratify a really important decision. This would be particularly appropriate if you want to cover all bases before committing the LLC to a substantial financial commitment, or if the decision at hand may provoke controversy (such as a contract with an outside company owned by a current LLC member or manager). Normally, you will not wish to take this extra precaution unless it is legally required or the decision is important enough to warrant the extra time and effort.

HOW TO SELECT AND USE LLC RESOLUTIONS

- Scan the table of contents at the beginning of the chapter to find resolutions of interest to you.

- When you find one you need, read the background material that precedes the pertinent LLC resolution.

- Follow the instructions included with the sample resolution to complete a draft of the resolution using your computer. If you need guidance on selecting and using the computer disk files, see Appendix A. (You'll have to fill in the tear-out resolution included in Appendix D if you don't have a computer.)

- Complete any needed attachment forms, such as account authorization forms or lease agreements.

- If the resolution involves complex issues that will benefit from expert analysis, have your legal or tax adviser review your paperwork and conclusions.

- Prepare minutes of meeting or written consent forms as explained in Chapters 5–7, inserting the completed resolution into the minutes or consent form.

- Have the LLC secretary sign the printed minutes or have members and/or managers sign any written consent forms. Then place the signed forms, together with any attachments, in your LLC records binder.

B. BANK ACCOUNT RESOLUTIONS

One of the first items of business any LLC will undertake is to open an LLC account from which checks can be written. Checks may be drawn against a standard bank checking account, a stock brokerage money-market account, or another type of interest-bearing account set up to provide a reasonable return on the LLC's funds.

Opening and maintaining financial accounts in the name of the LLC is not just a practical nicety, it's a legal safeguard. If you, as a member or manager of an LLC, intermingle LLC funds with your own personal money, a court may hold you personally liable for LLC debts or taxes. One of the reasons you organized an LLC was to gain personal protection from legal liability for your business. You don't want to let sloppy financial habits destroy the benefit of this important LLC attribute.

In small, closely held LLCs, the first deposit to the LLC account is often money advanced by the LLC organizers to help pay initial LLC organizational and operational costs. This advanced money can be reimbursed by the LLC after the company is fully organized, or it can be applied toward members' initial capital contributions. The second deposit into an LLC bank account often consists of personal checks from members who paid cash for their capital interests (memberships).

START-UP MONEY: FUNDING YOUR LLC BANK ACCOUNT

When you should deposit operating funds into your LLC checking account, and how much you should deposit, is often a matter of common sense. Generally, under state LLC statutes, you can fund ("capitalize" in legal jargon) your LLC with as little or as much as you wish.

Take heed, however. If you fail to pay into your LLC at least enough money to cover its foreseeable short-term debts and liabilities, and you're later sued, a court may decide to "pierce the LLC veil" and hold the owners personally liable for LLC debts. This is more likely to occur if a court sees holding the owners personally liable as a way to prevent fraud or injustice to creditors or other outsiders.

Example: The principals of Think Thin, LLC, begin doing business with no money or assets, hoping to obtain initial receipts (income) by franchising a national chain of hypnotherapy weight-reduction clinics. A few outsiders buy initial franchises in the mistaken belief (reinforced by the Think Thin sales force) that the LLC has sufficient operating capital to advertise and otherwise actively promote the franchise chain. In a later lawsuit brought by the franchisees, a court holds the LLC business owners personally liable for monetary damages to the franchise purchasers, stating that it would be unfair to let the LLC business structure protect LLC principals from personal liability under these circumstances.

Now, let's look at the resolutions provided with this book that can record authorization for the opening of one or more LLC financial accounts at banks and other financial institutions.

1. General Resolution to Open LLC Bank Account

This resolution will work well for most small LLCs that have a treasurer who handles the LLC's day-to-day finances, such as writing checks and making deposits. The resolution authorizes the treasurer to open one or more unspecified accounts in the name of the LLC. The treasurer alone is permitted to withdraw funds from these accounts, although anyone authorized by the treasurer may make deposits.

If you wish to designate a person different than the treasurer to deal with LLC funds, you can change the title of the officer in this resolution (and also in the resolutions that follow). For example, you may substitute the title "vice president of LLC finance" for the word "treasurer."

Below is a sample of the resolution you can use to authorize the treasurer to open and use accounts on behalf of the LLC. You'll find this resolution on the CD-ROM and as a tear-out form in Appendix D. (See Appendix A for information on selecting and using the CD-ROM files.)

AUTHORIZATION OF TREASURER TO OPEN AND USE LLC ACCOUNTS

The treasurer of the LLC is authorized to select one or more banks, trust companies, brokerage companies, or other depositories, and to establish financial accounts in the name of this LLC. The treasurer and other persons designated by the treasurer are authorized to deposit LLC funds in these accounts. However, only the treasurer is authorized to sign checks and withdraw funds from these accounts on behalf of the LLC.

The treasurer is further authorized to sign appropriate account authorization forms as may be required by financial institutions to establish and maintain LLC accounts. The treasurer shall submit a copy of any completed account authorization forms to the secretary of the LLC, who shall attach the forms to this resolution and place them in the LLC records binder.

CERTIFICATION OF BANK ACCOUNT RESOLUTION BY LLC SECRETARY

Banks usually provide their own account authorization form(s) to be completed by the LLC secretary or treasurer. The form(s) will ask for the signature(s) of the person(s) authorized to sign LLC checks, according to the terms of one of the bank account resolutions in this chapter.

Some banks may ask you to submit a copy of your LLC bank account resolution with its authorization form, certified as authentic by your LLC secretary. If required, complete a certification form and submit it, along with the resolution, to the bank with your completed bank account authorization form. (Instructions for preparing a certification form are provided in Section G1, below.)

2. Specific LLC Bank Account Resolution

The next resolution authorizes the LLC treasurer to open an account with specific banks or other institutions. Again, the resolution allows only the treasurer to write checks drawn against the funds in this account, although anyone authorized by the treasurer may make deposits. Once again, you may delegate this authority to someone other than the treasurer by changing the resolution.

Below is a sample of the resolution you can use to authorize the treasurer to open and use specific accounts. You'll find this resolution on the CD-ROM and as a tear-out form in Appendix D. (See Appendix A for information on selecting and using the CD-ROM files.) Fill the form out, following the special instruction provided below.

AUTHORIZATION OF TREASURER TO OPEN AND USE SPECIFIC LLC ACCOUNT(S)

The treasurer of this LLC is authorized to open the following account(s), in the name of the LLC, with the following depositories:

Type of account: ___["checking," "petty cash," or other]___

Name, branch, and address of financial institution:

_____

_____

_____

Type of account: ___["checking," "petty cash," or other]___   **❶**

Name, branch, and address of financial institution:

_____

_____

_____

The treasurer and other persons authorized by the treasurer must deposit the funds of the LLC in this account. Funds may be withdrawn from this account only on the signature of the treasurer.

The treasurer is authorized to complete and sign standard authorization forms for the purpose of establishing the account(s) according to the terms of this resolution. A copy of any completed account authorization form(s) must be submitted by the treasurer to the secretary of the LLC, who will attach the form(s) to this resolution and place them in the LLC records binder.

Special Instructions

❶ If you wish to authorize only one account, delete the additional account information lines. For three or more accounts, add additional account information lines.

3. Bank Account Resolution With Multiple Signers

This LLC account authorization resolution allows you to authorize one or more persons, such as officers and staff personnel, to sign LLC checks in order to withdraw LLC funds from the LLC accounts. You also can specify how many persons from this list are required to sign each LLC check.

Below is a sample of the resolution you can use to authorize the treasurer to open a bank account and designate one or more persons who may sign checks for the LLC. You'll find this resolution on the CD-ROM and as a tear-out form in Appendix D. (See Appendix A for information on selecting and using the CD-ROM files.) Fill the form out following the special instruction provided below.

AUTHORIZATION OF LLC ACCOUNT AND DESIGNATION
OF AUTHORIZED SIGNERS

The treasurer of this LLC is authorized to open a ___[type of account, such as "checking" or "petty cash"]___ account in the name of the LLC with ___[name and branch address of bank or other institution]___.

Any officer, employee, or agent of this LLC is authorized to endorse checks, drafts, or other evidences of indebtedness made payable to this LLC, but only for the purpose of deposit.

All checks, drafts, and other instruments obligating this LLC to pay money must be signed on behalf of this LLC by ___[number]___ of the following:___[names and titles of persons authorized to sign checks]___. ❶

The above institution is authorized to honor and pay any and all checks and drafts of this LLC signed as provided in this authorization.

The persons designated above are authorized to complete and sign standard account authorization forms for the purpose of establishing the account(s), provided that the forms do not vary materially from the terms of this resolution. The treasurer must submit a copy of any completed account authorization forms to the secretary of the LLC, who will attach the forms to this resolution and place them in the LLC records binder.

Special Instructions

❶ You may designate two or more persons allowed to write checks payable out of LLC accounts. One or more—or all of them—may be required to sign each check.

> **EXAMPLE 1:** "All checks, drafts, and other instruments obligating this LLC to pay money must be signed on behalf of this LLC by any one of the following: Janice Spencer, President; James Williams, Treasurer; William Yarborough, Assistant Treasurer."

> **EXAMPLE 2:** "All checks, drafts, and other instruments obligating this LLC to pay money must be signed on behalf of this LLC by any two of the following: Janice Spencer, President; James Williams, Treasurer; William Yarborough, Assistant Treasurer."

Add terms or conditions if you wish

You may customize this resolution to add other conditions or requirements for check-writing. For example, an additional sentence could be added to the above paragraph in Example 2 to require the approval of the president for all checks written for amounts above $1,000, $5,000, $10,000, or any amount you choose.

> **EXAMPLE OF ADDITIONAL TERMS:** "All checks, drafts, and other instruments obligating this LLC to pay money must be signed on behalf of this LLC by any one of the following: Janice Spencer, President; James Williams, Treasurer; William Yarborough, Assistant Treasurer. However, the verbal or written approval of the LLC president is required prior to the signing by the treasurer or assistant treasurer for checks with a face amount of or above the amount of one thousand dollars ($1,000)."

4. Authorization of LLC Safe Deposit Account

Some LLCs decide to open a safe deposit box at a local bank or other financial institution to store important LLC documents, such as promissory notes, investment securities owned by the LLC, or trade secrets. LLCs who run their shop formally may want to use the resolution shown below to authorize this item of business.

Below is a sample of the resolution you can use to authorize the rental of a safe deposit box. You'll find this resolution on the CD-ROM and as a tear-out form in Appendix D. (See Appendix A for information on selecting and using the CD-ROM files.) Fill the form out following the special instruction provided below.

AUTHORIZATION OF RENTAL OF SAFE DEPOSIT BOX

The treasurer of the LLC is authorized to rent a safe deposit box in the name of the LLC with an appropriate bank, trust company, or other suitable financial institution, and to deposit in this box any securities, books, records, reports, or other material or property of the LLC that he or she decides is appropriate for storage and safekeeping in this box.

C. ASSUMED OR "FICTITIOUS" LLC NAME RESOLUTION

Sometimes an LLC wishes to do business under a name different from the one stated in its articles of organization (or similar organizing document, such as the certificate of formation), without giving up its formal LLC name.

EXAMPLE: An LLC files articles of organization under the name "Accelerated Business Computer, LLC." Later, the mangers decide to use stationery, advertise, and otherwise do LLC business under the abbreviated name ABC, LLC. However, the managers still wish to keep the formal LLC name stated in its articles.

The easiest solution is to register the new name you want to use as an assumed LLC name. Assumed names (also called fictitious or "dba" names—for "doing business as") will need to be filed with a state and/or local office. In most states, the filing is made in the county clerk's office for each county in the state where the assumed LLC name will be used. For example, an LLC that sells goods and services locally would file assumed LLC name documents in the office of the county where the principal office of the LLC is located.

To find out how to register your assumed LLC name, call or email the state LLC filing office first. (A list of each state's LLC filing offices, including Web addresses at which you can email them, is provided in Appendix B.) This office should provide fictitious or "dba" forms if you must register the name at the state level, or will refer you to a local state office (county clerk) if the assumed name must be registered locally instead of (or as well as) at the state level. To register locally, you may be required to publish a notice of assumed name and file a proof of publication with the local county clerk's office. Your local county clerk's office can provide instructions.

If an assumed LLC name must be filed with the state office, it should be different from names of other LLCs registered in the state. The state will refuse to accept the name for filing if it finds the name already taken, on a master list that includes registered LLCs. For local filings, the new name is normally not checked against other names. However, it's worth a little research, both in your county and in the state, to avoid using a name that's too similar to an existing business's name. See "Perform a Trade Name and Trademark Search Before Adopting or Charging Your LLC Names," below.

Changing the LLC's formal name

If an LLC wishes to change to a completely new name, which it will use exclusively to conduct business, the best way to do this is to change its formal name in the articles of organization (or similar organizing document). An amendment to the articles showing the new LLC name will need to be filed with the LLC filing office. (See Chapter 10, Section B, for a resolution to approve an amendment to the LLC articles.)

Below is a sample of the resolution you can use to adopt an assumed or fictitious LLC name. You'll find this resolution on the CD-ROM and as a tear-out form in Appendix D. (See Appendix A for information on selecting and using the CD-ROM files.)

ADOPTION OF ASSUMED LLC NAME

It was decided that the LLC will do business under a name that is different from the formal name of the LLC stated in its articles of organization (or similar organizational document that was filed with the state to commence the legal existence of the LLC). The assumed name selected for the LLC is _____

_____ [assumed name] _____ .

The secretary of the LLC was instructed to register the assumed LLC name as required by law.

PERFORM A TRADE NAME AND TRADEMARK SEARCH BEFORE ADOPTING OR CHANGING YOUR LLC NAME

Registering an assumed LLC name, just like registering a formal LLC name by filing LLC articles of organization, does not guarantee that you have the absolute legal right to use the name. If another business has been using this name or a similar name in connection with its business, products, or services, a court can award the other business the right to the name. The court may also hold your LLC liable for damages, including any profits the other business lost because you used the name.

In other words, it makes sense to be reasonably sure before adopting a new name that another business is not using a name similar to it. This involves checking business names in your county and state and, if your business involves interstate commerce, business names used in other states where you operate. You can perform a search in your own state by checking telephone books, business directories, and names registered with the state trademark office. (Typically, this office is a division within the state Secretary or Department of State's office.) In addition, you can check nationwide by using the Federal Register maintained by the U.S. Patent and Trademark office in Washington, DC, which contains a list of nationally registered names. You can do a free federal trademark search over the Internet—point your Internet browser to www.uspto.gov and go to the trademarks area. You can also just put parts of the name you want to use into a search engine like Google, Yahoo, or MSN and see what comes up. For more information on performing your own name search, see *Trademarks: Legal Care for Your Business & Product Name,* by Stephen Elias (Nolo).

D. RESOLUTION TO APPROVE AN LLC CONTRACT

Before one of your LLC members or officers signs an important contract, you may want to obtain formal approval from your LLC members and/or managers, and record this approval in a written resolution. It's a good idea to obtain this type of formal approval of a contract ahead of time if the contract concerns an important undertaking by the LLC or obligates it to expend substantial funds. Other types of contracts that are appropriate for formal approval include:

- business deals that extend over a period of time, such as a five-year purchase-option contract on a building

- complicated business arrangements that would benefit from formal review and approval, and

- contracts where the other party wants the LLC to back up its commitment with a formal approval process—for example, a potential long-term supplier or service provider requests formal LLC management approval in writing before fulfilling the order.

The resolution below allows you to record approval by LLC management of a proposed contract between your LLC and an outside person or business and to delegate an LLC officer to enter into the contract on the LLC's behalf.

Resolutions for granting specific authority to LLC members, managers, officers, or employees For a discussion of resolutions specifically geared to authorizing LLC officers to transact business in general for the LLC, or to ratify a contract made by an LLC member or manager after it has been signed, see Section F, below.

Below is a sample of the resolution you can use to approve a proposed contract. You'll find this resolution on the CD-ROM and as a tear-out form in Appendix D. (See Appendix A for information on selecting and using the CD-ROM files.)

APPROVAL OF CONTRACT

The __["members" and/or "managers"]__ were presented a proposed contract to be entered into between the LLC and __[name of outside business or party]__ for the purpose of __[subject matter of contract, such as "the renovation of LLC offices"]__, together with the following attachments: __[specify additional material submitted with contract for approval, such as "building plans, schedule for performance of services under the contract, etc."]__.

Next, a report on the proposed contract was given by __[name of LLC officers or other employees]__, who made the following major points and concluded with the following recommendation: ____[if applicable, cite major points provided in verbal or written reports given at meeting and the conclusions of the reports]__.

After discussion, __[If you wish, you may add: "including discussion of the following points:" and cite specific statements or conclusions given by individual members or managers.]__, it was decided that the transaction of the business covered by the contract was in the best interests of the LLC, and the proposed contract and attachments were approved.

The ____[title of LLC officer]____ was instructed to execute the contract submitted to the meeting in the name of and on behalf of the LLC, and to see to it that a copy of the contract executed by all parties, together with all attachments, be placed in the records of the LLC.

E. REAL PROPERTY RESOLUTIONS

These resolutions address the lease, purchase, or sale of real property (real estate) by the LLC. Because transactions involving land normally involve a lot of money and/or long-term commitments, all LLCs will want to formally approve these transactions with the resolutions we provide below.

1. Resolution Approving Lease by LLC

Your LLC should pass a formal resolution to approve a lease of business premises by the LLC, particularly if the lease is long-term or involves a substantial deposit or payments by the LLC, or if the members and/or managers need to discuss the lease terms.

Commercial leases generally specify either rent calculated as a fixed rental amount or as a percentage of gross or net profits earned by the business. Of course, lease terms vary, depending on market conditions, bargaining positions, and state law requirements.

Use the following resolution to show LLC approval of lease terms negotiated with a property owner or manager. Attach a copy of the lease to the resolution and file both documents in your LLC records binder.

Below is a sample of the resolution you can use to approve a commercial lease. You'll find this resolution on the CD-ROM and as a tear-out form in Appendix D. (See Appendix A for information on selecting and using the CD-ROM files.)

CONSIDER A LEASE OF PERSONALLY OWNED REAL ESTATE TO YOUR LLC

A member of a small LLC may wish to lease property to the LLC to get cash out of the LLC and obtain favorable tax benefits. Of course, the IRS will expect the rent charged to be reasonable (since the LLC can deduct the rent as a business expense in computing net LLC income, which is then allocated to the owners). The LLC member-lessor reports the rent payments as ordinary income on his or her tax return. A portion of the rental income, in turn, can be offset by depreciation deductions taken by the leasing member. Ask your tax adviser before deciding to rent, rather than sell, real property to your LLC; the tax implications can be complex. If an LLC manager or member does rent property to the LLC, you may want to read Chapter 15, "Self-Interested Business Dealings Between the LLC and Its Members or Managers."

APPROVAL OF LEASE OF PREMISES BY LLC

A proposed lease agreement between _____[name of LLC]_____ and _____[name of owner]_____ for the premises known as _____[address of property]_____ was presented for approval. The lease covered a period of __[term of lease]__, with __[interval of lease payments, such as "monthly" or "quarterly"]__ rent payments payable by the LLC of __[dollar amount or formula used to compute rent payments]__.

After discussion, it was decided that the lease terms were commercially reasonable and fair to the LLC and that it was in the best interests of the LLC to enter into the lease.

The lease and all the terms contained in it were approved, and the secretary of the LLC was instructed to see to it that the appropriate officers of the LLC execute the lease on behalf of the LLC, and that a copy of the executed lease agreement be attached to this resolution and filed in the LLC records binder.

WHO IS AUTHORIZED TO TRANSFER REAL PROPERTY?

The LLC Acts of some states specifically say that all LLC members (in a member-managed LLC) or LLC managers (in a manager-managed LLC) are automatically empowered under law to transfer real property on behalf of the LLC. Of course, your articles of organization or operating agreement can restrict this transfer authority so that only specific members or managers have this right.

In that case, however, you would be wise to give a copy of any such limitation of authority to anyone who is considering buying or selling real property to or from the LLC. The reason is that other LLC statutes, enacted by a majority of the states, typically say that the LLC will be bound (obligated) to any business deal made by *any* member or manager of the LLC with an outsider— as long as the deal is the type an outsider would reasonably expect to be within the authority of the member or manager, and the outsider has no knowledge of any limitation of the authority of the member or manager with whom the outsider is dealing.

If you are worried that an unauthorized LLC member or manager may approach an outsider to discuss the sale or purchase of LLC real property, and you have not given certain members or managers the authority to transfer LLC real estate, make sure to give the outsider a copy of any such limitation language in your articles or operating agreement. Some states go even farther and allow an LLC to file a statement with the Secretary of State (or similar state LLC filing office) that lists the persons who may deal in real estate on behalf of the LLC. You can also record a resolution, the articles, or a separate state form that limits who can transfer LLC real estate interests with the county recorder. The idea behind this filing (and recording) is to put all outsiders on notice that only specific LLC members or managers may sign real estate transfer papers on behalf of the LLC. This sort of "constructive notice" means that a contract for the sale or purchase of LLC property made by an unauthorized LLC member or manager should not legally bind the LLC, even if the outsider did not actually know of the filing. We think it's best, if you make this sort of filing, to show any potentially interested outsiders a copy of the filed statement to make sure they receive actual notice of who may deal in real estate on behalf of your LLC.

If you want to authorize LLC members, managers, and officers to enter into a *particular* real estate deal, use one of the real property resolutions covered in Sections 2 or 3, below. If instead you simply wish to authorize just one LLC member, manager, officer, or employee to enter into LLC real-estate transactions in general, use the delegation of authority resolution discussed in Section F, below.

---

2. Resolution Authorizing Purchase of Real Property by LLC

The members or managers may want to formally authorize a purchase of real property by the LLC. This is not only a significant business transaction that warrants a little extra formality, but title and trust companies may require a members' or managers' (for a manager-managed LLC) resolution before escrow papers are finalized.

The purchase of real property gives rise to significant mortgage interest and depreciation deductions for the LLC and, if a building or other property is pur-

chased from an LLC member, a source of cash to the selling member. Of course, to ward off possible challenges from other members, the selling price of any land transferred to the LLC by a member should be its fair market value. (See Chapter 15, "Self-Interested Business Dealings Between the LLC and Its Members or Managers.") The tax ramifications of a purchase of real property by the LLC are complex, both for the LLC and its members (particularly if one or more members own the property being sold to the LLC). In all cases, check with your tax adviser before deciding to go ahead with an LLC real estate purchase.

Below is a sample of the resolution you can use to approve the purchase of real property by the LLC. You'll find this resolution on the CD-ROM and as a tear-out form in Appendix D. (See Appendix A for information on selecting and using the CD-ROM files.)

PURCHASE OF REAL PROPERTY BY LLC

The purchase by the LLC of real property commonly known as _____ [street address of property] _____

_____ was discussed. The president announced that the property had been offered to the LLC for sale by the owner at a price of __$ [seller's asking price]__ . After discussing the value of the property to the LLC and comparable prices for similar properties, it was agreed that the LLC should __["accept the offer" or "make a counteroffer for the property at a price of $(counteroffer price)"]__ .

It was also agreed that the LLC will seek financing for the purchase of the property on the following terms: _____ [insert, if applicable, the terms and interest rate of financing the LLC will seek for financing the purchase of the property, for example, "This offer or counteroffer is contingent on the LLC's ability to obtain financing for the purchase under a 30-year note carrying an interest rate not to exceed 10%"]_____ .

The president was instructed to see to it that the appropriate LLC officers prepare all financial and legal documents necessary to submit the offer or counteroffer to the seller and to seek financing for the purchase of the property according to the terms discussed and agreed to in this resolution.

---

3. Resolution Authorizing Sale of Real Property by LLC

Another important LLC transaction that should be formally approved by management is the sale of real property owned by the LLC. As with a purchase of real estate, a sale of real estate is a significant business transaction that warrants a little extra formality. Title and trust companies may also require a formal LLC resolution that approves the sale before final escrow papers can be prepared. The resolution shown below can be used for this purpose.

 Below is a sample of the resolution you can use to approve the sale of real property by the LLC. You'll find this resolution on the CD-ROM and as a tear-out form in Appendix D. (See Appendix A for information on selecting and using the CD-ROM files.) Fill in the resolution as you follow the sample below.

AUTHORIZATION OF SALE OF REAL PROPERTY BY LLC

After discussion, it was agreed that the president of this LLC is authorized to contract to sell real property of the LLC commonly known as: _____ [street address of the property to be sold] _____ on the following conditions and terms: _____ [provide price and other terms that the president should seek to obtain; for example: "at a sales price of at least $100,000, with at least 10% down and the balance carried through a 10-year or shorter note at current commercial interest rates"] .

The president of the LLC and any other officers of the LLC authorized by the president can execute all instruments on behalf of the LLC necessary to make and record a sale of the above property according to the above terms.

F. DELEGATION OF AUTHORITY AND APPROVAL OF INDIVIDUAL CONTRACTS

State law typically says that any member in a member-managed LLC and any manager in a manager-managed LLC is an "agent" of the LLC. An agent can legally act on the LLC's behalf to accomplish any business reasonably within its general business purposes. This also goes for officers and key employees. In other words, an LLC is bound by the acts of its members (in a member-managed LLC), its managers (in a manager-managed LLC), and other agents (including officers and other key employees), as long as the transaction is within the apparent authority of the person—that is, the transaction is the type of action or decision an outsider would reasonably expect the person to be able to perform or make for the LLC—and as long as the outsider has no knowledge of a limitation on the authority of the LLC member, manager, officer, or employee.

For major actions or decisions, however, you may wish to limit LLC authority to enter into a particular transaction or type of transaction to one or more individuals. There's no "bright-line" test to use here. Simply use your own business and common sense. If the matter is important enough, and your LLC will benefit by having it handled only by a particular LLC person with the necessary expertise, then using a "delegation of authority" resolution makes sense. For example, if the LLC wishes to allow a talented employee to commit significant funds for certain projects or to handle a critical area of LLC operations—such as purchasing real prop-

erty or signing long-term service contracts—it makes sense to have the LLC officially delegate authority to the employee for these actions. Doing this can be useful to emphasize to the employee the limits of his or her authority. And it can provide a paper trail of the decision if it is later questioned by others. Finally, if you are worried that an outsider may inadvertently deal with the wrong LLC member, manager, officer, or employee, you can give the outsider a copy of the resolution, to put the outsider on notice that the person specified in your resolution is the person the outsider should deal with.

In the following sections, we provide resolutions your LLC can use to approve the authority of an LLC member, manager, officer, or employee to undertake LLC business or enter into LLC contracts. We also cover ratification resolutions that can be used to approve business transactions already undertaken by individuals on behalf of the LLC. Such after-the-fact approval can be helpful, as explained below in Section 2.

1. Resolution Delegating LLC Authority

The following resolution can be used by the LLC to delegate specific authority for one or more contracts, decisions, or business matters to an LLC member, manager, officer, or employee. This resolution can help make the authorized individual aware of his or her primary role in upcoming business transactions, as well as let the person and others know how far the person can go in acting for the LLC.

EXAMPLE: Tired Treads, LLC, a used-car leasing company, wants one of its LLC officers to negotiate and sign a long-term, wholesale, car rental agreement with a used-car dealer. Before the dealer will close the deal, however, he wants to see a formally approved resolution from Tired Treads, LLC, that sets out the LLC officer's authority to close the deal. The LLC approves a resolution that delegates authority to the LLC officer to handle this particular transaction.

Below is a sample of the resolution you can use to delegate LLC authority. You'll find this resolution on the CD-ROM and as a tear-out form in Appendix D. (See Appendix A for information on selecting and using the CD-ROM files.) Fill in the resolution as you follow the sample below.

DELEGATION OF LLC AUTHORITY

After discussion, it was agreed that the following individual, whose LLC title is indicated below, is granted authority to perform the following tasks or transact the following business by and on behalf of the LLC, or to see to it that such tasks are performed for the LLC under his or her supervision as follows:

_____[state the name and title of LLC member, manager, officer, or employee and the specific authority granted to the person, including any limitations to his or her authority]_____ . ❶

This person is also granted the power to perform any and all incidental tasks and transact incidental business necessary to accomplish the primary tasks and business described above.

Special Instruction

❶ You can limit the individual's authority to specific business transactions, within specific monetary or time limits or in any other way you wish.

EXAMPLE: GyroCopter Tours Ltd. Liability Co. uses this resolution to help define the authority of an LLC vice president to negotiate the renewal of its flight insurance policies with its insurer. Specific minimum terms are set out in the resolution—the VP can only make a deal that covers the entire gyro fleet, for a minimum term of one year, with a minimum insured amount per gyro of $1 million. The resolution further states that if the policy is not obtained within the following 90 days, the delegation of authority automatically terminates, and the vice president must request additional approval from LLC management to continue the insurance negotiations on behalf of the LLC.

2. Resolution Ratifying a Contract or Other Business Approved by an Individual

When a business decision needs to be made in a hurry, an LLC member, manager, officer, or employee sometimes does not have time to obtain management's prior approval of the transaction. If the transaction is important or potentially controversial—that is, some members or managers may object without hearing more about the business deal or transaction made by the individual—it is wise to seek formal approval of the transaction after the fact. This gives the person who made the deal a chance to explain his or her reasons and obtain formal approval from the LLC members or managers. Legally, this sort of after-the-fact approval—called a ratification—takes the individual off the hook personally for any monetary loss from the transaction, and, as a practical matter, helps ease personal tensions by bringing management in on the deal.

EXAMPLE: The treasurer of Master Mind Enterprises, LLC, gets a large cash payment from a client. It's Friday, just before closing—too late to talk to management—and the treasurer decides to maximize the yield from the funds by depositing the check in a short-term certificate of deposit rather than in the LLC's interest-bearing checking account, which currently pays a lower interest rate. On Monday, the treasurer asks the managers to approve the transaction.

Below is a sample of the resolution you can use to ratify a transaction entered into by an LLC member, manager, officer, or employee. You'll find this resolution on the CD-ROM and as a tear-out form in Appendix D. (See Appendix A for information on selecting and using the CD-ROM.) Fill in the resolution as you follow the sample below.

Other uses for this resolution

This resolution also can be used to approve joint decisions, not just those undertaken by a particular individual. For example, by changing the language of the resolution slightly, you can use this resolution to have all members approve a contract or transaction that was made by the LLC managers (in a manager-managed LLC) or by some, but not all, members (in an LLC with one or more nonmanaging members).

EXAMPLE: The managers of Ovoid Egg Supply L.L.C. recently approved and paid for the renovation of its packaging plant, even though final cost exceeded the contracted price by 25%. The managers decide it would be wise to explain to the members the reasons for paying the excess amount, followed by a membership vote on a resolution to ratify the final payment.

RATIFICATION OF CONTRACT OR TRANSACTION

After discussion, it was agreed that the following contract or other business transaction undertaken on behalf of the LLC by the following individual whose title appears below is hereby adopted, ratified, and approved as the act of the LLC and is accepted as having been done by, on behalf of, and in the best interests of the LLC:

[insert the name and title of the LLC member, manager, officer, or employee and the date and nature of the contract or other business transaction] .

THE RIGHT WAY FOR OFFICERS AND OTHER EMPLOYEES TO SIGN LLC CONTRACTS

Whenever an LLC member, manager, officer, or employee signs a contract for the LLC—whether before or after obtaining LLC authority for the contract—the document should always be signed as follows:

    _____[name of LLC]_____ ,

by_ _[signature]_____

    [name and title of individual]

For example:

Ovoid Egg Supply L.L.C._____ ,

by _____ *Bud Breedy*_____

  _Bud Breedy, Secretary_____

If the individual fails to do this and signs a contract in his or her own name instead, a third party may be able to hold the individual personally responsible for performance under the contract.

---

3. Resolution Rescinding Employee's Authority

An LLC may wish to cancel the previously approved authority of an individual to transact business or negotiate the terms of a contract. This may happen, for instance, if the original LLC resolution was open-ended—that is, it did not specify a time limit for the individual's authority. Business conditions may have since rendered the delegation of authority to the person unnecessary or inappropriate. For example, the LLC rescinds the authority of the treasurer to seek loan funds, since the treasurer has now borrowed sufficient funds under the prior open-ended authority.

Below is a sample of the resolution you can use to revoke previously approved authority of an LLC member, manager, officer, or employee. You'll find this resolution on the CD-ROM and as a tear-out form in Appendix D. (See Appendix A for information on selecting and using the CD-ROM files.) Fill in the resolution as you follow the sample below.

RESCISSION OF AUTHORITY

After discussion, it was agreed that prior authority granted to __[name and title of LLC member, manager, officer, or employee]__ on __[date of approval of authority]__ for the purpose of __[describe the authority granted to the individual]__ is no longer necessary to the interests of the LLC and that any and all authority granted under the prior approval of authority is hereby rescinded and no longer in effect.

G. CERTIFICATION, AFFIDAVIT, OR ACKNOWLEDGMENT OF LLC DECISION OR DOCUMENT

Your LLC members, managers, officers, or employees may need to certify to others that a given LLC decision, act, or document was properly approved by your LLC. For example, prior to granting a loan, a bank may require the LLC secretary to certify that the LLC members (or managers in a manager-managed LLC) approved taking out the loan.

We provide three forms your LLC secretary (or other officer) can use to make this showing. Note that the forms do not require approval by members or managers—the secretary's signature certifies that the members or managers previously approved an act or decision; in other words, none is a resolution. The first two forms are ways to validate or certify a resolution that is attached to or quoted in the form; the third is a legal statement that can be added to the end of another legal document, such as a contract.

1. Certification of LLC Resolution

The following form is used by the LLC secretary to certify to outsiders that an action by the LLC is being properly performed. This is the least formal of the three forms in this section, and the most common means of certification.

You'll find this resolution on the CD-ROM and as a tear-out form in Appendix D. (See Appendix A for information on selecting and using the CD-ROM files.) Fill in the certification as you follow the sample below.

CERTIFICATION OF LLC RESOLUTION

The undersigned, duly elected and acting _____ ["secretary" or title of other officer] _____ ❶ of

_____ [name of LLC] _____ , certifies that the attached resolution ❷ was adopted by the

__ ["members" and/or "managers"] __

    ☐   at a duly held meeting at which a quorum was present, held on ___ [date of meeting] ___

    or,

    ☐   by written consent(s) dated on or after ___ [date of first written consent] ___ ,

and that it is a true and accurate copy of the resolution and that the resolution has not been rescinded or modified as of the date of this certification. ❸

Dated: _____

_____ [signature] _____

_____ [typed or printed name] _____ , Secretary [or other title]

Special Instructions

❶ Although it is most common for the secretary to sign this form, any officer, member, or manager can do so. Insert the title of the officer, member, or manager who is certifying the LLC decision in the first blank and the last blank of the certification.

❷ Fill in the name of the LLC and attach a copy of the LLC resolution or written consent approved by the members and/or managers before submitting this resolution form. Remember to place copies in your LLC records binder.

❸ Fill in the rest of the blanks as indicated.

2. Affidavit of LLC Resolution

A more formal way for the LLC secretary to certify that a particular LLC decision was formally approved by the LLC is through the use of an affidavit. This is a sworn statement, signed by the secretary in the presence of a notary, that attests to the truth of statements made in the affidavit. The legal language for affidavits varies from state to state, but a typical affidavit follows the format of the sample below.

You'll find this resolution on the CD-ROM and as a tear-out form in Appendix D. (See Appendix A for information on selecting and using the CD-ROM files.) Fill in the affidavit as you follow the sample below.

AFFIDAVIT OF LLC RESOLUTION

STATE OF _____

COUNTY OF _____

Before me, a Notary Public in and for the above state and county, personally appeared
_____ [name of LLC secretary] _____ who, being duly sworn, says:

    1. That he/she is the duly elected and acting _____ [title] _____ of _____ [name of
LLC] _____ , a _____ [name of state] _____ LLC.

    2. That the following is a true and correct copy of a resolution duly approved by the __ ["members"
and/or "managers"] __ of the LLC __ ["at a duly held meeting at which a quorum was present, held on __ [date
of meeting]" or "by a sufficient number of written consents dated on or after [date of first written consent obtained for approval of resolution]"] __ :

_____ [insert language of resolution here] _____

    3. That the above resolution has not been rescinded or modified as of the date of this affidavit.

    [signature of secretary taken in the presence of Notary]

    [typed or printed name] __ , Secretary

    Sworn to and subscribed before me this _____ [date] _____ day of _____ .

_____ [signature of Notary Public] _____

Notary Public

My commission expires: _____

Notary Seal

⚠️ **Check your state's notarization form**
Before using this form, ask a notary in your state for a copy of your state's standard affidavit. Make any necessary modifications so that the language of your affidavit conforms to your state's standard language. (Of course, you can also use the state's standard form instead.)

3. Acknowledgment of LLC Document

An LLC officer, member, or manager may be asked to acknowledge a legal document, such as a lease or deed. An acknowledgment states that the person is who he or she claims to be and that he or she actually signed the document in question. Acknowledgments, like affidavits, often must be signed in the presence of a notary.

An acknowledgment form is appended or attached to the end of a legal document signed by an LLC officer, member, or manager.

⚠️ **Check your state's acknowledgment form**
Before using this form, ask a notary in your state for a copy of your state's standard acknowledgment language, then make any necessary changes to have your acknowledgment language conform to state requirements.

💾 You'll find this resolution on the CD-ROM and as a tear-out form in Appendix D. (See Appendix A for information on selecting and using the CD-ROM files.) Fill in the acknowledgment as you follow the sample below.

ACKNOWLEDGMENT

STATE OF _____

COUNTY OF _____

    I hereby certify that on _____[date]_____, before me, a Notary Public in and for the above state and county, personally appeared __[name of officer, member, or manager]__, who acknowledged himself/herself to be the _____[title]_____ of _____[name of LLC]_____ and that he/she, having been authorized to do so, executed the above document for the purposes contained therein by signing his/her name as _____[title]_____ of _____[name of LLC]_____.

[signature of Notary Public]
    Notary Public

My commission expires: _____

Notary Seal

LLC Tax Resolutions

This chapter contains a few common LLC tax resolutions to be approved by members or managers. Of course, this is not an extensive treatment of the various tax issues that can come before the management of an LLC during its life. Often, the LLC's tax advisor will provide the impetus to consider and approve tax matters. We simply present these few resolutions as examples of ways to formally approve tax elections or decisions. More commonly, tax decisions are made informally, at both the LLC and the individual member levels. In later chapters, we discuss other common tax issues that arise during the course of LLC operations, such as contributions of capital and loans made by members to the LLC, the admission of new members, the withdrawal of existing members, and the transferring of a membership interest by a current member to an outsider.

The persons managing the LLC should approve resolutions

Unless otherwise noted below, the LLC resolutions contained in this chapter need to be approved by the person or persons responsible for managing the LLC. In a member-managed LLC, this means the voting members; in a manager-managed LLC, this means the person or persons appointed as managers. Of course, in a member-managed LLC you may choose to have all members (including nonvoting members if you have them), or in a manager-managed LLC both members and managers, approve or ratify a really important tax decision. Normally, you will not wish to take this extra step unless this additional approval is legally required or the decision is important enough to warrant the extra time and effort.

See Appendix C for a summary of significant changes in the 2003 federal tax act that affect small businesses, including LLCs, and small business owners.

HOW TO SELECT AND USE LLC RESOLUTIONS

- Scan the table of contents at the beginning of the chapter to find resolutions of interest to you.

- When you find one you need, read the background material that precedes the pertinent LLC resolution.

- Follow the instructions included with the sample resolution and complete a draft using your computer. If you need guidance on selecting and using the computer disk files, see Appendix A. (You'll have to fill in the tear-out resolution included in Appendix D if you don't have a computer.)

- Complete any needed attachment forms, such as tax forms.

- If a resolution involves complex issues that will benefit from expert analysis, have your legal or tax adviser review your paperwork and conclusions.

- Prepare minutes of meeting or written consent forms as explained in Chapters 5–7, and insert the completed resolution into the appropriate form.

- Have the LLC secretary sign the printed minutes or have members and/or managers sign any written consent forms. Then place the signed forms, together with any attachments, in your LLC records binder.

A. LLC CORPORATE TAX TREATMENT ELECTION

By default, a multimember LLC is taxed by the IRS as a partnership, and a single-owner LLC is taxed as a sole proprietorship. But that's only by default: An LLC can also elect to be treated by the IRS as a corporation. Most LLCs will not wish to do this—after all, one of the advantages of forming an LLC is the benefit of being treated as a "pass-through" tax entity. (LLC profits and losses and credits and deductions "pass through" the business and are allocated to members at the end of each LLC tax year.) But your tax adviser may decide that the time has come for your LLC to elect corporate tax treatment. Generally, this happens if LLC profits are substantial, and the owners wish to shelter business income in the LLC. If you do elect corporate tax treatment, the retained income in the LLC is taxed at lower corporate tax rates (15% and 25% for taxable net corporate incomes up to $75,000), instead of the sometimes higher individual tax rates that can apply to income allocated to members of a regular pass-through LLC.

If you want corporate tax treatment for your LLC, you must file IRS Form 8832, "Entity Classification Election," and check the corporation box on the form (the actual language of this box is "a domestic eligible entity electing to be classified as an association taxable as a corporation"). The form must be signed by all LLC members unless the members have authorized a particular officer, member, or manager to sign it on their behalf.

Below is a sample of the resolution you can use to approve a corporate tax election by the LLC. You'll find this resolution on the CD-ROM and as a tear-out form in Appendix D. (See Appendix A for information on selecting and using the CD-ROM files.) Fill out the resolution as you follow the sample and special instruction below.

Note that this resolution needs to be approved by all members, even in a manager-managed LLC.

LLC ELECTION OF CORPORATE TAX TREATMENT

After consultation with the LLC's tax adviser, the LLC treasurer recommended that the LLC elect to be taxed as a corporation, starting ____[insert date when election is to start]____. ❶ After discussion, all members agreed that this election should be made, and the treasurer was authorized by the members to complete IRS Form 8832, "Entity Classification Election," to accomplish this election, and to sign the form on behalf of each of the members of this LLC, and to file it with the IRS.

It was also agreed that, if applicable, the treasurer file any additional forms necessary to elect corporate tax treatment of the LLC for state income tax purposes. ❷

Special Instructions

❶ Your tax adviser should advise you when your election should start, and this date should be inserted here. The start date of the corporate tax treatment election must also be specified on IRS Form 8832.

❷ Most states that impose a corporate income tax follow the federal tax rules, treating an LLC that has elected corporate tax treatment as a corporate tax entity for state income tax purposes (if the state imposes a corporate income tax). But some states impose their own requirements, or have their own forms that must be completed to achieve corporate tax treatment at the state level. Ask your tax adviser for information on any special state requirements.

B. RESOLUTION FOR APPROVAL OF INDEPENDENT AUDIT

As a preliminary step to or part of the LLC's annual tax accounting procedures, a tax audit of the LLC's books may be necessary. Or, a special audit may be requested by the IRS or required by a bank prior to approval of a loan or credit application. Audits of this sort are called "independent audits," and they are usually done by an outside accounting firm that does not handle ongoing tax or bookkeeping chores for the LLC.

Alternatives to independent audits

To avoid the expense and hassles of a full-blown outside audit, financial institutions sometimes allow LLCs to submit financial statements that have been "reviewed" by the LLC's accountant, using standard auditing rules (Generally Accepted Accounting Practices or GAAP). If this alternative is available when you are preparing financial statements that will be examined by others, you will probably want to choose it.

Below is a sample of the resolution you can use to authorize an independent audit of the LLC's financial records and transactions. You'll find this resolution on the CD-ROM and as a tear-out form in Appendix D. (See Appendix A for information on selecting and using the CD-ROM files.) Fill out the resolution as you follow the sample below.

APPROVAL OF INDEPENDENT AUDIT OF LLC FINANCIAL RECORDS

After discussion, it was agreed that the accounting firm of ___[name of accountant or firm]___ was selected to perform an independent audit of the financial records of the LLC for the ___[year]___ fiscal year and to prepare all necessary financial statements for the LLC as part of its independent audit.

The LLC treasurer was instructed to work with the auditors to provide all records of LLC finances and transactions that may be requested by them, and to report to the LLC on the results of the audit on its completion.

C. APPROVAL OF LLC TAX YEAR

Choosing appropriate dates for your LLC's tax year is important—and best done with the guidance of the LLC's accountant. The deadlines for preparing and filing LLC informational tax returns, and the tax consequences of specific transactions made during the year, will turn on this decision. Further, the LLC's accounting period (the period for which the LLC keeps its books) must correspond to its tax year.

Generally, an LLC's tax year must be the same as the tax year of LLC members who hold a majority share of the LLC's profits and capital interests (individual members will have calendar tax years, corporate or other business entity members may not). If the members who own the majority of the LLC's interests do not share a common tax year (for example, one corporate member's tax year ends July 31 and another's tax year ends December 31), the LLC must choose the tax year of all of its "principal members." These are defined as members owning a 5% or greater share of LLC profits and capital. If the principal members don't share a common tax year, the LLC must choose a tax year that results in the least deferral of income. (A mathematical test is applied under Income Tax Regulation 1.706-1.)

Since LLC members typically are individuals, most LLCs have a calendar tax year (from January 1 to December 31). But special IRS rules allow LLCs to elect a noncalendar tax year—called a "fiscal year"—in a couple of instances:

- **Natural business year.** Revenue Procedure 74-33 allows an LLC to choose a noncalendar tax year if the LLC's natural business year concludes in a month other than December. (Generally, at least 25% of business revenue must occur within the last two months of the natural business year.) For example, a summer resort might choose a tax year that ends on September 30 if this is the end of the lodge's peak income season.

- **Three-month deferral of income.** LLCs can adopt a noncalendar tax year if it will result in a deferral of income of three months or less. For example, if a fiscal year ending September 30 is requested, this will generally be allowed, since it results in a three-month deferral of income when compared to the normal calendar tax year. Use of this three-month deferral exception comes at a price: It requires making an extra tax payment to the IRS each year in an amount equal to the estimated deferral of tax that results from the noncalendar year. This extra payment results in the payment of tax on deferred LLC income at the members' highest individual tax rate plus one percentage point. (See Sections 444 and 7519 of the Internal Revenue Code.) You must file an IRS Form 8752, "Required Payment of Refund under Section 7519," available at the IRS website, www.irs.gov.

For further information on these technical tax year rules, check with your accountant.

A change of tax year normally needs IRS approval

If your LLC has already adopted a tax year, and now wishes to approve a different one, you'll need IRS approval to make the change. Normally, the IRS will not approve a change of tax year unless you can show a substantial business purpose. (For example, you are converting from a calendar tax year to a tax year that meets the natural business year of your LLC.) However, there's an exception to this rule: An LLC can change its tax year without IRS approval if it adopts the tax year used by the members who hold a majority interest or by all the principal members (holders of 5% or more of the LLC's interests). To seek IRS approval for a change of tax year, the LLC must file IRS Form 1128, "Application to Adopt, Change, or Retain a Tax Year," available at the IRS website, www.irs.gov.

Below is a sample of the resolution you can use to approve the selection of a tax year for the LLC. You'll find this resolution on the CD-ROM and as a tear-out form in Appendix D. (See Appendix A for information on selecting and using the CD-ROM files.) Fill out the resolution as you follow the sample and special instruction below.

Note that the language of this resolution assumes that the LLC has consulted the LLC's accountant prior to making this decision.

APPROVAL OF LLC TAX YEAR

After discussion and a report from the treasurer, which included advice obtained from the LLC's accountant, it was resolved that the tax year of the LLC will end on <u>[ending date, such as "December 31" or the last day of another month if the LLC qualifies for a noncalendar tax year]</u> ❶ of each year. The treasurer was appointed to file the necessary tax forms on behalf of the LLC to adopt or change the tax year of the LLC with the IRS [add, if applicable, "and the appropriate state tax agency"].

Special Instruction

❶ If the LLC qualifies for a noncalendar tax year, it need not choose the last day of whatever month it picks to end its tax year—it may choose to have its tax year end on the same day each year, such as the last Friday of June. A tax year of this sort is called a 52-53 week tax year. ■

CHAPTER 10

Resolutions to Amend the LLC Articles and Operating Agreement

Many, if not most, LLCs eventually undertake the commonplace legal procedure of amending their articles of organization (referred to as a "certificate of formation" or a "certificate of organization" in some states) and their operating agreement. To do so, the LLC must follow rules contained in its state's LLC laws.

Membership approval is usually required
Under state law, typically, members must approve amendments to the LLC articles or to the LLC operating agreement, by either unanimous or majority approval. This can be arrived at by a vote or by written consent. Even if your state law allows less-than-unanimous consent, we think amendments to the articles or the operating agreement are important enough to warrant discussion and approval by all LLC members. Whether your operating agreement overrides state law or merely repeats it, it should indicate what is required for your LLC to approve amendments to your articles or operating agreement. If your operating agreement does not state this information, we summarize each state's amendment requirements in Appendix B, under the heading "Amendments."

In a manager-managed LLC, the managers normally need not approve the amendments (except in a few states). As a practical matter, however, it is usually the managers who decide on an amendment to the articles or operating agreement, then propose it to the members for approval.

HOW TO SELECT AND USE LLC RESOLUTIONS

- Scan the table of contents at the beginning of the chapter to find resolutions of interest to you.

- When you find one you need, read the background material that precedes the pertinent LLC resolution.

- Follow the instructions included with the sample resolution and complete a draft of the resolution using your computer. If you need guidance on selecting and using the computer disk files, see Appendix D. (You'll have to fill in the tear-out resolution included in Appendix C if you don't have a computer.)

- Complete any needed attachment forms.

- If a resolution involves complex issues that will benefit from expert analysis, have your legal or tax adviser review your paperwork and conclusions.

- Prepare minutes of meeting or written consent forms as explained in Chapters 5–7, and insert the completed resolution in the appropriate form.

- Have the LLC secretary sign the printed minutes or have members and/or managers sign any written consent forms. Then place the signed forms, together with any attachments, in your LLC records binder.

A. DECIDE WHETHER YOU NEED TO AMEND YOUR ARTICLES OR YOUR OPERATING AGREEMENT

If you want to add provisions to your articles of organization, state law may actually allow you to choose between placing them in your articles or your operating agreement. When you have this choice, it is best to add new provisions to your operating agreement rather than to your articles. That's because the operating agreement can be amended more easily and inexpensively than articles. Amendments to articles must be filed with your state's LLC filing office for a fee.

> **EXAMPLE:** The current members of Della Frattoria Wood-Fired Bread, LLC, wish to impose a requirement that all members be at least 18 years of age. In their state, member qualifications are not required to be placed in the articles. The LLC decides to amend the operating agreement to add this requirement.

To find out what provisions must be included in your articles of organization, take a look at your state's Business or LLC Law (available at a local law library or on the Internet through your state's home page. For your state's Web address, look in Appendix B for information on your state's LLC filing office; also see Chapter 1, Section C). Typically, one section of the law lists the provisions that *must* be included in articles. Usually the next section lists provisions that *may* be placed in articles. These are called optional article provisions and may be placed in either your articles or your operating agreement.

B. AMENDING ARTICLES OF ORGANIZATION

From time to time, LLCs may need to amend their original articles of organization to add, change, or delete provisions. Like the original articles, amendments to the articles must be filed with the state LLC filing office, accompanied by a filing fee. (Again, Appendix B lists each state's LLC filing office address and telephone number.)

LLCs often amend their articles because they wish to:

- change the structure of the LLC from member-management to manager-management or vice versa
- authorize special classes of membership, such as nonvoting memberships
- change the formal name of the LLC

- add additional provisions to the articles, such as limitations on the personal liability of members and managers officers, or
- delete provisions that the LLC wishes to repeal or that list outdated information. For example, an LLC may want to delete a provision that specifies the LLC will dissolve on a specified future date (no longer required under most LLC statutes).

AN EASIER WAY TO CHANGE AN LLC'S NAME

If you're planning to change your LLC's name—either to better identify your business or to benefit from a name that has become associated with your LLC's products or services—there's an easier way to change the name than amending your articles.

In most states, an LLC wishing to do business under a name different from that specified in the articles may file a fictitious or assumed business name statement with the state LLC filing office or local county clerk's office. This simple procedure allows the LLC to use the name locally without having to file a formal amendment to its articles. (A resolution for adopting an assumed or fictitious LLC name is covered in Chapter 8, Section C.)

> ### YOU CAN'T CHANGE CERTAIN ARTICLE PROVISIONS
>
> In most states, you can delete—but cannot change—article provisions that specify the initial agent, initial registered office, or initial members or managers of the LLC. The reason is simple: These people always remain the initial agent, members, or managers, and this address remains the initial registered office. You may delete any reference to them—for example, amend your articles to add unrelated provisions, and decide to take out the reference to your first registered agent, who has been replaced. You can't, however, specify other people or other office locations as the initial agent, members, managers, or initial registered office.
>
> To notify the state of any change in your registered agent or registered office, file a statement of change of agent or registered address with the state LLC filing office. If you request it, most state LLC offices provide a form for this purpose.

In a member-managed LLC, typically one or more members suggest a change to the articles, then ask the LLC secretary to call a membership meeting or circulate written consent forms to obtain membership approval of the amendment. In a manager-managed LLC, typically the managers first agree on the language of proposed amendments, then ask the members to approve the amendments. Amendments to articles almost always have to be approved by the members. Usually, all or a majority of the full membership must approve the amendment. (See the "Amendments" section for your state in Appendix B.)

Provide notice of a meeting to amend the articles

You will want to give all members ample notice of a meeting to amend the LLC articles, even if this isn't required under state law or your operating agreement. Disclose in the notice that the upcoming meeting is being held to amend the articles of the LLC, and include a copy of the proposed amendment along with the notice.

It's easy to prepare a resolution to amend your articles for membership approval, which you'll then insert in your minutes or written consent forms. The resolution can show approval of:

- only the specific language that you wish to change, or

- a restatement of your entire articles—which, of course, includes any changes you are making.

1. Specific Amendment to Articles Resolution

Below is a sample of the resolution you can use to approve a specific change to your articles (rather than to approve completely restated articles as explained later). You'll find this resolution on the CD-ROM and as a tear-out form in Appendix D. (See Appendix A for information on selecting and using the CD-ROM files.) Fill out the resolution as you follow the sample and special instructions below.

Because you are not changing the entire text of your articles, attach a copy of the approved resolution with the new articles language to the current articles in your LLC records binder.

APPROVAL OF AMENDMENT TO ARTICLES OF ORGANIZATION ❶

RESOLVED, that Article __[number or letter of Article that is being amended, added, or deleted]__ of the articles of organization of this LLC be __["amended to read," "added," or "deleted"]__ as follows: __[insert the language of the changed or new article, or show a struck-though version of the wording to be deleted]_____.❷

Special Instructions

❶ If your organizing document goes under another name, such as "certificate of organization" or "certificate of formation," change the references in the resolution to correspond to the name of your organizational document.

❷ Here are a few examples of ways to use this resolution:

EXAMPLE 1 (changing the LLC name): "RESOLVED, that Article ONE of the articles of organization be amended to read as follows: The name of this LLC is Big Wheels, LLC."

EXAMPLE 2 (changing from member-management to manager-management): "RESOLVED, that Article TWO of the articles of organization be amended to read as follows: Management of the LLC shall vest exclusively in one or more managers. The initial manager shall be: __[name and address of first manager]__."

EXAMPLE 3 (adding a new article): "RESOLVED, that Article TEN of the articles of organization be added as follows: One of the LLC managers shall be elected annually by the Hingham Investment Group, Ltd., with the initial election date to be determined by majority vote of the current LLC managers."

EXAMPLE 4 (deleting a limitation on the duration of the LLC that's no longer required to be included in articles under state law): "RESOLVED, that Article B of the articles of organization be deleted as follows: ~~The duration of this LLC shall be thirty years from the date of filing of these articles of organization.~~"

2. Amendment by Restatement of Articles Resolution

Members sometimes decide to approve a restatement of the entire articles, which contains all old and new provisions (minus any deletions also being made).

Below is a sample of the resolution you can use to approve a restatement of your articles. You'll find this resolution on the CD-ROM and **as a** tear-out form in Appendix D. (See Appendix A for information on selecting and using the CD-ROM files.) Fill out the resolution as you follow the sample and special instruction below.

APPROVAL OF RESTATEMENT OF ARTICLES OF ORGANIZATION ❶

RESOLVED, that the articles of organization be amended and restated to read in full as follows:

  [insert the entire text of your articles, including any new or changed provisions and minus any provisions that are being deleted   .

Special Instructions

❶ If your organizing document goes under another name, such as "certificate of organization" or "certificate of formation," change the references in the resolution to correspond to the name of your organizational document.

3. File Amendment of Articles With State LLC Filing Office

After obtaining the approval of your members to an amendment resolution, you'll need to file an Amendment of Articles form with your state's LLC filing office. A sample form for this purpose should be available from the LLC filing office in your state. A list of LLC filing office addresses and phone numbers, along with website addresses, can be found in Appendix B. Typically, the amendment form is referred to as an Amendment of Articles or Amendment of Certificate form. A nominal fee is usually charged for the filing.

The sample form below contains the basic information normally required in an amendment of articles. It provides space for the text of the amended or restated articles and how, when, and by whom the amendment was approved.

After filing your amendment form with your state's LLC filing office, remember to place a copy in your LLC records binder. Also include a copy of the minutes of a membership meeting or the written consent of members used to obtain approval of your amendment resolution.

We include the following sample amendment form as a guide, but you should use the form provided by your state's LLC filing office instead, if one is available. You'll find this form on the CD-ROM and as a tear-out form in Appendix D. (See Appendix A for information on selecting and using the CD-ROM files.)

AMENDMENT OF ARTICLES FORM

To: ___[name and address of state LLC filing office]___

Articles of Amendment

of

_____[name of LLC]_____

One: The name of the LLC is _____[name of LLC]_____.

Two: The following amendment to the articles of organization was approved by the members on ___[date of LLC meeting or written consent]___:

_____[insert language of amendment or full restatement of articles here]_____

_____

_____

_____

_____ .

Three: The number of members required to approve the amendment was ___[insert the membership vote required for approval, usually "all members"]___, and the number of members that voted to approve the amendment was ___[number of members (or percentage of membership interests) voting in favor of the amendment, again, usually "all members"]___.

Date: _____

By:

_____[signature of president]_____

_____[typed name]_____, President

_____[signature of secretary]_____

_____[typed name]_____, Secretary

C. AMENDING THE LLC OPERATING AGREEMENT

LLCs sometimes wish to add, delete, or change provisions in their operating agreement. As with amendments to LLC articles, the approval of all members is normally required. (See the "Amendments" heading for your state in Appendix B). Unlike articles amendments, amendments to the LLC operating agreement do not need to be filed with the state's LLC filing office.

You may wish to amend your existing operating agreement to accomplish one or more of the following items:

- After the admission of a new member, to show the capital, profits, and voting interests of the new member, as well as the changes in the existing members' interests brought about by the new member's admission.

- After the departure of a member, to show the recomputed capital, profits, and voting interests of the remaining members.

- To add comprehensive buy-sell provisions that specify how, when, and for how much a member may transfer a membership interest, and to control transfers of a membership interest by a member to family, heirs, or creditors.

- To change the date, time, or place of the annual or other regular members' or managers' meetings.

- To specify special notice, call, or voting rules for meetings of members or managers. For example, the members may wish to require written notice well in advance of all membership meetings, even if not required under state law.

- To change the authorized number of managers of the LLC (in a manager-managed LLC).

- To change the duties and responsibilities of one or more LLC officers.

In a member-managed LLC, one or more members normally ask the LLC secretary to arrange a members' meeting to discuss a proposed amendment to the operating agreement. If the wording of the amendment has already been worked out, and if the matter is one all members will readily agree to, the member may, instead, ask the secretary to circulate written consents to the members to obtain their approval to the proposed amendment. In a manager-managed LLC, one or more managers propose the amendment to the operating agreement. After the wording is worked out by the managers, the amendment is proposed at a meeting of members for full membership approval or is circulated to all members as part of a written consent.

Provide notice of a meeting to amend the operating agreement

If you hold a membership meeting to approve an amendment to your LLC operating agreement, we think it's best to provide written notice of the meetings well in advance to all members. Explicitly state in the notice that the meeting is being held to amend the operating agreement of the LLC. Also, include a copy of the proposed amendment with the notice. State law and your operating agreement may not require this much preliminary planning, but we think an operating agreement change warrants this extra measure of premeeting formality.

1. Resolution to Amend LLC Operating Agreement

Below is a sample of the resolution you can use to approve an amendment to your LLC operating agreement. You'll find this resolution on the CD-ROM and as a tear-out form in Appendix D. (See Appendix A for information on selecting and using the CD-ROM files.) Fill out the resolution as you follow the sample and special instruction below.

AMENDMENT OF LLC OPERATING AGREEMENT

RESOLVED, that ___[number and/or letter designation of amended operating agreement provision]___ of the operating agreement of the LLC is ___["added," "amended" or "deleted"]___ as follows:

___[insert language of new or changed operating agreement provision or show a struck-though version of wording to be deleted]___ . ❶

Special Instructions

❶ Here are examples of the completed resolution:

EXAMPLE 1: RESOLVED, that Article TWELVE of the operating agreement of the LLC is added as follows: "Article TWELVE: Nontransferability of Shares. All shares of this LLC are nontransferable, except with the written approval of all members."

EXAMPLE 2: RESOLVED, that Article II, Section A (3), of the operating agreement of the LLC is amended as follows:

"Article II: Meetings of LLC Managers, Section A (3): The managers of this LLC must meet annually on the first Wednesday of June of each year, and also on the same day as, and immediately following, the annual members' meeting required under other provisions of this operating agreement."

Make sure to update your operating agreement on file with the LLC

An operating agreement is a contract among your LLC members. Therefore, you will want to make sure that the agreement on file with the LLC reflects the changes approved by resolution or written consent of the members.

There are two ways to do this: First, you can retype the entire operating agreement (including the approved changes), then have it signed by all current members (and their spouses, if spouses signed your original agreement). A second way is to attach the resolution or written consent that contains the new language to the appropriate section of your current operating agreement, and to have all members initial or sign the resolution to show their approval (spouses should also sign or initial the attached resolution or written consent if they signed the original agreement). ■

LLC Membership Resolutions

This chapter covers LLC resolutions that approve changes in the rights and interests of members, plus other items of business that directly affect LLC members. For example, during the life of an LLC a member might be added. Or, one or more members might withdraw or sell their membership interests (whether to insiders or outsiders). In other membership matters, the LLC might approve distributions of profits to members or ask for additional capital contributions to fund ongoing LLC operations. These membership matters are discussed here, along with their legal and tax consequences.

LLC members should approve resolutions

The LLC resolutions contained in this chapter should be approved by the LLC members (as well as by managers in a manager-managed LLC). You'll see that we recommend that all members approve these resolutions, not just a majority of members or another percentage specified in your LLC operating agreement. Although unanimous approval is not always legally necessary, we think that it is the most practical choice for these important membership decisions. The surest way to avoid future disputes within the membership ranks, particularly when approving resolutions that affect one or more member's share of LLC capital or profits, is to have all members agree first.

HOW TO SELECT AND USE LLC RESOLUTIONS

- Scan the table of contents at the beginning of the chapter to find resolutions of interest to you.

- When you find one you need, read the background material that precedes the pertinent LLC resolution.

- Follow the instructions included with the sample resolution to complete a draft of the resolution using your computer. If you need guidance on selecting and using the computer disk files, see Appendix A. (You'll have to fill in the tear-out resolution included in Appendix D if you don't have a computer.)

- Complete any needed attachment forms.

- If a resolution involves complex issues that will benefit from expert analysis, have your legal or tax adviser review your paperwork and conclusions.

- Prepare minutes of meeting or written consent forms as explained in Chapters 5–7, and insert the completed resolution into the appropriate form.

- Have the LLC secretary sign the printed minutes, or have members and/or managers sign any written consent forms and waivers. Then place the signed forms, together with any attachments, in your LLC records binder.

Check tax issues with a professional
Though we'll give you an overview here, we don't deal with the more complex tax issues that inevitably arise in connection with the membership transactions discussed below. These unexplored issues include the "inside basis" of assets contributed to an LLC (the LLC's basis in its assets, as opposed to a member's individual basis in the member's LLC interest), as well as tax elections that can be made to change how this basis is computed. Extra tax complexities also surround the purchase and sale of a member's interest if property is or was contributed to the LLC for part or all the interest. And going gets *really* interesting when you want to reward an active member or manager with an increase in his or her LLC ownership share. In short, we remind you to check the full tax consequences of any of the transactions covered in this chapter before approving and implementing them.

A. DISTRIBUTIONS OF LLC PROFITS TO MEMBERS

People invest and work in LLCs to receive a share of their profits. Sure, when LLC cash is short, profits are often kept and used in the business. But most LLC owners don't wait too long before paying themselves a fair share of the revenue earned by the LLC. The members and/or managers of an LLC should consider several factors before deciding whether to pay out distributions of profits—including the legal rules for when an LLC can pay distributions and the tax ramifications of such distributions. Because the tax effects of LLC distributions of profits have an impact on the decision to pay profits to owners, let's look at the tax side of this transaction.

1. Tax Effects of LLC Distributions

At the end of the LLC tax year, profits (or losses) of the LLC are automatically allocated to LLC members in proportion to each member's "distributive share," or "profits (and losses) interest," in the LLC. The distributive share for each member should be defined in your operating agreement—it simply means the percentage of profits and losses to be allocated to each member. Normally, a member's distributive share of profits and distributive share of losses is the same—that is, a member with a 10% distributive share is allocated 10% of the LLC's profits and 10% of its losses. But this is not always so. For example, your operating agreement may say that a particular member's distributive share is set at 15% of the profits and 20% of the losses.

ALLOCATIONS OF LOSSES TO LLC MEMBERS

Planning to make profits in an LLC is a pleasant prospect, but planning for initial losses also is important. In the startup phase of an LLC, the business may generate losses—that is, business expenses may exceed profits. This is not always a bad thing.

Unlike a corporation, the LLC can pass businesses losses through the business onto the individual tax returns of the owners, where these losses can be used to offset other income of the owners, whether from a salaried day job or an investment portfolio. (Your tax adviser can tell you about special loss rules that place limits on how business losses can be used to reduce active or passive income.)

In contrast, business losses are "locked into" a corporation. Even though they may be carried back and forward (within limits) to offset corporate income in earlier or later corporate tax years, the shareholders can't use corporate losses to offset income on their individual income tax returns.

Exception: If a corporation makes an S corporation election—which turns a corporation into a special type of pass-through tax entity—losses (and profits) of the corporation pass through the corporation and are reported on the individual income tax returns of the corporate shareholders, where they can reduce other individual income, subject to special rules. [Note that an LLC obtains the same pass-through tax treatment with greater flexibility and fewer restrictions. S corporations are limited in the types of owners they can have and types of stock they can issue.]

S corporation shareholders only can report losses on their individual income tax returns to the extent of their basis in their stock plus any loans personally made by the shareholder to the corporation. Basis is calculated according to what a shareholder pays for stock, plus and minus adjustments made to basis when profits and losses are allocated to the shareholder or distributions are paid out of the corporation to the shareholder.

In an LLC, an owner also gets to use entity-level debt (for example, a loan taken out on property that the LLC owns) to increase the owner's basis in his or her LLC interest. This means the LLC owner has a greater ability than an S corporation owner to deduct business losses on an individual tax return.

Example: Big Plans, LLC is a property development LLC owned by Sam and Zena, who each contributed $50,000 to start it. Big Plans buys a $500,000 property for $100,000 down (the total amount of cash paid in by the two members) and a $400,000 mortgage. After the sale, each owner has a $250,000 basis in his or her LLC interest ($50,000 initial basis plus $200,000, which is each owner's 1/2 share of the $400,000 entity-level debt).

Let's assume that because of property development costs (mortgage payments and other costs) the LLC reports a loss of $140,000 in its first year. Each member shares 50/50 in profits and losses, so each is allocated a $70,000 loss. Because each member has $250,000 of basis, each can use the entire amount of the loss on his or her individual tax return to offset other income (assuming other technical tax rules are met). The allocation of this loss to each owner reduces each owner's basis to $180,000 ($250,000 minus $70,000).

If Sam and Zena had formed a corporation, the loss would not flow through to them personally unless their corporation had elected S corporation tax status. And even then, Sam and Zena would only be able to use $50,000 of the $70,000 loss, since they would not get the benefit of the $400,000 entity-level mortgage. In an S corporation, their basis (for purposes of claiming losses) is increased only by loans they personally make to their corporation, not loans taken out by the corporation such as loans from a bank or other non-shareholder source.

MEASURING MEMBERSHIP INTERESTS IN THE LLC

To help keep the terminology straight, we reprint this sidebar from Chapter 3 here.

Capital interests. A member's current capital interest is the percentage of capital contributed to the LLC, relative to total capital contributions made by all members. For example, if two LLC members form an LLC, with one member contributing $10,000 in cash and the second paying $20,000 in property, the first member has a one-third (33%) capital interest in the LLC, and the second a two-thirds (67%) capital interest. These numbers get adjusted from time to time if members make additional contributions (raising the members' capital account balances) or the LLC distributes cash or property to members (reducing members' capital account balances). This is why some statutes speak in terms of a member's current capital account balance with the LLC, rather than each member's initial capital contribution to the LLC.

Profits interests. One of the rights of LLC ownership (membership) is the right to receive a percentage of the profits (and losses) of the LLC. Generally, unless so-called "special allocations" of profits and losses are made to members in the LLC operating agreement, each member is entitled to the same percentage of LLC profits and losses as the member's capital interest. (Check your operating agreement to be sure.) So a member with a 10% capital account balance also will have a 10% profits interest in the LLC. But LLCs sometimes do make special (disproportionate) allocations of profits and losses, perhaps giving a 20% profits interest to a member paying 10% of the capital in cash, in recognition of the extra liquidity the cash-paying member provides (compared to the property contributions made by other members). Your operating agreement should specify the profits interests of all members. Many agreements simply say that profits (and loss) interests simply follow the capital interests of the members.

Capital and profits interests. Many state statutes specify membership rights in terms of each member's share of the capital *and* profits interests of each member. In other words, you must average each member's share of total capital and total profits interests in the LLC. For example, if Sam has a 10% capital interest and 20% profits interest in his LLC, he has a 15% capital and profits interest (the average of the two). In most LLCs, profits interests follow capital interests, so capital interest and profits interest will be the same—for example, Jerry has a 10% capital interest and a 10% profits interest, yielding an average capital and profits interest of 10%.

Distributive shares (profits and loss interests of members) are most commonly tied to each member's capital interest in the LLC. A member's capital interest is customarily referred to a member's "capital" or "percentage interest" in the operating agreement, but some agreements call it a member's "unit interest" or give it another name.

WHAT THE TERM "CAPITAL ACCOUNT" MEANS

The capital accounts of the members show, in bookkeeping terms, the current book value of each member's capital interest. When an LLC member contributes cash or property to a company, his or her capital account is credited with the cash amount or fair market value of the contribution.

When profits are allocated to the owner at the end of the LLC tax year, his or her capital account balance goes up (the business owes the owner this money); as distributions of profits are made, the owner's capital account balance goes down (the business no longer owes this money to him or her). Note that these adjustments to an LLC member's capital account are similar to the adjustments made to a member's basis as LLC profits are allocated (basis goes up) and distributed (basis goes down). But also note this difference: The initial tax basis an LLC member receives in his or her membership interest is equal to the amount of cash or the basis of any property that owner contributes to the LLC. The owner's capital account, on the other hand, is increased by the current fair market value of his or her capital contribution.

It is easy to confuse capital account balances with other accounting and tax terms, such as an owner's basis or distributive share of profits and losses. To avoid this, just think of a capital account balance as the amount of LLC assets that a member expects to be paid if the company is liquidated and split up among the members (assuming there is sufficient cash or other assets left after all creditors have been paid).

The key here is that, at the end of the tax year, the IRS treats profits as belonging to the LLC members, whether the distributions are actually paid or not. As profits are allocated, they are taxed to the individual members.

EXAMPLE: Ted's LLC has net profits of $20,000 at the end of its tax year on November 30, 2004. Ted has a 50% capital interest in the LLC and his distributive share is 50% of LLC profits and losses. Half the profits—$10,000—are allocated to him at the end of the LLC tax year, although these funds are not distributed. (He doesn't get a $10,000 check from the LLC.) On his 2004 individual tax return, Ted reports and pays taxes on the $10,000 of allocated profits at his individual marginal tax rate. (This is the individual tax rate that applies to the $10,000 of additional LLC income Ted must report.)

TAX BASIS OF OWNERSHIP INTERESTS

Tax basis refers to the value assigned to an LLC ownership interest for the purpose of determining the taxable gain or loss from it after it is sold. The member's basis in a membership interest is called the member's "outside basis"; the LLC's separate basis in any assets contributed by a member is called the LLC's "inside basis." An increase in basis generally results in lower capital gains taxes when an LLC member sells his or her interest; likewise, a decrease in basis generally results in higher taxes.

Basis also determines how much of the LLC's losses a member can claim on an individual tax return to offset other income. A member can only deduct LLC losses up to the amount of the member's tax basis in his or her interest (subject to other loss limitation rules involving recourse debts, discussed in Chapter 13, Section A1).

A member's basis is generally the cash amount a member pays, along with the member's current basis in any property he or she transfers, to buy the membership interest. If a member transfers property that's subject to a debt that the business assumes—for example, the member transfers real estate subject to a mortgage—the member's basis in his or her interest is decreased by the amount of the assumed debt. Over time, a member's original basis in her membership interest is adjusted up and down during the life of the LLC as profits (or losses) are allocated and paid to members and as the LLC's liabilities change.

Obviously, figuring your basis in an LLC membership interest at the time of LLC formation, during the course of its operations, and when a membership interest is sold or the LLC is liquidated is anything but easy. This is just one of the important tasks that should be referred to a tax adviser.

There's one more tax effect of the allocation of profits to an LLC member. When profits are allocated to a member, they increase the member's basis in his or her membership interest. (See "Tax Basis of Ownership Interests," above). Conversely, an allocation of LLC losses to a member decreases the member's basis in the membership interest, at least until the basis is reduced to zero. This is important, to make sure the member is not taxed twice on LLC profits. For example, if this adjustment of basis did not occur, a member who sells an interest would pay capital gains taxes on the value of the interest, and this gain would include any previously taxed profits retained in the LLC. By increasing a member's basis when profits are allocated, this double-tax result does not occur.

When previously allocated LLC profits are actually distributed to a member, they are not normally taxed to the member. Again, this is because they were taxed at the time they were allocated to the member. But the distribution does affect a member's basis, as follows: At the time of a distribution of LLC profits, a member decreases his or her basis by the amount of cash distributed. If the amount distributed exceeds a member's basis, only then is a tax due (on the amount by which the distributed profits exceed the member's basis). This downward adjustment of basis at the time of distribution offsets the upward adjustment that was made when profits were allocated to the member, and puts the member's basis back where it started before the distributed profits were earned by the LLC.

2. Legal Rules for LLC Distributions of Profits

State laws can also affect an LLC's decision to pay profits to its members.

a. When Distributions Can Legally Be Made

In many states, there are standards that dictate when LLC distributions can legally be made. Here are the main points found in state LLC Acts.

A distribution of profits is valid if, after the distribution, both of the following are true:

> 1. The LLC remains solvent—that is, the LLC will be able to pay its bills as they become due in the normal course of business.

> 2. Generally, LLC assets remain at least equal to or exceed liabilities (or conform to a higher asset-to-liability ratio set out in a state statute).

Managing members or managers can rely on financial statements, such as a balance sheet, of the LLC in making their determination of the appropriateness of a distribution. (Some states specifically allow an LLC to revalue its assets and liabilities prior to a distribution, as long as it discloses this fact to members.) More generally, managing members or managers should be allowed to base their decision to distribute profits on financial information from reliable sources such as the LLC's treasurer or tax adviser.

⚠ Watch out

Managing members or managers who approve a distribution in violation of the statutory standard can be held personally liable for the amount of the invalid distribution.

Some states have no statutory standards for paying out profits. In these states it's a safe bet that a state court, when faced with a legal challenge to a distribution brought by a disgruntled member or creditor, will apply standards similar to those listed above.

💡 Check your articles and your operating agreement

Check your articles and operating agreement to see if any rules are set out for when and how distributions may be made. If you need more information, check your state LLC Act. (See Chapter 1, Section C.)

b. How Distributions Must Be Made

Okay, we've established that distributions can be made only when the LLC can meet certain financial tests. Are there any standards that apply to *how* LLC distributions should be made? In many states, there are statutes covering the manner of LLC distributions.

Most states allow LLC operating agreements to set out how profits should be distributed. Generally, unless the LLC operating agreement sets out special allocations of profits and losses, each member is given a share of profits and losses (their distributive share) according to the member's capital interest with the LLC (but check your operating agreement to be sure). In the absence of a provision in the operating agreement, some states require distributions to be allocated in proportion to members' profit-sharing interests in the LLC. Here's an example.

Oregon LLC Act, Sec. 63.195

[…]

If neither the articles of organization nor any operating agreement provides for [… allocations of LLC distributions of cash or assets prior to LLC dissolution], such distributions shall be allocated among the members in proportion to their right to share in the profits of the limited liability company.

Other states require LLCs to allocate distributions of profits in proportion to the members' capital account balances.

Ohio LLC Act, Section 1705.11

[…]

Unless otherwise provided in the operating agreement, distributions that are made shall be made to the members in proportion to the value as stated in the records of the company […] of the contributions made by each member to the extent the contributions have been received by the company and have not been returned.

State law typically requires that each distribution of profits be made proportionately to all LLC members (according to their distributive shares). In other words, the LLC can't give one member his share of the profits in one distribution, and a second member her share in another. Members cannot normally be forced to accept distributions from the LLC that are disproportionate to their distributive shares.

Lastly, LLCs typically make distributions of profits in cash, not LLC property. In fact, many states specifically prohibit members from demanding distributions in property. Likewise, members usually do not have to accept property distributions from the LLC. This is because members don't have to accept LLC distributions that are disproportionate to their distributive shares. The nature of property distributions would normally require distributions that are disproportionate to members' shares since the value of property parceled out to members rarely matches their exact distributive share. Here's a typical statute that embodies these requirements.

Ohio LLC Act, Section 1705.13

Except as provided in writing in the operating agreement and regardless of the nature of his contribution, a member has no right to demand and receive any distribution from a limited liability company in any form other than cash. Except as provided in writing in the operating agreement, a member may not be compelled to accept a distribution of any asset in kind from a limited liability company if the percentage of the asset distributed to him is greater or less than the percentage in which he shares in distributions from the company.

3. Resolution to Approve LLC Distribution of Profits

State law does not normally require LLC members or managers to formally approve a resolution to distribute profits. A simple verbal consensus to do so is normally sufficient. As usual, it's up to you to decide when it makes sense to prepare and approve a formal LLC resolution. For smaller LLCs with plenty of cash, it may not be necessary to prepare this paperwork. But if the LLC is short of funds and a distribution may affect LLC performance, or if all members are not in agreement on the amount or other terms of distribution, the preparation and approval of a formal resolution can be helpful to show the distribution was lawfully made (according to the standards discussed above). For larger LLCs, it usually makes sense to formally approve distributions to avoid controversies later.

In actuality, if the LLC is making a cash distribution that all members readily agree to, there is little likelihood of a legal challenge to the distribution, unless the LLC is in debt and an unpaid creditor makes a fuss. (In that case, you will want to be sure your LLC can continue to pay off the debt after the distribution.) A formal resolution, in this case, can document how the LLC is able to afford the payout of cash, plus show that a sufficient number of members voted to approve it.

The following resolution can be used to approve a management decision to make a distribution of LLC profits to members.

Fill in the resolution as you follow the sample and special instructions below. You'll find this resolution on the CD-ROM and as a tear-out form in Appendix D. (See Appendix A for information on selecting and using the CD-ROM files.)

APPROVAL OF LLC DISTRIBUTION

The LLC resolves that the LLC will make the following distribution of profits of the LLC to the following members: ❶

Name of Member   Amount ❷

_____ $_____

_____ $_____

_____ $_____

_____

_____ $_____

　　　It was announced that the above distribution of LLC profits was in accordance with the requirements for the allocation of distributions to members as set out in the LLC operating agreement, or as required under state law. The treasurer presented a current balance sheet of the LLC at the meeting for review by the attendees, and announced that he/she had consulted the LLC's tax adviser. It was agreed that, after giving effect to the distribution, the LLC would continue to be able to pay its obligations as they become due in the normal course of its operations, and that the LLC would meet any applicable financial and legal tests under state law for making distribution to members. The treasurer was instructed to attach a copy of the balance sheet to this resolution for inclusion in the LLC's records binder. ❸

　　　The treasurer of the LLC is instructed to prepare and deliver or mail a check drawn on the LLC's account in the appropriate amount to each member entitled to the distribution no later than __ [date of distribution payment]__ . ❹

Special Instructions

❶ Check your operating agreement to see how many managers or members are required to approve distributions to members. Again, we repeat the suggestion that you obtain full membership approval for distributions. For example, some members with sufficient personal cash reserves may object to the distribution, preferring that money be kept in the business to help the LLC grow. It's best to deal with these objections before, not after, making a distribution.

❷ Insert the name of each member and the amount of cash distribution to be made to each. Of course, you can adapt this resolution to show the distribution of LLC assets to members, but such property distributions are less common and may invoke special state law requirements, as discussed in the text.

❸ This resolution states that the LLC members have consulted a current balance sheet presented by the treasurer prior to approving a distribution, and that a copy of the balance sheet was attached to the resolution. This precaution is recommended to show that members had good reason to conclude that the LLC would be solvent after the distribution. It also assumes that the treasurer consulted a tax adviser to make sure the distribution makes sense. You can delete or change these assertions as you see fit. Again, if you are making a cash distribution that all members readily agree to, there is little likelihood of a legal challenge to the distribution unless your LLC is in debt.

❹ The distribution date should be shortly after the date of the LLC decision, usually within one or two weeks. If you wait too long—say, more than one month—the financial condition of your LLC may change and you will need to analyze whether your LLC still meets the applicable financial tests for making the payout.

B. ADDITIONAL CAPITAL CONTRIBUTIONS BY MEMBERS

During the life of an LLC, there may be times when cash flow is low, and the LLC may need to seek additional operating funds from its existing members. One way to do this is by asking members to make loans to the LLC (covered in Chapter 13). Another way is to ask members to make additional capital contributions. If the LLC is on track to being successful over the long term, and added funds would benefit the LLC, some or all members may agree to pay additional cash into the LLC as capital.

1. Tax Considerations

Normally, a capital investment in an LLC is tax-free—the members do not owe any taxes on the membership interests they receive, nor does the LLC pay any taxes on the cash or property it accepts in exchange. Additional capital contributions simply increase each contributing member's tax basis in their membership interests (See Section A, above, for a discussion of basis.) In effect, the tax effects of paying capital into an LLC are deferred until a later time. The tax basis of a member in his or her LLC interest is used to determine the amount of taxes the member owes when the interest is sold or the LLC is liquidated.

EXAMPLE 1: Dianne capitalizes her one-person advertising consulting LLC with $50,000 in cash. Her initial $50,000 basis is adjusted up and down over the next seven years, and is equal to $40,000 seven years later when she decides to sell her LLC. She sells the LLC for $150,000. Her taxable profit on the sale is $110,000: $150,000 minus her $40,000 tax basis.

Simply put, when you sell your ownership interest, your profit (gain) is calculated by subtracting your tax basis in your ownership interest (your original basis, plus or minus adjustments) from your sale proceeds.

EXAMPLE 2: Barbara is a member and vice president of Biz Wiz, a small member-managed LLC. As part of its formation, Barbara's LLC issues her a 30% capital (membership) interest in exchange for her cash payment of $70,000, plus the patent she owns for "Biz Wiz" software. Barbara's $30,000 basis in her patent plus her cash payment of $70,000 are added to make up her starting basis of $100,000 in her LLC membership.

When Barbara leaves the company several years later, her LLC basis is $150,000, reflecting her share of LLC liabilities as well as allocations of profits made to her during the LLC's prior tax years. The LLC has done well, and expects to do better, so the remaining LLC members value Barbara's interest at $200,000 and pay her this amount. Barbara recognizes a taxable gain of $50,000 on her sale of her LLC interest—the $200,000 sales price minus her basis of $150,000.

You can expect to pay a tax on any gain you make when you sell your ownership interest. In most cases, your profit should be eligible for capital gains tax rates. Without listing the various capital gains rates and holding periods, the main point about capital gains is this: Capital gains rates are normally lower than ordinary individual income rates paid by the owners. Therefore, it's almost always an advantage to have the profit from a sale of an ownership interest taxed at capital gains rates.

EXAMPLE: Let's revisit Barbara, and assume her sale of her membership interest is eligible for long-term capital gains treatment (assume a 15% capital gains tax rate), rather than ordinary income tax treatment. Had Barbara's sale not qualified for capital gains tax rates, she would have been taxed on the sale proceeds at a 28% rate—her personal income tax bracket.

We'll discuss tax effects in the realm of selling or liquidating an interest a bit more in Sections C and D of this chapter.

Taxes also result from distributions of members' distributive shares

Member's may owe taxes when members realize profits from their LLC in the form of distributions (which are usually tied to members' capital contributions or capital accounts). We discussed the tax effects of distributions of profits and losses in Section A, above.

2. Legal Considerations

On the legal side, LLCs are generally free to ask for additional capital as needed, unless special requirements are contained in the LLC articles or operating agreement. For example, before a request for additional capital can be made, an LLC's operating agreement might require the unanimous or majority vote of members, or the specific approval of any members who won't pay in additional contributions (since contributions by the other members will lower noncontributing members' percentages of capital interest in the LLC, as discussed below). Before asking members to contribute additional capital, check your operating agreement to make sure it allows the LLC to make the request, and to see if any special voting or other requirements apply.

Commonly, members are asked to make capital contributions in proportion to their current capital interests (as shown by their capital account balances). Doing this maintains the status quo of the LLC, since LLC operating agreements normally provide that allocations and distributions of profits and losses and voting rights are meted out according to members' current capital account balances. But if your LLC needs cash, and some members are cash-rich and others are cash-poor, you may want to go ahead and accept the capital contributions of the members who can afford to make them. Sure, this will diminish the relative capital percentage of the noncontributing members. But, that may be acceptable to them. After all, the added funds will benefit the LLC, and they want the business to succeed as long as they hold any interests in it.

Of course, if a noncontributing member is suspicious and sees the request for additional capital as a scheme for the cash-rich members to increase their relative capital interests, he or she may object. The best way to handle scenarios of this sort is to discuss the reasons for the capital request with the entire membership, and to allow additional contributions only if all members agree. If you can convince all members—including those who cannot afford to make additional cash contributions—that there is a valid and pressing need for additional LLC capital, they probably will approve the pay-in by the other members, despite the fact that their relative capital and profit-sharing interests in the LLC will be diminished afterwards.

Update your operating agreement, if necessary

The relative capital contributions (or capital account balances) of your members may change after obtaining additional capital. This can happen because members disproportionately contribute additional capital, or some contribute and some don't, with the result that the voting and profit-and-loss-sharing ratios may change under your operating agreement. If out-of-date profit-and-loss-sharing ratios are hardwired into your agreement, you will want to update your agreement. Also, if your agreement includes a schedule of capital contributions, you will want to update it to show the additional capital contributions. For these reasons, make sure to review your agreement and make any necessary changes after you get extra capital from your members. (See Chapter 10, Section C1, for a resolution to use to approve amendments to your LLC operating agreement.)

SHOULD YOU PAY INTEREST ON ADDITIONAL CAPITAL OBTAINED FROM MEMBERS?

One way to reward members who make additional capital contributions to the LLC is to have the LLC pay interest on the contributed capital. This is particularly true if members are already receiving interest payments for their initial capital contributions to the LLC. If the LLC decides to pay interest on additional capital contributions made by members, make sure your operating agreement allows this; many agreements say that interest cannot be paid on contributed capital. If your agreement says this, you will need to amend it to allow interest payments on capital. (See Chapter 10, Section C1, for a resolution to use to approve amendments to your LLC operating agreement.)

From a tax standpoint, if interest payments to members are not dependent on profits, which is normally the case, they are treated as a "guaranteed payment" by the LLC. (For a discussion of guaranteed payments vs. distributive share payments, see Chapter 12, Section A1.) This means that the LLC can deduct or capitalize the payments, and each member reports the interest as income on his or her tax return. (A "capitalized" payment is put on the balance sheet as an asset cost. This reduces taxes later when LLC assets or interests are sold.) If the interest is payable to members only if profits of the LLC are sufficient that year, interest payments are treated as allocations and distributions of a member's distributive share of profits.

3. Resolution to Approve Additional Capital Contributions by Members

The following resolution can be used to approve additional contributions of capital by members.

Fill in the resolution as you follow the sample and special instructions below. You'll find this resolution on the CD-ROM and as a tear-out form in Appendix D. (See Appendix A for information on selecting and using the CD-ROM files.)

APPROVAL OF ADDITIONAL CONTRIBUTIONS OF CAPITAL BY MEMBERS

It was agreed that the following members will make the following contributions of capital to the LLC, on or by ___[date for payment]___ : ❶

Name of Member	Amount ❷
_____	$_____
_____	$_____
_____	$_____
_____	$_____
_____	$_____

☐ It was agreed that the operating agreement of the LLC will be amended, if necessary, to reflect the capital, profits, voting, and other interests of all members of the LLC as a result of the making of the above capital contributions.

☐ It was agreed that the LLC will pay interest at the rate of ___% per year on the above capital contributions, subject to the following terms: ___[specify time for payments and whether interest payments are dependent on sufficient LLC profits]___ . ❸

Special Instructions

❶ At a minimum, follow any voting requirements in your operating agreement for approval of additional capital contributions. We recommend that all members approve additional capital contributions, even if a smaller number is allowed under your operating agreement.

❷ List the names of members and their additional capital contributions. We assume cash contributions will be made, but, if appropriate, the fair market value of property contributions can be shown instead.

❸ If you wish to pay interest to members on their additional capital contributions, check this box and complete this paragraph. Specify the annual interest rate and show the terms for payment of the interest. For example, if the interest will be dependent on sufficient LLC profits, you can provide: "Interest is payable within one month following the close of each tax year of the LLC only if LLC profits are sufficient to pay the interest. If LLC profits are not sufficient in a given year, the in-terest will not be payable for that year." Or, if interest is guaranteed, regardless of LLC profits: "Interest payments will be paid yearly, within one month of the close of the LLC tax year."

C. Admission of LLC Members

The admission of a new member is a big change in the life of an LLC. An LLC may need a new member's additional capital investment to fund future growth, or perhaps a relative or friend of a current member has asked to be let in. Another scenario is that a current member decides to sell his or her interest to another person, and the remaining members are asked to approve the new member. If all current members agree that the new person would get along well with LLC management and add to LLC productivity, the admission of the new member makes sense. In this section, we look at these situations and present a resolution LLC members can use to formally admit a new member.

1. Admission of a New Member

Let's outline the general tax and legal treatment of the admission of a new member to an LLC. We assume the person being added is a brand new, additional member. (In contrast, we discuss admitting a new member to replace an existing member in Section 2, below.)

a. Tax Consequences

The treatment of a new member for tax purposes is handled just like the original admission of the founding LLC members. The new member makes a capital contribution in return for an interest in the capital, profits, and losses of the LLC. The transaction is normally nontaxable to the member, but the member is given a basis in his or her interest that affects the amount of taxes the member will pay when the membership interest or LLC is later sold or liquidated. The new member's basis normally equals the amount of cash paid, plus the member's tax basis in any property transferred to the LLC. (See Section A, above, for a discussion of basis.)

⚠️ **Taxes may be owed if a new member will work for the LLC**

If you admit a new member in return for the performance of services, that member may owe taxes on his or her membership interest. If the member receives a "capital interest" in an LLC (which generally means a right to share in the assets of the LLC on its liquidation in return for services), the interest is treated like income and is taxable. The same goes if the person receives a predictable payment of LLC profits. Either way, the member immediately owes taxes on the fair market value of the membership interest. If this tax result is likely to occur, the member may be better off borrowing the money necessary to buy into the LLC, and paying off the debt as he or she or she receives an LLC salary or a distributive share of LLC profits. We discuss this more in Chapter 12, Section A1.

When you admit a new member, the member's capital contribution is carried in the member's capital account on the LLC books. (For an explanation of capital accounts, see "What the Term 'Capital Accounts' Means" in Section A1, above.) But a new member's capital contribution can cause distortion of the relative capital account balances of the members. Since a member's share of LLC assets and profits and losses is normally tied to the new member's proportionate capital interest in the LLC, this distortion can be unfair to the existing members. As a result, your LLC may need to adjust its balance sheet, perhaps adding a value for goodwill, before the new member is brought in. Here's an example.

> **EXAMPLE:** Janet is being admitted as a new member to Icarus Films, LLC, a company with three existing members (Sally, Justin, and Barbara), each of whom has a current capital account balance of $40,000. Janet is to become an equal member of the company, so, after her contribution, her capital account should represent 25% of the total capital account balances of all members. The existing members agree that the current value of the film company is $200,000, and that Janet should pay $50,000 for her one-quarter stake in the business. If Janet's $50,000 contribution is simply reflected on the LLC books, her capital account balance will equal approximately 29% of all LLC capital accounts ($50,000/$170,000), meaning that Janet would own more of the company than any of the others.
>
> One way to handle this is to "capitalize" the goodwill (or reputation) of the company prior to Janet's admission. This means adding goodwill to the balance sheet as a new asset. The amount of the goodwill should be equal to the excess of the value of the company after Janet's admission over the member's total capital account balances. In other words, the goodwill amount is the difference between the value of the company ($200,000) and the sum of the current account balances ($120,000) plus Janet's contribution ($50,000). In this case, goodwill equals $30,000 ($200,000 value of LLC minus $170,000). This $30,000 worth of goodwill should be divided equally among the three members on the balance sheet so that, just prior to Janet's admission, Sally, Justin and

Barbara each have capital account balances of $50,000 ($40,000 plus a $10,000 share of the newly capitalized goodwill).

There is no basis change, no allocation or distribution, and no tax arising from this balance sheet event. Total capital account balances before Janet's admission should equal $150,000. When Janet is admitted, her capital account balance is $50,000, exactly one-quarter of the total capital account balances of all members after her admission ($200,000): the desired result.

You don't need to get involved with these calculations when admitting a member to your LLC—your tax person can handle the details for you. Our basic message is this: Capital account balances are affected by the admission of a new member, so adjustments may need to be made to capital accounts to make sure the members end up with their fair share of total LLC capital interests after the admission.

b. Legal Requirements for Admitting New Members

As elsewhere, your LLC operating agreement is your first and best source of the requirements for admitting new members to your LLC. Most agreements restate the default state LLC rule, typified by the following statute.

District of Columbia LLC Act, Section 29-1032

[...]

(b) Unless otherwise provided in the articles of organization or an operating agreement, after the formation of a limited liability company, *a person may be admitted as a member* [...] in the case of a person acquiring a membership interest directly from the limited liability company, *upon the unanimous consent of the members* [...]

This statute uses the standard state rule that all existing members must approve the admission of a new member into an LLC unless the articles or operating agreement provide otherwise. It's a sensible rule. It's important that all members are included in the discussion to admit a new member and agree to it. This avoids forcing the existing LLC members to share ownership and management responsibilities with an incompatible person.

Look up your state's default admission rule in Appendix B

We list the default state laws for admitting new members into an LLC for each state in Appendix B, under the heading "Admission of Members." This section includes the state rules for admitting both new members and members who have been transferred an interest from a prior member (discussed in Section 2, below). However, because state laws may change, it's important to look at your state's LLC Act as well—you'll find instructions for accessing it online in Appendix B.

There is another important legal implication to admitting a new member. As you know, the basic rights, responsibilities, and interests (capital, profits, and voting interests) of members and managers are spelled out in your LLC operating agreement. You'll want a new member to consent to the terms of the operating agreement, since it is, after all, a contract between the members of the LLC. Also, the admission of a new member changes the relative capital, profits, and voting interests of all members, so your operating agreement may need to be updated to reflect these new numbers (if actual capital, profits, and voting interests are specified for each member in the operating agreement). For both reasons, when you admit a new member it's important to take a close look at your operating agreement to see if it needs to be updated. In all cases, make sure the new member agrees to be bound by the LLC operating agreement. To accomplish this, have the new member sign a statement consenting to be bound by all terms of the current operating agreement. Or, if you are updating your operating agreement, have all members, including the new member, sign the updated agreement. Getting the signatures of all members' spouses is also recommended, since a member's spouse may have a property right in a membership interest. (To formally approve changes to your operating agreement, use the amendment resolution covered in Chapter 10, Section C1.)

EXAMPLE: Ninja Programming Consultants Group, LLC, is bringing in Jeff, a new master C++ programmer with a Black Belt in the Java language. He will be given a one-third capital interest in exchange for his contribution of a Java code kernel, which will form the basis for an advanced Internet search engine the LLC plans to market to clients. He will also receive a one-third profits interest in the business for maintaining this kernel plus creating other cutting-edge code critical to the continued success of the company. Obviously, Jeff's newly created capital and profits interests change the relative capital and profit-sharing interests of the existing members. They agree to admit Jeff as a new member, so a new LLC operating agreement is prepared that reflects the new capital and profits interests of all members. The existing members and Jeff, together with their spouses, sign the new operating agreement.

⚠ Watch out for securities laws
An investment in a business, including a capital interest in an LLC, may be defined under state and federal law as a "security." If it is, the sale of the interest must be registered with the federal Securities and Exchange Commission and the state securities agency, unless an exemption from federal and state registration applies. Fortunately, states are starting to say that an investment in an LLC where all members are active in the business is not a "security," since securities are traditionally defined as investments to reap profits from the work or energies of others. Also, federal and state securities laws contain exemptions for small, private sales of securities. Our main point is this: Proceed with caution in offering and selling LLC memberships to outsiders. To be sure you can safely issue a membership interest under the securities law, a consultation with a knowledgeable small business lawyer is recommended.

If you are considering selling an interest to a passive (inactive) member, be particularly careful, because the securities laws were set up to protect just this type of outside investor. If the investor became dissatisfied with the performance of her investment in your LLC, as a way to recover her losses from your LLC, she could sue you, claiming that issuance of her membership interest was in violation of the securities laws.

c.   Resolution to Admit a New LLC Member

The following resolution can be used by the LLC to formally approve the admission of a new, additional member, (To admit a member who has bought a membership from a existing member, see Section 2, below.)

Fill in the resolution as you follow the sample and special instruction below. You'll find this resolution on the CD-ROM and as a tear-out form in Appendix D. (See Appendix A for information on selecting and using the CD-ROM files.)

Special Instruction

❶ Insert the name of the new member and a description of the cash or property to be paid or transferred to the LLC by the new member. If the member is contributing property, state the fair market value of the property in your description. (The property will be carried on the LLC's books at this value.) In describing any property transferred, be as specific as you can. For example, give the year, make, and vehicle ID number for a truck or the make, model, and serial number of a computer. As an alternative to writing this information in the resolution, you can attach a receipt or other description of the property to the resolution, and refer to this paperwork in the resolution, such as "computer equipment listed in attached Schedule 1."

ADMISSION OF NEW MEMBER

After discussion, it was agreed that the LLC will issue the following membership interest to the following person for the following payment or transfer of property to the LLC:

Name   Payment

___[insert name of new member]___ ❶   ___[insert amount paid for membership interest]___

It was agreed that the operating agreement of the LLC will be amended, if necessary, to reflect the capital, profits, voting, and other interests of all members of the LLC as a result of the admission of the person named above. It was also agreed that, as a condition to being formally accepted as a member of this LLC, the new member agrees to the rights and responsibilities associated with membership by signing the most current LLC operating agreement or by signing a statement, attached to the most current LLC operating agreement, in which the new member agrees to be bound by the terms of the agreement. ❷

If the member will sign a promissory note to pay for his or her interest in installments, refer to the promissory note in the description. The note should carry commercially reasonable terms, such as rate of interest and repayment schedule. (See Chapter 14, Section D, for several forms of promissory notes you can adapt for use for this purpose.)

How to transfer assets to the LLC

Additional legal paperwork is needed to transfer some types of property to the LLC. For example, to transfer a car to an LLC, the new member must sign over a title slip and send a copy to the Department of Motor Vehicles in your state. For transfers of real estate, new deeds transferring the property to the LLC should be prepared and recorded at your county recorder or deeds office. Check with a real estate broker or office supply store for copies of standard deed or transfer forms. An excellent source of deed forms and legal information on transferring real property interests in California is *Deeds for California Real Estate*, by Mary Randolph (Nolo).

If the new member will pay for the membership interest by canceling a debt

Sometimes, the LLC will issue a new member an interest in return for canceling a debt that the LLC

owed to him or her. For example, the new member loaned the LLC startup funds under a note, but decides to exchange the note for an interest in the LLC rather than seek repayment under the note. If this is the case, describe the specifics of the debt cancellation in this resolution—for example, "cancellation of loan to LLC issued on October 1, 2000, principal and accrued unpaid interest owing in the amount of $35,500." Or, if the loan was documented with a promissory note, you can refer to the note instead—for example, "see attached promissory note dated October 1, 2000." Make sure the new member (the former lender) marks the note "paid in full," signs and dates the note, and attaches a copy of it to the resolution. Alternatively, the new member can sign a release. (For instructions on preparing promissory notes to document loans made by members, see Chapter 13, Sections C and D. A Release of Promissory Note form is covered in Chapter 14, Section F.)

❷ Make sure to obtain the signature of the new member to an updated operating agreement or to have the new member sign a statement agreeing to be bound by your current operating agreement after the new member reads a copy of the agreement. Place copies of the paperwork in your LLC records binder.

2. Admission of a Transferee to the LLC

Sometime during the life of your LLC a member may want to leave and cash out his or her membership interest by selling it to an outsider. Of course, this scenario presupposes that the member can find someone who is willing to buy the member's stake in the LLC, manage or work for it, and perform any other duties required under the LLC's operating agreement.

A Sale of Economic Rights Is Different From a Sale of All Membership Rights

When we discuss the sale of a membership interest in this chapter, we are talking about the sale of all of a departing member's membership rights—economic (profits and capital), managerial, voting—the whole ball of wax, with all associated membership rights and responsibilities. It is also possible for a member to transfer all or part of the member's economic rights to an outsider but remain a managing, voting member of the LLC. This sort of transfer of economic rights is normally allowable under state LLC law without consent by the other LLC members, unless the LLC operating agreement says otherwise.

Example: Billy is one of two members of Taxi-Cology Cab Company LLC, which owns two taxicab licenses and oversees a fleet of electric-powered cabs, contracted for use under an experimental clean-the-air program funded by a nonprofit ecology consortium. Billy, short of funds for his son's college tuition, pledges his membership interest as collateral for a personal loan. LLC profits are adequate for Billy to make loan repayments, but Billy has difficulty budgeting his finances and falls behind on the loan. The bank does not wish to foreclose, and its loan department suggests that Billy transfer his right to collect his share of LLC profits to the bank until the loan principal will reduced to a specified amount. Any excess of LLC profits over the loan payments will be applied to loan principal unless Billy requests a return of the excess. Billy agrees to the temporary transfer of economic rights in his membership, committing himself to keeping a closer track of his finances at least until his LLC's profits substantially increase.

---

a. Tax Consequences

The basic tax consequences for a new member who receives a former member's interest are similar to those that apply to a new member who buys an interest from the LLC. The transaction is normally nontaxable to the new member, but the new member is given a basis in the interest that affects the amount of taxes the new member will pay when the membership interest or LLC is later sold or liquidated. The transferee (the buying member) takes a tax basis in the interest equal to the amount of cash paid to the transferor (the selling member) plus the buyer's tax basis in any property that he transferred to the selling member. (See Section A, above, for a discussion of tax basis.)

But, the way a transfer of a membership interest is handled is different from the way an admission of a new member is handled on the LLC side—since the selling member rather than the LLC itself receives the payment for the interest. One common way to treat the transfer of a former member's interest to a new member is to keep the transfer "off the books" of the LLC. In other words, the old member's capital account balance is simply transferred to the new member's capital account. The actual amount paid for the interest by the transferee is not reflected on the LLC capital accounts.

> **EXAMPLE:** Dominic buys Alicia's LLC membership interest for its fair market value, $60,000. When she sells her interest, Alicia's capital account balance was $45,000. This $45,000 balance is zeroed out of Alicia's account when she withdraws and is posted to Dominic's new capital account. Note that the payment of $60,000 for the interest is not reflected on the LLC books; it is a private transaction between the former and new member.

There are other ways to handle a transfer of membership interest. For example, the LLC can take the opportunity to record the amount by which the LLC's fair market value has increased over its book value at the time of the transfer. In the above example, Alicia's stake in the net assets of the LLC as reflected in her capital account was only $45,000, but she was able to sell it for $60,000. One of the ways to update the LLC balance sheet at the time of the transfer is to account for the goodwill of the LLC—the excess of its fair market value over its net asset value—on its balance sheet. This is done in a manner similar to the Icarus Films example given in Section 1, above, where adjustments for goodwill were made to the existing member's capital accounts when a new member bought an interest in the LLC. The same sort of adjustments can be made when a former member sells an interest to a new member.

EXAMPLE: Let's still assume that Alicia wants to sell her LLC interest to Dominic for $60,000. Let's also assume that Alicia is a 25% owner and Rachel is a 75% owner of the LLC. Their capital account balances, respectively, are $45,000 and $135,000, making total LLC capital—the "net asset" or "book value" of the LLC—$180,000. But, since Alicia can sell her 25% interest for $60,000, the LLC is really worth $240,000 ($60,000/25%)—$60,000 more than its book value. This additional amount represents the LLC's "goodwill," an additional LLC asset.

Prior to the transfer of Alicia's membership, this goodwill asset is posted on the LLC books at $60,000, and the capital account of each member increases proportionately according to their relative interest in the LLC—Alicia's capital account increases by $15,000 ($60,000 x 25%), Rachel's by $45,000 ($60,000 x 75%). The result is that Alicia has a capital account balance of $60,000 ($45,000 + $15,000) and Rachel $180,000 ($135,000 + $45,000). The capital accounts are now properly established to reflect the terms of the sale of Alicia's membership to Dominic. He pays Alicia $60,000 for her interest, and Alicia's $60,000 capital account balance is transferred to his new LLC capital account. This amount is equal to 25% of the total capital of the LLC, which now equals $240,000.

Again, you don't need to worry about bookkeeping adjustments when a member sells an interest. Just make sure the LLC's tax adviser goes over the options and adjustments to the LLC books prior to a transfer of a member's interest to a new member.

WHEN A MEMBER TRANSFERS A 50% OR GREATER MEMBERSHIP INTEREST

When a member who owns a 50% or greater interest in an LLC sells or transfers the member's interest, special IRS rules kick in. These can have significant tax effects on the LLC and its members. Specifically, Section 708 of the Internal Revenue Code says that an LLC is "terminated for tax purposes" if, within a 12-month period, there is a sale or exchange of 50% or more of the total capital and profits interests in the LLC. Transfers of interests by gift, will, inheritance, or buyouts by the LLC itself (where the LLC buys the interest of a departing member) do not count, but sales of interests to outsiders (who become new members) or to the continuing LLC members do.

Here's the problem: If this type of transfer of a 50% or greater interest does occur, the IRS says that the LLC is terminated for tax purposes. This means the books of the company are closed and all assets are considered to have been distributed to the LLC members, who then are assumed to have recontributed the distributed assets to a new LLC owned by the same LLC members (not counting the member whose 50% or greater transfer triggered the tax termination). Since a deemed distribution to members can result in recognition of their taxable gain and the payment of taxes, the tax effect of this type of forced tax termination can be enormous and costly. Make sure you plan ahead.

In all cases, when a member is planning to transfer an interest, even if the member's stake in capital and profits of your LLC is less than 50%, check with your tax adviser well in advance to handle or minimize any tax results that may occur, including a possible tax termination of the LLC.

Under current Internal Revenue Code 708 regulations, a tax termination also occurs when an LLC is left with one member only (or when the LLC stops doing business). But, when one member of a two-member LLC dies, the LLC does not terminate as long as the deceased member's estate, or an inheritor of the interest, continues to share in the profits or losses of the LLC.

b. Legal Issues on the Transfer of a Membership

State statutes vary, but most require that nontransferring members approve a sale by a member to a new member, unless the articles or operating agreement say otherwise. Typically, the law requires the consent of all or a majority of the nontransferring members (either per capita, or according to capital and/or profits interests in the LLC).

If the transfer of a membership interest to a new member is not covered in your articles or your operating agreement, and your members do not agree to admit a transferee (the person who buys an LLC interest), state law usually says the buyer gets only an economic interest in the LLC membership. In other words, the buyer receives a right to profits and capital distributions, but not full LLC membership voting or management rights. Obviously, a buyer normally wants the whole kit and caboodle, so you will want to poll your members to get their consent for the buyer to join the membership ranks.

Here's a typical state statute covering the transfer of membership rights.

Georgia LLC Act, Sec. 14-11-503

Except as otherwise provided in the articles of organization or a written operating agreement:

(1) An assignee [a transferee—the person who buys a membership interest] of a limited liability company interest may become a member only if the other members unanimously consent;

(2) An assignee who has become a member has, to the extent assigned, the rights and powers, and is subject to the restrictions and liabilities, of a member under the articles of organization, any operating agreement, and this chapter [the state LLC Act]; [...]

A related statute indicates what happens if the nontransferring members do not consent to the admission of a transferee.

Georgia LLC Act, Sec. 14-11-502

[...]

(2) An assignment [sale of an LLC interest] entitles the assignee [transferee] to share in the profits and losses and to receive the distributions to which the assignor [selling member] was entitled, to the extent assigned;

(3) An assignment of a limited liability company interest does not of itself [...] entitle the assignee to participate in the management and affairs of the limited liability company or to become, or exercise any rights of, a member *until admitted as a member* [italics added] pursuant to Code section 14-11-505 [which eventually refers to Section 14-11-503, cited above].

 How to find your state's approval rule for admitting new members

We list each state's membership voting requirement for approving the admission of a transferee in Appendix B under the heading "Admission of Members." (This heading also shows the approval requirement for issuing a new membership to someone who contributes capital directly to the LLC.) Make sure to also check your operating agreement, and, if you want to be sure of the most current state rules, your state LLC Act.

The admission of a new member is an important decision. Because the nontransferring members may not have had any dealings with the proposed admitee in the past, we recommend that you have all members approve the admission of the new member, no matter what your operating agreement or state law has to say on the subject. This is particularly true when the LLC is member-managed. If the new member is not compatible personally and managerially with the other members, LLC business can suffer severely. As part of this approval process, the existing members can let the new member know what they expect, and the members can try to work out any differences at the outset. If it is clear that the new member is not compatible, it's probably best to handle the problem head-on, letting the selling or transferring member know that his or her choice of buyer is not satisfactory to the other members. In this case, the transferring member can decide to transfer only economic rights in the membership to the buyer or continue the search for a new buyer (if the member is determined to transfer all membership rights in order to be completely free of the LLC).

There is another important legal implication to admitting a new member. As you know, the basic rights, responsibilities, and interests (capital, profits, and voting interests) of members and managers are spelled out in your LLC operating agreement. You'll want a new member to consent to the terms of the operating agreement, since it is, after all, a contract between the members of the LLC. Also, since the admission of a new member may change the relative capital, profits, and voting interests of all members, your operating agreement may need to be updated to reflect these new numbers (if actual capital, profits, and voting interests are specified for each member in the operating agreement). For both reasons, it's important to take a close look at your operating agreement when you admit a new member. It may need to be updated.

In all cases, make sure the new member agrees to be bound by the LLC operating agreement. To accomplish this, either have the new member sign a statement consenting to be bound by all terms of the current operating agreement or, if you are updating your operating agreement, have all members, including the new member, sign the updated agreement. We also recommend that all members' spouses sign, since a member's spouse may have a property right in a membership interest. (To formally approve changes to your operating agreement, use the amendment resolution covered in Chapter 10, Section C1.)

State law also may require the specific consent of nontransferring members to continue the LLC

Some states' LLC statutes say that an LLC automatically dissolves, or "legally terminates," when a member sells or otherwise disposes of a membership interest, unless the remaining (nontransferring) members agree in writing to continue the LLC. We know this seems like a strange and unnecessary requirement, but your state may have enacted this sort of provision to comply with old tax rules. Since it's easy to comply with this requirement if it's imposed in your state, we suggest that you assume it applies to you. (But you can check if your state has this type of provision in Appendix B, under the heading "Continuation of the LLC"). Simply use the resolution shown below for approving the transfer of a member's interest. Paragraph 4 covers the nontransferring members' consent to continue the LLC after the transfer.

c. Resolution to Approve Transfer of Membership to a New Member

The following resolution can be used by the LLC to formally approve the transfer of an LLC membership interest by a departing member to a new member. Under typical state statutes, unless the remaining members approve the transfer, the buyer only gets economic rights (rights to profits and losses and, when the LLC dissolves, liquidated distributions), but not full membership voting and management rights.

Fill in the resolution as you follow the sample and special instructions below. You'll find this resolution on the CD-ROM and as a tear-out form in Appendix D. (See Appendix A for information on selecting and using the CD-ROM files.)

APPROVAL OF TRANSFER OF MEMBERSHIP

After discussion, it was agreed that the LLC approves the transfer of the membership interest of
_____[name of transferring member]_____, "former member," to _____[name of new member]_____, "new member." ❶ The new member is admitted as a full member of this LLC, with all economic, management, voting, and any other rights associated with the membership interest of the former member.

It was agreed that the books of this LLC will be adjusted to show the termination of membership rights of the departing member and the establishment of membership rights of the new member.

The operating agreement of the LLC will be amended, if necessary, to reflect the capital, profits, voting, and other interests of all members of the LLC as a result of the admission of the new member named above. It was also agreed that, as a condition to being formally accepted as a member of this LLC, the new member must agree to the rights and responsibilities associated with membership by signing the most current LLC operating agreement or by signing a statement, which will be attached to the most current LLC operating agreement, agreeing to be bound by the terms of the agreement. ❷

It was further resolved that the nontransferring members of the LLC, whose signatures appear below, consent to the continuance of the business and legal existence of the LLC following the withdrawal of the former member and the admission of the new member. ❸

Date: _____

Signature: _____

Signature: _____

Signature: _____

Signature: _____

Special Instructions

❶ Insert the names of the former member and the new member.

❷ Make sure to obtain the signature of the new member to an updated operating agreement, or to have the new member sign a statement agreeing to be bound by your current operating agreement after the new member reads a copy of the agreement. Place copies of the paperwork in your LLC records binder.

❸ As mentioned in the text, state statutes and/or the LLC operating agreement may require the written consent of the nontransferring members to continue the LLC after a member sells an interest. If so, the written consent of the nontransferring members must be obtained within 90 days after the former member withdraws. We assume you will approve and sign this resolution in advance of a member's sale to a new member, and therefore meet any deadline imposed in your operating agreement or under state law for obtaining this consent.

To make it clear that you wish to continue your LLC after a member sells an interest, have all nontransferring members sign in the space provided, and indicate the date of their signatures. (If they sign at different times, show the date of the first signature.) If you have any questions about your state's current default rule for voting to continue your LLC after a member sells an interest, check your state LLC Act or ask a lawyer for guidance.

D. WITHDRAWAL OF LLC MEMBERS

This section applies to a member who withdraws from the LLC without transferring the member's interest to a new member. (When a member transfers his or her membership interest to a new member and then withdraws is covered in Section C2, above.)

The flip side of the admission of a member is the withdrawal of a member. A member may withdraw from a LLC in any one of the following scenarios:

• The LLC is not sufficiently profitable, and the member wishes to withdraw capital and invest it elsewhere.

• The member needs funds to meet other business or personal needs, and wants to cash out the membership interest now rather than waiting for the LLC to be sold or liquidated (which could take some time, of course).

• The member is having a personal or business conflict with the other members, isn't enjoying working in the LLC any longer, or wants to depart for other personal reasons.

• The member is disabled and is no longer able to manage and/or work for the LLC as a result.

• The member is a thorn in the side of the other members and is being expelled. Expulsions are not common; they can only occur in LLCs with more than two members. (In a two-member LLC, if a member wants to expel the other against his wishes, this really means forcing a dissolution of the LLC.)

When a member wishes to leave, the first place to look is your LLC articles and operating agreement. In many LLCs, the members have agreed in their operating agreement that a member is not allowed to cash out prior to the liquidation or sale of the LLC or may cash out only if the member accepts a discounted value for her membership interest. Often the operating agreement contains comprehensive "buy-sell provisions" that specify exactly when a member's interest may be bought, how a member's interest will be valued, and how the LLC will pay for it. These provisions may give both the LLC and/or the remaining members a chance to buy the withdrawing member's interest.

For more information on buy-sell provisions If you want to learn more about the options typically included in LLC (as well as partnership and corporate) buy-sell provisions—perhaps to include in your own LLC operating agreement—see *Buy-Sell Agreement Handbook: Plan Ahead for Changes in the Ownership of Your Business*, by Anthony Mancuso and Bethany K. Laurence (Nolo).

Often, however, buy-sell provisions of this sort have not been adopted by the members, and the LLC documents are silent on a member's withdrawal. In this situation, you will need to check your state's LLC Act to explore the legal options and consequences of the departure of an LLC member. We discuss some of these options and consequences in Section 2, below, but first let's look at the basic tax consequences of the departure of a member.

1. Tax Effects of a Member's Withdrawal

The buyout of a member's interest, by the LLC or the remaining members, is, of course, a taxable event. The withdrawing member calculates any gain he or she realizes on the sale—the amount by which the sales price for the interest exceeds the member's basis—and pays taxes on the gain. (For a general discussion of tax basis, see Section A1, above.) Normally, the member's gain is taxed at capital gains rates, which are generally lower than the normal individual income tax rates. If the amount paid to the withdrawing member is less than his or her basis in the interest, the member realizes a loss on the sale, which the member may be allowed to deduct on his or her individual tax return. (The IRS "at-risk" and "passive income" rules affect the deductibility of losses by a member. Your tax adviser can tell you more about these loss limitation rules.)

Effect of LLC liabilities on a withdrawing member

An LLC member's basis in an LLC interest includes the member's share of LLC liabilities. When the member's interest is sold, the member is relieved of these liabilities. Therefore, the tax rules say that a member's share of LLC liabilities is added to the amount received in a sale of the LLC interest. In effect, the member is treated as having received an additional cash payment equal to the member's share of LLC debts at the time of departure.

> **EXAMPLE:** José withdraws from his LLC, and the remaining members buy out his interest for $40,000. José's basis in his interest was $25,000, and his share of LLC liabilities at the time of his withdrawal was $5,000. His gain on the transfer of his interest is $20,000 ($40,000 payment plus $5,000 liabilities minus $25,000 basis).

These standard tax rules regarding basis and gain apply when a withdrawing member sells a membership interest back to one or more of the remaining LLC members or to an outsider (who is then admitted into the LLC as discussed in Section C2, above). But special tax rules kick in if a withdrawing member sells an interest back to the LLC, not to one or more of the remaining LLC members or to an outsider. The payment made by the LLC to buy back the interest of a withdrawing member is known as a "liquidating distribution." Essentially, the rules regarding liquidating distributions allow more wiggle room than the standard rules. They let the LLC and its members structure the tax consequences of the sale in more than one way.

Here's how the liquidating distribution rules generally work: When the LLC itself buys back a withdrawing member's interest, capital gains treatment only applies to payments made by the LLC for the book value of actual LLC assets.

> **EXAMPLE:** Chuck withdraws from his LLC, which pays for his interest according to its book value. This value is computed as the balance sheet value of LLC assets minus LLC liabilities, multiplied by Chuck's percentage of LLC ownership (the percentage of his capital interest compared to total LLC capital interests).
>
> If LLC assets equal $150,000, and liabilities equal $75,000, the balance sheet (net asset) value of the LLC is $75,000. If Chuck holds a 25% capital interest in the company, the LLC pays him $18,740 ($75,000 x 25%) for his interest. In this situation, Chuck is being paid for his proportionate interest in the net assets of the LLC, and the sale is eligible for capital gains tax treatment—that is, Chuck pays capital gains taxes on the amount of gain he realizes on the sale of his interest back to the LLC.

Of course, withdrawing members usually want to get more for their membership interest than the book value of the interest. That's because the book value of LLC assets does not normally include appreciation on the assets that has occurred since the transfer of the assets to the LLC (unless the assets have recently been revalued to update the balance sheet). It does reflect depreciation deductions taken by the LLC on its assets. Also, book value does not normally include the "goodwill" of the business—the added value of a business due to its recognition by its customers and its continuing ability to earn profits because of this recognition. Because of this, the buy-sell provisions of LLC operating agreements often provide for additional payments to a withdrawing member. For example, the agreement may provide that a withdrawing member is entitled to the book value of the member's interest plus an additional amount, which may be a set amount or a percentage of book value or LLC profits. This bonus amount is intended to compensate the withdrawing member for his or her share of the fair market value of the LLC over and above its book value. (We discuss the legal side of how much a withdrawing member should be paid in Section 2, below.)

Here's what the IRS rules say (under IRC Section 736) regarding liquidating payments for a member's interest by the LLC over and above book value: This extra amount will be treated as ordinary income to the withdrawing member, taxable at the member's individual income tax rates instead of the lower capital gains rates (unless the LLC operating agreement specifically provides for and allocates an extra payment as "goodwill," discussed below). The LLC gets to treat the additional payment for goodwill as a payout of profits, which reduces the distributive share of income payable to the other members, or as an expense, which reduces the net income of the LLC. In either case the LLC (and, therefore, the continuing members) get the tax benefit of the additional payout, since it reduces its net taxable income passed along to the other members.

EXAMPLE: Using Chuck again as an example, if the buy-sell provisions of Chuck's LLC operating agreement stated that Chuck should be paid his 25% share of the net asset value of the LLC on his withdrawal, plus a bonus of 15% of this balance sheet figure, this extra 15% bonus amount is taxable to him as ordinary income, and reduces the net income reported by the LLC on its tax return. (Chuck pays ordinary income tax rates on the 15% amount, but still gets to treat the 25% share as capital gains, taxable at the lower capital gains tax rates).

The big exception to this rule is that any additional payment by the LLC (over and above a payment for the LLC assets) will be treated under the capital gains rules if the LLC's operating agreement specifically says that the extra payment is for the "goodwill" of the business. An example best illustrates this important tax exception.

EXAMPLE: Using the previous LLC example, if the LLC's operating agreement says that the extra 15% payment to a withdrawing member is payment for a member's share of the LLC's "goodwill," the extra amount will be taxed at capital gains rates to Chuck, and the LLC can't use the extra payment to reduce its taxable income.

The whole idea behind this exception to the IRS rules is to allow LLCs to structure the tax consequences of a payout to a withdrawing member in a way the members decide best: If they agree to have the withdrawing member pay the tax cost of an additional payment by paying ordinary income tax on it, then there's no need to say anything in the operating agreement. But if the members agree that the LLC should bear the tax cost of these additional payments (payments over and above the book value of LLC assets) to withdrawing members, they can allocate the extra payments to goodwill in their operating agreement. By doing so, a withdrawing member gets favorable capital gains tax treatment on the additional payment, but the LLC can't use it to reduce its income.

⚠ **Prior to a buyout of a withdrawing member, check your operating agreement** As always, our examples are simple, and the tax rules are complicated. For example, special rules apply to liquidating payments made for a member's share of an LLC's inventory and accounts receivable. Our discussion is intended simply to lead to the following point: Because the tax consequences of a buyout of a withdrawing member can generate very different tax outcomes depending on the exact wording of your operating agreement, make it a point to have your operating agreement checked before a withdrawing member leaves your LLC.

Specifically, a lawyer or tax adviser may decide to amend your agreement to include (or exclude) magic language relating to payments for goodwill, which can be critical to achieve a tax result in favor of your LLC or a withdrawing member.

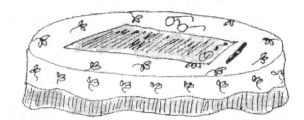

2. Legal Issues on the Withdrawal of an LLC Member

State law varies concerning a member's right to withdraw from an LLC at any time, particularly when the LLC operating agreement is silent on the issue. The various state statutes also differ with respect to the amount of compensation a member is legally entitled to when he or she withdraws from an LLC (again, assuming the operating agreement is silent on this). This leads us to emphasize the following point: Because it's important to all members to know in advance how much a withdrawing member will be paid by the LLC if it buys back an interest, take a fresh look at your operating agreement to see if it is clear on this issue. If not, it's probably time to give your agreement a tune-up. As discussed above, this once-over is also important from a tax perspective. You'll want to make sure the language of your agreement leads to the desired tax result when a departing member's interest is bought back by your LLC.

How to prepare basic buy-sell provisions One self-help resource that shows you how to prepare basic buy-sell provisions to include in your operating agreement is Nolo's *Buy-Sell Agreement Handbook: Plan Ahead for Changes in the Ownership of Your Business,* by Anthony Mancuso and Bethany K. Laurence. This book shows you how to prepare provisions that specify how, when, and how much to pay a business owner who withdraws, dies, or proposes to sell an interest to an outsider. It applies to LLCs as well as small corporations and partnerships.

Of course, the best and surest way to know how your state handles membership withdrawal is to check out your state's LLC Act. We summarize each state's default rule for the withdrawal of members in Appendix B, under the heading "Withdrawal of Members." That section indicates your state's rules, if any, for the procedures when a member wishes to withdraw from the LLC, as well as the rules for payments to a withdrawing member. Check your state LLC Act for the latest information. Generally, these default rules apply only if the LLC articles and operating agreement are silent on these issues. Note that we specifically list the rules that apply to a member who withdraws from the LLC without transferring his or her interest to a new member. (The rules that apply when a member transfers a membership interest to a new member and then withdraws are covered under "Admission of Members," in Appendix B; see Section C2, above, for a further discussion of this scenario.)

A state may allow members to withdraw without notice. Some states require six months' notice.

Other states have shorter notice requirements. For example, Indiana requires only 30 days' prior notice by a withdrawing member; Missouri, 90 days. But when a member leaves, what does the D.C. statute have to say about the member's right to payment from the LLC?

District of Columbia LLC Act, 29-1027

(a) Except as otherwise provided in [this LLC Act], upon resignation, any resigning member is entitled to receive any distribution to which such member is entitled under the articles of organization or an operating agreement, and, if not otherwise provided in the articles of organization or an operating agreement, such member is entitled to receive, within a reasonable time after resignation, the fair value of such member's membership interest as of the date of resignation.

(b) If the resignation of the member is a breach of an operating agreement, or the resignation occurs as a result of otherwise wrongful conduct of the member, the limited liability company may recover from the resigning member damages for breach of the operating agreement or as a result of the wrongful conduct, including the reasonable costs of obtaining replacement of the services that the resigning member was obligated to perform, and may offset the damages against the amount otherwise distributable to the resigning member, in addition to pursuing any remedies provided for in an operating agreement or otherwise available under applicable law.

This, too, is a typical state statute. First of all, it says that a member is entitled to current distributions—that is, a member's distributive share of profits earned but unpaid prior to the withdrawal of the member. It goes on to require that, unless the articles or operating agreement say otherwise, a member must get the *fair value* of his or her interest. What does this mean? The LLC Act does not define this important standard, but court cases involving partnerships—which, it is safe to assume, apply to LLCs as well—generally say that the fair value of a business interest is its fair market value, not just its book value.

In other words, if an LLC's operating agreement is silent on the rights of withdrawing members and a member resigns from an LLC, the withdrawing member is probably entitled to more than the balance of the member's capital account or the book value of his or her interest. In fact, the member may decide to sue for more if it appears likely that the fair market value of the member's interest is more than he or she received. (See the discussion of appreciation of assets and goodwill in Section D1, above, for why the fair market value of an interest is usually higher than its book value.) And, the member may have a fair chance of winning, particularly if the operating agreement is not clear on how much a departing member is entitled to be paid and if state law does not specifically limit the amount a departing member is entitled to receive.

The second portion of the D.C. statute is also typical of how states handle member withdrawal. Obviously, state law cannot prohibit a member from leaving an LLC, no matter what the statutes or the LLC operating agreement say. This section addresses this problem. It says that a member who resigns in violation of a provision of the LLC operating agreement (or leaves due to wrongful conduct—for example, a member is expelled for violation of standards specified in the operating agreement) can be required to pay for the cost of replacing himself or for other monetary damages caused to the LLC because of the withdrawal. These costs can be deducted from the amount the LLC is otherwise required to pay the withdrawing member.

EXAMPLE: Hilda is a one-third member of Goody-Goody Two Shoes Supply, LLC. (She has a one-third capital and profits interest.) In addition to her initial capital contribution of $10,000, her deal with her LLC is that she work full-time, including weekends if needed, running the business in return for her share of the profits.

Hilda becomes tired of working day-in, day-out for her less-than-adequate, one-third share of LLC profits. She hands in her walking papers to her fellow members, giving them six months' advance notice of her departure. Since the LLC operating agreement forbids Hilda from leaving without finding a replacement member who will work in the business and is suitable to the other members, Hilda tries to find a replacement. She has no luck finding anyone willing to work the number of hours required for her current level of profit-sharing, but she leaves anyway.

The remaining members understand Hilda's need to leave, but want to be fair to the LLC as well as Hilda. They value the business at a fair market value of $240,000, which makes Hilda's capital interest worth $80,000. The LLC has to hire and train a replacement for Hilda, at least until another member willing to invest and work in the business comes along. They estimate these training costs at $10,000 and deduct this amount from the check they issue to Hilda on her departure. (They don't deduct the ongoing salary of the replacement worker—after all, the LLC receives value for these services.) Hilda is happy getting $70,000 back on her investment of money and time in the LLC and moves on to greener— that is, more profitable—pursuits.

TAX NOTE: Because Goody-Goody's LLC operating agreement does not allocate to goodwill any part of an LLC's payments made to a withdrawing member (discussed above), the LLC will be able to deduct the amount of the payment that exceeds Hilda's share of the book value of the business. They remind Hilda in their cover letter sent with the check that the portion of the LLC payment that exceeds her share of the book value of the business is likely taxable to her as ordinary income, and that her tax person can help her meet the requirements for reporting the payment on her tax return.

It is common for states to allow the LLC to offset the amount paid to a departing member if the LLC has to find a replacement worker to perform the withdrawing member's services or if the member is withdrawing in violation of the operating agreement or for other wrongful conduct. Some states allow the LLC in such cases to reduce the payment otherwise required under the operating agreement by the amount of profits lost by the LLC or, in the alternative, by the portion of the goodwill, or "going concern" value, of the LLC otherwise allocated to the member's interest.

Other states take an approach to payments that's less generous to a withdrawing member, even one who gives the LLC adequate notice. For example, the Tennessee LLC Act (Section 48-216-101) says a withdrawing member is entitled to the fair market value of the member's interest (determined on a going-concern basis or a liquidation basis, whichever is less). Liquidation value means the amount the LLC assets would bring when sold separately at a liquidation of the LLC (when a buyer is simply paying for assets, not paying to step into a going business)—and is likely to be the lowest measure of a business's worth. Other states may limit the amount a withdrawing member receives to the balance of the member's capital account. This is normally substantially less than the fair market value of the member's interest in a profitable company. Here is a rather wordy example of this type of provision (as usual, it applies only when the operating agreement is silent on the issue).

Florida LLC Act, 608.427. Withdrawal or Reduction of Members' Contributions to Capital

(2) Upon withdrawal, … a withdrawing member is entitled to receive any distribution to which the withdrawing member is entitled under the articles of organization or operating agreement, and, if not otherwise provided in the articles of organization and operating agreement, the withdrawing member is entitled to receive, within a reasonable time after withdrawal, the fair value of the withdrawing member's interest. […]

A number of states take an even less generous approach—that is, they don't even allow withdrawing members to be paid for their membership interest unless and until the LLC dissolves (as always, unless otherwise provided in the LLC operating agreement). Instead, the withdrawing member is given the status of a transferee or assignee of a membership interest. This means that the withdrawing member can no longer vote or manage the LLC, but only retains a right to receive ongoing allocations and distributions of the LLC profits, losses, credits, and deductions passed along to all LLC members. In other words, the withdrawing member is not paid the value of the member's membership interest until the LLC is later sold or liquidated in its entirety. Here's an example, which provides that a withdrawing member is treated as a transferee.

Nebraska LLC Act, 21-2619. Withdrawal or Reduction of Member's Contribution to Capital

[…]

(3) A member of the limited liability company who has withdrawn from membership, but whose capital account has not been liquidated pursuant to the articles of organization or the operating agreement, shall have the status of a transferee as provided in section 21-2621 [which lists the rights to profits and other eco-

nomic rights of transferees] unless otherwise provided in the operating agreement.

Lastly, a number of states (such as Delaware) simply say that a member may not withdraw from the LLC unless allowed to do so under the operating agreement or by consent of the remaining members. But, remember: Even in a state that disallows membership withdrawal without the consent of other members, a member whose departure violates the operating agreement is always free to leave, as long as that member is willing to live with (or challenge in court) not receiving payment for the membership interest or receiving a reduced amount.

Sometimes, an LLC can't legally pay for a withdrawing member's interest

Don't forget that state LLC law usually contains restrictions on LLC management's ability to make distributions to members. As discussed in Section A2, above, if a distribution will lower the book value of LLC assets below the current liabilities of the LLC, or if a distribution is likely to make it difficult for an LLC to be able to pay its bills as they become due, an LLC should not make the distribution. These distribution restrictions apply not just to the payout of LLC profits; they apply to all LLC distributions, including the payout to a withdrawing member to purchase a membership interest.

If the LLC is unable to pay cash to a departing member because of these legal requirements, and if it cannot borrow the money from a bank, it may be forced to pay for the departing member's interest in installments. It would do so either by signing a promissory note to pay the member monthly or quarterly or, if the future liquidity of the LLC is difficult to predict, by forestalling payments until the LLC has more cash on hand. If this happens—if the LLC cannot buy back the departing member's interest, even under an installment payment plan—the withdrawing member will continue to own an economic interest in the LLC and will continue to share in LLC profits and losses until his or her membership is bought out by the LLC.

Check your state's statutes

Because state statutes are subject to change, you should refer to your state's LLC Act for the most current rules. (See Chapter 1, Section C for tips on finding your state's law.) Typically, state LLC Acts contain a section entitled "Withdrawal of a Member," or a similarly titled provision, that specifies when a member may withdraw from an LLC and how much the member is entitled to receive in the absence of a provision in the LLC operating agreement.

3. Resolution to Approve LLC Purchase of a Withdrawing Member's Interest

The following resolution can be used to approve the purchase by the LLC of a withdrawing member's interest (and to agree to continue the LLC after a member withdraws).

Fill in the resolution as you follow the sample and special instructions below. You'll find this resolution on the CD-ROM and as a tear-out form in Appendix D. (See Appendix A for information on selecting and using the CD-ROM files.)

APPROVAL OF LLC PURCHASE OF INTEREST OF WITHDRAWING MEMBER

The LLC resolves that the LLC will purchase the entire membership interest of _____ [name of withdrawing member]_____, a member of this LLC, on the terms specified below. It was agreed that the purchase of the membership interest will terminate all capital, profits, loss, and voting, and all other management, ownership, and economic interests of the member in this LLC.

The date of purchase is: _____ [insert proposed purchase date]_____

The terms of the purchase are as follows: ___[specify amount, type, and timing of payment, plus any other terms]_____. ❶

After a report of the treasurer, which included an analysis of the most recently prepared balance sheet of the LLC and LLC operations since its preparation, it was agreed that the LLC was able financially and in accordance with any applicable state legal requirements to purchase the withdrawing member's interest according to the terms set out above. ❷

The treasurer was instructed to prepare a balance sheet of the LLC as of the date set for purchase of the withdrawing member's interest, and to see to it that a copy of the balance sheet, plus any additional supporting documentation, be given to the member prior to the date of purchase for the member's review and, if requested, signature. A copy of the balance sheet and any supporting documentation, signed by the withdrawing member if appropriate, will be attached to this resolution and placed in the LLC records binder.

On completion of the necessary paperwork, the treasurer will pay, or make appropriate arrangements for payment, on behalf of the LLC to purchase the withdrawing member's interest on the terms specified above.

It was further resolved that the remaining members of the LLC, whose signatures appear below, consent to the continuance of the business and legal existence of the LLC following the withdrawal of the member named above. ❸

Date: _____

Signature: _____

Signature: _____

Signature: _____

Signature: _____

Special Instructions

❶ In the first blank, specify the name of the withdrawing member. In the second blank, put the date of the purchase of the departing member's interest by the LLC. In the third, spell out the terms of purchase of the interest, including the form of payment (cash or property—usually cash) and whether the payment will be in installments. (If payment is to be in installments, specify repayment terms, and attach a promissory note embodying the terms of repayments. See Chapter 13, Section D, for promissory note forms.)

❷ Attach a balance sheet to the resolution. It should show that the LLC is financially able to buy back the departing member's interest according to the terms set out in the resolution. If you have questions about your LLC's ability to afford the buyback or about your state's legal distribution requirements, check out your state LLC Act or see a lawyer or tax person for help.

❸ Some state statutes and/or LLC operating agreements may require the written consent of the remaining members to continue the LLC after a member withdraws. If this is true of your LLC, then to avoid a legal dissolution, have the remaining LLC members sign in the space provided, and indicate the date of their signatures. (If they sign at different times, show the date of the first signature.) Remember, state requirements vary, but typically the written consent of the remaining members must be obtained, if at all, within 90 days of the member's withdrawal. We assume you will approve and sign this resolution in advance of a member's departure, and therefore meet any deadline imposed in your operating agreement or under state law for obtaining this consent. ■

CHAPTER 12

LLC Hiring and Compensation Resolutions

An important part of any LLC's business is to hire LLC personnel and set salaries. This is true for small, closely held LLCs as well as big companies with large payrolls.

Another increasingly important issue is when and how to contract for services offered by outside individuals and companies (independent contractors). Hiring independent contractors can be a cost- and tax-effective strategy for obtaining help with an LLC project without having to place the worker on the payroll.

Also, LLCs may decide to pass special compensation resolutions for members, managers, and officers, such as approving year-end salary increases and bonuses, payment for attending meetings, and indemnification for members, managers, and employees. This chapter covers all of the above issues and provides instructions for selecting and using resolutions to approve these and related matters.

LLC management generally approves resolutions

The LLC resolutions contained in this chapter normally need to be approved by LLC management—that is, by the members of a member-managed LLC or by the managers of a manager-managed LLC.

How to Select and Use LLC Resolutions

- Scan the table of contents at the beginning of the chapter to find resolutions of interest to you.

- When you find one you need, read the background material that precedes the pertinent LLC resolution.

- Follow the instructions included with the sample resolution to complete a draft of the resolution using your computer. If you need guidance on selecting and using the computer disk files, see Appendix A. (You'll have to fill in the tear-out resolution included in Appendix D if you don't have a computer.)

- Complete any needed attachment forms.

- If a resolution involves complex issues that will benefit from expert analysis, have your legal or tax adviser review your paperwork and conclusions.

- Prepare minutes of meeting or written consent forms as explained in Chapters 5–7, and insert the completed resolution in the appropriate form.

- Have the LLC secretary sign the printed minutes or have members and/or managers sign any written consent forms and waivers. Then place the signed forms, together with any attachments, in your LLC records binder.

A. Approving LLC Salaries of Members and Employees

In this section, we provide resolutions to approve the hiring and compensation of LLC members and nonmember employees. These resolutions can be useful to explain the payment of substantial salaries and to list the responsibilities of member and nonmember workers.

Before getting into the language of the resolutions, let's overview the tax ramifications of paying salaries to LLC members.

1. Tax Treatment of Salaries Paid to Members

Even though a member of an LLC, like a partner in a partnership, may be paid a salary, the member is not generally considered an employee for legal and tax purposes. So while it is customary for some LLCs to give members a guaranteed salary in return for the performance of services, these payments (if not tied to the net income of the LLC) are classified as "guaranteed payments" under the tax rules. This means that the payments are taxed as ordinary income to the member at the close of the LLC's tax year in which the payments accrue (become payable), even if they are distributed to the member at a later time. Of course, the LLC gets to deduct (or capitalize in some cases) the payments as a business expense.

On the other hand, if a member's salary is tied to the net income of the LLC, it is treated as a member's "distributive share" of LLC profits. That means the salary payments are taxed to the member when allocated to him or her by the LLC (again, normally at the end of the LLC's tax year)

Although both guaranteed payments and distributive share payments are taxed as ordinary income to the member, the net tax results to the members as a whole are a bit different. For example, allocations and distributions of members' distributive shares of profits can affect the members' basis in their membership interests; guaranteed payments do not. And, guaranteed payments come off the top. In other words, they are deducted by the LLC before the net LLC income available for distribution to all members is computed—that is, before the members' distributive shares are allocated. This means that guaranteed payments affect all LLC members, since they lower the net income that will be allocated to the members at the end of the LLC tax year.

So (you may be asking) should an LLC member who works for the company be compensated with guaranteed payments or distributive shares? The answer will vary. It is common to allocate profits to a working member in recognition of the fact that the member is entitled to compensation (like wages or salary) in return for working for the business, separate from what he or she might receive for merely being an owner.

EXAMPLE: Jeff and Roberta form the Magic Carpet Cleaning LLC. Each pays equal cash to start the LLC in return for a 50% capital interest. Since Jeff will work for the business, and Roberta won't, they agree that the first $30,000 of annual net profits, if any, go to Jeff, and any remaining profits are divided equally between Jeff and Roberta. In other words, Jeff receives a greater distributive share of profits in recognition of his work as a member of the LLC.

It is also common to give a mix of guaranteed payments and a percentage of profits to a member who works for the LLC.

EXAMPLE: Magic Carpet Cleaning LLC (MCC) decides to guarantee Jeff a yearly payment of $30,000. It does this by providing in its LLC operating agreement that Jeff will receive 50% of the annual profits of MCC, but no less than $30,000 each year. First-year profits of MCC are $50,000, so Jeff is allocated half of the profits at the end of the year—$25,000—as his distributive share of profits for the year, plus he is given $5,000 to reach his minimum of $30,000 for the year. Only the $5,000 is treated for tax purposes as a guaranteed payment to Jeff (since actual profits were not sufficient to pay the $5,000). In its second tax year, MCC's net income is $60,000. Jeff is allocated $30,000 in profits at the end of the year—half of the profits. This allocation is treated for tax purposes as Jeff's distributive share of profits (since profits were sufficient to pay Jeff's guarantee of $30,000).

What about the employment tax status of working LLC members?

As discussed above, LLC members who work for the LLC are normally not considered employees for tax purposes, even if they are paid salaries. It follows that payments to members are not considered wages; rather, payments to these working members are considered guaranteed payments or payments of the member's distributive share of LLC profits, as discussed above. However, members who are actively involved in LLC operations must normally report all money received from the LLC as self-employment income. That includes allocations of all profits, not just profits paid in return for services, plus any guaranteed payments. Ask your tax adviser for more information on the self-employment tax rules that apply to LLC members..

Payments to a member as an outside consultant

If an LLC member is paid for services in a nonmember capacity—for example, a member is paid for providing occasional legal or accounting services as a consultant—the payment usually can be handled like any payment for outside services by the business. That is, the LLC deducts the payment from its income (or capitalizes it if required to do so), and the member only reports and pays income tax on the payment when the member actually receives it. (See Section B, below, on independent contractors.)

Other tax issues related to member services

There are other possible tax consequences to members who perform services for the LLC. For example, if a member receives a "capital interest" in an LLC—this generally means a right to share in the assets of the LLC on its liquidation—in return for the performance of services, the capital interest is treated like income and is taxable. The member immediately owes taxes on the fair market value of the member-

ship interest. If a member who provides services receives an interest only in the profits of the LLC in return for services—called a "profits" interest—the profits interest is normally not taxed, unless the amount of profits the member will receive is clearly discernible or predictable. (See Revenue Procedure 93-27.)

Check with your tax advisor before compensating members

Obviously, the tax issues related to payments for members' services can become involved, and you will want to check with your tax adviser prior to deciding on the best way to pay a member for performing services for your LLC.

2. Resolution Approving LLC Hiring

The following resolution can be an excellent means of formalizing the hiring of an LLC worker (who can be an LLC member, manager, officer, or employee). However, think twice before putting the terms of any employment relationship, particularly with a nonmember, in writing—whether in this resolution, an employment contract, or other LLC paperwork. Here is the reason: State law will most likely impose limits on terminating the employment relationship of a nonmember worker who is hired for a set employment term (as opposed to an "at-will" nonmember employee, who is hired for an unspecified period).

Employment laws

 For an excellent resource in understanding employment law requirements, see *The Employer's Legal Handbook*, by Fred Steingold (Nolo). It contains a wealth of information, including rules on hiring and firing employees of a business.

Below is a sample of the resolution you can use to approve the hiring of an LLC worker. You'll find this resolution on the CD-ROM and as a tear-out form in Appendix D. (See Appendix A for information on selecting and using CD-ROM files.) Fill it out as you follow the sample and special instruction below.

APPROVAL OF LLC HIRING

After discussion, the hiring of _____ [name of member or employee] _____ to the position of _____ [job title] _____ was approved.

It was agreed that the duties of this position and compensation for performing these services will be as follows: _____ [specify job duties and compensation] _____ .

Special Instruction

❶ This is an optional paragraph. If you include this paragraph, a court may decide that your language gives a nonmember employee extra rights to work for your LLC. But you may decide to use this clause to specify the duties of an executive you know will be around for a while—for example, an organizing member and key employee of your LLC.

3. Resolution for Salary Increases or Bonuses

It is customary for LLCs to increase the pay of top executives from time to time and to award annual bonuses to working members, managers, and employees as well. If the increase or bonus is substantial, you may wish to pass a resolution showing LLC approval of the additional payment. Doing so helps show that the additional expenses were approved after due consideration by the LLC, a formality that may help in case any nonworking members wonder whether the pay increases were warranted.

 Below is a sample of the resolution you can use to approve bonuses and salary increases. You'll find this resolution on the CD-ROM and as a tear-out form in Appendix D. (See Appendix A for information on selecting and using the CD-ROM files.) Fill it out as you follow the sample below.

APPROVAL OF BONUSES AND SALARY INCREASES

The LLC considered the question of salary increases and bonuses to persons who performed compensated services for the LLC. After discussion, the LLC approved the following salary increases and bonuses, to be paid to the following persons:

Name and Title	Amount	Type	
_____	$ _____	☐ Salary Increase	☐ Bonus
_____	$ _____	☐ Salary Increase	☐ Bonus
_____	$ _____	☐ Salary Increase	☐ Bonus
_____	$ _____	☐ Salary Increase	☐ Bonus
_____	$ _____	☐ Salary Increase	☐ Bonus
_____	$ _____	☐ Salary Increase	☐ Bonus
_____	$ _____	☐ Salary Increase	☐ Bonus

The above salary amounts or bonuses will be paid as follows: __[specify when bonuses will be paid, such as "on December 15, 2010," or the LLC tax year when salary increases are effective, such as "for the year 2010"]__ .

B. Using Independent Contractors

As a way to keep costs down, LLCs often hire outside individuals (called independent contractors, or ICs) to perform work for their LLC, thus saving on payroll taxes, workers' compensation insurance, health insurance, disability insurance, and other employment costs.

1. IRS Filing Requirements

Even though you do not need to withhold or pay employment taxes for independent contractors, you must prepare and file IRS Form 1099-MISC for each independent contractor to whom you pay more than a small threshold amount during the tax year. Keep tabs on this 1099 requirement if you hire independent contractors; the threshold amount for this filing is subject to change and is posted each year on the IRS website at www.irs.gov.

⚠ The IRS may assess substantial penalties for misclassification of independent contractors

The IRS and state tax agencies are becoming increasingly concerned about companies that treat too many workers as "independent contractors." These agencies routinely perform employment audits that result in independent contractors being reclassified as employees, with back taxes and penalties being assessed against the employer (even if the worker filed tax returns and paid income taxes and self-employment taxes on the earnings).

If you misclassify an employee as an independent contractor, the unpaid payroll taxes and withholding amounts can easily equal 20% to 40% of the compensation paid to the worker. Worse, after additional penalties and interest are added, the total employer liability resulting from an employment tax audit can exceed the amount of compensation paid to the worker.

IRS INDEPENDENT CONTRACTOR CLASSIFICATION CRITERIA

The IRS uses a number of tests when deciding whether a worker is an independent contractor or an employee. (Remember: Members who work for their LLC are not treated as employees. See Section A, above.) Here are some of the more important independent contractor (IC) tests:

- *If it looks like the worker runs a separate business.* One of the most heavily weighted factors the IRS uses to determine IC status is whether the person who provides the services for the LLC has a substantial investment in his or her own business and facilities (in a business other than the LLC) and is pursuing personal profit motives in performing the work. If so, the person will likely be treated as an IC.

- *If the worker does outside work.* Does the worker work for other companies while working for your LLC? If so, this helps establish IC status.

- *If the worker is supervised like an employee.* If the worker must account for his or her actions on an ongoing basis or is directed not just as to the results of the work, but when and how it must be done, the worker looks more like an employee.

- *If the work is very important to the LLC.* If the success or failure of the LLC's business hinges in a major way on the outcome of the work being performed, or if it is the primary business of the company, this will weigh heavily toward a finding of employee status.

- *If the worker is hired by the LLC continually.* If you constantly employ the same person to perform the same task over an extended period of time, this factors against IC status.

- *If the worker needs help from the LLC to perform the services.* If you must give the worker extra help or training to perform the task, this figures in favor of employee tax status.

- *If the worker's business is incorporated.* If the outside worker has incorporated his or her business (or, perhaps, has formed an LLC), this is often persuasive evidence that the person should be treated as in independent contractor. In fact, more and more companies that use outside help—for example, firms that contract for programming services—are requiring individuals to be incorporated (or to have established another type of business entity, such as an LLC) to help dispose of any employment tax issues that would otherwise arise.

2. Resolution Approving Independent Contractor Services

In many situations, you can use your regular procedure for hiring outside contractors without worrying about formalities. But if you want to obtain formal approval of the arrangement—for example, if an outside IC requests formal approval of her arrangement by your LLC—our general resolution can come in handy.

Below is a sample of the resolution you can use to approve the hiring of ICs. You'll find this resolution on the CD-ROM and as a tear-out form in Appendix D. (See Appendix A for information on selecting and using the CD-ROM files.) Fill it out as you follow the sample and special instruction below.

APPROVAL OF INDEPENDENT CONTRACTOR SERVICES

After discussion, the following independent contractor services were approved to be performed by   [name of independent contractor firm or individual] :

_____[specify services and payment schedule for services to be performed]_____ **❶**

Special Instruction

❶ If the outside firm or individual has submitted a schedule of services or an agreement for approval, you can refer to it here and attach it to your resolution after the resolution is approved. In that case, insert the following language in this portion of the resolution: "See attached schedule/agreement, which was approved and attached to this resolution."

The advantage of independent contractor agreements

An independent contractor agreement not only sets the terms of the work to be performed and the schedule for payments for the work by the LLC, but can also help the arrangement qualify for independent contractor status with the IRS. Standard independent contractor agreements reference many of the tax factors used by the IRS for classifying the worker as an outside contractor. For example, agreements often make the service provider liable for all employment taxes, withholding, and the like. To prepare an independent contractor agreement and learn more about the various tax criteria used by the IRS in classifying workers as employees and independent contractors, you'll need outside help. One excellent resource is *Hiring Independent Contractors: The Employer's Legal Guide*, by Stephen Fishman (Nolo).

C. APPOINTING AND PAYING LLC OFFICERS

State LLC law normally allows an LLC to appoint whatever officers it decides are necessary or convenient to carry out its business. Typically, an LLC has a president, a treasurer, and a secretary, plus any additional officer positions it decides to fill. In a small one- or two-owner LLC, more than one officer position might be held by one person. State law typically allows this. In many instances, officer titles such as president and secretary are formal, administrative titles only. They are used by the officer only when signing or approving LLC legal or tax papers. In other words, even though a person may be granted the title of LLC president or treasurer, he or she is typically paid a salary in connection with other full-time work for the LLC.

> **EXAMPLE 1:** Beth is the president of the Dynamite Deli LLC, and Bob is its treasurer/secretary. Beth is paid a salary as the manager of the deli and Bob as the counter chief. (Their formal LLC officer positions are unpaid.)

> **EXAMPLE 2:** Nate, Nancy, and Nick are the three members of a member-managed financial planning services LLC. Nate is the CEO (chief executive officer, which can be an alternate title for president), Nancy is the CFO (chief financial officer, an alternate title for treasurer), and Nick is the CIO (chief information officer—in charge of the financial software systems of the company). He also doubles formally as the LLC secretary. Each is paid a salary for filling these traditional officer positions (president, vice president, and secretary). Nick should get paid for performing both jobs.

Use the resolution shown below to appoint LLC officers and to set any compensation (hourly or salary) if an officer is to be paid for officer duties. Generally, officers are appointed at the same time, as shown in the resolution presented here.

Below is a sample of the resolution you can use to approve the appointment of LLC officers. You'll find this resolution on the CD-ROM and as a tear-out form in Appendix D. (See Appendix A for information on selecting and using the CD-ROM files.) Fill it out as you follow the sample and special instruction below.

APPOINTMENT OF LLC OFFICERS

After discussion, the following individuals were appointed to serve in the following LLC officer positions. Any annual salary to be paid to any officer and approved is shown below next to the name of the officer:

Title of Officer	Name	Compensation, if any
_____ :	_____	$_____ **❶**
_____ :	_____	$_____
_____ :	_____	$_____
_____ :	_____	$_____

Each officer has the duties that are specified in the operating agreement of the LLC and as may be designated from time to time by the LLC management. An officer serves until his or her successor is elected and is qualified to replace the officer.

Special Instruction

❶ In the case where a person will be paid for serving as an officer, fill in the annual salary. If salaries will be set later, insert "to be determined" in the appropriate salary blanks. If officers will not receive salaries in their capacities as officers, fill in "N/A" or "none" in the salary blanks.

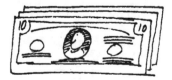

D. COMPENSATION FOR ATTENDING LLC MEETINGS

Your LLC may authorize the payment of compensation to members or managers for attending LLC meetings, as well as for incurring travel and other expenses. Note that all types of special compensation paid to managers are taxable income to the individual. They are also deductible by the LLC in determining its net income that is distributable to members on its annual information return.

1. Resolution Authorizing Payment for Attending LLC Meetings

Members and managers may be paid a per diem (per day) amount for attending LLC manager or member meetings. In addition, members or managers who must travel to attend these meetings may be reimbursed additional reasonable travel expenses. This occurs most often where closely held LLCs have outside members—perhaps an out-of-state relative who holds a membership interest in the LLC and attends annual membership meetings.

Below is a sample of the resolution you can use to authorize special compensation. You'll find this resolution on the CD-ROM and as a tear-out form in Appendix D. (See Appendix A for information on selecting and using the CD-ROM files.) Fill it out as you follow the sample and special instruction below.

AUTHORIZATION OF PAYMENT FOR ATTENDING LLC MEETINGS

After discussion, it was agreed that all of the following persons will be paid the following amounts for each day, or fraction of a day, during which they attend a meeting of the LLC.

Name and Title	Per Diem Amount
_____	$_____
_____	$_____
_____	$_____
_____	$_____

It was also discussed and agreed that the following persons will be __["advanced" or "reimbursed"]__ the following reasonable and necessary travel expenses incurred to attend meetings of the managers and/or members of the LLC:

Name and Title	Per Meeting Travel Allotment ❶
_____	$_____
_____	$_____
_____	$_____
_____	$_____

Special Instruction

❶ You can specify a set travel expense allotment, or you can simply set a maximum amount to be advanced or reimbursed (for example, "actual travel expenses up to a maximum amount of $500").

2. Resolution Authorizing Stipend for Attending LLC Meetings

Another way to compensate members or managers for attending LLC meetings is by authorizing the payment of an annual amount, regardless of the number of meeting days per year or the actual travel expenses incurred.

Below is a sample of the resolution you can use to authorize annual stipends. You'll find this resolution on the CD-ROM and as a tear-out form in Appendix D. (See Appendix A for information on selecting and using the CD-ROM files.) Fill it out as you follow the sample and special instruction below.

ANNUAL STIPEND FOR ATTENDANCE AT LLC MEETINGS

After discussion, it was agreed that, on or by ____[date of payment]____ ❶ of each year, the following persons will be paid the following annual amounts, which comprise a yearly travel allotment for traveling to and attending regular and special meetings of the LLC:

Name and Title	Annual Stipend and Travel Allotment
_____	$ _____
_____	$ _____
_____	$ _____
_____	$ _____

Special Instruction

❶ Insert a month and date, such as "March 31." Do not include a year.

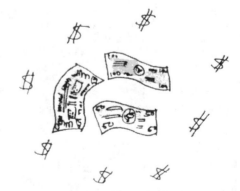

E. APPROVAL OF INDEMNIFICATION FOR LLC MEMBERS, MANAGERS, OFFICERS, AND EMPLOYEES

Indemnification means that the LLC will pay any fines, settlements, court awards or judgments, attorney fees, penalties, or other amounts that are personally assessed against:

- a member
- a manager
- an officer
- an employee, or
- another person acting as an agent of the LLC.

These amounts might be assessed because of unwise decisions or omissions made while performing services for the LLC. They usually emerge as the result of lawsuits or investigations.

In other words, indemnification is an LLC's way of guaranteeing LLC members, managers, employees, and other agents that the LLC will pay certain costs and amounts that may be assessed against them as a result of working for the LLC. Some LLCs only indemnify certain categories of LLC representatives, such as managers or officers, or set certain conditions that must be met before indemnification occurs.

> **EXAMPLE:** Tosh Imato, the sole manager of Lox Box LLC, approved the LLC's use of certain suppliers, who turned out to be lax in their refrigeration procedures. A customer sues Tosh personally for medical bills resulting from a food poisoning incident. Tosh wins the suit, after a finding by the court that he could not have reasonably known of or foreseen the inferior food-processing procedures used by the supplier. The victory is not complete, since Tosh is liable for hefty lawyers' fees incurred in his own defense. Because the LLC has authorized indemnification for all legal costs associated with lawsuits that are resolved in favor of managers, the LLC—not Tosh—pays these fees.

The extent and amount of indemnification that can or must be paid by LLCs to managers, members, and officers may be set by state LLC statutes. Some states are silent on indemnification; others have lengthy statutes covering this issue. Typically, if a state LLC Act has a provision for indemnification, it requires the LLC to indemnify an LLC member, manager, officer, employee, or agent of the LLC for legal expenses, including attorney fees, if that LLC representative is sued and wins the lawsuit. Other types of indemnification, such as payment of a court judgment or settlement if an LLC representative doesn't win a lawsuit, may or must be paid if certain conditions are met. For example, indemnification might be authorized if the LLC determines that the person acted in good faith and in the best interests of the LLC and, in criminal cases where fines are levied, that the person did not believe the conduct was unlawful.

Here is a typical statute.

Minnesota Limited Liability Company Act, Section 322B.699

[…] a limited liability company shall indemnify a person made or threatened to be made a party to a proceeding, by reason of the former or present official capacity of the person, against judgments, penalties, fines, including, without limitation, excise taxes assessed against the person with respect to an employee benefit plan, settlements, and reasonable expenses, including attorney's fees and disbursements, incurred by the person in connection with the proceeding, if, with respect to the acts or omissions of the person complained of in the proceeding, the person:

1. has not been indemnified by another organization or employee benefit plan for the same judgments, penalties, fines, [etc.];

2. acted in good faith;

3. received no improper personal benefit . . .

4. in the case of a criminal proceeding, had no reasonable cause to believe the conduct was unlawful; and

5. in the case of acts or omissions occurring [when the person was acting as a governor/manager, member, or employee of the LLC], reasonably believed that the conduct was in the best interests of the limited liability company ....

[The provision goes on to say that this otherwise mandatory indemnification can be denied by an express provision in the Articles or operating agreement of the LLC as long as the denial of indemnification applies to all persons within a given class (such as all managers or members).]

Your articles or your operating agreement might already contain a summary or restatement of the mandatory or permissible indemnification rules in your state. Or it might authorize indemnification payments for your LLC's principals and agents according to its own preference. In either case, you will not need to use the resolution below. But if your articles and your operating agreement are silent on indemnification, we suggest you use the following resolution as a starting point only. Because state indemnification rules vary, you should check the resolution against the rules in your state's LLC Act and, if you need more information, ask a small business lawyer for guidance.

WHY MANAGERS' AND MEMBERS' LIABILITY INSURANCE MAY BE IMPORTANT

Even if your LLC indemnifies you to the maximum extent possible under state LLC statutes, this may not be enough. If a manager, member, or officer loses a lawsuit, state law may not allow indemnification unless an independent committee of the LLC or a judge finds that the person acted in good faith. Moreover, even if indemnification can be authorized in a particular case, the LLC may not have the funds to pay indemnification.

Consequently, some LLCs decide that the best way to protect members and managers from personal liability for their LLC acts or omissions is to purchase a special managers', members' and officers' liability policy. (In the corporate world, this type of insurance is called a D & O liability policy, which stands for "directors and officers" liability policy.) These policies can be used instead of, or in conjunction with, indemnification by the LLC. For example, they can pick up the cost of legal expenses not paid directly by the LLC, or they can pay in addition to any indemnification made. Policies of this sort may be costly, or they may contain too many exclusions to be worthwhile. So if obtaining this type of coverage is important to you, do some insurance shopping. Check with different insurance brokers to find a suitable and affordable policy.

The general indemnification resolution provided below can be used by the LLC to authorize the maximum indemnification for LLC members, managers, officers, and other LLC agents permitted by state law. It also authorizes the LLC to purchase managers' and members' liability insurance to cover legal expenses, settlements, fines, and other costs not covered by indemnification.

There's more to indemnification than meets the eye

Again, this general resolution is not tailored to meet the details of each state's indemnification scheme. If indemnification is of crucial concern to you—perhaps because your particular line of business or the legal climate in your field means that you can expect lawsuits directed against your managers, members, or officers—check with a small business lawyer to explore just how helpful your state's indemnification statutes really are. Also check into buying a manag-

ers' and members' liability policy to cover any non-indemnified legal costs. (See "Why Managers' and Members' Liability Insurance May Be Important," above.)

Below is a sample of the resolution you can use to provide for indemnification and insurance. You'll find this resolution on the CD-ROM and as a tear-out form in Appendix D. (See Appendix A for information on selecting and using the CD-ROM files.) Fill it out as you follow the sample below.

LLC INDEMNIFICATION AND INSURANCE

The LLC will indemnify its current and former __[insert "members," "managers," "employees" and/or "other agents"]__ to the fullest extent permitted under the laws of this state. Such indemnification is not deemed to be exclusive of any other rights to which the indemnified person is entitled, consistent with law, under any provision of the LLC Articles of Organization (or similar organizing document of this LLC) or the LLC operating agreement; as a result of any general or specific action of the members or managers of this LLC; under the terms of any contract; or as may be permitted or required by law.

The LLC may purchase and maintain insurance or provide another arrangement on behalf of any person who is or was a __[insert "member," "manager," "employee," and/or "other agent"]__ of this LLC against any liability asserted against him or her and incurred in such a capacity or arising out of his or her official capacity with this LLC, whether or not the LLC would have the power to indemnify him or her against that liability under the laws of this state.

Loans to the LLC

When an LLC needs money, it typically applies to a bank for a loan or asks its members for additional funds, in the form of additional capital contributions or as loans. Some smaller LLCs may prefer to borrow funds from members, since they are usually active in the business and willing to help out when cash flow is tight. (If your LLC wishes to lend money to—rather than borrow from—an LLC member, manager, officer, or employee, see Chapter 14.)

This chapter discusses the tax and legal ins and outs of borrowing money. We provide resolutions that allow the LLC to formally approve finalized LLC loans taken out from financial institutions, existing members, or their family and friends. Setting out this type of specific borrowing approval in a formal resolution helps an LLC control the borrowing behavior of its principals. It also helps everyone in the LLC agree on how much to borrow when cash is short.

This chapter also includes resolutions that can be used to authorize LLC members, managers, or officers to go out and borrow funds on behalf of the LLC. These resolutions are preliminary in nature—that is, they grant LLC officers permission to seek a loan, sometimes with a limit placed on the maximum amount that may be borrowed or other restrictions on the terms of the financing.

Finally, to help you keep your loans in order, we show you how to select and use different types of promissory notes (included with this book) to help you document the payback terms of your LLC's loans.

Tax and legal considerations

LLC borrowing is a serious business, even if the lender is a member, manager, or other LLC insider. We recommend you use the information gleaned from this chapter to discuss the tax, legal, and practical considerations of taking out loans with your tax adviser or business lawyer before approving any sizable LLC loan.

Who should approve loans to the LLC

Normally, only LLC management (the managing members of a member-manager LLC or the managers of a manager-managed LLC) needs to approve loan transactions. Nonetheless, if the loan transactions are substantial in amount or frequency, or if your LLC has outside investors (nonmanaging members) who might raise eyebrows at a particular loan transaction, we recommend you have all members (in addition to any managers) approve the loan.

<table>
<tr><td>

HOW TO SELECT AND USE LLC RESOLUTIONS

- Scan the table of contents at the beginning of the chapter to find resolutions of interest to you.

- When you find one you need, read the background material that precedes the pertinent LLC resolution.

- Follow the instructions included with the sample resolution to complete a draft of the resolution using your computer. If you need guidance on selecting and using the computer disk files, see Appendix A. (You'll have to fill in the tear-out resolution included in Appendix D if you don't have a computer.)

- Complete any needed attachment forms, such as promissory notes.

- If a resolution involves complex issues that will benefit from expert analysis, have your legal or tax adviser review your paperwork and conclusions.

- Prepare minutes of meeting or written consent forms as explained in Chapters 5–7, and insert the completed resolution into the appropriate form.

- Have the LLC secretary sign the printed minutes or have members and/or managers sign any written consent forms. Then place the signed forms, together with any attachments, in your LLC records binder.

</td></tr>
</table>

Another reason to formally approve LLC borrowing

State LLC law is another reason to take the time to formally approve the amount and extent of borrowing authority granted to LLC members, managers, and officers. The law typically grants any member of a member-managed LLC, any manager of a manager-managed LLC, and any LLC officer the legal authority to bind the LLC. This means that the LLC will normally be legally committed to a loan agreement executed by any of these LLC representatives. One exception occurs when an outside lender knows that a proposed loan is outside the authority actually granted to an LLC member, manager, or officer. Of course, we don't expect you to give each proposed lender a copy of an LLC resolution that shows who may borrow money on behalf of the LLC. We do think, however, that preparing resolutions that give specific people specific authority to borrow funds will act as a effective internal check on their otherwise unlimited authority. In other words, once you approve a resolution that sets out the specific borrowing authority of a member, manager, or officer, chances are that he or she will abide by the terms of the resolution and not seek to commit the LLC to loan agreements outside the scope of the resolution.

A. BANK LOANS TO THE LLC

Many LLCs borrow funds from time to time from banks and other commercial institutions such as savings and loans and credit unions. In this chapter, we generally refer to all of these institutions as "banks."

There are two common ways LLCs borrow from banks:

- **Lump-sum loan.** The LLC receives the entire amount of borrowed funds all at once and repays it over time, usually over two to five years. Banks often charge the prime interest rate currently in effect plus two or three percentage points or an adjustable rate that changes in step with a particular financial index. Especially at the start of its relationship with a bank, your LLC should also expect to be asked to pay a point or two as a loan fee and to pledge either the personal assets of LLC principals, the LLC's accounts receivable, or the LLC's inventory as collateral for the loan. As your LLC's credit history develops with the bank, you should be able to negotiate lower points on future loans and might get away without a pledge of personal collateral. (This is a good thing, of course, because when an LLC member pledges personal assets for a loan, he or she gives up the limited liability protection that otherwise applies to LLC debts and is personally liable for the loan if the LLC fails to repay it.)

- **Revolving line of credit.** Funds may be borrowed by the LLC, paid back, and reborrowed over a period of time (usually one year) on an as-needed basis, up to the LLC credit limit. Interest rates and fees are similar to those for a loan, but for the credit limit to be renewed for another year, the bank may require that the line of credit be paid off at least for part of the year. "Out of debt for thirty days once in each 12 months" is a typical requirement for renewal.

As with lump-sum loans, your LLC may be required to pledge either the personal assets of LLC principals, the LLC's accounts receivable, or the LLC's inventory as collateral for the line of credit.

EXAMPLE: The Hinterland Campwear LLC finds it needs additional funds to take up the slack in cash flow during slow periods of its yearly business cycle. It applies for and obtains a $75,000 line of credit at a local bank. Throughout the year, authorized officers may call the bank and ask to have funds transferred to the LLC account. Requests for additional funds may be made as often as needed, as long as cumulative borrowing under the line of credit does not exceed the credit limit of $75,000 in a fiscal year. Hinterland may pay back as little or as much of the amount borrowed as it chooses, which allows the LLC to save on interest payments when it has extra cash.

UNDERSTANDING IMPORTANT LOAN TERMS

Make sure you fully understand the terms of any LLC loan before you sign on the dotted line. Here are some loan terms to read carefully:

- **Security pledge.** Depending on the LLC's and its members' net worth and credit history, as well as the amount of the LLC loan, the bank may ask members to pledge personal assets as collateral for the note—such as equity in a house. If the LLC defaults on repayment of the note, the bank can foreclose on the house and sell the property to satisfy the delinquent debt.

- **Right of setoff.** In case of default, the bank will have the right to reach all of the money, securities, and other property that the LLC and the guarantors have deposited as security for the debt with the bank.

- **Subordination agreement.** If the LLC signs a subordination agreement and then defaults on its bank loan, the bank has a legal right to be paid before other lenders (including LLC members) listed in this agreement. In other words, if you previously loaned money to your LLC, either during the LLC's formation or at a later date, the bank has a right to be paid before you.

1. Tax Effects of a Bank Loan to an LLC

The money an LLC borrows from the bank (also called the principal of the loan) is not considered income. Therefore, it is not allocated to members and taxed to them. After all, the principal amount of a loan must be repaid—the LLC and its members don't really get to keep this money. The interest that the LLC pays on a bank loan can be deducted from the LLC's income as an LLC business expense. This reduces the LLC's net profits, which are allocated and taxed to members at the end of the LLC's tax year.

A bank loan to an LLC can also affect the members' tax basis in their membership interests. This is a complicated area, so we'll just scratch the surface.

First, as we discussed in Chapter 11, the term " income tax basis," or simply "basis," refers to the value assigned to your LLC ownership interest for the purposes of determining the taxable gain or loss from it after it is sold. Generally, your income tax basis in an ownership interest is the cash amount you pay, along with your current basis in any property you transfer, to buy the interest. If you transfer property that's subject to a debt that the business assumes—for example, you transfer real estate subject to a mortgage—your basis in your interest is decreased by the amount of the assumed debt.

An increase in basis generally results in lower capital gains taxes when an LLC member sells his or her interest; likewise, a decrease in basis generally results in higher taxes. In addition, members sometimes want to increase their basis in a membership interest so they can deduct losses of the LLC on their individual income tax returns. Here's how it works: Members generally get to deduct LLC losses allocated to them, up to the amount of their basis in their interest. If the loss exceeds the basis amount, the loss cannot be deducted on the member's tax return for that tax year but must be held by the member for deduction in future years.

A member's basis can be affected when a member personally guarantees repayment of a bank loan—that is, when the member agrees to pay off the loan balance if the LLC defaults and the LLC assets pledged as collateral don't cover it. The tax rules classify this type of loan as a "recourse debt," because the lender has recourse to seek repayment from the member who made a personal guarantee. When a member takes on a "recourse debt," the tax rules allow that member to increase his or her basis in a membership interest by the full amount of the loan. (This tax treatment is similar to the increase of basis that occurs when a member makes a capital contribution to an LLC as discussed in Section B1, below). Of course, any time a member's basis increases because of an LLC loan, the member's basis decreases as the loan is paid off.

There are other ways that a member's basis in a membership interest can be increased when the LLC takes out a loan. Bank loans can sometimes be classified as recourse debt of the members, even if they don't personally guarantee the loans. For example, if the bank that has loaned money to the LLC can force the members to pay cash into the LLC to bring their capital account balances back up to zero any time they are negative, the bank loan can be classified as recourse debt. In this situation, a member's basis is increased by multiplying the total loan amount by the member's percentage of profits interest in the LLC.

If a loan to an LLC does not qualify as recourse debt, the tax rules call it "nonrecourse debt." Even nonrecourse debt can allow LLC members to increase their basis in their membership interests (we don't go into the details here), but the benefit of this basis increase may be limited by other tax rules. (See "Why an Increase in a Member's Tax Basis Because of a Loan Doesn't Always Allow Members to Deduct More LLC Losses," below.)

WHY AN INCREASE IN A MEMBER'S TAX BASIS BECAUSE OF A LOAN DOESN'T ALWAYS ALLOW MEMBERS TO DEDUCT MORE LLC LOSSES

As mentioned above, members can deduct LLC losses allocated to them up to the amount of their basis in their interest. If the loss exceeds the basis amount, the loss cannot be deducted on the member's tax return for that tax year, but must be held by the member for deduction in future years.

Here's the rub: Another set of IRS loss-deduction rules—called the "at-risk" loss rules—say that even if a member has sufficient basis to absorb a loss, no deduction can be made unless the member's "at-risk" basis is equal to or more than the amount of the loss the member seeks to claim. At-risk basis is generally the amount of money an LLC member stands to lose as a result of an investment in the LLC, including his or her liability for any LLC debt. However, most nonrecourse LLC loans—loans taken out by an LLC for which no member is personally responsible—do not increase a member's at-risk basis (with the exception of some secured real estate loans).

There are other loss limitations rules that can kick in when a member seeks to use losses and deductions generated by LLC loans to offset income on a member's individual tax return.

See your tax adviser for further information
We'll stop here, having introduced you to the complexities surrounding this area of LLC operations. We strongly recommend that you talk to your tax adviser if you wish to learn more about the various ways loans affect a member's basis in an LLC interest and the tax a member must pay on his or her individual income tax return.

2. Resolutions to Approve Loans to the LLC by Lending Institutions

If you plan to borrow money from a bank or other financial institution, a formal resolution will probably be required by the bank. But check with its loan department before preparing any of the resolutions provided in this chapter. You may find that the bank may do much or all of the paperwork for you. All banks will at least provide you with a promissory note to sign. Some use their own loan resolution forms for signature by LLC members or managers.

If a bank does not provide its own resolution form, it may ask you to submit a copy of an LLC resolution that shows approval by the LLC members and managers of the loan or line of credit. Below, we present samples of various resolutions that you can use to record LLC approval of loans from banks and other outside lending institutions. Pick the one that applies best to your situation.

Certification by LLC secretary

A bank may require that a loan approval resolution be certified by your LLC secretary. This means the secretary attaches a statement to the resolution stating that it was properly approved by the LLC and is still in effect. See Chapter 8, Section G1, for a certification form the LLC secretary may use to certify the LLC's approval of a resolution.

a. Resolution Authorizing Bank Loan to LLC at Specific Terms

Use this resolution if you are seeking approval of a loan already negotiated with a local bank or other lender. This resolution shows approval of the specific terms of the loan.

Fill in this resolution as you follow the sample and special instructions below. You'll find this resolution on the CD-ROM and as a tear-out form in Appendix D. (See Appendix A for information on selecting and using the CD-ROM files.)

AUTHORIZATION OF LOAN TO LLC AT SPECIFIC TERMS

It was announced that the officers of the LLC have received a loan commitment from the following bank, trust company, or other financial institution on the following terms:

Name of Lender: __[name of bank or other financial institution]__

Loan Amount: __[principal amount of the loan—amount you plan to borrow, not including interest]__

Terms of the Loan: ____[state the terms of the loan, including rate of interest, the full repayment period, number and amount of installment payments, and date and amount of final payment if different from other payments]____ ❶

It was resolved that the proposed terms of the loan are fair and reasonable to the LLC and that it is in the best interests of the LLC to borrow the funds on the terms stated above.

It was further resolved that the following member, manager, or officer is authorized to execute the notes and documents necessary to make the above loan on behalf of the LLC:

Name   Title ❷

_____   _____

_____   _____

Special Instruction

❶ As a shortcut, on the line "Terms of the Loan," you can use the words "terms according to the attached promissory note" and attach a copy of the promissory note to your resolution.

❷ Normally, a member, manager, or officer, such as the president or treasurer, is authorized by the LLC to borrow loan funds on behalf of the LLC. However, you may specify another officer or employee if you wish.

b. Resolution Authorizing Maximum Loan to LLC on General Terms

The next resolution allows the LLC to authorize an LLC member, manager, or officer to go out and secure a bank loan (one that has not yet been arranged with a bank). This resolution allows the designated LLC representative to seek financing from a bank or other financial institution for a maximum loan amount on currently available terms, without limiting the transaction to a specific interest rate or other repayment provisions.

Fill in this resolution form as you follow the sample and special instructions below. You'll find this resolution on the CD-ROM and as a tear-out form in Appendix D. (See Appendix A for information on selecting and using the CD-ROM files.)

AUTHORIZATION OF MAXIMUM LOAN AMOUNT TO LLC

It was resolved that it is in the best interests of the LLC to borrow up to the following amount from the following bank, trust company, or other financial institution:

Name of Lender: _____ [name of bank] _____

Loan Amount: _____ [principal amount of the loan not including interest] _____

On behalf of the LLC, the following member, manager, or officer is authorized to sign the appropriate notes and documents necessary to borrow an amount that does not exceed the amount noted above, on terms commercially reasonable to the LLC:

Name   Title ❶

_____   _____

_____   _____

Special Instruction

❶ Again, a member, manager, or officer, such as the president or treasurer, is typically authorized by the LLC to borrow loan funds on its behalf.

c. Resolution Authorizing LLC Representative to Borrow Funds on Behalf of LLC as Needed

You may use this resolution to give an LLC member, manager, or officer unlimited authority to borrow money on behalf of the LLC from one or more banks whenever necessary for LLC business. The delegation of this much financial leeway by the LLC to an LLC principal should be reserved for LLCs that have a significant amount of personal trust in an LLC principal. Such trust is most typically found in small LLCs where the person in question is actively involved with day-to-day operations.

Fill in this resolution as you follow the sample and special instruction below. You'll find this resolution on the CD-ROM and as a tear-out form in Appendix D. (See Appendix A for information on selecting and using the CD-ROM files.)

AUTHORIZATION OF LLC REPRESENTATIVE TO BORROW FUNDS ON BEHALF OF LLC AS NEEDED

It was resolved that the following member, manager, or officer of the LLC is authorized to borrow funds on behalf of the LLC from one or more banks or other financial institutions in the amounts he or she decides are reasonably necessary to meet the business needs of the LLC:

Name   Title

_____   _____

_____   _____

Special Instruction

❶ Again, a member, manager, or officer, such as the president or treasurer, is typically authorized by the LLC to borrow loan funds on its behalf.

d. Resolution Authorizing Specific Loan Terms Secured by LLC Property

You may use the following resolution to approve and document an LLC loan that is secured by personal or real property owned by the LLC. While the earlier loan resolutions can be modified to allow you to do this, here you can specifically list the LLC assets pledged as secu-

rity. This extra bit of detail makes sense if the LLC is pledging significant LLC assets, such as LLC real estate, accounts receivables, or inventory, as collateral for the loan.

Get permission from members before pledging substantial LLC assets

To avoid member discontent if the LLC can't repay the debt, and the lender liquidates the LLC assets that secured the loan, we suggest you have all members approve this resolution, whether your LLC is managed by some (or all) members or by managers.

Fill in this resolution as you follow the sample and special instructions below. You'll find this resolution on the CD-ROM and as a tear-out form in Appendix D. (See Appendix A for information on selecting and using the CD-ROM files.)

AUTHORIZATION OF LOAN TERMS SECURED BY LLC PROPERTY

It was resolved that the following LLC member, manager, or officer is authorized to borrow the sum of __$ [principal amount of loan]__ on behalf of the LLC from _____ [name of bank] _____:

Name　　　　　　　　　　　　　　　　Title ❶

_____　　_____

_____　　_____

The person named above is authorized to execute a promissory note for the principal amount shown above, together with a mortgage, deed of trust, or security agreement and any other documents necessary to secure payment of the note with the pledge of the following LLC property:

Property Used as Security for Note:_____ [insert a description of the property]_____ ❷

The terms for repayment of the note will be as follows:

Terms of Note: _____ [specify loan terms or refer to promissory note]_____ ❸

Special Instructions

❶ Again, a member, manager, or officer, such as the president or treasurer, is typically authorized by the LLC to borrow loan funds on its behalf.

❷ Describe the LLC property pledged for the loan. For personal property, provide serial or ID numbers and a description of the property. An example might be "1994 Jeep Grand Cherokee, ID # XXX0099." For real estate, a street address (rather than a legal description) will do fine.

❸ Spell out the terms of loan, such as the rate of interest and the number and amount of monthly payments. If terms have not been arranged, insert the following statement: "on best terms available from lender." If you prepare a promissory note for the loan, you may refer to it here as follows: "See the terms of the promissory note between the LLC and _____ [name of lender]_____, attached to this resolution" and attach a signed copy to the resolution.

e. Resolution Authorizing Line of Credit

The next resolution authorizes an LLC member, manager, or officer to arrange for and use an ongoing line of credit at a bank. It's important to realize that, with this resolution, once the authority is granted, an authorized person may tap the line at any time, up to the credit line limit that the bank authorized. (If you want a resolution that places a cap on the amount of money that an LLC principal may borrow from a line of credit in any one transaction, see the resolution that follows this one.)

Note that the authority granted under this resolution is more limited than the authority given under the previous resolution. (See Subsection c, above.) Here, the designated person may enter into repeated borrowing transactions only after the LLC obtains a line of credit.

The result is that the person can't borrow more than the maximum amount authorized by the credit line. By contrast, in the previous resolution, an LLC member, manager, or officer is given the power to apply repeatedly for different bank loans, with no maximum overall limit established.

Fill in this resolution as you follow the sample and special instructions below. You'll find this resolution on the CD-ROM and as a tear-out form in Appendix D. (See Appendix A for information on selecting and using the CD-ROM files.)

AUTHORIZATION OF LINE OF CREDIT

It was resolved that it is in the best interests of the LLC to obtain a line of credit for borrowing funds from
_____ [name of bank] _____ .

The following LLC member, manager, or officer is authorized to complete all necessary forms, documents, and notes and to pledge as security for the loan any LLC assets necessary to obtain and use the line of credit:

Name   Title ❶

_____   _____

_____   _____

It was further decided that the authority granted by this resolution be limited and that the person named above not be allowed to establish a line of credit that exceeds _____ [credit line limit] _____ . ❷

Special Instructions

❶ Again, a member, manager, or officer, such as the president or treasurer, is typically authorized by the LLC to borrow loan funds on its behalf.

❷ You can use this paragraph to restrict the amount the LLC representative can borrow from the credit line during a certain period.

Example: Execuflex Time Management Systems, LLC, authorizes its treasurer to establish and borrow against an LLC line of credit as she sees fit, subject to an annual borrowing limit of $100,000 or up to $50,000 in a given quarter. Here's how to complete this provision:

"It was further decided that the authority granted by this resolution is limited and that the person named above is not allowed to borrow funds against the line of credit that exceed $100,000 per year or $50,000 in any calendar quarter."

If you don't wish to limit the credit line limit, simply delete the last paragraph. If you wish to limit the per-transaction amount of borrowing under a line of credit, see the next resolution.

f. Resolution Authorizing Line of Credit With Cap on Each Transaction

The sample resolution below authorizes a line of credit but restricts the amount that may be borrowed in any given transaction under this line of credit.

Fill in this resolution as you follow the sample and special instructions below. You'll find this resolution on the CD-ROM and as a tear-out form in Appendix D. (See Appendix A for information on selecting and using the CD-ROM files.)

AUTHORIZATION OF LINE OF CREDIT WITH CAP ON EACH TRANSACTION

It was resolved that it is in the best interests of the LLC to obtain a line of credit from

_____ [name of bank] _____.

The following LLC member, manager, or officer was authorized to complete all necessary forms, documents, and notes necessary to obtain and use the line of credit to allow borrowing by the LLC in an aggregate amount that does not exceed $[credit line limit and period if you wish—for example, $50,000 per fiscal year] : ❶

Name   Title ❷

_____   _____

_____   _____

It was further resolved that the amount borrowed under the line of credit in one transaction will not exceed $[maximum amount that can be borrowed against the line of credit in one transaction, such as $10,000]   unless any excess amount is specifically approved by further resolution of the LLC. ❸

Special Instructions

❶ You can use this paragraph to restrict the amount the LLC representative can borrow from the credit line during a certain period.

EXAMPLE: Execuflex Time Management Systems, LLC, authorizes its treasurer to establish and borrow against an LLC line of credit as she sees fit, subject to an annual borrowing limit of $100,000 or up to $50,000 in a given quarter. Here's how to complete this provision:

It was further decided that the authority granted by this resolution is limited and that the person named above is not allowed to borrow funds against the line of credit that exceed <u>$100,000 per year or $50,000 in any calendar quarter.</u>"

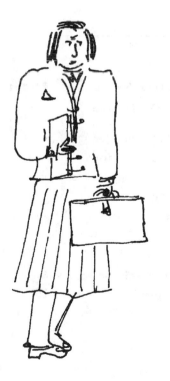

❷ Again, a member, manager, or officer, such as the president or treasurer, is typically authorized by the LLC to borrow loan funds on its behalf.

❸ You can use this paragraph to restrict the amount the LLC representative can borrow from the credit line in any one transaction. If you don't wish to limit the authority of the person named in this resolution in this way, simply delete the last paragraph.

g. Resolution Authorizing a Line of Credit Secured by LLC Property

You may use the following resolution to approve and document an LLC line of credit that is secured by personal or real property owned by the LLC. While the earlier line of credit resolutions can be modified to allow you to do this, here you can specifically list the LLC assets pledged as security. This extra bit of detail makes sense if the LLC is pledging significant LLC assets, such as LLC real estate, accounts receivables, or inventory, as collateral for the line of credit.

💡 Get permission from members before pledging substantial LLC assets

To avoid member discontent if the LLC can't repay the debt and the lender liquidates the LLC assets that secured the line of credit, we suggest you have all members approve this resolution, whether your LLC is managed by some (or all) members or by managers.

Fill in this resolution as you follow the sample and special instructions below. You'll find this resolution on the CD-ROM and as a tear-out form in Appendix D. (See Appendix A for information on selecting and using the CD-ROM files.)

AUTHORIZATION OF LINE OF CREDIT SECURED BY LLC PROPERTY

It was resolved that it is in the best interests of the LLC to obtain a line of credit for borrowing funds from

_____[name of bank]_____.

The following LLC member, manager, or officer is authorized to complete all necessary forms, documents and notes and to pledge as security for the loan any LLC assets necessary to obtain and use the line of credit:

Name   Title ❶

_____   _____

_____   _____

The person named above is authorized to execute a promissory note for the line of credit amount shown above, together with a mortgage, deed of trust, or security agreement and any other documents necessary to secure payment of the note with the pledge of the following LLC property:

Property Used as Security for Note: _____[insert a description of the property]_____ ❷

The terms for repayment of the note will be as follows:

TermlÄof Note: __[specify line of credit terms or refer to promissory note]__ ❸

Special Instructions

❶ Again, a member, manager, or officer, such as the president or treasurer, is typically authorized by the LLC to open a line a credit on its behalf.

❷ Describe the LLC property pledged for the line of credit. For personal property, provide serial or ID numbers and a description of the property. An example might be "1994 Jeep Grand Cherokee, ID # XXX0099." For real estate, a street address (rather than a legal description) will do fine.

❸ Spell out the terms of the line of credit, such as the rate of interest and how monthly payments are calculated. If terms have not been arranged, insert the following statement: "on best terms available from lender." If you prepare a promissory note for the credit line, you may refer to it here as follows: "See the terms of the promissory note between the LLC and _____ [name of lender]_____, attached to this resolution" and attach a signed copy to the resolution.

B. Loans to the LLC by Members and Other Insiders

In small LLCs, the members often have a choice as to how to fund their business endeavors. They may pay money into the business as "capital" or they may lend funds to the LLC as "debt." This choice applies whether the funds are obtained at the startup of the LLC enterprise or after the LLC has been in business for a while.

⚠ **It's very important to formally approve an insider loan to the LLC**

Insider loans are loans from an LLC member, officer, or manager to (or by) the LLC. This is not one of the areas of LLC decision making where you should consider formal approval with a resolution to be optional. All LLCs should use resolutions and promissory notes (provided in Appendix D and on disk) to formally approve and record insider loan transactions. This precaution will maintain the limited liability of the members, will avoid internal controversy among the members and will help combat problems with the IRS.

1. Legal Issues on Insider Loans

Some LLCs borrow funds from time to time from their members or managers (or sometimes from an LLC member's family or friends). These loans may supplement bank loans or replace them. The purpose is usually to increase the LLC's cash reserves or to cover operational expenses. These insider loans can benefit both the LLC and a lending member or other insider.

As opposed to an additional capital contribution, a loan payable with interest results in an immediate investment return to the lending member. (In comparison, a capital contribution is a "risk" investment that depends on the success of the LLC—when you make a capital payment to your LLC, you are paying for the right to receive a share of any profits of the LLC as well as a portion of LLC assets when the LLC is sold or liquidated—if any assets remain after paying off creditors.) Obviously, unlike an interest-bearing loan made to an LLC, a capital contribution does not guarantee you a return on your money.

Even a loan signed by the LLC, however, doesn't always assure the lender an investment return on the loaned funds. It's always possible that the LLC could fail to turn a profit and not be able to make repayments on the loan. And unlike a bank, an LLC insider probably won't have asked the other members to sign personal guarantees for the loan. For this reason, in larger LLCs, it may be difficult to find members or other individuals willing to offer funds unless the LLC is doing well and the lender feels assured of receiving timely interest and principal payments under the loan. That's why loans of this sort from individuals mostly occur in the context of smaller, closely held LLCs. In such cases, there is considerable overlap between the fortunes of the LLC and the personal finances of its main members.

EXAMPLE: Larry's Reality, LLC, is a one-person computer arcade and virtual reality parlor in the Westmont Mall complex. To keep his adolescent clientele interested in making return visits to the arcade, Larry must purchase the latest in expensive computer and virtual reality game gear, regardless of the current condition of his business's bottom line. As a result, he finds that he must occasionally make short-term (one- to three-month) personal loans to his LLC.

It is particularly important to document this type of insider loan transaction with LLC resolutions. If you don't do any extra paperwork when you routinely lend your one-person or small LLC operational funds by writing checks out of your personal checking account, a court could well decide that your LLC is simply your alter ego. The court could then hold you personally liable for LLC debts.

EXAMPLE: For each of the personal loans made by Larry to his LLC, he prepares an LLC loan resolution and a basic promissory note to place in his LLC records binder. These should stand him in good stead should he ever land in court. Even if a disgruntled creditor claims that Larry's Reality operation is nothing more than his own personal limited liability checking account, this should be disregarded by the court.

Another reason to prepare resolutions for insider loan transactions is to avoid internal controversy among your members. While LLC members or managers usually lend funds to help the LLC, not themselves, it is natural that repeated loan transactions between an LLC and a principal member or manager may arouse the curiosity of other LLC insiders. They may wonder if the lending member or manager is taking advantage of his or her LLC leverage to get too good a deal on repayment terms, essentially making money at the expense of the LLC. Getting formal approval for these loan transactions can answer nonborrowing members' questions and avoid this type of insider controversy.

EXAMPLE: Larry's brother-in-law, Fred, invests in Larry's Reality for a 20% nonvoting (nonmanaging) membership share. Larry calls an annual LLC membership meeting. At the meeting, he assures Fred that all personal loans made by Larry to the LLC carry commercially competitive interest rates and other repayment terms. Larry gives Fred copies of the loan resolutions and promissory notes. After examining the loan terms, Fred is satisfied that Larry has made the loans simply to help the business succeed, not to receive a special individual benefit.

Interest rates charged by members

A member may wish to lend money to the LLC at no or low interest rates (though this may raise the hackles of IRS auditors, as discussed in Section 2, below). More sensibly, a member might wish to charge a commercially reasonable rate of interest for going to the trouble of lending personal funds to the LLC. But while commercial banks commonly charge variable interest rates that float two or three points above prime, members usually do not like to set up loans with fluctuating rates, because it's too complicated to do all the calculations. Instead, member loans usually contain a fixed interest rate. This is often fixed at a point or two above the prime rate that's in effect when the loan documents are signed. Or, members can choose a commercial rate, such as the "applicable federal rate." See "Federal Loan Rates," below.

FEDERAL LOAN RATES

The federal rates are the rates paid by the federal government on borrowed funds. They are set monthly. There are three federal rates: short term for loans with a three-year term or less (or for demand notes that can be called due at any time); mid term for loans from three years to nine years; and long term for loans with a term over nine years.

The applicable federal rates are changed each month, and can be found online at www.irs.gov as the current month's "imputed interest rates" or "AFR rates" (technically called the "applicable federal rates under Section 1274(d) of the Internal Revenue Code"). Major business newspapers also list the current applicable fed rates, typically in their stock quotations section.

Beware of state usury laws

Be aware that, whatever rate you come up with for an individual loan to your LLC, it must comply with your state's usury law. This law limits the maximum interest rate individuals can charge on loans, usually to 10%–12% per year but sometimes much less. Check with your accountant or your local bank or other financial institution if you're not sure of the usury regulations in your state. You can also check the Caine-Weiner resource center at www.caine-weiner.com for a 50-state chart of permitted interest rates.

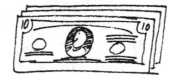

OTHER WAYS MEMBERS CAN HELP THEIR LLC FINANCIALLY

Investing capital or making loans to an LLC is not the only means members have to fund their LLC or make assets available for its use. Here are a few other ways:

- The LLC may not need to go to the trouble of raising money to buy property that is currently owned by a member. Instead, the member can lease property to the LLC and receive rental income in return. Rent payments, like interest payments for a loan, are deductible by the LLC as business expenses (and, like interest income, rental income is taxed to the member who leases out the property).

- If the LLC needs funds to buy property (real estate or personal property, such as equipment or automobiles), it may be more advantageous for a member to purchase the property and lease it to the LLC (similar to the previous scenario).

- If the LLC needs cash, it can borrow from a bank rather than from its members, using the members' personal collateral to qualify for the loan. In other words, the members help out by pledging personal assets to guarantee repayment of the loan in case the LLC defaults on its payments. (Bank loans are covered in Section A, above.)

2. Tax Effects of Insider Loans

The basic tax effects of a member loan to the LLC are straightforward (and are the same as the tax effects of loans made to an LLC by a bank, discussed in Section A, above), as long as the loan is legitimate.

As a quick review: The money the LLC borrows (the principal of the loan) is not considered business income, and so is not taxed to the LLC; nor is it allocated to members or taxed to them. The LLC gets to deduct the interest it pays on the loan as a business expense.

This, in turn, reduces the net profit of the LLC allocated and taxed to members at the end of its tax year. The member who lends the money to the LLC reports the interest payments received from the LLC on his or her individual income tax return, and is taxed at his or her individual income tax rate. Of course, the repayment of principal by the LLC to the member is simply a return of loan proceeds, and is not taxable to the member.

Potential problems arise only when an LLC or an LLC member is selected for a tax audit. In that case, the IRS may carefully scrutinize a loan made to the LLC by a member, particularly if the LLC is closely held by just a few members.

If the IRS thinks a loan is just a disguised capital investment in the LLC, it will treat it as such. This means that interest payments made by the LLC to the member will be considered "guaranteed payments" (much like fixed salary payments), which have certain technical differences in their tax treatment that can be important to some LLCs. (We discussed guaranteed payments and fixed salary payments briefly in Chapter 12, Section A1.)

More important, if the IRS regards a loan as a capital contribution to the LLC, the loan principal repayments by the LLC to a member will be treated as distributions of LLC profits from the member's capital account. Generally, distributions of profits lower the member's basis in his or her interest. If the distributions exceed the member's basis, the member will have to pay taxes on the amount of distributions that exceed the member's basis. A lower basis also results in higher capital gains taxes, if and when a member sells the membership interest or the LLC is liquidated. A lower basis can also limit the amount of LLC losses a member can claim on an individual tax return to offset other income.

One reason the IRS is leery of insider loans is that some LLC members use unpaid LLC debts to generate immediate deductions and losses, instead of waiting to claim them when the business folds. We know this is an unlikely scenario for readers of this book, who actively engage in a business to make a profit, not to generate deductible losses on their individual tax return. Nevertheless, here's an example of what the IRS is worried about:

EXAMPLE: Tradewinds Travel Agency, LLC, is in the financial doldrums. It's short on profits due to a downturn in the economy, which resulted in less discretionary travel spending by the agency's regular clientele. To shore up the agency over the short-term, Sarah and Lewis, the two equal member-managers of the LLC, each lend the company $20,000. This will keep the office open and pay the salary of their sole booking agent. (Sarah and Lewis do have other income from other, more lucrative businesses.) They do not prepare formal promissory notes for the loans, deciding to treat them informally as non-interest-bearing demand notes—meaning that they will wait until the LLC is profitable before paying themselves back.

After two years, the LLC still hasn't turned around, and Sarah and Lewis realize that the LLC is unlikely to ever pay them back on the loans. They claim the loans as bad-debt deductions on their individual tax returns, using them to offset other income on their tax returns to save on taxes. Unfortunately for them, the IRS audits the LLC's and Sarah and Lewis's tax returns, disallowing the bad-debt losses. Why? Because the loans look to the IRS like investment of additional capital by the owners, which should depend on profits of the business for payback. After all:

- The loans did not carry a set rate of interest.

- There was no repayment schedule.

- They were made in proportion to the member's capital interests in the business.

- They were commercially unreasonable loans (a bank would have required collateral for the loans and interest payments).

Since the IRS treats the loans as capital contributions, Sarah and Lewis will have to wait until they liquidate or sell their LLC membership interests to take their losses on the loan.

To avoid this kind of trouble with the IRS, below we discuss a few basic rules you should keep in mind. Following these rules will help ensure that the IRS treats loans from your members as legitimate lending transactions rather than capital contributions. These guidelines mostly come from court cases that judged the validity of loans made by shareholders of closely held corporations to their corporation. But the Tax Court has made it clear that these rules also apply to the validity of loans made by a partner to a partnership—a leading case is *Hambuechen v. Commissioner of Internal Revenue*, 43 Tax Court 90 (1964). (Since an LLC is treated as a partnership for most tax purposes, these partnership rules should apply to member loans to an LLC as well.)

As always, don't overemphasize these precautions. They are mostly meant as signposts to paths that can lead to trouble if you lend your LLC too much money at ridiculously low rates.

The overriding idea behind these rules is simple: If all the facts and circumstances of a loan transaction show that money is advanced to an LLC by a member with a reasonable expectation of repayment regardless of the success of the LLC, the transaction will be treated as a loan. If the facts show otherwise, the loan will be treated as a capital contribution.

The main key to making a loan that passes possible IRS audit scrutiny is to make the loan *commercially reasonable*. The loan should be backed up by a written promissory note that includes at least the following terms:

- An unconditional promise by the LLC to repay the loan amount. If the LLC can delay payment to a member until the member liquidates his or her interest, the IRS is more likely to see the loan as a capital contribution.

- A fixed maturity date. The IRS prefers short-term notes over long-term notes, although repayment terms as long as ten years are usually considered acceptable. If a promissory note lacks a maturity date (a demand note, for instance) or if payments are contingent on earnings of the LLC, the IRS is more likely to disregard the loan.

- Interest payments at or close to the prevailing commercial rates. For small businesses, this hovers around, or perhaps a little above, the prime rate.

- A pledge of collateral as security for repayment, if a commercial lender probably would have required collateral.

Also, if loans are made by more than one member in proportions that correspond roughly to their capital interests, the "loans" start looking to the IRS more like capital contributions than valid loan transactions.

To avoid such conflicts with the IRS (and to maintain your limited liability and avoid controversy among the members), it's important to record LLC management's approval of an insider loan in a resolution and to use a promissory note, discussed below.

3. Resolution to Approve Loan to the LLC by Insider

If your LLC is borrowing funds from an LLC member, manager, or other individual, rather than a bank or other outside business, you should always get LLC approval of a formal resolution. Back this up with a promissory note that spells out the terms for repayment. Doing this creates a paper trail that the LLC and the individual lender can refer to later to handle any disputes. It's surprising how often undocumented loans to and from individual owners can lead to trouble. Lenders and borrowers might remember the terms of the deal differently or walk away from the transaction with different expectations. If you put all loan transactions in writing, you can resolve later controversies with a quick look at your LLC records. Preparing proper LLC loan documentation can also, of course, help avoid problems with the courts and the IRS.

The resolution below records the LLC's acceptance of a loan of funds to the LLC from one or more members, managers, or other individuals (friends or relatives of a member, for instance). This resolution uses language designed to verify that the loan is properly documented by a written promissory note, is being made on commercially acceptable terms, and is capable of being paid without jeopardizing the financial viability of the

LLC. These recitals help establish the loan as a valid debt transaction.

💡 **You may wish to use a special resolution to approve a member or manager loan to the LLC**

If the LLC borrows from a member or manager at payback terms that are generous to the lending member or manager (for example, the lending member will receive a high rate of interest from the LLC), you may want to have the loan approved by the nonlending members. They will first want to verify that the loan terms do not unduly benefit the lending members (that is, the terms are similar to the terms that any outsider would insist on when making a loan to the the LLC).

An easy way to do this is to approve the loan by using the resolution form contained in Chapter 15, Section B1, for the approval of self-interested business, instead of the standard loan approval resolutions presented below. The self-interested business approval resolution in Chapter 15 includes extra space to show disclosure of the member's or manager's interest in the loan transacation and allows the LLC to state why the loan transaction is fair to the LLC.

💿 Fill in this resolution as you follow the sample and special instructions below. You'll find this resolution on the CD-ROM and as a tear-out form in Appendix D. (See Appendix A for information on selection and using the CD-ROM files.)

APPROVAL OF LOAN TO THE LLC

It was resolved that it is in the best interests of the LLC to borrow the following amount(s) from the following individuals:

Name of Lender   Amount ❶

_____ $_____

_____ $_____

  The terms of each loan were included in a proposed promissory note presented for approval at the meeting. ❷ The LLC determined that these terms were commercially reasonable. The LLC also determined that LLC earnings should be sufficient to pay back the loan(s) to the lender(s) according to the terms in the note(s), and that such repayment would not jeopardize the financial status of the LLC.

  Therefore, the LLC approved the terms of each note and directed the treasurer to sign each note on behalf of the LLC. The secretary was directed to attach a copy of each note, signed by the treasurer, to this resolution and to place the resolution and the attachment(s) in the LLC records binder.

Special Instructions

❶ Specify the amount to be lent along with the name of each member, manager, or other individual making the loan to the LLC. If a loan is made jointly by spouses, show the names of both spouses on one line.

❷ Before presenting the resolution to the LLC, prepare a proposed promissory note, which contains the proposed loan terms, and present it for approval by LLC. After approval, it should be signed by the LLC treasurer and the lender, and a copy should be attached to the resolution. We show you how to prepare basic promissory notes in Section D, below.

C. Promissory Notes Overview

A promissory note is, of course, the contract behind a particular loan—a written promise by the borrower to pay back the lender the principal amount borrowed, with interest, in a specific time frame.

Before looking at the various promissory note forms included with this book, let's explore the different ways notes are commonly structured. This discussion will help you select the most appropriate form for your loan transaction.

➡ For LLC loans from individuals only

All banks will provide you with a promissory note to sign when your LLC borrows money from them. Use the promissory notes below only for loans to the LLC by members, managers, and other individual lenders.

OUR PROMISSORY NOTES USE SIMPLE INTEREST

The notes discussed in this chapter call for simple, rather than compound, interest. With simple interest, interest is charged on the remaining unpaid principal due under the note, but not on any unpaid interest that accumulates during the term of the loan.

As a practical matter, compound interest is usually not necessary for LLC loans from insiders. If the loan is paid off in installments, the LLC will usually pay off all accrued interest with each installment. For long-term loans that don't call for any payments for quite a while (perhaps a year or more), it's possible to compound the interest due, although most smaller LLCs won't choose to do so. If you want to figure out compound interest, you can use a future value table; check with your tax adviser, your bank, or a real estate broker.

1. Lump-Sum Repayment With Interest

If your note provides for a lump-sum repayment, both principal and interest are repaid at the end of the agreed repayment period. To compute the interest due with the repayment, multiply the full amount of principal owed under the note times the annual interest rate times the number of years (and any fraction of a year) the loan will be outstanding.

EXAMPLE: Kyle will lend $10,000 to his LLC at an annual interest rate of 9%. Under the terms of the promissory note, repayment of principal plus interest is due in one lump sum at the end of a five-year period. To compute the interest due with the lump-sum payment, Kyle multiplies $10,000 x .09 x 5 to arrive at an interest payment of $4,500. The total lump-sum payment due at the end of the loan period will be $14,500.

It may be necessary to calculate the interest on a monthly basis, such as when a note calls for a 15- or 30-month repayment period. In that case, figure out the monthly interest and multiply it by the appropriate number of months. Then add that amount to the principal.

EXAMPLE: Kyle will lend $10,000 to his LLC at an annual interest rate of 9%. Repayment of principal plus interest is due in one lump sum at the end of an eight-month period. To compute the interest due, Kyle multiplies $10,000 x .09 to arrive at an annual interest payment of $900. He then divides that by 12, to get monthly interest of $75, which he multiplies by 8, for a total of $600. Finally, he adds the total interest to the principal to calculate the total lump-sum payment due at the end of the loan period: $10,600.

2. Periodic Payment of Interest Only

If your note provides for periodic payments of interest only with a lump-sum payment of principal at the end of an agreed period, you have to figure out the amount of interest that should be paid periodically. The easiest way to do this is to figure out the total amount of interest the LLC will end up paying. As you'll see, the LLC will pay the same total amount of interest as it would if it repaid the entire amount (principal and interest) at the end of the repayment period, as in the case discussed just above.

To compute the total interest charged under this type of note, multiply the principal amount times the annual interest rate times the number of years (and any fraction of a year) of the loan term. Then divide this total interest amount by the number of periodic interest payments required under the note. The result is the amount of each interest-only payment the LLC must pay each payment period.

> **EXAMPLE:** Maria, an LLC manager, lends $15,000 to her LLC. The note provides for quarterly interest-only payments at the rate of 9% over the three-year life of the note. That's 12 quarterly interest payments the LLC will make. Total interest due on the $15,000 over the three-year period is $4,050 ($15,000 x .09 x 3). The amount of each monthly interest payment is $337.50—the total $4,050 interest amount divided by 12.

3. Periodic Payments of Interest Plus Principal (Amortized Loans)

This next type of repayment plan, which allows for monthly or quarterly payments of principal and interest, along with its accompanying promissory note, is probably the most common one used by small LLCs.

When both principal and interest are paid in periodic installments under a note, the interest owed under the note usually declines with each payment, because the outstanding principal balance declines wtih each payment. It's possible, however, to charge equal payments for principal and interest if the amount of principal is raised with each payment.

Fortunately, it's not difficult to figure out the amount required for each payment. To help you do this, we provide a basic amortization schedule below. If you can't find the interest rate and time period you want, real estate brokers, banks, credit unions, financial publications, and business books have amortization schedules that show amortization multipliers for other interst rates and periods. In addition, standard computer spreadsheets such as Microsoft Excel and others can compute interest due on amortized loans, as can online calculators, which can be found on numerous websites, including www.timevalue.com.

To use the amortization schedule below, you need to know the annual interest rate and term of the note in years. Find your interest rate percentage in the left-hand column of the schedule and the number of years for the terms of your note in the top row. Then, extend the column and row until they intersect. Multiply this number by the total principal amount of your loan. The result is the monthly principal and interest payment under the note that will pay off the principal in the specified number of years.

> **EXAMPLE:** Martina, an LLC member, plans to lend her LLC $20,000 at 8% over a period of ten years, to be paid back in equal monthly principal and interest payments. She finds the 8% row on the left side of the schedule and follows it to the right to meet the ten-year column extending down from the top row of the schedule. She multiplies the resulting number, .0121, by $20,000 to arrive at the monthly principal plus interest payment amount of $242.

AMORTIZATION SCHEDULE FOR MONTHLY PAYMENTS

Number of Years

	1	1.5	2	2.5	3	4	5	6	7	8	9	10	11	12	13	14	15	20
3.0%	.0847	.0569	.0430	.0346	.0291	.0221	.0180	.0152	.0132	.0117	.0106	.0097	.0089	.0083	.0077	.0073	.0069	.0055
3.5%	.0849	.0571	.0432	.0349	.0293	.0224	.0182	.0154	.0134	.0120	.0108	.0099	.0091	.0085	.0080	.0075	.0071	.0058
4.0%	.0851	.0573	.0434	.0351	.0295	.0226	.0184	.0156	.0137	.0122	.0110	.0101	.0094	.0088	.0082	.0078	.0074	.0061
4.5%	.0854	.0576	.0436	.0353	.0297	.0228	.0186	.0159	.0139	.0124	.0113	.0104	.0096	.0090	.0085	.0080	.0076	.0063
5.0%	.0856	.0578	.0439	.0355	.0300	.0230	.0189	.0161	.0141	.0127	.0115	.0106	.0099	.0092	.0087	.0083	.0079	.0066
5.5%	.0858	.0580	.0441	.0358	.0302	.0233	.0191	.0163	.0144	.0129	.0118	.0109	.0101	.0095	.0090	.0085	.0082	.0069
6.0%	.0861	.0582	.0443	.0360	.0304	.0235	.0193	.0166	.0146	.0131	.0120	.0111	.0104	.0098	.0092	.0088	.0084	.0072
6.5%	.0863	.0585	.0445	.0362	.0306	.0237	.0196	.0168	.0148	.0134	.0123	.0114	.0106	.0100	.0095	.0091	.0087	.0075
7.0%	.0865	.0587	.0448	.0364	.0309	.0239	.0198	.0170	.0151	.0136	.0125	.0116	.0109	.0103	.0098	.0094	.0090	.0078
7.5%	.0868	.0589	.0450	.0367	.0311	.0242	.0200	.0173	.0153	.0139	.0128	.0119	.0111	.0106	.0101	.0096	.0093	.0081
8.0%	.0870	.0591	.0452	.0369	.0313	.0244	.0203	.0175	.0156	.0141	.0130	.0121	.0114	.0108	.0103	.0099	.0096	.0084
8.5%	.0872	.0594	.0455	.0371	.0316	.0246	.0205	.0178	.0158	.0144	.0133	.0124	.0117	.0111	.0106	.0102	.0098	.0087
9.0%	.0875	.0596	.0457	.0373	.0318	.0249	.0208	.0180	.0161	.0147	.0135	.0127	.0120	.0114	.0109	.0105	.0101	.0090
9.5%	.0877	.0598	.0459	.0376	.0320	.0251	.0210	.0183	.0163	.0149	.0138	.0129	.0122	.0117	.0112	.0108	.0104	.0093
10.0%	.0879	.0601	.0461	.0378	.0323	.0254	.0212	.0185	.0166	.0152	.0141	.0132	.0125	.0120	.0115	.0111	.0107	.0097
10.5%	.0881	.0603	.0464	.0380	.0325	.0256	.0215	.0188	.0169	.0154	.0144	.0135	.0128	.0122	.0118	.0114	.0111	.0100
11.0%	.0884	.0605	.0466	.0383	.0327	.0258	.0217	.0190	.0171	.0157	.0146	.0138	.0131	.0125	.0121	.0117	.0114	.0103
11.5%	.0886	.0608	.0468	.0385	.0330	.0261	.0220	.0193	.0174	.0160	.0149	.0141	.0134	.0128	.0124	.0120	.0117	.0107
12.0%	.0888	.0610	.0471	.0387	.0332	.0263	.0222	.0196	.0177	.0163	.0152	.0143	.0137	.0131	.0127	.0123	.0120	.0110

Interest Rate

4. Securing Loans With Interests in LLC Property

Sometimes, although not often, individual lenders (members, managers, their friends or family) may ask for the repayment of a loan to be secured with collateral. After all, this is exactly what outside commercial lenders often require. Securing a loan with collateral means that property owned by the LLC is pledged as security for the loan. In the event the LLC defaults, the lender may take the collateral and keep it or sell it as repayment for the debt.

Collateral for loans typically consists of the LLC's equity and share in real or personal property such as land or a building, a boat, a car, or computers. The accounts receivable of the LLC—amounts owed to the LLC and carried on the LLC books as an asset—also may be pledged for a loan. Product inventory owned by the LLC is another likely source of collateral for loans. In all cases, lenders must make sure that the property has not already been pledged for the repayment of another LLC loan, such as a bank loan or line of credit.

After assuring that the property is "unencumbered" (that is, has not been used to secure another note), the lender should request that paperwork be prepared to put third parties on notice that the property is being used to secure a note, thus making it more difficult for the LLC (the debtor) to dispose of the secured property without the lender's (creditor's) permission. This is always done when real estate is used as security: A mortgage or deed of trust is prepared and recorded at the office of the county recorder. A legal stationer who carries legal forms, a local real estate broker, a bank officer, or your legal or tax adviser may have copies of these forms available. We provide a basic secured, amortized promissory note in Section D2, below, to which you can attach copies of any security agreements (deeds of trust or mortgages) necessary in your state.

5. Demand Notes

A demand note allows the lender to "call the loan due" (request repayment of the entire loan) at any time. Rather than specifying a particular date in the future for repayment, the lender is given the power to call the loan due by making a written demand for payment. The borrower is usually given a short period of time, 30 to 60 days, for instance, after the written demand in which to pay off the loan balance.

Some demand notes limit when the lender can demand repayment. For example, a note might prohibit a lender from demanding repayment until at least three years have elapsed from the date of signing of the loan.

⚠ Proceed cautiously with a demand note
Although relations within the LLC may be cozy now, it's possible that there could be a falling out between your LLC and the lender. It's not unheard of for a lender to decide to get even by making an unexpected demand on a demand note. If you think there's a reasonable chance that this may happen when the LLC may not have the cash necessary to fulfill the loan repayment demand, choose another type of promissory note.

⚠ The IRS may look askance on demand notes
As we mentioned in Section B2, above, if a promissory note lacks a maturity date and a repayment schedule, the IRS is more likely to regard a loan from an LLC member to the LLC as a capital contribution to the LLC rather than a valid loan transaction.

D. PROMISSORY NOTES FOR LOANS TO LLC

Let's look at the promissory note forms included with this book. As discussed earlier, we suggest you prepare a promissory note for each loan transaction made by an individual to your LLC. Attach it to your LLC resolution approving the loan.

 **When to get outside help**

It's always a good idea to have your tax adviser or lawyer given an LLC note the once-over before using it, to ensure favorable legal and tax treatment. This is particularly important if you decide to add additional provisions to your note or wish to make any of the changes discussed in "Changing the Terms of the Basic Note Forms," directly below.

CHANGING THE TERMS OF THE BASIC NOTE FORMS

There are a great many terms and variations of terms that may be included in promissory notes, including interest rates, maturity dates, collateral, default provisions, and periodic payments of interest, principal, or both. The promissory notes included with this bok contain the most common terms used by smaller LLCs. However, you may wish to add, delete, or change provisions on these forms to suit your own loan transaction. Here are some examples:

- **Acceleration clause.** All notes we provide contain an acceleration clause that allows the lender to declare the entire unpaid amount of the loan due if the LLC misses a payment for a specified number of days after its due date. While it's unlikely that an individual lender closely associated with the LLC will actually enforce this provision if one payment is missed, the fact that he or she has the right to do so helps establish that the lender and the LLC intend to create a valid creditor/debtor relationship. If, however, you don't want your LLD to be obligated by this type of instant repayment provision, you can delete this clause

- **Collection costs.** Another provision we include in our notes allows the lender to charge collections costs in the event of a default by the LLC. This also helps establish the commercial reasonableness of the loan transaction. These collection costs include "reasonable attorney fees." Some readers may wish to define or place a limit on these fees, perhaps limiting the attorney fees that the LLC will pay in the event of a default to 10%–15% of the principal amount of the loan.

1. Promissory Note: Installment Payments of Principal and Interest (Amortized Loan)

Most smaller LLCs will prefer to use a promissory note that provides for periodic payments of principal plus interest until the principal amount of the loan is paid off.

Fill in this note as you follow the sample and special instructions below. You'll find this resolution on the CD-ROM and as a tear-out form in Appendix D. (See Appendix A for information on selecting and using the CD-ROM files.)

LLC PROMISSORY NOTE:
INSTALLMENT PAYMENTS OF PRINCIPAL AND INTEREST
(AMORTIZED LOAN)

For value received, _____[name of LLC]_____, the borrower, promises to pay to the order of __[name of member, manager, or other individual lender]__, the noteholder, the principal amount of $ __[principal amount of loan]__, together with simple interest on the unpaid principal balance from the date of this note until the date this note is paid in full, at the annual rate of __[annual rate of interest]__%. Payments will be made at _____[address of lender]_____.

Principal and interest will be paid in equal installments of $__[amount of each payment]__, ❶ beginning on __[date of first payment]__, and continuing on __[day for ongoing payments, for example, "the fifteenth day of each month"]__ until the principal and interest are paid in full. Each payment made by the borrower shall be applied first to accrued but unpaid interest, and the remainder will be applied to unpaid principal.

This note may be prepaid by the borrower in whole or in part at any time without penalty. This note is not assumable without the written consent of the noteholder. Consent will not be unreasonably withheld. This note is nontransferable by the noteholder. ❷

If any installment payment due under this note is not received by the noteholder within __[number of days]__ of its due date, the entire amount of unpaid principal and accrued but unpaid interest due under this note will, at the option of the noteholder, become immediately due and payable without prior notice by the noteholder to the borrower. In the event of a default, the borrower is responsible for the costs of collection, including, in the event of a lawsuit to collect on this note, the noteholder's reasonable attorney fees as determined by a court hearing the lawsuit.

Date of Signing: _____

Name of Borrower: _____[name of LLC]_____

Address of Borrower:_____[address of principal office of LLC]_____

City, or County, and State Where Signed _____

Signature of Borrower: _____[signature of treasurer]_____, Treasurer
on behalf of _____[name of LLC]_____

Special Instructions

❶ Use an amortization schedule to calculate the monthly payment. (See Section C3, above.) Payments are usually made on a monthly basis, but you can establish a different interval if you choose. If you do, you'll need to use an amortization table based on your loan's repayment interval, such as quarterly or every other month. Check with a library, bookstore, or bank for other amortization tables.

❷ This paragraph specifies that the loan may be repaid by the LLC at any time without triggering a prepayment penalty. This allows your LLC to pay back the loan whenever it makes economic sense to do so. The loan is also made assumable (meaning another company or person can take over the payment obligation for the LLC) with the permission of the noteholder. However, this is probably academic, since it is unlikely that another company or person will wish to assume payments under the loan. Finally, the note is nontransferable—the individual lender may not transfer the note to another person to collect the payments from the LLC. This provision is normal for insider loans in a small LLC. You can easily change this sentence to allow transfers if you wish, though it's highly unlikely that a noteholder will wish to transfer an LLC loan.

2. Promissory Note: Installment Payments of Principal and Interest (Amortized Loan) Secured by LLC Property

This promissory note is the same as the previous note but adds a clause that pledges LLC property as security for repayment of the loan. Again, loans that individuals make to your LLC are not normally secured, but this may be necessary in some cases to help make the individual lender feel more comfortable.

How to use the security clause in other note forms

To allow the LLC to pledge property as security for the repayment of a different type of note, you may copy the security clause in this note—the last paragraph in the text of the note shown below—to any of the other note forms covered below.

Fill in this note as you follow the sample and special instructions below. You'll find this resolution on the CD-ROM and as a tear-out form in Appendix D. (See Appendix A for information on selecting and using the CD-ROM files.)

LLC PROMISSORY NOTE:
INSTALLMENT PAYMENTS OF PRINCIPAL AND INTEREST
(AMORTIZED LOAN) SECURED BY LLC PROPERTY

For value received, _____ [name of LLC] _____ , the borrower, promises to pay to the order of __[name of member, manager, or other individual lender]__ , the noteholder, the principal amount of __$[principal amount of loan]__ , together with simple interest on the unpaid principal balance from the date of this note until the date this note is paid in full, at the annual rate of __[annual rate of interest]%__ . Payments will be made at _____ [address of lender] _____ .

Principal and interest will be paid in equal installments of __$[amount of each payment]__ , ❶ begin-ning on ____[date of first payment]____ , and continuing on __[day for ongoing payments, for example, "the fifteenth day of each month"]__ until the principal and interest are paid in full. Each payment made by the borrower will be applied first to accrued but unpaid interest, and the remainder will be applied to unpaid principal.

This note may be prepaid by the borrower in whole or in part at any time without penalty. This note is not assumable without the written consent of the noteholder. Consent will not be unreasonably withheld. This note is nontransferable by the noteholder. ❷

If any installment payment due under this note is not received by the noteholder within __[number of days]__ of its due date, the entire amount of unpaid principal and accrued but unpaid interest due under this note will, at the option of the noteholder, become immediately due and payable without prior notice from the noteholder to the borrower. In the event of a default, the borrower is responsible for the costs of collec-tion, including, in the event of a lawsuit to collect on this note, the noteholder's reasonable attorney fees as determined by a court hearing the lawsuit.

Borrower agrees that until the principal and interest owed under this note are paid in full, the note is secured by the following described mortgage, deed of trust, or security agreement: __[describe security agreement, deed of trust, or mortgage used to pledge security of the property, including a description of the property]__ . ❸

Date of Signing: _____

Name of Borrower:_____ [name of LLC] _____

Address of Borrower:_____ [address of principal office of LLC] _____

City, or County, and State Where Signed: _____

Signature of Borrower:_____ [signature of treasurer] _____ , Treasurer

on behalf of _____ [name of LLC] _____

Special Instructions

❶ Use an amortization schedule to calculate the monthly payment. (See Section C3, above.) Payments are usually made on a monthly basis, but you can establish a different interval if you choose. If you do, you'll need to use an amortization table based on your loan's repayment interval, such as quarterly or every other month. Check with a library, bookstore, or bank for other amortization tables.

❷ This paragraph specifies that the loan may be repaid by the LLC at any time without triggering a prepayment penalty. This allows your LLC to pay back the loan whenever it makes economic sense to do so. The loan is also made assumable (meaning another company or person can take over the payment obligation for the LLC) with the permission of the noteholder. However, this is probably academic, since it is unlikely that another company or person will wish to assume payments under the loan. Finally, the note is nontransferable—the individual lender may not transfer the note to another person to collect the payments from the LLC. This provision is normal for insider loans in a small LLC. You can easily change this sentence to allow transfers if you wish, but it's highly unlikely anyway that a noteholder will wish to transfer an LLC loan.

❸ This is the security clause. Specify the security agreement used to pledge the property as repayment for the loan in case of default, together with a description of the property. For real estate, you will want to complete and record a mortgage deed or deed of trust with the county recorder. For personal property, under state law you may need to complete and file a security agreement to enforce the security clause in your note. A legal forms stationer may have security agreements on hand, or you can contact a real estate broker, tax adviser, or lawyer to obtain these forms or have them prepared for you. Attach a completed copy of the security document to the resolution.

EXAMPLE (Real Estate Used as Security): "Deed of Trust to real property commonly known as _____ [address] _____, owned by _____ [name of LLC] _____, executed on __[date of signing of deed of trust]_, at __[city and state where signed]__, and recorded at __[place recorded]_, in the records of __[name of recording office]__, _____ [name of county and state] _____."

EXAMPLE (LLC-Owned Automobile Used as Security): "Security Agreement signed by _____ [name of officer] _____, on behalf of__ [name of LLC] __, on__ [date of signing]__, pledging title to ____[make and model and year of automobile with Vehicle ID #]___."

3. Promissory Note: Installment Payments of Principal and Interest (Amortized Loan) With Balloon Payment

The next promissory note differs from the standard amortized note (covered in Section 1, above) by requiring a "balloon payment" at the end of the repayment term. A balloon payment is a complete payoff of all remaining principal on a specified installment date, one that's prior to the date the loan would normally be paid off by regular installment payments. Use this note if the lender wishes to receive regular payments of principal and interest for a period of time, but then wants full repayment of principal on a particular future date. You will need to use an amortization guide that includes a remaining loan balance table, which will allow you to calculate the amount of the balloon payment (see the special instructions to the note form, below).

Fill in this note as you follow the sample and special instructions below. You'll find this resolution on the CD-ROM and as a tear-out form in Appendix D. (See Appendix A for information on selecting and using the CD-ROM files.)

LLC PROMISSORY NOTE:
INSTALLMENT PAYMENTS OF PRINCIPAL AND INTEREST
(AMORTIZED LOAN) WITH BALLOON PAYMENT

For value received, _____ [name of LLC] _____, the borrower, promises to pay to the order of __[name of member, manager, or other individual lender]__, the noteholder, the principal amount of __$[principal amount of loan]__, together with simple interest on the unpaid principal balance from the date of this note until the date this note is paid in full, at the annual rate of ___[annual rate of interest]%___. Payments will be made at _____ [address of lender] _____.

Principal and interest will be paid in equal installments of __$[amount of each payment]__, beginning on __[date of first payment]__, and continuing on __[day for ongoing payments, for example, "the fifteenth day of each month"]__. On the installment payment date on __[date of final (balloon) payment]__, a balloon payment of $___[amount of remaining principal owed on the loan on final installment date]___ ❶ will be added to the installment amount paid by the borrower in order to pay off this note in its entirety on this final installment payment date. Each payment made by the borrower will be applied first to accrued but unpaid interest, and the remainder will be applied to unpaid principal.

This note may be prepaid by the borrower in whole or in part at any time without penalty. This note is not assumable without the written consent of the noteholder. Consent will not be unreasonably withheld. This note is nontransferable by the noteholder. ❷

If any installment payment due under this note is not received by the noteholder within __[number of days]__ of its due date, the entire amount of unpaid principal and accrued but unpaid interest due under this note will, at the option of the noteholder, become immediately due and payable without prior notice from the noteholder to the borrower. In the event of a default, the borrower is responsible for the costs of collection, including, in the event of a lawsuit to collect on this note, the noteholder's reasonable attorney fees as determined by a court hearing the lawsuit.

Date of Signing: _____

Name of Borrower:_____ [name of LLC] _____

Address of Borrower:_____ [address of principal office of LLC] _____

City, or County, and State Where Signed: _____

Signature of Borrower:_____ [signature of treasurer] _____, Treasurer

on behalf of _____ [name of LLC] _____

Special Instructions

❶ You start by calculating the periodic payments using an amortization schedule, as in Sections 1, 2, and 3, above. The major difference is that you will amortize the loan for a longer period than the loan will be outstanding; the balloon payment date will occur before the end of the full amortization term. For example, if the LLC plans to provide for a balloon payment in seven years, it may wish to amortize monthly payments over ten or fifteen years, which will allow the lender to make relatively low payments. Choose the amortization term for the loan, then find the monthly payment amount under the interest rate on the amortization schedule. (See Section C3, above.) Payments are usually made on a monthly basis, but you can establish a different interval if you choose. If you do, you'll need to use an amortization table based on your loan's repayment interval, such as quarterly or every other month. Check with a library, bookstore, or bank for other amortization tables.

Next, figure the amount of the balloon payment to be added to the last installment payment—this will be the principal balance owed on the note on this date.

Remaining loan balance table

The easy way to find the remaining principal balance is to use a table called a "remaining loan balance table" that is included in standard loan amortization pamphlets and books. This table will show the percentage of the principal remaining in a given year of a loan. These percentages vary according to the interest rate and the full amortization term of the loan, as well as the date when the balloon payment is made. *McGraw-Hill's Interest Amortization Tables*, by Jack Estes and Dennis Kelley, gives remaining loan balance tables for five- to 30-year loans.

Insert into the last blank in this section of the note the additional principal payment amount—the balloon payment—due on the last installment payment date.

EXAMPLE 1: Sheryl Shore, the sole member of For Shore Electronics, LLC, proposes to lend $10,000 to her LLC at a 5% interest rate. The loan will be amortized over 15 years, with the LLC making regular monthly payments of principal and interest for the first seven years, until a balloon payment becomes due—exactly seven years from the original loan date. Using the amortization schedule shown in Section C3, above, Sheryl multiplies the principal amount of the loan by .0079 to arrive at a monthly payment amount of $79. Next, Sheryl looks at a remaining loan balance table. She finds that the percentage of the original principal amount owed after seven years on a loan amortized over 15 years at a 5% interest rate is 62.464% (the same as .62464). Sheryl multiplies .62464 by $10,000, and comes up with $6,246.40. This is the principal amount that will be owed on the date the last installment is due (on the date the LLC makes the last payment of $79, at the end of seven years). Sheryl adds the remaining principal payment of $6,246.40 to $79 to come up with a total final (balloon) payment of $6,325.40. The LLC will end up paying a total of $12,882.40— that's ($79 x 12 x 7) plus $6,246.40.

EXAMPLE 2: Sheryl's LLC wants to amortize the monthly interest and principal amounts over ten years instead of 15. Looking at the amortization table in Section C3, above, the loan payments will be $106 per month ($10,000 x .0106). A remaining loan balance table shows that the remaining loan balance after seven years is 35.390% of the original principal amount. In this case, $3,539 ($10,000 x .35390) will be owed on the seven-year anniversary balloon payment date, plus the regular amortized payment of $106. This balloon payment is less than the balloon payment in the previous example because here the loan is paid off more quickly ($106 per month instead of $79 per month), so less principal remains on the note on the pay-off date.

❷ This paragraph specifies that the loan may be repaid by the LLC at any time without triggering a pre-payment penalty. This allows your LLC to pay back the loan whenever it makes economic sense to do so. The loan is also made assumable (meaning another company or person can take over the payment obligation for the LLC) with the permission of the noteholder. However, this is probably academic, since it is unlikely that another company or person will wish to assume payments under the loan. Finally, the note is nontransferable—the individual lender may not transfer the note to another person to collect the payments from the LLC. This provision is normal for insider loans in a small LLC. You can easily change this sentence to allow transfers if you wish, though it's highly unlikely that a noteholder will wish to transfer an LLC loan.

4. Promissory Note: Periodic Payments of Interest Only With Lump-Sum Principal Payment

This promissory note provides a designated period of monthly payments of interest only, to be followed by a lump-sum payment of the entire principal amount of the loan. This form of loan makes sense if the loan amount is not excessive and the LLC will be able to come up with the entire principal amount of the loan funds at the end of the loan period.

EXAMPLE: Gerard, as sole member, lends his LLC $10,000 at a 7.5% rate for five years. Gerard uses the amortization table in Section C3, above, to calculate that the total interest owed by the LLC for these funds will be $3,750 ($10,000 x .075 x 5). The amount of each monthly interest installment under the note is thus $62.50 (total interest for the five-year loan period—$3,750—divided by the 60 installments made in this period). At the end of the five-year period during which the LLC pays monthly interest only, the LLC must pay Gerard the entire $10,000.

Fill in this note as you follow the sample and special instructions below. You'll find this resolution on the CD-ROM and as a tear-out form in Appendix D. (See Appendix A for information on selecting and using the CD-ROM files.)

LLC PROMISSORY NOTE:
PERIODIC PAYMENTS OF INTEREST
WITH LUMP-SUM PRINCIPAL PAYMENT

For value received, _____[name of LLC]_____, the borrower, promises to pay to the order of __[name of member, manager, or other individual lender]__, the noteholder, the principal amount of __$[principal amount of loan]__, together with simple interest on the unpaid principal balance from the date of this note until the date this note is paid in full, at the annual rate of ___[annual rate of interest]%___. Payments will be made at _____[address of lender]_____.

Interest will be paid in equal installments of __$[amount of each interest payment]__, ❶ beginning on __[date of first payment]__, and continuing on the __[day for ongoing payments, for example, "the fifteenth day of each month"]__ until __[ending date of loan period]__, on which date the entire principal amount, together with total accrued but unpaid interest, will be paid by the borrower.

This note may be prepaid by the borrower in whole or in part at any time without penalty. This note is not assumable without the written consent of the noteholder. Consent will not be unreasonably withheld. This note is nontransferable by the noteholder. ❷

If any installment payment due under this note is not received by the noteholder within __[number of days]__ of its due date, the entire amount of unpaid principal and accrued but unpaid interest due under this note will, at the option of the noteholder, become immediately due and payable without prior notice from the noteholder to the borrower. In the event of a default, the borrower is responsible for the costs of collection, including, in the event of a lawsuit to collect on this note, the noteholder's reasonable attorney fees as determined by a court hearing the lawsuit.

Date of Signing: _____

Name of Borrower:_____[name of LLC]_____

Address of Borrower:_____[address of principal office of LLC]_____

City, or County, and State Where Signed: _____

Signature of Borrower:_____[signature of treasurer]_____, Treasurer

on behalf of _____[name of LLC]_____

Special Instructions

❶ Multiply the principal amount by the interest rate. That is the amount of interest payable per year. Divide that number by 12 to come up with a monthly interest payment. Payments are usually made on a monthly basis, but you can establish a different interval if you choose. If you do, divide the annual interest payable by the amount of payments to be made in one year.

❷ See Section D3, above, Special Instruction #2.

5. Promissory Note: Lump-Sum Payment of Principal and Interest on Specified Date

This promissory note is similar to the previous note in that the entire amount of principal is paid in one lump sum at the end of the loan period. However, unlike the previous note, where interest payments are made in installments during the loan period, here the entire interest amount is paid along with the entire principal amount at the end of the loan term.

> **EXAMPLE:** Ubiquity Movers, LLC, borrows $10,000 for three years at 9% interest. Using the amortization table in Section C3, above, to calculate the total interest owed by the LLC for these funds, a one-time payment of $12,700 ($10,000 principal plus the entire $2,700 interest amount) is due at the end of the three-year loan term.

Fill in this note as you follow the sample and special instruction below. You'll find this resolution on the CD-ROM and as a tear-out form in Appendix D. (See Appendix A for information on selecting and using the CD-ROM files.)

LLC PROMISSORY NOTE:
LUMP-SUM PAYMENT OF PRINCIPAL
AND INTEREST ON SPECIFIED DATE

For value received, _____ [name of LLC] _____, the borrower, promises to pay to the order of __[name of member, manager, or other individual lender]__, the noteholder, the principal amount of __$[principal amount of loan]__, together with simple interest on the unpaid principal balance from the date of this note until the date this note is paid in full, at the annual rate of __[annual rate of interest]%__. Payments will be made at _____[address of lender]_____.

The entire principal amount of the loan, together with total accrued but unpaid interest, will be paid by the borrower on __[due date for payment of all principal and interest]__. Any payment made by the borrower prior to the due date specified above will be applied first to accrued but unpaid interest, and the remainder will be applied to unpaid principal.

This note may be prepaid by the borrower in whole or in part at any time without penalty. This note is not assumable without the written consent of the noteholder. Consent will not be unreasonably withheld. This note is nontransferable by the noteholder. ❶

In the event of a default, the borrower is responsible for the costs of collection, including, in the event of a lawsuit to collect on this note, the noteholder's reasonable attorney fees as determined by a court hearing the lawsuit.

Date of Signing: _____

Name of Borrower:_____[name of LLC]_____

Address of Borrower:_____[address of principal office of LLC]_____

City, or County, and State Where Signed: _____

Signature of Borrower:_____[signature of treasurer]_____, Treasurer

on behalf of _____[name of LLC]_____

Special Instruction

❶ This paragraph specifies that the loan may be repaid by the LLC at any time without triggering a prepayment penalty. This allows your LLC to pay back the loan whenever it makes economic sense to do so. The loan is also made assumable (meaning another company or person can take over the payment obligation for the LLC) with the permission of the noteholder. However, this is probably academic, since it is unlikely that another company or person will wish to assume payments under the loan. Finally, the note is nontransferable—the individual lender may not transfer the note to another person to collect the payments from the LLC. This provision is normal for insider loans in a small LLC. You can easily change this sentence to allow transfers if you wish, though it's highly unlikely that a noteholder will wish to transfer an LLC loan.

6. Promissory Note: Lump-Sum Payment of Principal and Interest on Demand by Noteholder

Here is a classic "demand note" that allows the noteholder (lender) to call the note due at any time. A demand note may make sense when an LLC has only one or two members who borrow money for personal uses from time to time when the LLC has positive cash flow.

Fill in this note as you follow the sample and special instruction below. You'll find this resolution on the CD-ROM and as a tear-out form in Appendix D. (See Appendix A for information on selecting and using the CD-ROM files.)

LLC PROMISSORY NOTE:
LUMP-SUM PAYMENT OF PRINCIPAL
AND INTEREST ON DEMAND BY NOTEHOLDER

For value received, _____ [name of LLC] _____, the borrower, promises to pay to the order of __[name of member, manager, or other individual lender]__, the noteholder, the principal amount of __$[principal amount of loan]__, together with simple interest on the unpaid principal balance from the date of this note until the date this note is paid in full, at the annual rate of ___[annual rate of interest]%___. Payments will be made at _____ [address of lender] _____.

The entire principal amount of the loan, together with total accrued but unpaid interest, will be paid within __[period, for example "30 days or other period agreeable to the LLC and borrower"]__ of receipt by the LLC of a demand for repayment by the noteholder. A demand for repayment by the noteholder shall be made in writing and will be delivered or mailed to the borrower at the following address: _____ [address of principal office of LLC] _____. If demand for repayment is mailed, it will be considered received by the borrower on the third business day after the date when it was deposited in the U.S. mail as registered or certified mail. ❶

Any payment made by the borrower prior to the due date specified above will be applied first to accrued but unpaid interest, and the remainder will be applied to unpaid principal.

This note may be prepaid by the borrower in whole or in part at any time without penalty. This note is not assumable without the written consent of the noteholder. Consent will not be unreasonably withheld. This note is nontransferable by the noteholder. ❷

In the event of a default, the borrower is responsible for the costs of collection, including, in the event of a lawsuit to collect on this note, the noteholder's reasonable attorney fees as determined by a court hearing the lawsuit.

Date of Signing: _____

Name of Borrower:_____ [name of LLC] _____

Address of Borrower:_____ [address of principal office of LLC] _____

City, or County, and State Where Signed: _____

Signature of Borrower:_____ [signature of treasurer] _____, Treasurer

on behalf of _____ [name of LLC] _____

Special Instruction

❶ Specify how much time the LLC has to pay the loan off after the demand by the noteholder. This period will vary depending on the cash flow requirements of the LLC and the lender. Thirty days is often specified as the period, but up to three months or more may be allowed if the loan amount is substantial. A longer period is appropriate if the LLC might need to seek a bank loan to satisfy the call on the note by the noteholder.

You can, if you wish, add language to the note limiting when the lender can demand repayment. For example, you can prohibit the lender from demanding repayment on the loan until at least three years have elapsed from the date of signing of the loan. You might make an exception to this prohibition by allowing a member-lender to make a demand for repayment at any time during the life of the note if he or she no longer owns an interest in the LLC.

❷ This paragraph specifies that the loan may be repaid by the LLC at any time without triggering a prepayment penalty. This allows your LLC to pay back the loan whenever it makes economic sense to do so. The loan is also made assumable (meaning another company or person can take over the payment obligation for the LLC) with the permission of the noteholder. However, this is probably academic, since it is unlikely that another company or person will wish to assume payments under the loan. Finally, the note is nontransferable—the individual lender may not transfer the note to another person to collect the payments from the LLC. This provision is normal for insider loans in a small LLC. You can easily change this sentence to allow transfers if you wish, though it's highly unlikely that a noteholder will wish to transfer an LLC loan.

7. Promissory Note: Special Schedule of Payments of Principal and Interest

This promissory note allows you to specify a special (nonuniform) schedule for repayment of principal and interest under the loan. For example, your schedule may show changes in principal and/or interest payments over the life of the note, often ending with a final balloon payment of the remaining principal plus all accrued and unpaid interest due on a certain date. The options here are unlimited, but here's one example to give you the general idea.

> **EXAMPLE:** On July 1, Laura lends her LLC $10,000 for five years at 8% interest. She and the LLC agree that Laura will receive nothing until the end of the second year. Using the amortization table in Section C3, above, they agree she'll then receive $1,600 in interest-only payments for the first two years of the loan ($10,000 x .08 x 2). The LLC will then make an interest-only payment of $800 at the end of the third year. At the end of the fourth year, it will make an $800 interest payment along with a payment of $4,000 in principal, leaving a principal balance of $6,000. Finally, at the end of the fifth year, the LLC will make its last payment, consisting of the balance of $6,000 principal along with $480 interest ($6,000 x .08 x 1). Here is the repayment schedule:

June 31, 2nd year:	$1,600	(interest)
June 31, 3rd year:	$800	(interest)
June 31, 4th year:	$4,800	($4,000 principal; $800 interest)
June 31, 5th year:	$6,480	($6,000 principal; $480 interest)
Total Payments:	$13,680	($10,000 principal; $3,680 interest)

An LLC may pay less with an amortized loan

If the same loan had been amortized over five years, Laura's LLC would have paid $203 per month in principal and interest—or $2,436 per year—for a total of $12,180 over five years. In that case, the LLC would have paid only $2,180 in interest.

Fill in this note as you follow the sample and special instruction below. You'll find this resolution on the CD-ROM and as a tear-out form in Appendix D. (See Appendix A for information on selecting and using the CD-ROM files.)

LLC PROMISSORY NOTE:
SPECIAL SCHEDULE OF PAYMENTS OF PRINCIPAL AND INTEREST

For value received, _____ [name of LLC] _____, the borrower, promises to pay to the order of __[name of member, manager, or other individual lender]__, the noteholder, the principal amount of __$[principal amount of loan]__, together with simple interest on the unpaid principal balance from the date of this note until the date this note is paid in full, at the annual rate of __[annual rate of interest]%__. Payments will be made at _____ [address of lender] _____.

Principal and interest will be paid as follows:

__[Include schedule of payments here. For the last payment, you can insert the following: "The borrower will make a final payment in the amount of all remaining principal and all accrued but unpaid interest on (date)."]__

This note may be prepaid by the borrower in whole or in part at any time without penalty. This note is not assumable without the written consent of the noteholder. Consent will not be unreasonably withheld. This note is nontransferable by the noteholder. ❶

If any installment payment due under this note is not received by the noteholder within __[number of days]__ of its due date, the entire amount of unpaid principal and accrued but unpaid interest of the loan will, at the option of the noteholder, become immediately due and payable without prior notice by the noteholder to the borrower. In the event of a default, the borrower is responsible for the costs of collection, including, in the event of a lawsuit to collect on this note, the noteholder's reasonable attorney fees as determined by a court hearing the lawsuit.

Date of Signing: _____

Name of Borrower: _____ [name of LLC] _____

Address of Borrower: _____ [address of principal office of LLC] _____

City, or County, and State Where Signed: _____

Signature of Borrower: _____ [signature of treasurer] _____, Treasurer

on behalf of _____ [name of LLC] _____

Special Instruction

❶ This paragraph specifies that the loan may be repaid by the LLC at any time without triggering a prepayment penalty. This allows your LLC to pay back the loan whenever it makes economic sense to do so. The loan is also made assumable (meaning another company or person can take over the payment obligation for the LLC) with the permission of the noteholder. However, this is probably academic, since it is unlikely that another company or person will wish to assume payments under the loan. Finally, the note is nontransferable—the individual lender may not transfer the note to another person to collect the payments from the LLC. This provision is normal for insider loans in a small LLC. You can easily change this sentence to allow transfers if you wish, though it's highly unlikely that a noteholder will wish to transfer an LLC loan. ■

Loans by the LLC

In this chapter, we cover loans made by an LLC to LLC insiders such as members, managers, officers, and other employees. This is the flip side of the loan transactions covered in the previous chapter (Chapter 13 covers loans made to the LLC). We also provide a promissory note for LLC insiders to fill out and sign, along with explanations and an example, and a "Release of Promissory Note" form, for the LLC to sign when the loan is paid off.

A. OVERVIEW OF LOANS TO INSIDERS

Unless your LLC is in the business of making loans to outsiders—and in most states, it needs special permission from the state to do so—a loan made by an LLC will normally be made to an individual associated with the LLC, such as a member, manager, or key employee. This type of insider loan transaction is not common. Instead, if a member needs cash, the usual way of meeting this need is for the LLC to distribute the member's "distributive share" of profits to him or her. And if a member wants a cash distribution of profits before these profits have been earned by the LLC and allocated to the member (which happens at the end of the LLC's tax year), the member can seek an advance payment (draw) of these profits instead of seeking a personal loan from the LLC.

Loans made by an LLC to nonmember managers, officers or employees are also not a normal business practice. LLC profits are more productively reinvested in the business of the company, rather than loaned out to LLC individuals. In addition, nonborrowing members in a co-owned LLC are likely to cast a leery eye on special loans made to a particular LLC person. They may feel that such a loan deal smacks of unacceptable favoritism and an inappropriate diversion of LLC operating funds.

Despite all of this, there may be circumstances where your LLC decides it really does make sense to grant an LLC loan to a member, manager, officer, or employee. For example, if an LLC member is experiencing a personal cash crunch, management may decide that making a personal loan will help keep the person focused on LLC business, especially if the LLC is flush with profits. In that situation, making the loan can serve the best interests of both the LLC and the borrowing member. Here's another example, one that relates more to the LLC business, where the approval of a program of personal loans by the LLC makes sense.

EXAMPLE: A small semiconductor chip fabricator, MegaChips, LLC, decides to entice LLC officers to relocate close to its main headquarters by lending funds to newly hired officers for the purchase of nearby residential housing. Doing this benefits the LLC by making it easier to attract key employees. The loans should be considered fair to the LLC as long as they:

• carry a reasonable rate of interest (which may be slightly lower than the rates charged by commercial lenders)

- are secured by the property purchased by the officers (a second deed of trust or mortgage on the purchased property)

- are approved by the members, and

- will not impair the LLC's ability to pay its ongoing bills.

LOANS TO OUTSIDERS

This chapter deals with loans to LLC insiders (members, managers, officers, and other employees). Your LLC also may decide to make loans or extend credit to outsiders—customers, clients, purchasers, and others. Arm's-length transactions of this sort are governed by the credit and consumer loan laws in your state. We do not cover them here, since there is normally no need to observe extra precautions to head off charges of favoritism.

Also keep in mind that your LLC probably will have to be organized and operated under special laws if it seeks to make outside loans as a regular part of its business (like a bank, credit or finance company, real estate agency, and the like). The commercial lending and credit area is a broad one. Obviously, if you plan to set up shop as a commercial lender or finance company, you will need to check the legal resources at your law library, and consult a knowledgeable lawyer or tax adviser who specializes in your area of operation.

How to Select and Use LLC Resolutions

- Scan the table of contents at the beginning of the chapter to find resolutions of interest to you.

- When you find one you need, read the background material that precedes the pertinent LLC resolution.

- Follow the instructions included with the sample resolution to complete a draft of the resolution using your computer. If you need guidance on selecting and using the computer disk files, see Appendix A. (You'll have to fill in the tear-out resolution included in Appendix D if you don't have a computer.)

- Complete any needed attachment forms, such as promissory notes.

- If a resolution involves complex issues that will benefit from expert analysis, have your legal or tax adviser review your paperwork and conclusions.

- Prepare minutes of meeting or written consent forms as explained in Chapters 5–7, and insert the completed resolution into the appropriate form.

- Have the LLC secretary sign the printed minutes or have members and/or managers sign any written consent forms. Then place the signed forms, together with any attachments, in your LLC records binder.

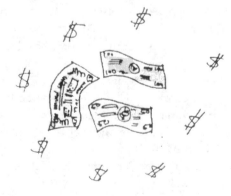

B. LEGAL CONSIDERATIONS FOR LOANS ISSUED TO INSIDERS

State law, either explicitly or implicitly, usually permits LLCs to make loans to members and other individuals. But check your state's LLC Act to be sure, and to see if any special approval requirements must be met. Regardless of state requirements, we recommend you confirm the following before approving an LLC loan:

- The terms of the loan are commercially competitive—or at least reasonable.

- The disbursal of loan funds will not impair the financial condition of the LLC.

- All the members will approve the loans to non-members.

- If the loan is to a member, you can also use the self-interested business resolution discussed in Chapter 15, Section B.

Also, keep the following tips in mind when approving a loan by your LLC:

- Over and above your state's LLC laws, your LLC articles and operating agreement may impose conditions on LLC loans made to insiders. Before approving an insider loan, make sure loans to members, managers, officers, or employees are not prohibited or limited by your articles or operating agreement.

- In LLCs owned and operated by one or just a few managing members, if all members agree to lend money to themselves, they can be more relaxed about formalities. After all, if there are no non-managing members, who's to complain that the interest rates are noncompetitive? But you still need to think about the IRS—more on this later in Section C, below—and whether the LLC could invest its money more productively elsewhere.

- Avoid making loans during hard times. If your LLC is on shaky financial footing when it considers making a loan, or you suspect it soon may be, we suggest you wait until the LLC is more solvent. Making an insider loan when your LLC is cash-poor risks financial, as well as legal, trouble.

- Get outside help if you need it. As just noted, any time your LLC makes a loan, you will want to make sure that it can afford to do so. You should discuss with your tax adviser or business lawyer any special tax or legal or practical considerations that may make a loan problematical. The information in this chapter should help you when seeking this advice.

COURT CASES: WHEN ARE LLC INSIDER LOANS APPROPRIATE?

The LLC is a relatively new type of legal entity, and few court cases have been published that clarify the legal concepts that apply to loans from LLCs. But there are some court cases dealing with corporate loans that help illuminate the standards that probably apply to LLC loans. Generally, the corporate cases say a corporate loan to a corporate insider is legal as long as it benefits the company. A loan benefits the company if it is both commercially reasonable (for example, the LLC lends money at a rate close to banks' lending rates to members for the purchase of laptop computers) and reasonably likely to further its business operations (the members will get more work done if they can use the laptops when working from home or traveling).

Courts have ruled that some loans fall outside the limits of appropriate corporate lending. For example, one court struck down interest-free loans made by a closely held corporation to a director and majority shareholder who admitted he did not intend to repay them. (*Oberhelman v. Barnes Investment Corporation*, 690 P.2d 1343, 236 Kan. 335 (1984).) Another case disallowed loans made by a corporation to the president and majority shareholder because they were made primarily to allow the president to buy additional shares of corporate stock and increase his ownership percentage. (*Milam v. Cooper Co.*, 258 S.W.2d 953 (1953).) Another case set aside an unsecured loan as unfair where it was made to a director at less-than-market interest rates (4%). (*Washington National Trust Co. v. W.M. Dary Co.*, 116 Ariz. 171, 568 P.2d 1069 (1977).) A different case, however, has broadly held that below-market interest rate loans to controlling directors are allowable if there is no evidence that the corporation could have obtained a better return by investing the funds elsewhere. (*Tovrea Land & Cattle Co. v. Linsenmeyer*, 100 Ariz. 107, 412 P.2d 47 (1966).) Again, by analogy, these corporate cases can apply to an LLC's lending as well.

C. TAX CONSIDERATIONS AND CONSEQUENCES OF INSIDER LOANS

A legitimate LLC loan to an insider usually has minimal tax consequences. On the lender's (LLC's) side of the transaction, the LLC does not deduct the disbursement of loan funds from its income, nor does it report the re-payment of principal from the borrower as income. The LLC does, however, report interest it collects from the borrower as income on its LLC tax return. This increases revenue and thereby affects the amount of net income allocated to members at the end of the LLC tax year.

The borrower (member, manager, or officer), similarly, does not report the loan funds as income, since, of course, they must be paid back. And the borrower cannot normally deduct interest payments made on the loan for federal income tax purposes. However, there is a exception if the borrower legitimately uses the income for business or investment purposes (in which case, it's a normal business expense) or secures it with an interest in the borrower's residence. A legitimate loan usually does not affect the borrower's tax basis in his or her membership interest. (But see Section 1, "Illegitimate Member Loans Treated as Distributions of Profit," below).

Interest and federal tax returns
If LLC loan funds secured by a borrower's residence will not be used to purchase or improve a residence (for instance, the member/borrower uses the funds for educational expenses), interest on only the first $100,000 of the loan is deductible. Generally, the interest a borrower pays on a personal loan may be deducted on federal income tax returns if it is secured by the borrower's first or second residence. Interest deductions are itemized on the borrower's 1040 income tax return and are subject to a 2% floor—that is, they can only be deducted in a given tax year to the extent that they exceed 2% of the taxpayer's adjusted gross income. Interest may also be deducted if charged on a loan made for busi-ness or investment by the taxpayer in certain circum-stances. For the latest interest deductibility rules, check IRS publications or ask your tax adviser.

Check tax issues with an expert
No matter how straightforward and sound your LLC loan to an insider may appear to be, you still risk IRS problems. The IRS often scrutinizes insider loans as a part of business audits. In Sections 1 and 2 below, we summarize some tax issues that can arise. But please treat this discussion as an introduc-tion, not a thorough treatment. As always, for au-thoritative tax advice, see your tax adviser. (Chapter 16 discusses finding a tax adviser to work with.)

1. Illegitimate Member Loans Treated as Distributions of Profit

One risk with insider loans is that the IRS might decide that a loan to an LLC member was not a bona fide loan transaction but a distribution of a member's distributive share of LLC profits—in other words, an advance against future LLC profits. If this happens, the member's basis in his or her membership interest would be re-duced by the amount of the loan disbursement.

A reduced basis can lead to several results (as dis-cussed more thoroughly in Chapter 13):

- More taxes are owed when the membership in-terest is sold.

- If the loan amount exceeds the member's basis, the member will have to pay income taxes on the excess.

- In addition, a low basis can limit the amount of LLC losses a member can claim on his or her in-dividual tax return to offset other income.

REVIEW: TAX BASIS OF OWNERSHIP INTERESTS

Tax basis refers to the value assigned to an LLC ownership interest for the purpose of determining the taxable gain or loss from it after it is sold. Basis also determines how much of the LLC's losses a member can claim on an individual tax return to offset other income—a member can only deduct LLC losses up to the amount of the member's basis in his or her interest.

     A member's basis is generally the cash amount a member pays, along with the member's current basis in any property transferred, to buy the membership interest. Over time, a member's original basis in the membership interest is adjusted up and down during the life of the LLC as profits (or losses) are allocated and paid to members and as the LLC's liabilities change. (Allocations of a member's share of profits and losses occur automatically at the end of the LLC tax year, and are called the member's "distributive share" of profits and losses. The percentage of each member's distributive share of profits and losses is set in the LLC operating agreement.)

     Figuring your basis in an LLC membership interest at the time of LLC formation, during the course of its operations, and when a membership interest is sold or the LLC is liquidated is anything but obvious to most of us. This is just one of the important tasks that should be referred to a tax adviser.

To make sure the IRS accepts a loan as a loan, rather than a distribution of profits, the transaction should include as many of the following features as possible (these are the same basic tax guidelines that we mentioned in Chapter 13, Section B2, with respect to loans made by insiders *to* an LLC):

- A promissory note to document the loan. It should state a commercially reasonable rate of interest and a maturity date—either payable on de-

mand by the LLC, or, better yet, at a specific date or in specified installments.

- Formal approval of the loan transaction by the LLC and by all members (even in a manager-managed LLC or in a member-managed LLC managed by less than all members). The transaction should also be documented in LLC minutes or written consents, which are placed in the LLC records binder.

- The debt should be carried on the LLC books and reported on its tax returns as a loan transaction.

- The insider-borrower should make interest and principal payments according to the terms of the note.

- If the note is a demand note (as opposed to one with a due date or payment schedule), demand for payment should be made by the LLC within a reasonable time (two to three years, for instance). In other words, the loan should not be carried on the books indefinitely.

- Repeated loans to members should not be made (and paid off) on a regular schedule. To the IRS, repeated loans to members on a regular basis look more like payments of LLC profits.

- Avoid issuing loans to members in proportion to capital or profits interests in the LLC, which makes the loan transactions look like taxable payments of members' distributive shares of profits.

2. Below-Market Member Loans

Another possible problem the IRS can have with an insider loan is a too-low interest rate. The IRS doesn't like to see LLC loans to insiders that call for inadequate interest, or none at all, for this reason: The IRS loses taxes on interest income that the LLC would normally receive in connection with the loan transaction. As a result, if the IRS determines that the LLC has made this type of loan, called a "below-market loan" under IRC Section 7872, it will tax the borrower on the interest saved.

That is, the borrower will have to pay taxes on the interest he or she would have had to pay on a commercially reasonable loan. Generally, a "below-market" loan is one that carries a rate of interest lower than the "applicable federal rate" in effect at the time the loan is made.

Below-market loans arise mostly in the corporate context where a closely held corporation makes low-interest loans to shareholders instead of reinvesting the money and paying corporate taxes on returns from the investments. But it can also apply to LLCs that devise a clever scheme to lend money at low or no interest to LLC members so that the LLC members can save on taxes.

FEDERAL LOAN RATES

The federal rates are the rates paid by the federal government on borrowed funds. They are set monthly. There are three federal rates: short term for loans with a three-year term or less (or for demand notes that can be called due at any time); mid term for loans from three years to nine years; and long term for loans with a term over nine years.

The applicable federal rates are changed each month, and can be found online at www.irs.gov as the current month's "imputed interest rates" or "AFR rates" (technically called the "applicable federal rates under Section 1274(d) of the Internal Revenue Code"). Major business newspapers also list the current applicable fed rates, typically in their stock quotations section.

You may want to charge competitive interest on insider loans anyway

For business reasons, your LLC may want to charge competitive interest rates on all LLC loans to insiders. For example, your LLC may decide to make an LLC loan to members at the current prime interest rate plus two percentage points to provide your LLC with interest income on the loan amounts and to en-courage a timely payback by borrowing members (the longer they take to repay the loan, the more interest they end up paying to the LLC). Competitive loans made to members are also more likely to be acceptable to nonborrowing members and other LLC principals.

See your tax adviser

We don't belabor this below-market loan area or cover the technical consequences if the IRS finds an insider loan to have too low an interest rate. Just be aware that low-interest loans may be challenged by the IRS in some cases. Ask your tax adviser for guidance if this is a potential tax issue for your LLC.

D. RESOLUTION FOR LLC AND MEMBER APPROVAL OF LLC LOANS TO INSIDERS

As mentioned above, preparing resolutions for insider loan transactions can avoid internal controversy among your members. It is natural that repeated loan transactions between an LLC and a principal member or manager may arouse the curiosity of other LLC insiders, who may wonder if the borrowing member or manager is taking advantage of his or her LLC leverage to get too good a deal on interest and repayment terms. Getting formal approval for these loan transactions can answer nonborrowing members' questions and avoid this type of insider controversy.

Use the following resolution to show approval of a loan made by the LLC to a member, manager, officer, employee, or other LLC insider. To summarize: If you can, get the approval of all managers (in a manager-managed LLC) and all members (in both manager- and member-managed LLCs) who are not borrowing money from the LLC. In all cases, make sure that the LLC can afford to make the loan and that the loan terms are fair to the LLC. Use a commercially reasonable rate of interest and repayment schedule.

Fill in the resolution as you follow the sample and special instructions below. You'll find this resolution on the CD-ROM and as a tear-out form in Appendix D. (See Appendix A for information on selecting and using the CD-ROM files.)

APPROVAL OF LLC LOAN TO INSIDER

It was resolved it is in the best interests of the LLC to make the following loan to the following persons under the following terms:

Name and Title of Borrower: __[name and title of member, manager, officer, employee, or other individual who is borrowing the funds]__

Principal Amount of Loan: $ __[principal amount of the loan—or refer to promissory note: "see attached note for terms of loan" and leave all loan terms below blank]__ ❶

Rate of Interest: __[interest rate]__ %

Term of Loan: __[number of months or years if the loan has a set term, or "payable on demand by LLC" if it's a demand loan]__

Payment Schedule: __[number and amount of payments (whether they consist of interest only or principal and interest) and date and amount of final payment]__ ❷

It was further resolved that the above loan could reasonably be expected to benefit the LLC and that the LLC would be able to make the loan without jeopardizing its financial position, including its ability to pay its bills as they become due.

Therefore, the LLC approved the terms of the note and directed the borrower to sign the note. The secretary was directed to attach a copy of the note, signed by the borrower, to this resolution and to place the resolution and the attachment(s) in the LLC records binder.

Special Instructions

❶ You may insert the specific terms of the loan in the blanks, or you can simply refer to the terms of the promissory note that you complete and attach to your resolution. (Promissory notes are discussed in Section E, below.) If you refer to the promissory note, either leave all loan terms blank or delete them from the resolution.

❷ Here's an example of a repayment schedule for a five-year $10,000 member loan carried at a 7% annual interest rate: "Four interest-only payments of $700 shall be made on June 15 of each year, starting on June 15, 2011. The fifth annual payment shall be made on June 15, 2015, consisting of $700 in remaining accrued but unpaid interest, plus the full amount of the unpaid principal of $10,000, for a total final payment of $10,700." For further examples of repayment options and terms, as well as an amortization table, see Chapter 13, Sections C and D.

E. PROMISSORY NOTES FOR LOANS BY LLC

We recommend that you prepare a promissory note for each loan transaction and attach it to your LLC resolution approving the loan. Doing this records the terms of the loan and can be used to help convince the IRS and others that the loan was a bona fide business transaction between the LLC and its member, manager, officer, or employee.

In the sections below, we discuss the variety of promissory notes included with this book that can be used to document the terms of LLC loans to insiders. These forms are similar to the promissory notes covered in Chapter 13 for loans to the LLC by insiders. However, key wording, instructions, and commentary are a bit different, since the underlying loan transaction is reversed here. For example, instead of being titled "LLC Promissory Notes," the notes below are entitled "Individual Promissory Notes"—that is, they are signed by individual persons, not the LLC.

All promissory note forms in this section allow two borrowers to sign for the loan. Normally, two borrowers will only take out the same loan when they are spouses, who are jointly liable for repayment of the note. This means that, if there is a default, the LLC may seek to collect against either spouse for the full amount owed under the note. By doing this, each borrower agrees to the repayment obligation—something that can avoid later legal complications should there be a default, a dissolution of marriage, or other change in the spouses' legal status. If the borrower is unmarried, the person signs the note alone.

To select a note appropriate for your situation, scan the promissory notes that follow and choose one that suits the lending arrangement at hand. Most of the notes are self-explanatory, but we include additional information as needed in instructions below each note. (For additional background information on the various loan repayment terms reflected in the notes below, see Chapter 13, Sections C and D.)

OUR PROMISSORY NOTES USE SIMPLE INTEREST

The loans provided in this chapter call for simple, rather than compound, interest. With simple interest, interest is charged on the remaining unpaid principal due under the note, but not on any unpaid interest that accumulates during the term of the loan.

As a practical matter, compound interest is usually not necessary for LLC loans to insiders, anyway. If the loan is paid off in installments, the borrower will usually pay off all accrued interest. For long-term loans that don't call for any payments for quite a while (perhaps a year or more), it's possible to compound the interest due, although most smaller LLCs won't choose to do so. If you want to figure out compound interest, you may use a future value table; check with your tax adviser, bank, or real estate broker.

---

1. Individual Promissory Note: Installment Payments of Principal and Interest (Amortized Loan)

Let's start with the most familiar note form, which provides for the regular payments of principal plus interest over the term of the loan. Typically, payments are scheduled to be made monthly, but you can decide on any payment plan you wish.

 Fill in the note as you follow the sample and special instructions below. You'll find this resolution on the CD-ROM and as a tear-out form in Appendix D. (See Appendix A for information on selecting and using the CD-ROM files.)

INDIVIDUAL PROMISSORY NOTE:
INSTALLMENT PAYMENTS OF PRINCIPAL
AND INTEREST (AMORTIZED LOAN)

For value received, _____ [name of member, manager, officer, employee, or other individual (plus name of spouse if the LLC borrower is married)]_____ , the borrower(s), promise(s) to pay to the order of _____[name of LLC]_____ , the noteholder, the principal amount of $__[principal amount of loan]__ , together with simple interest on the unpaid principal balance from the date of this note until the date this note is paid in full, at the annual rate of __[annual rate of interest]__%. Payments will be made at _____[address of LLC]_____ .

    Principal and interest will be paid in equal installments of $__[amount of each payment]__ , beginning on __[date of first payment]__ , and continuing on __[day for ongoing payments, for example, "the fifteenth day of each month"]__ until the principal and interest are paid in full. Each payment made by the borrower(s) will be applied first to accrued but unpaid interest, and the remainder will be applied to unpaid principal. ❶

    This note may be prepaid by the borrower(s) in whole or in part at any time without penalty. This note is not assumable without the written consent of the noteholder. Consent will not be unreasonably withheld. This note is nontransferable by the noteholder. ❷

    If any installment payment due under this note is not received by the noteholder within __[number of days]__ of its due date, the entire amount of unpaid principal and accrued but unpaid interest due under this note will, at the option of the noteholder, become immediately due and payable without prior notice by the noteholder to the borrower(s). In the event of a default, the borrower(s) is/are responsible for the costs of collection, including, in the event of a lawsuit to collect on this note, the noteholder's reasonable attorney fees as determined by a court hearing the lawsuit.

    If two persons sign below, each is jointly and severally liable for repayment of this note. ❸

Name of Borrower #1:

_____

Address: _____

City, or County, and State Where Signed: _____

Date of Signing: _____

Name of Borrower #2:

_____

Address: _____

City, or County, and State Where Signed: _____

Date of Signing: _____

Special Instructions

❶ For instructions on computing the amount of installment payments due under your note, see Chapter 13, Section C3.

❷ This paragraph specifies that the loan may be repaid by the borrower at any time without triggering a prepayment penalty. This allows the borrower to pay off the loan at any time. The loan is assumable (meaning another company or person can take over the payment obligation for the borrower) with the permission of the noteholder (the LLC), but it is unlikely that another person will wish to assume payments under the loan. Finally, the note is nontransferable—the LLC may not transfer the note to another company or person to collect payments from the borrower. This provision is customary for loans from a small LLC. You can easily change this sentence to allow transfers if you wish, though it's highly unlikely that anyone would wish to buy this type of note anyway, even at a discount.

❸ The borrower should complete and sign the first set of signature lines. If the borrower is married, the spouse should complete and sign the second set; otherwise, it should be deleted.

2. Individual Promissory Note: Installment Payments of Principal and Interest (Amortized Loan) Secured by Property

This promissory note is the same as the previous note but adds a clause that secures the loan with the borrower's real estate or personal property.

💡 How to use the security clause in other note forms

To allow the borrower to pledge property as security for the repayment of a different type of note, you may copy the security clause in this note—the last paragraph in the text of the note shown below—to any of the other note forms covered below.

Fill in the note as you follow the sample and special instructions below. You'll find this resolution on the CD-ROM and as a tear-out form in Appendix D. (See Appendix A for information on selecting and using the CD-ROM files.)

INDIVIDUAL PROMISSORY NOTE:
INSTALLMENT PAYMENTS OF PRINCIPAL AND INTEREST
(AMORTIZED LOAN) SECURED BY PROPERTY

For value received, _____ [name of member, manager, officer, employee, or other individual (plus name of spouse if LLC person is married)] _____ , the borrower(s), promise(s) to pay to the order of _____ [name of LLC] _____ , the noteholder, the principal amount of $ [principal amount of loan] , together with simple interest on the unpaid principal balance from the date of this note until the date this note is paid in full, at the annual rate of ___ [annual rate of interest] ___%. Payments will be made at _____ [address of LLC] _____ .

   Principal and interest will be paid in equal installments of $ [amount of each payment] , ❶ beginning on ___ [date of first payment] ___ , and continuing on ___ [day for ongoing payments, for example, "the fifteenth day of each month"] ___ until the principal and interest are paid in full. Each payment made by the borrower(s) will be applied first to accrued but unpaid interest, and the remainder will be applied to unpaid principal.

   This note may be prepaid by the borrower(s) in whole or in part at any time without penalty. This note is not assumable without the written consent of the noteholder. Consent will not be unreasonably withheld. This note is nontransferable by the noteholder. ❷

   If any installment payment due under this note is not received by the noteholder within __ [number of days] __ of its due date, the entire amount of unpaid principal and accrued but unpaid interest of the loan will, at the option of the noteholder, become immediately due and payable without prior notice by the noteholder to the borrower(s). In the event of a default, the borrower(s) is/are responsible for the costs of collection, including, in the event of a lawsuit to collect on this note, the noteholder's reasonable attorney fees as determined by a court hearing the lawsuit.

   Borrower(s) agree(s) that until such time as the principal and interest owed under this note are paid in full, the note will be secured by the following described mortgage, deed of trust, or security agreement: __ [describe security agreement, deed of trust, or mortgage used to pledge security of the property, including a description of the property] __ . ❸

   If two persons sign below, each is jointly and severally liable for repayment of this note. ❹

Name of Borrower #1: _____

Address: _____

City, or County, and State Where Signed: _____

Date of Signing: _____

Name of Borrower #2: _____

Address: _____

City, or County, and State Where Signed: _____

Date of Signing: _____

Special Instructions

❶ For instructions on computing the amount of installment payments due under your note, see Chapter 13, Section C3.

❷ This paragraph specifies that the loan may be repaid by the borrower at any time without triggering a prepayment penalty. This allows the borrower to pay off the loan at any time. The loan is assumable (meaning another company or person can take over the payment obligation for the borrower) with the permission of the noteholder (the LLC), but it is unlikely that another person will wish to assume payments under the loan. Finally, the note is nontransferable—the LLC may not transfer the note to another company or person to collect payments from the borrower. This provision is customary for loans from a small LLC. You can easily change this sentence to allow transfers if you wish, though it's highly unlikely that anyone would wish to buy this type of note anyway, even at a discount.

❸ This is the security clause. (For general information, see Chapter 13, Section C4.) Specify the security agreement used to pledge the property as repayment for the loan in case of default, together with a description of the property. Again, for real estate, you will want to complete and record a mortgage deed or deed of trust with the county recorder. For personal property, under state law you may need to complete and file a security agreement to enforce the security clause in your note. A legal forms stationer may have security agreements on hand, or you can contact a real estate broker, tax adviser, or lawyer to obtain these forms and/or have them prepared for you. Attach a completed copy of the security document to the resolution.

Example (Real Estate Used as Security):
"Deed of Trust to real property commonly known as _____[address]_____ , owned by _____[name of borrower(s)]_____ , executed on _[date of signing of deed of trust]_ , at _____[city and state where signed]_____ , and recorded at ____[place recorded]____ , in the records of ____[name of recording office]____ , ____[name of county and state]____ ."

Example (Automobile Used as Security):
"Security Agreement signed by _____[name of borrower(s)]_____ , on _____[date of signing]____ , pledging title to ____[make and model and year of automobile with Vehicle ID #]____ ."

❹ The borrower should complete and sign the first set of signature lines. If the borrower is married, the spouse should complete and sign the second set; otherwise, it can be deleted.

3. Individual Promissory Note: Installment Payments of Principal and Interest (Amortized Loan) With Balloon Payment

The next promissory note differs from the standard amortized note (covered in Section 1, above) by requiring a "balloon payment" to be made at the end of the repayment term. A balloon payment is a complete payoff of all remaining principal on a specified installment date, one that's prior to the date the loan would normally be paid off by regular installment payments. Use this note if the lender wishes to receive regular payments of principal and interest for a period of time, but then wants full repayment of principal on a particular future date. You will need to use an amortization guide that includes a remaining loan balance table, which will allow you to calculate the amount of the balloon payment. (See the special instructions to the note form, below.) For more information on computing the balloon payment amount, see Chapter 13, Section D3.

Fill in the note as you follow the sample and special instructions below. You'll find this resolution on the CD-ROM and as a tear-out form in Appendix D. (See Appendix A for information on selecting and using the CD-ROM files.)

INDIVIDUAL PROMISSORY NOTE:
INSTALLMENT PAYMENTS OF PRINCIPAL AND INTEREST
(AMORTIZED LOAN) WITH BALLOON PAYMENT

For value received,_____ [name of member, manager, officer, employee, or other individual (plus name of spouse if LLC person is married)]_____ , the borrower(s), promise(s) to pay to the order of _____ [name of LLC] _____ , the noteholder, the principal amount of $____ [principal amount of loan]___ , together with simple interest on the unpaid principal balance from the date of this note until the date this note is paid in full, at the annual rate of ____ [annual rate of interest]_____ %. Payments will be made at _____ [address of LLC] _____ .

    Principal and interest will be paid in equal installments of $ ___ [amount of each payment]___ , beginning on ___ [date of first payment]___ , and continuing on ___ [day for ongoing payments, for example, "the fifteenth day of each month"]___ . On the installment payment date on ___ [date of final (balloon) payment]___ , a balloon payment of $___ [amount of remaining principal owed on the loan on final installment date]___ ❶ will be added to the installment amount paid by the borrower in order to pay off this note in its entirety on this final installment payment date. Each payment made by the borrower(s) will be applied first to accrued but unpaid interest, and the remainder will be applied to unpaid principal.

    This note may be prepaid by the borrower(s) in whole or in part at any time without penalty. This note is not assumable without the written consent of the noteholder. Consent will not be unreasonably withheld. This note is nontransferable by the noteholder. ❷

    If any installment payment due under this note is not received by the noteholder within ___ [number of days]___ of its due date, the entire amount of unpaid principal and accrued but unpaid interest of the loan will, at the option of the noteholder, become immediately due and payable without prior notice by the noteholder to the borrower(s). In the event of a default, the borrower(s) is/are responsible for the costs of collection, including, in the event of a lawsuit to collect on this note, the noteholder's reasonable attorney fees as determined by a court hearing the lawsuit.

    If two persons sign below, each is jointly and severally liable for repayment of this note. ❸

Name of Borrower #1: _____

Address: _____

City, or County, and State Where Signed: _____

Date of Signing: _____

Name of Borrower #2: _____

Address: _____

City, or County, and State Where Signed: _____

Date of Signing: _____

Special Instructions

❶ For instructions on computing the balloon payment, see the special instructions in Chapter 13, Section D3.

❷ This paragraph specifies that the loan may be repaid by the borrower at any time without triggering a prepayment penalty. This allows the borrower to pay off the loan at any time. The loan is assumable (meaning another company or person can take over the payment obligation for the borrower) with the permission of the noteholder (the LLC), but it is unlikely that another person will wish to assume payments under the loan. Finally, the note is nontransferable—the LLC may not transfer the note to another company or person to collect payments from the borrower. This provision is customary for loans from a small LLC. You can easily change this sentence to allow transfers if you wish, though it's highly unlikely that anyone would wish to buy this type of note anyway, even at a discount.

❸ The borrower should complete and sign the first set of signature lines. If the borrower is married, the spouse should complete and sign the second set; otherwise, it should be deleted.

4. Individual Promissory Note: Periodic Payments of Interest Only With Lump-Sum Principal Payment

This promissory note provides for regular payments of interest only for a designated period, to be followed by a lump-sum payment of the entire principal amount of the loan. This form of loan makes sense if the loan amount is not excessive and the borrower can come up with the entire principal at the end of the loan period. For more information on this type of payment plan, see Chapter 13, Section C2.

> **EXAMPLE:** Frank's LLC lends him $10,000 at a 7.5% rate for five years. The LLC uses the amortization table in Chapter 13, Section C3, to calculate that the total interest owed by Frank for these funds will be $3,750 ($10,000 x .075 x 5). The amount of each monthly interest installment under the note is thus $62.50 (total interest for the five-year loan period— $3,750—divided by the 60 installments made in this period). At the end of the five-year period during which Frank pays monthly interest only, Frank must pay the LLC the entire $10,000 amount.

Fill in the note as you follow the sample and special instructions below. You'll find this resolution on the CD-ROM and as a tear-out form in Appendix D. (See Appendix A for information on selecting and using the CD-ROM files.)

INDIVIDUAL PROMISSORY NOTE:
PERIODIC PAYMENTS OF INTEREST
WITH LUMP-SUM PRINCIPAL PAYMENT

For value received,_____ [name of member, manager, officer, employee, or other individual (plus name of spouse if LLC person is married)]_____ , the borrower(s), promise(s) to pay to the order of _____ [name of LLC]_____ , the noteholder, the principal amount of $ [principal amount of loan] , together with simple interest on the unpaid principal balance from the date of this note until the date this note is paid in full, at the annual rate of [annual rate of interest] %. Payments will be made at _____ [address of LLC]_____ .

Interest will be paid in equal installments of $ [amount of each payment] , beginning on [date of first payment] , and continuing on [day for ongoing payments, for example, "the fifteenth day of each month"] until [ending date of loan period] , on which date the entire principal amount, together with total accrued but unpaid interest, will be paid by the borrower(s). ❶

This note may be prepaid by the borrower(s) in whole or in part at any time without penalty. This note is not assumable without the written consent of the noteholder. Consent will not be unreasonably withheld. This note is nontransferable by the noteholder. ❷

If any installment payment due under this note is not received by the noteholder within [number of days] of its due date, the entire amount of unpaid principal and accrued but unpaid interest of the loan will, at the option of the noteholder, become immediately due and payable without prior notice by the noteholder to the borrower(s). In the event of a default, the borrower(s) is/are responsible for the costs of collection, including, in the event of a lawsuit to collect on this note, the noteholder's reasonable attorney fees as determined by a court hearing the lawsuit.

If two persons sign below, each is jointly and severally liable for repayment of this note. ❸

Name of Borrower #1: _____

Address: _____

City, or County, and State Where Signed: _____

Date of Signing: _____

Name of Borrower #2: _____

Address: _____

City, or County, and State Where Signed: _____

Date of Signing: _____

Special Instructions

❶ For instructions on computing the interest-only payments, see the special instructions in Chapter 13, Section D4.

❷ This paragraph specifies that the loan may be repaid by the borrower at any time without triggering a prepayment penalty. This allows the borrower to pay off the loan at any time. The loan is assumable (meaning another company or person can take over the payment obligation for the borrower) with the permission of the noteholder (the LLC), but it is unlikely that another person will wish to assume payments under the loan. Finally, the note is nontransferable—the LLC may not transfer the note to another company or person to collect payments from the borrower. This provision is customary for loans from a small LLC. You can easily change this sentence to allow transfers if you wish, though it's highly unlikely that anyone would wish to buy this type of note anyway, even at a discount.

❸ The borrower should complete and sign the first set of signature lines. If the borrower is married, the spouse should complete and sign the second set; otherwise, it should be deleted.

5. Individual Promissory Note: Lump-Sum Payment of Principal and Interest on Specified Date

This promissory note is similar to the previous note in that the entire amount of principal is paid in one lump sum at the end of the loan period. However, unlike the previous note, where interest payments are made in installments during the loan period, here the entire interest amount is paid along with the entire principal amount in one lump sum at the end of the loan term. For more information on this type of payment plan, see Chapter 13, Section C1.

> **EXAMPLE:** Rosie borrows $10,000 for three years at 9% interest from her LLC. Using the amortization table in Chapter 13, Section C3, above, to calculate the total interest owed by Rosie for these funds, a one-time payment of $12,700 in ($10,000 principal plus the entire $2,700 interest) is due at the end of the three-year loan term.

Fill in the note as you follow the sample and special instructions below. You'll find this resolution on the CD-ROM and as a tear-out form in Appendix D. (See Appendix A for information on selecting and using the CD-ROM files.)

**INDIVIDUAL PROMISSORY NOTE:
LUMP-SUM PAYMENT OF PRINCIPAL
AND INTEREST ON SPECIFIED DATE**

For value received,_____ [name of member, manager, officer, employee, or other individual (plus name of spouse if LLC person is married)]_____, the borrower(s), promise(s) to pay to the order of _____ [name of LLC]_____ , the noteholder, the principal amount of $__ [principal amount of loan]__ , together with simple interest on the unpaid principal balance from the date of this note until the date this note is paid in full, at the annual rate of [annual rate of interest] %. Payments will be made at _____ [address of LLC]_____

The entire principal amount of the loan, together with total accrued but unpaid interest, will be paid by the borrower(s) on __ [due date for payment of all principal and interest]__ . Any payment made by the borrower(s) prior to the due date specified above will be applied first to accrued but unpaid interest, and the remainder will be applied to unpaid principal.

This note may be prepaid by the borrower(s) in whole or in part at any time without penalty. This note is not assumable without the written consent of the noteholder. Consent will not be unreasonably withheld. This note is nontransferable by the noteholder. ❶

In the event of a default, the borrower(s) is/are responsible for the costs of collection, including, in the event of a lawsuit to collect on this note, the noteholder's reasonable attorney fees as determined by a court hearing the lawsuit.

If two persons sign below, each is jointly and severally liable for repayment of this note.❷

Name of Borrower #1: _____

Address: _____

City, or County, and State Where Signed: _____

Date of Signing: _____

Name of Borrower #2: _____

Address: _____

City, or County, and State Where Signed: _____

Date of Signing: _____

Special Instructions

❶ This paragraph specifies that the loan may be repaid by the borrower at any time without triggering a prepayment penalty. This allows the borrower to pay off the loan at any time. The loan is assumable (meaning another company or person can take over the payment obligation for the borrower) with the permission of the noteholder (the LLC), but it is unlikely that another person will wish to assume payments under the loan. Finally, the note is nontransferable—the LLC may not transfer the note to another company or person to collect payments from the borrower. This provision is customary for loans from a small LLC. You can easily change this sentence to allow transfers if you wish, though it's highly unlikely that anyone would wish to buy this type of note anyway, even at a discount.

❷ The borrower should complete and sign the first set of signature lines. If the borrower is married, the spouse should complete and sign the second set; otherwise, it should be deleted.

6. Individual Promissory Note: Lump-Sum Payment of Principal and Interest on Demand by Noteholder

Here is a "demand note" that allows the noteholder (LLC) to call the note due at any time. Rather than specifying a particular date in the future for repayment, the LLC is given the power to call the loan due and payable by making a written demand for payment. Obviously, you want to be sure the borrower has sufficient cash resources to comply with a demand for repayment prior to making a loan of this sort. Make sure to call any demand loans you make to members within a reasonable period of making the loan. If you don't, and the IRS audits your LLC, it is likely to claim that the demand loans were really a distribution of profits to a member (See Section C1, above.)

Fill in the note as you follow the sample and special instructions below. You'll find this resolution on the CD-ROM and as a tear-out form in Appendix D. (See Appendix A for information on selecting and using the CD-ROM files.)

INDIVIDUAL PROMISSORY NOTE:
LUMP-SUM PAYMENT OF PRINCIPAL AND INTEREST
ON DEMAND BY NOTEHOLDER

For value received, _____ [name of member, manager, officer, employee, or other individual (plus name of spouse if LLC person is married)] _____ , the borrower(s), promise(s) to pay to the order of _____ [name of LLC] _____ , the noteholder, the principal amount of $__ [principal amount of loan]__ , together with simple interest on the unpaid principal balance from the date of this note until the date this note is paid in full, at the annual rate of [annual rate of interest] %. Payments will be made at _____ [address of LLC] _____ .

The entire principal amount of the loan, together with total accrued but unpaid interest, will be paid within __[period, for example "30 days or other period agreeable to the LLC and borrower"]__ of receipt by the borrower(s) of a demand for repayment by the noteholder. A demand for repayment by the noteholder will be made in writing and delivered or mailed to the borrower(s) at the following address: _____ [address of borrower(s)] _____ . If demand for repayment is mailed, it will be considered received by the borrower(s) on the third business day after the date when it was deposited in the U.S. mail as registered or certified mail.

Any payment made by the borrower(s) prior to the due date specified above will be applied first to accrued but unpaid interest, and the remainder will be applied to unpaid principal.

This note may be prepaid by the borrower(s) in whole or in part at any time without penalty. This note is not assumable without the written consent of the noteholder. Consent will not be unreasonably withheld. This note is nontransferable by the noteholder. ❶

In the event of a default, the borrower(s) is/are responsible for the costs of collection, including, in the event of a lawsuit to collect on this note, the noteholder's reasonable attorney fees as determined by a court hearing the lawsuit.

If two persons sign below, each is jointly and severally liable for repayment of this note. ❷

Name of Borrower #1: _____

Address: _____

City, or County, and State Where Signed: _____

Date of Signing: _____

Name of Borrower #2: _____

Address: _____

City, or County, and State Where Signed: _____

Date of Signing: _____

Special Instructions

❶ This paragraph specifies that the loan may be repaid by the borrower at any time without triggering a prepayment penalty. This allows the borrower to pay off the loan at any time. The loan is assumable (meaning another company or person can take over the payment obligation for the borrower) with the permission of the noteholder (the LLC), but it is unlikely that another person will wish to assume payments under the loan. Finally, the note is nontransferable—the LLC may not transfer the note to another company or person to collect payments from the borrower. This provision is customary for loans from a small LLC. You can easily change this sentence to allow transfers if you wish, though it's highly unlikely that anyone would wish to buy this type of note anyway, even at a discount.

❷ The borrower should complete and sign the first set of signature lines. If the borrower is married, the spouse should complete and sign the second set; otherwise, it should be deleted.

7. Individual Promissory Note: Special Schedule of Payments of Principal and Interest

This promissory note allows you to specify a special (nonuniform) schedule for repayments of principal and interest under the loan. Typically, the schedule will require principal and/or interest payments of unequal amounts and at irregular intervals during the life of the note, ending with a final payment of principal and all accrued and unpaid interest due.

⚠ You can make your own payment arrangements, but make sure to include interest

Remember, we assume all loans will make provisions for the payment of interest on the borrowed funds, unless, of course, you are purposely setting up a no-interest loan program. If you are, watch out for the below-market loan rules—see Section C2, above, and check with your tax adviser.

The options here are unlimited; but here's one example.

EXAMPLE: On July 1, Hamid's LLC lends him $10,000 for five years at 8% interest. They agree that Hamid will not make payments until the end of the second year. Using the amortization table in Chapter 13, Section C3, Hamid calculates that he'll pay $1,600 in interest-only payments for the first two years of the loan ($10,000 x .08 x 2). Hamid will make an interest-only payment of $800 at the end of the third year. At the end of the fourth year, he will make an $800 interest payment, along with a payment of $4,000 in principal, leaving a principal balance of $6,000. Finally, at the end of the fifth year, Hamid will make his last payment, which consists of the balance of the $6,000 principal along with $480 in interest ($6,000 x .08). Here is the special repayment schedule:

June 31, 2nd year	$1,600	(interest)
June 31, 3rd year	$800	(interest)
June 31, 4th year	$4,800	($4,000 principal; $800 interest)
June 31, 5th year	$6,480	($6,000 principal; $480 interest)
Total Payments	$13,680	($10,000 principal; $3,680 interest)

Fill in the note as you follow the sample and special instructions below. You'll find this resolution on the CD-ROM and as a tear-out form in Appendix D. (See Appendix A for information on selecting and using the CD-ROM files.)

INDIVIDUAL PROMISSORY NOTE:
SPECIAL SCHEDULE OF PAYMENTS
OF PRINCIPAL AND INTEREST

For value received,_____ [name of member, manager, officer, employee, or other individual (plus name of spouse if LLC person is married)]_____ , the borrower(s), promise(s) to pay to the order of _____ [name of LLC] _____ , the noteholder, the principal amount of $__ [principal amount of loan]__ , together with simple interest on the unpaid principal balance from the date of this note until the date this note is paid in full, at the annual rate of _[annual rate of interest]_ %. Payments will be made at _____ [address of LLC] _____ .

Principal and interest will be paid as follows:

___ [Include schedule of payments here. For last payment, you can insert the following: "The borrower(s) will make a final payment in the amount of all remaining principal and all accrued but unpaid interest on (date)."]___

This note may be prepaid by the borrower(s) in whole or in part at any time without penalty. This note is not assumable without the written consent of the noteholder. Consent will not be unreasonably withheld. This note is nontransferable by the noteholder. ❶

If any installment payment due under this note is not received by the noteholder within __[number of days]__ of its due date, the entire amount of unpaid principal and accrued but unpaid interest of the loan will, at the option of the noteholder, become immediately due and payable without prior notice by the noteholder to the borrower(s). In the event of a default, the borrower(s) will be responsible for the costs of collection, including, in the event of a lawsuit to collect on this note, the noteholder's reasonable attorney fees as determined by a court hearing the lawsuit.

If two persons sign below, each is jointly and severally liable for repayment of this note. ❷

Name of Borrower #1: _____

Address: _____

City, or County, and State Where Signed: _____

Date of Signing: _____

Name of Borrower #2: _____

Address: _____

City, or County, and State Where Signed: _____

Date of Signing: _____

Special Instructions

❶ This paragraph specifies that the loan may be repaid by the borrower at any time without triggering a prepayment penalty. This allows the borrower to pay off the loan at any time. The loan is assumable (meaning another company or person can take over the payment obligation for the borrower) with the permission of the noteholder (the LLC), but it is unlikely that another person will wish to assume payments under the loan. Finally, the note is nontransferable—the LLC may not transfer the note to another company or person to collect payments from the borrower. This provision is customary for loans from a small LLC. You can easily change this sentence to allow transfers if you wish, though it's highly unlikely that anyone would wish to buy this type of note anyway, even at a discount.

❷ The borrower should complete and sign the first set of signature lines. If the borrower is married, the spouse should complete and sign the second set; otherwise, it should be deleted.

F. RELEASE OF PROMISSORY NOTE

The next form can be used to show that a promissory note has been paid in full. A borrowing member or other LLC insider will usually want the LLC to fill out this release when the final payment has been received. When this occurs, the LLC should fill in and sign and date the form. The promissory note also should be marked "paid in full" by the LLC and attached to the release form. Copies of both should be placed in the LLC records binder. You also should record the release if the loan was secured by property and a security interest document, such as a deed of trust, was recorded for the loan transaction.

Fill in the note as you follow the sample and special instructions below. You'll find this resolution on the CD-ROM and as a tear-out form in Appendix D. (See Appendix A for information on selecting and using the CD-ROM files.)

RELEASE OF PROMISSORY NOTE

The undersigned noteholder, __[name and address of noteholder]__ , in consideration of full payment of the promissory note dated __[date of note]__ in the principal amount of $__[principal amount of note]__ , hereby releases and discharges the borrower(s), _____[name of borrower(s)]_____ , _____[address of borrower(s)]_____ , from any claims or obligations on account of the note.

Dated: _____

Name of Noteholder: _____

Signature: _____

[If the LLC is the noteholder, use the following signature lines instead:]

Name of Noteholder: _____[name of LLC]_____

By: _____[signature of treasurer]_____ , Treasurer

on behalf of _____[name of LLC]_____

Releases usually requested by borrowing members only

Note that we did not provide a Release of Promissory Note form in Chapter 13, for loans from an LLC insider to the LLC. That's because when an LLC borrows money from members and pays it back, the LLC normally will not request the noteholder to sign a release. ■

CHAPTER 15

Self-Interested Business Dealings Between the LLC and Its Members or Managers

A general principle of LLC law is that LLC members and managers must not advance their own personal interests at the expense of the LLC. This does not mean that a member or manager can't take part in any deal that benefits him or her personally. The key here is that a member or manager who is considering such a deal must disclose all the facts surrounding the deal to LLC comembers and/or managers, who must approve it. This chapter includes a resolution that the members and/or managers can use to approve an LLC business deal that may benefit a particular member or manager.

→ Formal approval of this sort is normally not necessary for one-owner or spousal-owned LLCs. If you have a single-member LLC, you can skip this chapter.

Approval can legally validate LLC business that benefits a member or manager and can help head off later conflict by disclosing upfront any personal financial benefit a member or manager stands to gain by doing business with the LLC.

Who approves self-interested business resolutions?

As discussed below, the self-interested business resolution presented in this chapter should be approved, if possible, by a disinterested majority of the LLC members (in a member-managed LLC) or a disinterested majority of LLC managers (in a manager-managed LLC). By a "disinterested majority," we mean by a majority of the group of members or managers who do not stand to derive a direct personal financial benefit from the business deal in question. If this isn't possible because most or all of the members or managers will benefit from the proposed business deal with the LLC, make sure you can show that the deal is fair and in the best interests of the LLC. Our resolution helps you make this showing.

For an important or potentially controversial deal, you may wish to seek approval of *all members* (if your LLC is either managed by managers or is member-managed by less than all members).

How to Select and Use LLC Resolutions

- Scan the table of contents at the beginning of the chapter to find resolutions of interest to you.

- When you find one you need, read the background material that precedes the pertinent LLC resolution.

- Follow the instructions included with the sample resolution to complete a draft of the resolution using your computer. If you need guidance on selecting and using the computer disk files, see Appendix A. (You'll have to fill in the tear-out resolution included in Appendix D if you don't have a computer.)

- Complete any needed attachment forms.

- If a resolution involves complex issues that will benefit from expert analysis, have your legal or tax adviser review your paperwork and conclusions.

- Prepare minutes of meeting or written consent forms as explained in Chapters 5–7, and insert the completed resolution in the appropriate form.

- Have the LLC secretary sign the printed minutes or have members and/or managers sign any written consent forms and waivers. Then place the signed forms, together with any attachments, in your LLC records binder.

A. Legal Duties Owed by Members and Managers

Let's start by looking at the legal duties LLC members and managers owe to their LLC. These duties apply to members who manage a member-managed LLC or to the managers of a manager-managed LLC. (Note that nonmanaging members of an LLC generally do not owe any statutory duty to their LLC, since they do not manage its affairs!)

1. Duties of Care and Loyalty

What are the duties of managing members or managers? The answer to this question is governed by state statutes, which try to define the duties of "care" or "loyalty" owed by LLC members or managers. These statutes vary from state to state. Most of them are couched in general terms, but their thrust is clear: LLC members and managers must deal honestly with the LLC and not use it as a vehicle to advance their own personal interests over the business interests of the LLC and the other members. Similarly, LLC members and managers must act based on sound business principles and with at least some attention to detail. While honest mistakes in business judgment are legally allowed, extremely sloppy, reckless, or unlawful decision making by a member or manager can result in personal liability.

> **EXAMPLE:** Ward, in his capacity as LLC manager, receives a call from an executive of an outside company asking about the availability of merchandise sold by the LLC. Rather than pass the request through normal LLC channels, Ward decides to broker the deal personally, giving the client a reduced contract price for the merchandise, with Ward secretly pocketing a 10% commission. Obviously, this deal is shady from a moral and honest business perspective. It also fails to meet the standard duty of loyalty that a managing LLC member or a manager owes to the company. Ward can be held personally liable to the LLC and its other members for the amount of his commission, plus any additional amount the LLC lost on the deal, plus interest.

Here is a typical state statute setting out an LLC member's duties of care and loyalty, taken from the Alabama LLC Act.

Alabama LLC Act, Section 10-12-21

[...]

(e) In a limited liability company managed by its members [...], the only fiduciary duties a member owes to the company or to its other members are the duty of loyalty and the duty of care imposed by sections (f) and (g).

(f) A member's duty of loyalty to a member-managed limited liability company and its members is limited to each of the following:

(1) To account to the limited liability company and to hold as trustee for it any property, profit, or benefit derived by the member in the conduct or winding up of the limited liability company's business or derived from a use by the member of the limited liability company's property, including the appropriation of the limited liability company's opportunity.

(2) To refrain from dealing with the limited liability company in the conduct or winding up of the limited liability company's business as or on behalf of a party having an interest adverse to the limited liability company.

(3) To refrain from competing with the limited liability company in the conduct of the limited liability company's business before the dissolution of the limited liability company.

(g) A member's duty of care to a member-managed limited liability company and its other members in the conduct or winding up of the limited liability company's business is limited to refraining from engaging in grossly negligent or reckless conduct, intentional misconduct, or a knowing violation of law.

2. Approval of Self-Serving Business by Members or Managers

The duties of care and loyalty owed by a managing LLC member or manager are not necessarily violated if, in the course of managing LLC business, a member or manager approves a business deal that gives him or her a personal financial benefit. For example, Ward in the previous example would not have compromised his duties of care and loyalty to the LLC if he had fully disclosed his proposed commission deal to the exec of the outside company and to his comanagers, who felt that the LLC would benefit in the longterm by allowing Ward a personal incentive to broker the deal with the outside company.

In fact, it is common for LLC members and managers to accept an LLC business deal that, as a side effect, produces a personal financial benefit for one or more of the members or managers. Some states (as part of their LLC statutes that define the duties of care and loyalty owed by a member or manager) use the following or similar wording, which makes it clear that members or managers may approve business in which they have a financial stake. (The sample wording, taken from Section 180/15-3 of the Illinois LLC Act, applies to members of a member-managed LLC, but Illinois and other states go on to say in their statutes that the rule also applies to managers of a manager-managed LLC).

Illinois LLC Act, 180/15-3

[…]

   (e) A member of a member-managed LLC does not violate a duty or obligation under this Act or under the operating agreement merely because the member's conduct furthers the member's own interest.

Other states take a more general approach, as seen in the following statute.

Maryland LLC Act, 4A-405

   Except as provided in the operating agreement, a member may lend money to and transact other business with the limited liability company and, subject to other applicable law, has the same rights and obligations with respect to the transaction as a person who is not a member.

To help clarify what types of self-interested business transactions are legally permissible, some states list the requirements for their approval. Here is a typical statute of this sort, taken from the Tennessee LLC Act (it applies to business deals between an LLC and its members, but similar standards typically apply to business deals between managers and the LLC).

Tennessee LLC Act, 48-240-103. Member Conflicts of Interest

   A contract or other transaction between an LLC and one (1) or more of its members […] is not voidable because the member or members […] are parties or because the member or members are present at the meeting of the members or of a committee at which the contract or transaction is authorized, approved, or ratified, if:

   (1) The contract or transaction was […] fair and reasonable as to the LLC at the time it was authorized, approved, or ratified; [or]

   (2) The material facts as to the contract or transaction and as to the member's or members' interest are fully disclosed or known to the members and […] the contract or transaction is approved in good faith by either:

      (A) The owners of a majority of the voting power of the membership interests entitled to vote that are owned by persons other than the interested member or members; or

      (B) The owners of a majority of the financial interest of the membership interests that are owned by persons other than the interested member or members….

This law (set out above) is typical of the statutory standard applied in various states to validate a matter of business between an LLC and a member or manager. Essentially, these statutes require either of the following:

- Approval by a majority of members (or managers) who are not benefited by the business deal, after full disclosure of how the deal will benefit the self-interested member.

- The business deal is fair to the LLC, even if not approved by a disinterested majority of members or managers. After all, in a smaller LLC, there may not be a majority of members who do not benefit from the proposed business deal.

In some states, the statutes make it clear that routine items of business that necessarily benefit a member or manager, such as the setting of salaries of members who work for the LLC, do not require a special vote or validation procedure. Obviously, it is assumed that the members or managers, when approving this type of routine business, will not overreach—that they will set salaries and make other routine decisions in a way that is both fair to the LLC as a whole and fair to the members and managers personally.

⚠️ Fair and honest dealing is required in every state

Even in states that seem to permit any sort of self-interested business between an LLC and an LLC member or manager, you can expect trouble if a member or manager derives an unfair or secret financial advantage from a transaction, or if a deal benefits a member or manager at the expense of the LLC. In other words, even if the duties of care and loyalty are not spelled out in a state statute, the general rules of fair and honest dealing will generally be enforced by any court in the matter of a self-interested business deal between a member or manager and the LLC.

Here is some advice that we recommend following when approving self-interested business deals in any state:

- Make sure the transaction is fair. If you are unjustly benefiting members at the expense of the LLC, and you have nonmanager members, you are just asking for trouble.

- Get unanimous approval. If at all possible, have self-interested transactions approved by all disinterested members or managers after full disclosure of the details of the deal and the member's or manager's potential financial interest in it. By taking these steps, you can help avoid future controversy and claims against the LLC and its members and managers.

- If unanimous approval is not possible, get majority approval by the disinterested members and/or managers.

EXAMPLE: AB LLC is managed by five members. (It also has two nonmanaging member-investors.) The president asks the managing members to approve a contract for the furnishing of supplies to the LLC by a company in which one member has a part ownership interest. After the disclosure of the interested member's ownership interest in the outside company, three of the four disinterested LLC managing members—a majority—vote to approve the transaction (only after making sure that the cost of supplies is at least as good as the lowest price available from independent suppliers). A statement of the disclosure of the member's interest and of the determination of fairness is included in the resolution approved at the membership meeting. Because of these precautions, it is unlikely that the managing and nonmanaging members who do not approve the deal will challenge the transaction later.

- If approval by the disinterested members and/or managers is not meaningful, take extra steps. As a practical matter, if yours is a small, closely held LLC, it's possible that a majority of your LLC members or managers will have a financial interest in the transaction. Even though you may be able to get the approval of all disinterested members or managers, their number may not be sufficient to pass the resolution by normal voting rules. In that case, you should have all members (not just disinterested members or managers) formally approve a resolution that states why the deal is fair to the LLC and is comparable to the type of deal that the LLC would make in a transaction with any other party.

- If your LLC has only one manager (as is common in small LLCs), the manager should get approval of the members before going ahead with a deal that would benefit him or her personally.

EXAMPLE: The sole manager of Threadbare Sofa Reconditioners, LLC, will benefit financially from a transaction. Obviously, there is no way for the manager alone to approve the deal by a disinterested majority vote. The manager can take two steps:

- formally approve a resolution (by signing it himself or herself) that states why the deal is fair to the LLC and is comparable to the type of deal that the LLC would make in a transaction with any other party and

- get formal approval from the members by having them sign a resolution or written consents that show their approval after full disclosure of the manager's personal financial interest in the deal.

B. Resolution for Approval of Member or Manager Self-Interested Business Deals

Here's our practical advice for approving transactions involving the financial interests of members or managers.

1. When Resolutions Are Necessary

Prepare resolutions whenever a particular member or manager (or two) is singled out. If a member or manager is going to benefit from a business deal that doesn't benefit other members or managers, it's best to prepare a formal resolution that shows you took a few extra precautions before approving the transaction (for example,

that you disclosed the member's or manager's interest in the deal and made sure that a majority of the disinterested members or managers approved the deal as fair to the LLC).

In addition, prepare resolutions any time there are secondary benefits to members or managers. This applies if one or more members or managers will clearly receive a significant, collateral financial benefit as a secondary effect of the transaction.

EXAMPLE: The LLC members approve an across-the-board 10% increase in salary for all LLC employees, but two of the LLC members also work for the LLC. As the highest-paid employees, these two will receive the highest salary increase in terms of actual dollars. A formal resolution will prevent arguments later.

2. Resolution to Approve Business That Benefits an LLC Member or Manager

Below is a basic resolution you can use to approve an LLC item of business in which one or more members or managers have a personal financial interest. As discussed above, approval should be sought only after a disclosure of the material facts of the transaction, including the financial benefit that will accrue to the interested members or managers.

Fill out the self-interested business resolution below following the special instructions provided. You'll find this resolution on the CD-ROM and as a tear-out form in Appendix D. (See Appendix A for information on selecting and using the CD-ROM.)

LLC APPROVAL OF TRANSACTION BENEFITING
A MEMBER OR MANAGER

The members and/or managers of the LLC have considered: [state nature of transaction or contract]   . ❶

It was understood that the following persons have a material financial interest in this transaction or contract

as follows: [state the name(s) of the member(s) or manager(s) and their personal financial interest in the

transaction or contract with the LLC]   .

   After discussion, it was agreed that the approval of this business was fair to and in the best interests of

the LLC because _____ [state why the transaction or contract was determined to be fair]   . ❷ Therefore,

it was approved by the votes of the members and/or managers as follows:

   Name   Vote ❸

   _____   _____

   _____   _____

Special Instructions

❶ Describe the business transaction or contract to be approved. If the terms of the transaction are contained in a separate agreement or contract (such as a lease, promissory note, or the like), refer to the agreement or contract (for example, "see attached lease agreement") and attach a copy to the resolution.

EXAMPLE: Shake and Rake Tree Trimmers, LLC, wishes to obtain full membership approval of a loan proposed to be made by the LLC to a member. Instead of describing the loan and the terms of the note here, the secretary fills in: "proposed loan by LLC to [name of member], with terms as described in a proposed promissory note attached to this resolution." (Chapters 13 and 14 contain specific promissory note forms.)

❷ As explained above, many self-interested decisions by members or managers do not violate state law, simply because they are also fair to the LLC. To give extra weight to your determination of fairness, insert the explicit reasons why the proposed deal is fair to the LLC (for example, "the rent amount under a lease of property by [name of member] to the LLC is the prevailing commercial rate in the area").

EXAMPLE: The Shake and Rake Tree Trimmers, LLC secretary inserts the following reason for the fairness of the proposed LLC loan to a member: "The LLC has sufficient cash reserves to make the loan without impeding ongoing LLC business, and the interest rate to be charged on the loan is the current rate charged on commercial loans by commercial lenders."

❸ Insert the names of the members and/or managers asked to approve the self-interested transaction, and show the vote cast by the member or manager—for or against the resolution. As discussed, normally you will seek approval of the managing members or managers of the LLC. But for an important or potentially controversial deal, you may wish to seek approval of all members (if your LLC is either managed by managers or is member-managed by less than all members). ■

Lawyers, Tax Specialists, and Legal Research

Much of the work in holding LLC meetings and documenting decisions is routine. Any knowledgeable and motivated business-person can competently do it. But there's no way around it—from time to time you are bound to need help from outside sources. Some LLC decisions involve complex areas of law or taxation. Others involve a mix of business and legal savvy and are likely to be best made with the input of an experienced small-business lawyer.

You may wish to turn to a lawyer for help in drafting resolutions to approve special items of business approved at meetings or with written consents of your members and/or managers. And, of course, there will be important legal consequences associated with ongoing LLC decisions that may require input from an experienced legal professional. One good way to learn more about any legal decision or form is to read up on these areas in a law or business library. (See Section C, below.) Or you can decide, as many busy business people do, to pay a lawyer, accountant, or financial adviser (such as a pension plan specialist, bank loan officer, or financial investment adviser) to check your conclusions about tricky legal areas and the completion of legal forms. In the sections below, we provide a few tips to help you in your search for competent expert information, assistance, and advice.

A. How to Find the Right Lawyer

Most small businesses can't afford to put a lawyer on retainer. Even when consulted on an issue-by-issue basis, lawyer's fees mount up fast—often way too fast to be affordable except for the most pressing problems. Just as with individuals, more and more small businesses are trying to at least partially close this affordability gap by doing as much of their own legal form preparation as possible. Often a knowledgeable self-helper can sensibly accomplish the whole task. Other times, it makes sense to briefly consult with a lawyer at an interim stage, or have the paperwork reviewed on completion.

You already have taken one positive step toward making your legal needs affordable by using this book to prepare standard LLC minutes and written consent forms. Depending on the size of your business and the complexity of your legal needs, your next step is likely to be to find a cooperative lawyer who will help you consider important legal decisions and review or draft specific resolutions you will insert in your minutes.

You obviously don't want a lawyer who is bent on taking over all your legal decision making and form-drafting while running up billable hours as fast as possible. Instead, you need what we call a legal coach, someone who is willing to work *with* you—not just *for* you. Under this model, the lawyer helps you take care of many routine legal matters yourself, while remaining available to consult on more complicated legal issues as the need arises.

You don't need a big-time LLC lawyer
There is a lawyer surplus these days, and many newer lawyers, especially, are open to nontraditional business arrangements. Look for a lawyer with some small business experience, preferably in your field or area of operations. For the most part, you don't want a lawyer who works primarily with big businesses. Not only will this person deal with issues that are far from your concerns, but he or she is almost sure to charge too much.

DON'T ASK A LAWYER FOR TAX ADVICE

When it comes to LLC decisions that have tax implications, accountants often have a better grasp of the issues than lawyers. And an added bonus is that although tax advice doesn't come cheap, accountants often charge less than lawyers.

---

1. Look and Ask Around

When you go looking for a lawyer, don't start with phone books, legal directories, or advertisements. Lawyer referral services operated by bar associations are equally unhelpful. These simply supply the names of lawyers who have signed on to the service, often accepting the lawyer's own word for what types of skills he or she has. A better approach is to talk to people in your community who own or operate businesses you respect. Ask them about their lawyer and what they think of that person's work. If you talk to half a dozen business people, chances are you'll come away with several good leads. Other people, such as your banker, accountant, insurance agent, or real estate broker, may be able to provide the names of lawyers they trust to help them with business matters. Friends, relatives, and business associates within your own company may also have names of possible lawyers.

Let your legal coach refer you to experts when necessary

What if you have a very technical legal question? Should you start by seeking out a legal specialist? For starters, the answer is probably no. First, find a good business lawyer to act as your coach. Then rely on this person to suggest specialized materials or experts as the need arises.

2. Talk to the Lawyer Ahead of Time

After you get the names of several good prospects, don't wait until two days before an important LLC meeting or until a legal problem arises before contacting a lawyer. Once enmeshed in a crisis, you may not have time to find a lawyer who will work with you at affordable rates. Chances are you'll wind up settling for the first person available at a moment's notice—which all but guarantees you'll pay too much.

When you call a lawyer, announce your intentions in advance—that you are looking for someone who is willing to review your papers from time to time, point you in the right direction as the need arises, serve as a legal adviser as circumstances dictate, and tackle particular legal problems as necessary. In exchange for this, let the lawyer know you are willing to pay promptly and fairly. If the lawyer seems agreeable to this arrangement, ask to come in to meet for a half-hour or so. Although many lawyers will not charge you for this introductory appointment, it's often a good idea to offer to pay for it. You want to establish that while you are looking for someone to help you help yourself, you are able to pay as you go.

At the interview, re-emphasize that you are looking for a nontraditional "legal coach" relationship. Many lawyers will find this unappealing—for example, saying they don't feel comfortable reviewing documents you have drafted using self-help materials. If so, thank the person for being frank and keep interviewing other lawyers. You'll also want to discuss other important issues in this initial interview, such as the lawyer's customary charges for services, as explained further below.

Pay particular attention to the rapport between you and your lawyer. Remember: You are looking for a legal coach who will work with you. Trust your instincts and seek a lawyer whose personality and business sense are compatible with your own.

3. Set the Extent and Cost of Services in Advance

When you hire a lawyer, get a clear understanding about how fees will be computed. For example, if you call the lawyer from time to time for general advice or to be steered to a good information source, how will you be billed? Some lawyers bill a flat amount for a call or a conference; others bill to the nearest six-, ten-, or twenty-minute interval. Whatever the lawyer's system, you need to understand it.

Especially at the beginning of your relationship, when you bring a big job to a lawyer, ask specifically about what it will cost. If you feel it's too much, don't hesitate to negotiate; perhaps you can do some of the routine work yourself, thus reducing the fee.

It's a good idea to get all fee arrangements—especially those for good-sized jobs—in writing. In several states, fee agreements between lawyers and clients must be in writing if the expected fee is $1,000 or more, or is contingent on the outcome of a lawsuit. But whether required or not, it's a good idea to get it in writing.

HOW LAWYERS CHARGE FOR LEGAL SERVICES

There are no across-the-board arrangements on how lawyers' fees are to be charged. Expect to be charged by one of the following methods:

- **By the hour.** In most parts of the United States, you can get competent services for your small business for $150 to $250 an hour. Newer attorneys still in the process of building a practice may be available for paperwork review, legal research, and other types of legal work at lower rates.

- **Flat fee for a specific job.** Under this arrangement, you pay the agreed-upon amount for a given project, regardless of how much or how little time the lawyer spends. Particularly when you first begin working with a lawyer and are worried about hourly costs getting out of control, negotiating a flat fee for a specific job can make sense.

- **Contingent fee based on settlement amounts or winnings.** This type of fee typically occurs in personal injury, products liability, fraud, and discrimination-type cases, where a lawsuit will likely be filed. The lawyer gets a percentage of the recovery (often 33%–

40%) if you win and nothing if you lose. A contingency fee can go as high as 50% if the case does not settle and goes to court. Since most small business legal needs involve advice and help with drafting paperwork, a contingency fee approach doesn't normally make sense. However, if your business becomes involved in a personal injury claim or lawsuit involving fraud, unfair competition, or the infringement of a patent or copyright, you may want to explore the contingency fee approach.

- **Retainer.** Some LLCs can afford to pay relatively modest amounts, perhaps $1,000 to $2,000 a year, to keep a business lawyer on retainer for ongoing phone or in-person consultations, routine premeeting minutes review or resolution preparation, and other business matters during the year. Of course, your retainer won't cover a full-blown legal crisis, but it can help you take care of ongoing minutes and other legal paperwork (for example, contract or special real estate paperwork) when you need a hand.

💡 Use nonlawyer professionals to cut down on legal costs

Often, nonlawyer professionals perform some tasks better and at lower cost than lawyers. For example, look to management consultants for strategic business planning, real estate brokers or appraisers for valuation of properties, financial planners for investment advice, insurance agents for advice on insurance protection, independent paralegals for routine LLC resolution- or form-drafting, and CPAs for help in setting up and maintaining the LLC's financial records and preparing its tax returns. Each of these matters is likely to have a legal aspect, and you may eventually want to consult your lawyer, but normally you won't need to until you've gathered information on your own.

4. Confront Any Problems Head-On

If you have any questions about a lawyer's bill or the quality of his or her services, speak up. Buying legal help should be just like purchasing any other consumer service—if you are dissatisfied, seek a reduction in your bill or make it clear that the work needs to be redone properly. If the lawyer runs a decent business, he or she will promptly and positively deal with your concerns. If you don't get an acceptable response, find another lawyer pronto. If you switch lawyers, you are entitled to get your important documents back from the first lawyer.

Even if you fire your lawyer, you may still feel unjustly wronged. If you can't get satisfaction from the lawyer, write to the client grievance office of your state bar association (with a copy to the lawyer, of course). Often, a phone call from this office to your lawyer will bring the desired results.

B. FINDING THE RIGHT TAX ADVISER

Many LLC minutes resolutions and ongoing LLC decisions involve tax issues and advice. To make good decisions in these and other tax areas often requires the expert advice of a tax adviser. Depending on the issue before you, this adviser may be a certified public accountant, financial or investment adviser, LLC loan officer at a bank, pension plan specialist, or inside or outside bookkeeper trained in employment and LLC tax reporting and return requirements.

Whatever your arrangement, consider the same issues for finding, choosing, using, and resolving problems with a tax professional as those discussed above for legal services. Shop around for someone recommended by small business people you respect, or who is otherwise known to you as qualified for the task. Again, you may be able to take advantage of the lower rates offered by newer local practitioners or firms. Your tax person should be available over the phone to answer routine questions, or by mail or fax to handle paperwork and correspondence, with a minimum of formality or ritual. It is likely that you will spend much more time dealing with your tax adviser than your legal adviser, so be particularly attentive to the personal side of this relationship.

Tax issues are often cloudy and subject to a range of interpretations and strategies, particularly in the LLC area, so it is absolutely essential that you discuss and agree to the level of tax-aggressiveness you expect from your advisor. Some small business owners want to live on the edge, saving every possible tax dollar, even at the risk that deductions and other tax practices will be challenged by the IRS or state tax agents. Others are willing to pay a bit more in taxes to gain an extra measure of peace of mind. Whatever your tax strategy, make sure you find a tax adviser who feels the same way you do, or is willing to defer to your more liberal or conservative tax tendencies.

As with legal issues that affect your business, it pays to learn as much as you can about LLC taxation. Not only will you have to buy less help from professionals, but you'll be in a good position to make good financial and tax planning decisions. IRS forms, business and law library publications, trade groups, and countless other sources provide accessible information on LLC tax issues. Your accountant or other tax adviser should be able to help you put your hands on good materials. Banks are an excellent source of financial advice, particularly if they will be LLC creditors—after all, they will have a stake in the success of your LLC. Further, the federal Small Business Administration can be an ideal source of financial and tax information and resources (as well as financing in some cases).

See Appendix C for a summary of significant changes in the 2003 federal tax act that affect small businesses, including LLCs, and small business owners.

C. How to Do Your Own Legal Research

Law is information, not magic. If you can look up necessary information yourself, you need not purchase it from a lawyer—although, for important issues, you may wish to check your conclusions with a lawyer, or use one as a sounding board for your intended course of action.

Much of the research necessary to understand your state's business LLC law can be done without a lawyer by spending a few minutes online browsing your state LLC Act or by visiting a local law or business library. We explain the few simple steps necessary to find LLC statutes in your state's business LLC law in Chapter 1, Section C; and list the Web links to each state's LLC Act in Appendix B. Even if you need to go to a lawyer for help in preparing an LLC resolution to insert in your minutes or to discuss the legal ramifications of a proposed LLC transaction, you can give yourself a head start by reading legal manuals prepared for lawyers, which are available at law libraries.

How do you find a law library open to the public? In many states, you need to look only as far as your county courthouse or, failing that, your state capital. In addition, publicly funded law schools generally permit the public to use their libraries, and some private law schools grant limited access to their libraries—sometimes for a modest user's fee. If you're lucky enough to have access to several law libraries, select one that has a reference librarian to assist you. Also look through the business or reference department of a major city or county public library. These often carry LLC statutes as well as books on LLC law and taxation useful to the small business owner.

In doing legal research for an LLC or other type of business, there are a number of sources for legal rules, procedures, and issues that you may wish to examine. Here are a few:

- **LLC Act.** These state statutes should be your primary focus for finding the rules for operating your LLC, including holding meetings and obtaining the approval of members and managers for ongoing legal, tax, business, and financial decisions. Your state LLC Act is probably available for browsing and/or downloading from your state-maintained Web page on the Internet. Appendix B includes the Web addresses, if available, for state LLC filing offices; these often link to a page where state statutes, including the state LLC Act, may be researched.

- **Other state laws, such as the Securities, Commercial, Civil, Labor, and Revenue Code.** These and other laws govern the issuance and transfer of securities; the content, approval, and enforcement of commercial contracts; employment practices and procedures; state tax requirements; and other aspects of doing business in your state. Depending on the type of business you have, you may also want to research statutes and regulations dealing with other legal topics such as environmental law, product liability, real estate, copyrights, and so on.

- **Federal laws.** These include the tax laws and procedures found in the Internal Revenue Code and Treasury Regulations implementing these code sections; regulations dealing with advertising, warranties, and other consumer matters adopted by the Federal Trade Commission; and equal opportunity statutes such as Title VII of the Civil Rights Act administered by the Justice Department and Equal Employment Opportunities Commission.

- **Administrative rules and regulations.** Issued by federal and state administrative agencies charged with implementing statutes, state and federal statutes are often supplemented with regulations that clarify the statute and contain rules for an agency to follow in implementing and enforcing the statutes.

- **Case law.** These are decisions of federal and state courts interpreting statutes—and sometimes making law, known as "common law," if the subject isn't covered by a statute. Annotated state LLC codes contain not only the statute itself, but references to any court cases interpreting and

implementing specific sections of the law. However, since LLC law is relatively new, annotations to court cases are just beginning to pop up in the codes.

- **Secondary sources.** Also important in researching LLC and business law are sources that provide background information on particular areas of law. One example is this book. Others are commonly found in the business, legal, or reference section of your local bookstore. Also see "Resources From Nolo," below.

Consider joining a trade group

As a final method of finding legal information, we suggest joining and participating in one or more trade groups related to your business. These groups often track legislation in particular areas of business and provide sample contracts and other useful legal forms. Some also retain law firms for trade association purposes that may refer you to competent local lawyers.

RESOURCES FROM NOLO

Below are a few titles published by Nolo with valuable information for the small business person:

- **LLCMaker** (software), by Anthony Mancuso. This interactive program assembles LLC articles and operating agreements for use in each state. Contains built-in links to each state's LLC filing office and LLC Act.

- **Form Your Own Limited Liability Company** (book with CD-ROM), by Anthony Mancuso. This national title shows you how to form an LLC under each state's LLC law and the latest federal tax rules.

- **Buy-Sell Agreement Handbook: Plan Ahead for Changes in the Ownership of Your Business** (book with CD-ROM), by Anthony Mancuso and Bethany K. Laurence. This book shows you how to adopt comprehensive buy-sell provisions to handle the purchase and sale of ownership interests in an LLC, partnership, or corporation when an owner withdraws, dies, becomes disabled, or wishes to sell an interest to an outsider. Comes with an easy-to-use agreement as a tear-out and on disk.

- **How to Form Your Own California Corporation,** by Anthony Mancuso. This book shows you how to form a corporation under the specific rules for California. Step-by-step instructions for preparing articles, bylaws, and organizational minutes. If you don't live in California, see *Incorporate Your Business: A 50-State Legal Guide to Forming a Corporation,* also by Anthony Mancuso.

- **Legal Guide for Starting & Running a Small Business,** by Fred S. Steingold. This book is an essential resource for every small business owner, whether you are just starting out or are already established. Find out how to form a sole proprietorship, partnership, or LLC; negotiate a favorable lease; hire and fire employees; write contracts; and resolve business disputes.

- **The Employer's Legal Handbook,** by Fred S. Steingold. Employers need legal advice daily—and can get it in this comprehensive resource.

The only book that compiles all the basics of employment law in one place, it covers safe hiring practices, wages, hours, tips and commissions, employee benefits, taxes and liability, insurance, discrimination, sexual harassment, and termination.

- **Tax Savvy for Small Business,** by Frederick W. Daily. Gives business owners information about federal taxes and shows them how to make the best tax decisions for their business, maximize profits, and stay out of trouble with the IRS.

- **How to Write a Business Plan,** by Mike McKeever. Whether starting a business or expanding an existing one, this book will show you how to write the business plan and loan package necessary to finance your idea and make it work. Includes up-to-date sources of financing.

- **Patent It Yourself,** by David Pressman. This state-of-the-art guide is a must for any inventor who wants to get a patent—from the patent search to the actual application. Patent attorney and former patent examiner David Pressman covers use and licensing, successful marketing, and infringement. This best-selling book is now available in software as well.

- **The Copyright Handbook: How to Protect & Use Written Works,** by Stephen Fishman. Provides forms and step-by-step instructions for protecting all types of written expression under U.S. and international copyright law. It also explains copyright infringement, fair use, works for hire, and transfers of copyright ownership.

- **Web & Software Development: A Legal Guide** (book with CD-ROM), by Stephen Fishman. A reference bible for people in the software industry, this book explores the legal ins and outs of copyright, trade secrets and patent protection, employment agreements, working with independent contractors and employees, development and publishing agreements, and multimedia developments. Sample agreements and contracts are included on the CD-ROM. ■

How to Use the CD-ROM

The tear-out forms in Appendix D are included on a CD-ROM in the back of the book. This CD-ROM, which can be used with Windows computers, installs files that can be opened, printed, and edited using a word processor or other software. It is *not* a stand alone software program. Please read this appendix and the README.TXT file included on the CD-ROM for instructions on using the Forms CD.

Note to Mac users: This CD-ROM and its files should also work on Macintosh computers. Please note, however, that Nolo cannot provide technical support for non-Windows users.

HOW TO VIEW THE README FILE

If you do not know how to view the file README.TXT, insert the Forms CD-ROM into your computer's CD-ROM drive and follow these instructions:

- Windows 9x, 2000, Me, and XP: (1) On your PC's desktop, double click the My Computer icon; (2) double click the icon for the CD-ROM drive into which the Forms CD-ROM was inserted; (3) double click the file README.TXT.

- Macintosh: (1) On your Mac desktop, double click the icon for the CD-ROM that you inserted; (2) double click on the file README.TXT.

  While the README file is open, print it out by using the Print command in the File menu.

A. INSTALLING THE FORM FILES ONTO YOUR COMPUTER

Word processing forms that you can open, complete, print, and save with your word processing program (see Section B, below) are contained on the CD-ROM. Before you can do anything with the files on the CD-ROM, you need to install them onto your hard disk. In

accordance with U.S. copyright laws, remember that copies of the CD-ROM and its files are for your personal use only.

Insert the Forms CD and do the following.

1. Windows 9x, 2000, Me, and XP Users

Follow the instructions that appear on the screen. (If nothing happens when you insert the Forms CD-ROM, then (1) double click the My Computer icon; (2) double click the icon for the CD-ROM drive into which the Forms CD-ROM was inserted; and (3) double click the file WELCOME.EXE.)

By default, all the files are installed to the \Limited Liability Company Forms folder in the \Program Files folder of your computer. A folder called "Limited Liability Company Forms" is added to the "Programs" folder of the Start menu.

2. Macintosh Users

Step 1: If the "LLC Forms CD" window is not open, open it by double clicking the "LLC Forms CD" icon.

Step 2: Select the "Limited Liability Company Forms" folder icon.

Step 3: Drag and drop the folder icon onto the icon of your hard disk.

B. USING THE WORD PROCESSING FILES TO CREATE DOCUMENTS

This section concerns the files for forms that can be opened and edited with your word processing program.

All word processing forms come in rich text format. These files have the extension ".RTF." For example, the form for the Meeting Summary Sheet discussed in Chapter 3 is on the file MEETSUM.RTF. All forms and their filenames are listed at the beginning of Appendix D.

RTF files can be read by most recent word processing programs including all versions of MS Word for Windows and Macintosh, WordPad for Windows, and recent versions of WordPerfect for Windows and Macintosh.

To use a form from the CD to create your documents you must: (1) open a file in your word processor or text editor; (2) edit the form by filling in the required information; (3) print it out; (4) rename and save your revised file.

The following are general instructions on how to do this. However, each word processor uses different commands to open, format, save, and print documents. Please read your word processor's manual for specific instructions on performing these tasks.

Do not call Nolo's technical support if you have questions on how to use your word processor.

Step 1. Opening a File

There are three ways to open the word processing files included on the CD-ROM after you have installed them onto your computer.

- Windows users can open a file by selecting its "shortcut" as follows: (1) Click the Windows "Start" button; (2) open the "Programs" folder; (3) open the "Limited Liability Company Forms" subfolder; and (4) click on the shortcut to the form you want to work with.

- Both Windows and Macintosh users can open a file directly by double clicking on it. Use My Computer or Windows Explorer (Windows 9x, 2000, Me, or XP) or the Finder (Macintosh) to go to the folder you installed or copied the CD-ROM's files to. Then, double click on the specific file you want to open.

- You can also open a file from within your word processor. To do this, you must first start your word processor. Then, go to the File menu and choose the Open command. This opens a dialog box where you will tell the program (1) the

type of file you want to open (*.RTF); and (2) the location and name of the file (you will need to navigate through the directory tree to get to the folder on your hard disk where the CD's files have been installed). If these directions are unclear you will need to look through the manual for your word processing program—Nolo's technical support department will *not* be able to help you with the use of your word processing program.

Where Are the Files Installed?

Windows Users

- RTF files are installed by default to a folder named \Limited Liability Company Forms in the \Program Files folder of your computer.

Macintosh Users

- RTF files are located in the "Limited Liability Company Forms" folder.

Step 2. Editing Your Document

Fill in the appropriate information according to the instructions and sample agreements in the book. Underlines are used to indicate where you need to enter your information, frequently followed by instructions in brackets. *Be sure to delete the underlines and instructions from your edited document.* If you do not know how to use your word processor to edit a document, you will need to look through the manual for your word processing program—Nolo's technical support department will *not* be able to help you with the use of your word processing program.

EDITING FORMS THAT HAVE OPTIONAL OR ALTERNATIVE TEXT

Some of the forms have check boxes before text. The check boxes indicate:

- optional text, where you choose whether to include or exclude the given text

- alternative text, where you select one alternative to include and exclude the other alternatives.

If you are using the tear-out forms in Appendix D, you simply mark the appropriate box to make your choice.

If you are using the Forms CD, however, we recommend that instead of marking the check boxes, you do the following.

Optional text

If you don't want to include optional text, just delete it from your document.

If you do want to include optional text, just leave it in your document.

In either case, delete the check box itself as well as the italicized instructions that the text is optional.

NOTE: If you choose not to include an optional numbered clause, be sure to renumber all the subsequent clauses after you delete it.

Alternative text

First delete all the alternatives that you do not want to include.

Then delete the remaining check boxes, as well as the italicized instructions that you need to select one of the alternatives provided.

Step 3. Printing Out the Document

Use your word processor's or text editor's "Print" command to print out your document. If you do not know how to use your word processor to print a document, you will need to look through the manual for your word processing program—Nolo's technical support department will *not* be able to help you with the use of your word processing program.

Step 4. Saving Your Document

After filling in the form, use the "Save As" command to save and rename the file. Because all the files are "read-only," you will not be able to use the "Save" command. This is for your protection. *If you save the file without renaming it, the underlines that indicate where you need to enter your information will be lost and you will not be able to create a new document with this file without recopying the original file from the CD-ROM.*

If you do not know how to use your word processor to save a document, you will need to look through the manual for your word processing program—Nolo's technical support department will *not* be able to help you with the use of your word processing program. ∎

State Information

This appendix provides the basic legal rules for major LLC decisions during the life of an LLC. Since most LLC statutes are flexible, most of the rules shown here are state default rules—that is, in most cases, they apply unless a contrary rule is set out in the LLC articles or operating agreement. (When we can, we'll tell you whether a rule can be changed in the articles, operating agreement, or both.)

Please use this information as a guide. LLC laws constantly change and are subject to different interpretations. Further, other statutes may affect different areas of LLC operations, such as the admission or departure of a member. If any area is particularly important to you, update this information with a reading of your state's latest LLC Act. (See the State LLC Act link in your state sheet, below.)

 Use the statute numbers to look up the law
We generally list the specific state statute or statutes that form the basis of the summarized rule or rules in this appendix. Use these section numbers to look up the provision of your state LLC Act.

This state-specific information is organized into different headings, which we summarize here.

LLC Filing Office

Here you'll find the address and phone number (subject to change) of the state office that handles LLC legal filings, such as the filing of the original articles of organization (or the certificate of formation or similar document) to start the legal existence of the LLC. Other filings that typically occur during the life of the LLC are:

- amendments or restatements of articles or certificate

- change of LLC registered agent or registered office, and

- articles or a certificate of dissolution (to dissolve the LLC).

Commonly, the Secretary of State or Department of State is the office that handles LLC filings, but some states use a different title for this office. Normally this office, or a separate division of this office, handles legal filings for other business entities, such as filings for corporations and limited partnerships.

We also show any Internet Web address currently available for this office. Links from this Web page usually bring you to a page from which you can download official LLC filing forms and instructions.

State LLC Act

Under this heading we list the State LLC Act and indicate whether the state provides a link from which you can browse and download sections of your state's LLC Act. If the state provides a link, we explain how to use it to locate and research your state's LLC Act.

 Related text section
For more information on researching your state's LLC Act, see Chapter 1, Section C.

State Tax Office

We list the location, telephone number, and website address (URL) of your state's revenue and taxation (or similar) office. We recommend you call this number early on in the life of your LLC and ask for tax forms and other tax materials.

LLC Management

This heading lists the state default rule for LLC management—that is, whether an LLC is managed by its members or by one or more managers in the absence of a specific provision in its LLC articles or operating agreement. Most LLCs will specifically choose their management structure in their articles, and the majority of smaller LLCs will choose member-management.

Related text section
For more informationt, see Chapter 2, Section B.

Manager Election

This heading is relevant to manager-managed LLCs—those that have designated one or more managers (who may be members, but normally do not need to be) to manage the LLC. We list the basic rules in each state for the election and re-election of managers—the number of members or the percentage of membership voting power that is necessary to elect managers and the managers' terms of office (which determine when they should be re-elected). The rules shown here are usually default rules—an LLC often can set its own rules for election and re-election of LLC managers, typically in its operating agreement.

Related text section

For more information, see Chapter 2, Section B.

Meeting Requirements

We list the state LLC Act requirements for calling, holding, and voting at LLC meetings of members and managers. There is significant variation among the states, particularly with regard to membership meeting rules. Of course, these are mostly state default rules, so you will want to look at your operating agreement first to determine if your LLC has any specific requirements for holding meetings of your LLC members or managers that may override your state's law.

Managers normally vote to approve a resolution or a decision to act at a meeting or by written consent on a one-manager, one-vote basis. Normally a majority of the managers is needed for approval. But pay particular attention to the default membership voting requirements listed here. These vary considerably from state to state. Some states give members per capita (one member, one vote) voting power, while others grant voting rights to members according to the members' current capital account balances. If your operating agreement is silent on how your members vote, you may need to rely on your state's default membership voting rules when seeking the approval of your members for a resolution presented at a members' meeting or contained in a written consent form. For the latest information on these rules, you will

want to consult the statute numbers shown in this section.

Regardless of how voting power is measured (per capita or by capital accounts balances), members and managers normally approve resolutions presented at meetings or included in a written consent form by a majority—the vote of a majority of members or managers or the vote of a majority of the capital accounts balances. But keep in mind that special super-majority voting requirements (such as a unanimous vote) may apply to special LLC decisions, particularly those involving structural changes to the LLC or changes in the relative interests of members, such as amendments to the articles or operating agreement or a vote to approve the admission of a member or the continuation of the LLC after a member departs. We cover special matters of this sort under special headings in this appendix (for example, see "Amendments," "Admission of Members," "Departure of Members," and "Continuation of the LLC," discussed below).

Related text section

For more information, see Chapter 3, Section B, Step 4.

Amendments

In this heading, we list the state requirements for amending the articles of organization (or similar organizing document such as a certificate of formation) and the LLC operating agreement. Note that the members of the LLC are usually required to approve these amendments by a unanimous or majority vote of the entire membership, unless otherwise provided in the LLC articles or operating agreement. Even if not required, we recommend obtaining the approval of all members to all amendments to the articles or operating agreement. These are the essential organizing and operating documents of the LLC, so changes to them can have significant effects on the legal and financial rights and responsibilities of all members.

Related text section

For more information, see Chapter 10.

Admission of Members

This heading contains the state rules for approving the admission of members. We provide two sets of rules for each state if possible. The first states the membership vote necessary for the LLC to issue a membership to a new member. The second shows the requirement for admitting a person who is transferred (sold, given, willed) a membership from a former member. This type of new member is called a transferee or assignee. Typically, all existing members must approve the admission of a new member of either type, unless the articles or operating agreement contain a different approval rule.

If a transferee is not approved for membership

If a new member who has been transferred a membership interest from a former member is not approved by the required vote, most state statutes give the transferee mere economic rights in the transferred membership. In other words, the new member only receives a right to share in profits and receive any other monetary distributions the former member had a right to receive. The transferee is not given voting rights, management rights or any other rights associated with the transferred membership. The other members would have to approve the admission of the transferee for such rights to accrue to the new member.

Related text section

For more information, see Chapter 11, Section C.

Withdrawal of Members

This heading lists the state rules for the withdrawal of a member from the LLC. Two basic items of information from the state statutes are provided, if available:

- whether a member is allowed to withdraw under the default state rules and, if so, the type and length of notice the member must give the LLC and/or the other members

- the amount the LLC must pay the withdrawing member, if the operating agreement is silent on this issue, and any costs or damages the LLC is entitled to subtract from this amount if the withdrawal violates the operating agreement or is otherwise wrongful.

Related text section

For more information, see Chapter 11, Section D.

These rules relate to a member who unilaterally resigns or otherwise withdraws from the LLC and expects payment for his or her membership interest from the LLC. For the rules that cover the withdrawal of a member who has transferred his or her interest to a person who wishes to be admitted as a new member, see "Admission of Members," above.

Continuation of the LLC

Some states require the remaining members to approve the continuation of the LLC after a member:

- withdraws from the LLC

- sells or otherwise transfers an interest

- is expelled, or

- otherwise terminates his or her membership interest in the LLC or has it terminated involutarily.

Membership-terminating events of this sort are referred to as the dissociation of a member. Some states say that in the absence of a contrary provision in the articles or operating agreement, the LLC is automatically dissolved by the dissociation of a member unless the remaining members formally vote to approve the continuance of the LLC.

This result may seem capricious and harsh. But the reason some states require a vote to continue the LLC is to help it look more like a partnership and less like a corporation under the traditional IRS entity classification rules. Fortunately, the IRS no longer uses these corporation/partnership classification rules, so many states that used to require a vote to continue the LLC after the dissociation of a member no longer do so. But there are some states that still require this vote, and this heading lists them.

Keep in mind, however, that if your articles or operating agreement say that the LLC continues without the need for a vote after a member is dissociated, you don't need to formally approve the continuance of the LLC. And if your remaining members must vote to continue your LLC, it's easy to formally approve such a vote by holding a membership meeting or preparing written consents to continue the LLC for the remaining members to sign.

Even if your state is listed as requiring a vote to continue the LLC after a member leaves, it may have repealed this vote requirement, or will soon do so, perhaps by the time a member leaves your LLC. The best way to check is to look up the section of the state LLC Act given in this heading to see if it still requires a vote, or if it has been changed or repealed.

It makes sense to review LLC operations after a member leaves

It's always a good idea to review the status of your LLC after a member leaves, to see where the company and the remaining members stand. In most cases, the fact that the LLC should stay in business will be a foregone conclusion, but you may want to discuss the prospect of admitting a new member or reassigning the departing member's management and operational duties.

Related text section

For more information, see Chapter 11, Sections C and D.

Special Statutory Rules

This heading lists any special statutory rules that struck our eye as we browsed each state's LLC Act. For example, we may list actions that must be approved by a unanimous vote of members under the state LLC Act (usually, unless the operating agreement provides otherwise) or a special statutory rule involving the approval of contracts or loans to LLC members or managers. The list here is not exhaustive—your state's LLC Act no doubt has other special voting rules for approving special transactions. Again, we list just a few rules that stood out from the rest.

ALABAMA

LLC Filing Office

Secretary of State
Corporate Section
Box 5616
Montgomery, AL 36103
Telephone: 334-242-5324
www.sos.state.al.us/business/corporations.cfm

State LLC Act

The Alabama LLC Act is contained in Title 10, Chapter 12 of the Alabama statutes, and is browseable from the following Web page (select Title 10, then Chapter 12):

www.legislature.state.al.us/CodeofAlabama/1975/coatoc.htm

State Tax Office

Department of Revenue, Montgomery
www.ador.state.al.us

LLC Management

An LLC is managed by its members unless the articles state that the LLC is to be managed by one or more managers. [Sections 10-12-10 and 10-12-22]

Manager Election

Unless otherwise provided in the operating agreement, managers are elected by at least one-half of the number of members. Managers hold office for an indefinite term unless otherwise provided in the operating agreement. [Section 10-12-22]

Meeting Requirements

Rules for the notice, time, place, quorum, and manner of voting by members or managers at a meeting, or by written consent, are to be specified in the articles or operating agreement. [Section 10-12-22]

Amendments

Unless the articles require a greater vote, amendment to articles must be approved by a majority vote of voting members. [Section 10-12-11] Unless otherwise stated in the operating agreement, the operating agreement must be amended by written consent of all members.

Admission of Members

Unless the operating agreement says otherwise, new members are admitted by written consent of all members. [Section 10-12-31] Unless otherwise provided in the operating agreement, the admission of transferees must be approved by unanimous written consent of all nontransferring members. [Section 10-12-33]

Withdrawal of Members

If not prohibited by the LLC operating agreement, a member can withdraw from the LLC at any time upon 30 days, written notice to the other members. If a member's withdrawal is in violation of the operating agreement or is due to wrongful conduct by the member, the member can be held personally liable for financial damages caused by the withdrawal from the LLC (including the cost of paying another person to perform services promised by the withdrawing member). [Section 10-12-36]

Continuation of the LLC

After the loss of a member, the LLC continues—a vote to continue the LLC is not required. But if the LLC loses its last member, it automatically dissolves unless the LLC's articles or operating agreement contain a provision that continues the existence of the LLC and provides for the appointment of one or more new members (or unless the holders of financial rights in the LLC, such as prior members, agree in writing within 90 days of the loss of the last member to continue the LLC and to appoint one or more new members). [Section 10-12-37]

ALASKA

LLC Filing Office

Department of Commerce and Economic Development
Corporations Division
Box 110808
Juneau, AK 99811-0808

Telephone: 907-465-2530

Anchorage Office: 907-269-8140

www.dced.state.ak.us/bsc/corps.htm

State LLC Act

The Alaska LLC Act is contained in Title 10, Chapter 10.50 of the Alaska statutes, starting at Section 10.50.010, and is browseable online. Go to the Web page listed below (the corporations section home page), select the link to Alaska Statutes and Regulations, then select The Current Alaska Statutes, expand the Title 10 heading, and select Chapter 10.50 to view the LLC Act.

www.dced.state.ak.us/bsc/corps.htm

State Tax Office

Department of Revenue, Juneau

www.revenue.state.ak.us/

LLC Management

An LLC is to be managed by its members unless the articles state that the LLC is to be managed by one or more managers. [Sections 10.50.075 and 10.50.110]

Manager Election

Unless otherwise provided in the operating agreement, managers are elected by at least one-half of the number of members. [Section 10.50.115] Managers hold office for an indefinite term unless otherwise provided in the operating agreement. [Section 10.50.125]

Meeting Requirements

Unless otherwise stated in the operating agreement or articles, members in a member-managed LLC approve LLC management decisions by consent of more than one-half of all of the members. Unless otherwise stated in the operating agreement, the managers of a manager-managed LLC must approve management decisions by more than one-half of the number of managers. [Section 10.50.150]

Amendments

All members must consent in writing to amendments of the articles or operating agreement, but the operating agreement may reduce this level of consent for amendments to a majority of the members (but no less than a majority). [Section 10.50.150]

Admission of Members

Unless the operating agreement says otherwise, new memberships are issued by written consent of all members. [Section 10.50.155] Unless otherwise provided in the operating agreement, the admission of a transferee as a member must be approved by unanimous written consent of nontransferring members. [Section 10.50.165]

Withdrawal of Members

Unless otherwise provided in the operating agreement, if the LLC has a limited term or is formed for a particular undertaking (project), the withdrawal of a member before the end of the term or the accomplishment of the undertaking is a breach of the operating agreement. [Section 10.50.190]

If the voluntary withdrawal of a member with the power to withdraw breaches the operating agreement, or if the withdrawal occurs as a result of otherwise wrongful conduct of the member, the LLC may recover from the withdrawing member damages that result from the breach of the operating agreement or the wrongful conduct, including the reasonable costs of obtaining replacement services the withdrawing member was obligated to perform. The LLC may offset these damages against the amount the withdrawing member is entitled to receive upon the member's withdrawal. [Section 10.50.195]

In addition to a distribution of profits owed to a member who withdraws or whose interest is terminated prior to the dissolution of the LLC (and except for removal of a member under other provisions of the LLC Act), the LLC shall distribute to the member the amount of the member's limited liability company interest. If the operating agreement does not specify the amount of the distribution or a method for determining the amount, the LLC shall make the distribution within a reasonable time after termination, and the amount of the distribution shall be the fair value of the member's interest as of the date of termination based upon the member's right to share in LLC distributions. [Section 10.50.335]

Continuation of the LLC

After the loss of a member, the LLC continues—a vote to continue the LLC is not required. [Section 10.50.400]

Special Statutory Rules

A contract or transaction that personally benefits a manager or managing member can be approved by members without a personal interest in the contract or transaction after disclosure of the interest to the members. [Section 10.50.140]

Loans by an LLC to an employee must be approved by managers or managing members. A loan by the LLC to a manager or managing member must be approved by two-thirds of the members (the vote of a managing member seeking a loan can be counted). [Section 10.50.145]

Any member of a member-managed LLC may transfer property of the LLC if the transfer is signed by the member in the name of the LLC. Property owned by a manager-managed LLC may only be transferred by a manager signing the transfer document in the name of the LLC. [Section 10.50.355]

ARIZONA

LLC Filing Office

Arizona Corporation Commission
Corporation Filing Section
1300 West Washington
Phoenix, AZ 85007-2996

Telephone: 800-345-5819 (in AZ only)
or 602-542-3135

Tucson Branch Office: 520-628-6560
(accepts LLC filings)

www.cc.state.az.us/corp/index.htm

State LLC Act

The Arizona LLC Act is contained in Title 29, Chapter 4 of the Arizona Statutes, starting at Section 29.601, and is browseable from the following Web page (scroll down to Chapter 4 in the Title 29 Web page list):

www.azleg.state.az.us/ars/29/title29.htm

State Tax Office

Department of Revenue, Phoenix
www.revenue.state.az.us

LLC Management

An LLC is managed by its members unless the articles state that the LLC is to be managed by one or more managers. [Sections 29-632 and 29-681]

Manager Election

Designation, election, replacement, and removal of managers are according to any rules set out in the operating agreement. If all managers resign, and the operating agreement is silent on how to elect new ones, a majority of members may elect a new manager or managers. [Section 29-681]

Meeting Requirements

Rules for the notice, time, place, quorum, and manner of voting by members or managers at a meeting, or by written consent, are to be specified in the operating agreement. [Section 29-682]

Amendments

Except as provided in the operating agreement, all members must approve an amendment to articles that changes the LLC from member-managed to manager-managed or from manager-managed to member-managed; otherwise, amendments to the articles must be approved by a majority of members (or majority of managers in a manager-managed LLC). Amendments to the articles that simply correct information in the articles, however, can be filed by any member or manager. Unless provided otherwise in the operating agreement, all members must approve amendments to the operating agreement. [Section 29-681]

Admission of Members

Except as provided in the operating agreement, new memberships must be issued with the consent of all members. [Section 29-681] Unless otherwise provided in the operating agreement, the admission of a transferee as a member must be approved by consent of all nontransferring members. [Section 29-731]

Withdrawal of Members

A member may withdraw from the LLC at any time by mailing or delivering a written notice of withdrawal to the other members, but, if the withdrawal violates the operating agreement, the LLC may recover from the member damages for breach of the operating agreement and offset the damages against any amount otherwise distributable to the member. [Section 29-734]

On any event of withdrawal of a member (which includes the withdrawal or expulsion of a member), except as otherwise provided in the operating agreement, the member does not have a right to a distribution because of the withdrawal, but does have the same right to continued distributions as would an assignee of the interest, and to a distribution when the LLC dissolves (less any amount recoverable from the withdrawing member because the withdrawal violated the operating agreement). [Section 29 707]

Continuation of the LLC

Except as provided in the operating agreement, a membership vote to continue the LLC after withdrawal of a member is not required, and the LLC continues. But if the last remaining member withdraws, unless a transferee of the member admits a new member into the LLC within 90 days, the LLC dissolves. [Section 28-781]

Special Statutory Rules

Except as provided in the operating agreement, under Section 29-681, a majority of members (or, in a manager-managed LLC, a majority of managers) must consent to:

1) settle differences on running the business of the LLC,

2) distribute LLC cash or property to members

3) authorize the repurchase by the LLC of a member's interest, and

4) authorize the filing of a notice to wind up the LLC. [Section 29-681]

Except as otherwise provided in the operating agreement, the approval of all members is required to fix or change the amount or type of capital contributions to be made by members. [Section 29-701]

Except as provided in the operating agreement, the approval of more than one-half the members and the member(s) entitled to receive upon dissolution of the LLC more than one-half the value of its assets is required to dissolve the LLC. [Section 29-781]

ARKANSAS

LLC Filing Office

Arkansas Secretary of State
Corporations Division
State Capitol
Little Rock, AR 72201-1094

888-233-0325

www.sosweb.state.ar.us/corp_ucc.html

State LLC Act

The Arkansas LLC Act (called the Small Business Entity Tax Pass Through Act) is located in Title 4 (Business and Commercial Law), Subtitle 3 (Corporations and Associations), Chapter 32, starting with Section 4-32-101, and is browseable from the following Web page (choose HTML or Java version, then select "Arkansas Code" to see a list of title headings; then select Title 4, then Subtitle 3, then Chapter 32):

www.arkleg.state.ar.us/Siteindex.asp?

State Tax Office

Department of Finance & Administration
Revenue Division, Little Rock

www.ark.org/dfa

LLC Management

An LLC is managed by its members unless the articles state that the LLC is to be managed by one or more managers. [Sections 4-32-202 and 4-32-401]

Manager Election

Unless otherwise provided in the operating agreement, designation, election, replacement, and removal of managers must be by the vote of more than one-half the number of members; terms of managers are indefinite unless otherwise stated in the operating agreement. [Section 4-32-401]

Meeting Requirements

Unless otherwise stated in the operating agreement, approval of more than one-half the members (or managers in a manager-managed LLC) is required to decide LLC business. [Section 4-32-403] We could not find specific rules for notice, time, place, or quorum for membership and management meetings in the LLC Act, so, presumably, any such rules are as provided in the operating agreement.

Amendments

Unless otherwise stated in the operating agreement, amendments to the operating agreement must be approved by all members. [Section 4-32-403] No specific rules for amendments of the articles were found in the LLC Act.

Admission of Members

Except as provided in the operating agreement, new memberships must be issued with the consent of all members. [Section 4-32-801] Unless otherwise stated in the operating agreement, the admission of a transferee as a member must be approved by unanimous written consent of nontransferring members. [Section 4-32-706]

Withdrawal of Members

Unless otherwise provided in the operating agreement, a member may withdraw upon 30 days' written notice to the other members. Exception: Unless otherwise stated in the operating agreement, if the LLC is established for a definite term or project, the member may not withdraw before the completion of the term or project. If a withdrawal is in violation of the operating agreement or due to wrongful conduct, the LLC may offset damages against the amount due a withdrawing member, including the cost of replacement services owed by the member, if the withdrawal was due to the member's wrongful conduct or was a breach of the LLC operating agreement. [Section 4-32-802(c)]

Unless provided otherwise in the operating agreement, and subject to exceptions involving assignments of a withdrawing member's interest, a withdrawing member is entitled to receive the fair value of the member's interest within a reasonable time after withdrawal. [Section 4-32-603]

Continuation of the LLC

After a member withdraws, the LLC continues automatically—a vote to continue the LLC is not required. [Section 4-32-901]

Special Statutory Rules

A vote of all members is required to voluntarily dissolve the LLC. [Section 4-32-901]

CALIFORNIA

LLC Filing Office

California Secretary of State
Limited Liability Company Unit
P.O. Box 944228
Sacramento, CA 94244-2280

Telephone: 916-653-3795

Branch offices of the Secretary of State are located in Fresno, Los Angeles, San Francisco, and San Diego. Currently, branch offices provide LLC forms over the counter only, and do not mail out forms or accept LLC filings.

www.ss.ca.gov/business/business.htm

Note: The practice of a California licensed profession cannot be organized as an LLC (accountants, attorneys, and architects can form a registered limited liability partnership, which is similar to an LLC).

State LLC Act

The California Beverly-Killea Limited Liability Company Act is contained in the California Corporations Code, Title 2.5 (Limited Liability Companies), starting with Section 17000, and is browseable from the following Web page (check the Corporations Code box, then click the search button at the bottom of the page; then scroll down to Section 17000 to find the LLC Act Sections):

www.leginfo.ca.gov/calaw.html

State Tax Office

Franchise Tax Board, Sacramento

www.ftb.ca.gov

LLC Management

An LLC is managed by its members unless the articles state that the LLC is to be managed by one or more managers. [Section 17051 of the Corporations Code]

Manager Election

Unless otherwise stated in the articles or operating agreement, managers are elected and removed by vote of majority in interest of members (if not defined in the operating agreement, this term means the vote of members who have a right to more than one-half of the current profits of the LLC). Managers are elected for an indefinite term unless otherwise provided in the articles or operating agreement. [Section 17152]

Meeting Requirements

Unless otherwise provided in the articles or operating agreement, members vote in proportion to their right to receive profits of the LLC (according to their profits interests in the LLC). [Section 17103]

Unless otherwise provided in the articles or operating agreement, the following default rules apply to LLC membership meetings:

- Meetings are held at the principal executive office of the LLC.

- Meetings can be called by any manager or by a member or members who hold more than 10% of the membership interests allowed to vote on the matters brought before the meeting.

- Notice of meetings must be given at least ten and no more than 60 days before the date of the meeting, and must state the time, date, place, and purpose of the meeting.

- Members may sign a waiver of notice to validate the actions taken at a meeting, however called and noticed.

- A quorum for a meeting consists of a majority in interest of the members (if not defined in the operating agreement, this term means the vote of members who have a right to more than one-half of the current profits of the LLC). [Section 17103]

Members also may take action by written consent if the number of members signing the consent is at least equal to the number of members who would have been required to approve the action at a membership meeting attended by all voting members. But the written consent of all members is required for special actions, such as the amendment of the LLC's articles or operating agreement or a dissolution of the LLC. [Section 17103]

Except as otherwise stated in the articles or operating agreement, managers approve decisions by a majority vote at a meeting, or by unanimous written consent. [Section 17156] Apparently, meetings of managers may be called, noticed, and held according to rules contained in the articles or operating agreement or as the managers see fit (no statutory rules were found in the LLC Act).

Amendments

Unless otherwise provided in the articles or operating agreement, amendments to the articles or operating agreement must be approved by all members. Note: The LLC articles or operating agreement cannot reduce the membership vote required to amend the articles below a majority in interest of members (if not defined in the operating agreement, this term means the vote of members who have a right to more than one-half of the current profits of the LLC). [Section 17103]

Admission of Members

Except as provided in the articles or operating agreement, new memberships must be issued with the consent of a majority in interest of the members, and only after the new member signs the LLC's operating agreement. [Section 17100] Except as otherwise provided in the articles or operating agreement, the admission of a transferee as a member must be approved by the consent of a majority interest of nontransferring members. [Section 17303]

Withdrawal of Members

A member may withdraw upon giving notice to the other members. Unless the articles or operating agreement provide otherwise, the member is not entitled to a distribution, but shall have the right of a holder of an economic interest in the LLC to receive continuing distributions. The LLC can offset these distributions by any damages recoverable against the member for breach of the LLC operating agreement. [Section 17252]

Continuation of the LLC

After a member withdraws, the LLC continues automatically—a vote to continue the LLC is not required. [Section 17350]

Special Statutory Rules

LLCs may be dissolved by vote of a majority in interest of the members or by any greater percentage of members stated in the articles or operating agreement. [Section 17350]

COLORADO

Secretary of State
Business Division
1560 Broadway, Suite 200
Denver, CO 80202

Telephone: 303-894-2200 (refers you to a 900 number for individual assistance)

www.sos.state.co.us/pubs/business/main.htm

State LLC Act

The Colorado LLC Act is contained in Title 7, Article 80 of the Colorado Statutes, starting with Section 7-80-101, and is browseable from the following Web page (select Colorado Statutes in the left pane, then select Title 7, then Limited Liability Companies):

http://198.187.128.12/colorado/
lpext.dll?f=templates&fn=fs-main.htm&2.0

State Tax Office

Revenue Department, Denver

www.revenue.state.co.us

LLC Management

An LLC is managed by its members unless the articles state that the LLC is to be managed by one or more managers. [Sections 7-80-204 and 7-80-401]

Manager Election

Managers are elected by a majority of the members for a one-year term. [Section 7-80-402] LLCs with six or more managers may elect managers for staggered terms, electing each group of managers for a two- or three-year term—this arrangement is called a classified management scheme. [Section 7-80-403] Managers may be removed by a majority of members, and manager vacancies may be filled by written agreement of a majority of remaining managers. [Sections 7-80-404 and 7-80-405] These manager election, removal, and replacement rules may be overridden in the LLC operating agreement. [Section 7-80-108]

Meeting Requirements

Members and managers vote according to any rules set out in LLC articles or operating agreement. [Sections 7-80-401 and 7-80-706]

Unless otherwise provided in the LLC operating agreement, the following rules apply to membership meetings:

- Meetings of members shall be held at the principal office of the LLC. [Section 7-80-707]
- An annual meeting of members shall be held for the election of managers. [Section 7-80-707]
- Meetings of the members may be called by any manager or by not less than 1/10 of all voting members. [Section 7-80-707]

- A majority of the LLC's voting members make up a quorum for purposes of membership meetings. [Section 7-80-708]

- The yes vote of a majority of members at which a quorum is present is required to approve membership decisions at a meeting. [Section 7-80-708]

- Written notice of regular (annual meetings scheduled in the operating agreement) and special meetings must be given to each voting member. The notice must state the time, date, and place (and, for special meetings, the purpose) of the meeting. It must be distributed no fewer than ten nor more than 50 days before the date of the meeting. [Section 7-80-709]

- Members may waive notice of a meeting by signing a written waiver before or after the membership meeting. [Section 7-80-710]

- Members may take action by unanimous written consent in lieu of a meeting. [Section 7-80-711]

Amendments

Unless otherwise stated in the LLC operating agreement, amendments to the articles must be approved by the written consent of all members. [Sections 7-80-209 and 7-80-108] No statutory rule was found for amendments to the operating agreement, so presumably the members can set their own rule within the agreement.

Admission of Members

Except as provided in the operating agreement, new memberships must be issued with the written consent of all members. [Section 7-80-701] Unless otherwise stated in a written operating agreement, the admission of a transferee as a member must be approved by unanimous written consent of nontransferring members. [Sections 7-80-702 and 7-80-108]

Withdrawal of Members

Unless prohibited in the operating agreement, a member can resign at any time from the LLC. If withdrawal is in violation of the operating agreement, distributions payable to the member may be offset by damages owed because of the breach. [Section 7-80-602]

A member who resigns has no right to participate in management of the LLC, and has a right to receive only that share of profits and distributions that are owed to nonresigning members (presumably, in the absence of a contrary provision in the operating agreement). [Section 7-80-603]

Continuation of the LLC

A membership vote to continue the LLC after dissociation of a member (cessation or termination of a membership interest) is not required under the LLC Act.

Special Statutory Rules

Except as otherwise provided under law, LLC debt may only be contracted by one or more LLC managers (or members in a member-managed LLC). [Sections 7-80-407 and 7-80-401]

Instruments for the purchase, mortgage, or sale of LLC property must be executed by one or more LLC managers (or members in a member-managed LLC). [Sections 7-80-408 and 7-80-401]

Except as provided in the LLC operating agreement, distributions to members prior to resignation from the LLC or before its dissolution must be approved by all members. [Section 7-80-601]

All members must vote in order to dissolve the LLC. [Section 7-80-801]

CONNECTICUT

LLC Filing Office

Connecticut Secretary of State
30 Trinity Street
P.O. Box 150470
Hartford, CT 06106
Telephone: 860-509-6002
www.sots.state.ct.us

State LLC Act

The Connecticut LLC Act is contained in Title 34, Chapter 613 of the Connecticut Statutes, starting with Section 34-100, and is browseable from the following Web page (click Title 34, then click Chapter 613):

www.cga.state.ct.us/2001/pub/titles.htm

State Tax Office

Department of Revenue Services, Hartford

www.drs.state.ct.us

LLC Management

An LLC is managed by its members unless the articles state that the LLC is to be managed by one or more managers. [Sections 34-121 and 34-140]

Manager Election

Unless otherwise stated in the operating agreement, managers are elected and removed by majority-in-interest (presumably, a majority of the profits and capital interests of members—we were unable to find a definition of this term in the Act) of members, and serve for an indefinite term. [Section 34-140]

Meeting Requirements

Except as provided in the articles or operating agreement, or as required under special provision of the LLC Act, members approve action by the vote of a majority in interest of the members (presumably, a majority of the profits and capital interests of members); if the LLC is manager-managed, managers approve decisions by more than one-half the total number of managers. [Section 34-142] The LLC Act seems open-ended with respect to procedures for holding membership and manager meetings—so, notice, time, place, quorum, and manner of voting by members or managers at a meeting or by written consent can be set as desired in the operating agreement. [Section 34-140]

Amendments

Except as otherwise provided in the articles, amendments to the articles must be approved by a vote of a majority in interest of the members (presumably, by members who hold at least a majority of the capital and profits interests in the LLC). Except as otherwise provided in the articles or operating agreement, amendments to the operating agreement must be approved by at least two-thirds in interest of members (presumably, by members who own at least two-thirds of the capital and profits interests in the LLC). [Section 34-142]

Admission of Members

Except as provided in the operating agreement, new memberships must be issued with written consent of a majority in interest of members. [Section 34-179] Unless otherwise provided in the operating agreement, the admission of a transferee as a member must be approved by approval of a majority in interest of the members, not counting the interests of the transferring member, or, if the transferring member is the only LLC member, if the transferor agrees that the buyer can become a member. [Section 34-172]

Withdrawal of Members

If not prohibited by the LLC operating agreement, a member can withdraw from the LLC at any time upon 30 days' notice to the other members. If the withdrawal is not prohibited by the operating agreement, but is otherwise in violation of the operating agreement, the member can be held personally liable for financial damages caused by the withdrawal from the LLC (including the cost of paying another person to perform services promised by the withdrawing member). [Section 34-180]

Generally, unless otherwise provided in the articles or operating agreement, a member who resigns is not entitled to be paid for her interest, but only has a right to receive a share of LLC profits and other distributions that would be paid to an assignee of an economic interest in the LLC (such as ongoing profits and capital distributions on liquidation of the LLC). [Section 34-159]

Continuation of the LLC

A vote to continue the LLC after dissociation of a member (cessation or termination of a membership interest) is not required under the LLC Act.

Special Statutory Rules

If an LLC is member-managed, transfers of LLC property may be transferred by a document signed by a member on behalf of the LLC; if manager-managed, only a manager can execute such a transfer document on behalf of the LLC. [Section 34-168]

A majority in interest of the members must vote to voluntarily dissolve the LLC. [Section 34-206]

DELAWARE

LLC Filing Office

Department of State
Division of Corporations
P.O. Box 898
Dover, DE 19903

Telephone: 302-739-3073

www.state.de.us/corp/index.htm

State LLC Act

The Delaware LLC Act is contained in Title 6 (Commerce and Trade), Chapter 18 of the Delaware Statutes, starting with Section 18-101, and is browseable from the following Web page (click Chapter 18. Limited Liability Company Act):

www.state.de.us/corp/DElaw.htm

State Tax Office

Delaware Franchise Tax Office, Dover

www.state.de.us/revenue

LLC Management

An LLC is managed by its members unless the operating agreement vests management in one or more managers. [Section 18-402]

Manager Election

Election of managers, and managers' terms of office, are as provided in the operating agreement. [Section 18-402]

Meeting Requirements

Members make management decisions by approval of the members owning more than 50% of the current profits interests in the LLC. Manager voting rules are as provided in the operating agreement. [Sections 18-402 and 18-404] Notice, time, place, and quorum requirements for membership and manager meetings are as specified in the operating agreement. Unless otherwise provided in the operating agreement, action by written consent of members or managers must be signed by members or managers having at least the minimum number of votes necessary to approve the action at a meeting. [Sections 18-302 and 18-404]

Amendments

No statutory requirements were found for amending the certificate of formation or operating agreement.

Admission of Members

Except as provided in the operating agreement, new memberships must be issued with written consent of all members and after the admission of the new member is reflected in the LLC records. [Section 18-301] Admission of a transferee as a member must be approved by vote of all nontransferring members of the LLC, or as provided in the LLC operating agreement. [Section 18-704]

Withdrawal of Members

Unless allowed by the LLC operating agreement, a member may not resign prior to the dissolution and winding up of the LLC. [Section 18-603]

Generally, upon resignation authorized by the LLC operating agreement, a resigning member is entitled to receive the fair value of his membership interest within a reasonable period after resignation (unless the operating agreement has its own provisions for payments to a resigning member). [Section 18-604]

Continuation of the LLC

Generally, a vote to continue the LLC after dissociation of a member (cessation or termination of a membership interest) is not required. Exception: If the sole remaining member of the LLC is dissociated, the LLC automatically dissolves unless, within 90 days, the personal representative of the last member agrees to continue the LLC and consents to serve as an LLC member or appoints another person in his or her place. [Section 18-801]

Special Statutory Rules

Unlike most other states, the LLC Act says that unless otherwise provided in the operating agreement, both members and managers are agents of the LLC (whether the LLC is manager- or member-managed), and both have the authority to bind the LLC. [Section 18-402]

Unless otherwise provided in the operating agreement, a vote to dissolve the LLC must be approved by members who own more than two-thirds of the current profits interests in the LLC. But, within 90 days after the termination of a member, remaining members who own more than 50% of the current profits interests in the LLC can approve the dissolution of the LLC. [Section 18-801]

The operating agreement may prohibit a member assigning her membership interest prior to the dissolution of the LLC. [Section 18-603]

DISTRICT OF COLUMBIA

LLC Filing Office

Department of Consumer and Regulatory Affairs
Business Regulation Administration
Corporations Division
941 North Capitol Street, N.E.
Washington, DC 20002

Telephone: 202-442-4411

http://dcra.dc.gov/information/build_pla/
business_services/coporations_division.shtm

State LLC Act

The DC LLC Act is contained in Title 29 (Corporations), Chapter 10 of the DC Code, starting with Section 29-1001, and is browseable from the following Web page (click DC, click Division 5, then Title 29, then Chapter 10):

www.michie.com/resources1.html

State Tax Office

Finance and Revenue Department
http://cfo.dc.gov/etsc/main.shtm

LLC Management

An LLC is managed by its members unless the articles state that the LLC is to be managed by one or more managers. [Section 29-1017]

Manager Election

Managers are elected by the members (no specific membership voting rules for election are given in the Act). But, unless otherwise stated in the articles or operating agreement, the removal of managers and the filling of vacancies in manager positions must be approved by those members owning at least a majority of profits interests in LLC. [Section 29-1019]

Meeting Requirements

Unless otherwise provided in the articles or operating agreement, members vote in proportion to their profits interests in the LLC, with the vote of members owning at least a majority of the profits interests necessary to take membership action. Rules for notice, time, place, and quorum for membership meetings or action by written consent of members are as specified in the articles or operating agreement. [Section 29-1017] Unless otherwise provided in the articles or operating agreement, managers take action by vote of a majority of the managers. [Section 29-1019] Other rules for manager meetings and action by written consent of the managers were not found in Act, and presumably should be stated in the LLC articles or operating agreement.

Amendments

Unless otherwise provided in the articles or operating agreement, amendments to the articles or operating agreement must be approved by members who own at least a majority of the profits interests in the LLC. [Sections 29-1007 and 29-1018]

Admission of Members

Except as provided in the articles or operating agreement, new memberships must be issued with unanimous consent of the members. [Section 29-1032] Unless otherwise provided (or restricted) by the articles or operating agreement, the admission of a transferee as a member must be approved by consent of the nontransferring members holding a majority of the interests in profits of the LLC. [Section 29-1036] If the articles or operating agreement restrict the rights of members to assign their interests, these restrictions must comply with Section 29-1037 of the LLC Act.

Withdrawal of Members

A member may resign from a limited liability company only at the time or upon the happening of such events as are specified in the articles of organization or the operating agreement. [Section 29-1034]

If not otherwise provided in the operating agreement, a resigning member is entitled to receive the fair value of the membership interest within a reasonable time after resignation. If the resignation is a breach of the operating agreement or the result of wrongful conduct, the LLC may offset the amount paid to the resigning member by the amount of damages caused by the breach or wrongful conduct, including the costs of obtaining replacement services owed by the resigning member. [Section 29-1027]

Continuation of the LLC

Generally, a vote to continue the LLC after dissociation of a member (cessation or termination of a membership interest) is not required. Note: Except as otherwise provided in the operating agreement, the LLC automatically dissolves when the limited liability company has had no members for 90 consecutive days. [Section 29-1047]

Special Statutory Rules

Voluntary dissolution of the LLC must be approved by unanimous consent of voting members. [Section 29-1047]

FLORIDA

LLC Filing Office

Florida Department of State
Division of Corporations
P.O. Box 6327
Tallahassee, FL 32314

Telephone: 850-245-6052

www.dos.state.fl.us/doc/index.html

State LLC Act

The Florida LLC Act is contained in Title XXXVI (Business Organizations), Chapter 608 of the Florida Statutes, starting with Section 608.401, and is browseable from the following Web page (click Statutes and Constitution tab, then select Title XXXVI, then Chapter 608 from the index):

www.leg.state.fl.us/Welcome/index.cfm

State Tax Office

Revenue Department, Tallahassee
http://sun6.dms.state.fl.us/dor

LLC Management

An LLC is managed by its members unless the articles state that it will be managed by one or more managers. [Sections 608.407 and 608.422]

Manager Election

Managers must be elected for one-year terms according to procedures contained in the articles or operating agreement (the LLC Act refers to the operating agreement as the regulations of the LLC). [Section 608.422]

Meeting Requirements

In a member-managed LLC, members vote according to the relative percentages of their capital accounts (the percentage of each member's capital contribution to all members' contributions, plus any additions and minus any withdrawals made to these accounts during the life of the LLC). If a member's capital account is zero or a negative amount, the member has one vote. Note: Unless otherwise provided in the LLC articles or operating agreement, only managers who are also members are allowed to vote on matters affecting the limited liability company (presumably, the operating agreement of a manager-managed LLC with one or more nonmember managers will give all managers the right to vote on and otherwise manage LLC business). [Sections 608.422 and 608.4231] Rules for notice, time, place, and quorum for membership and manager meetings and action by written consent by members and managers were not found in the Act, and are presumably as specified in the LLC's articles or operating agreement.

Amendments

Unless provided otherwise in the articles or operating agreement, only members of the LLC can amend the operating agreement (but even if not provided in the articles or operating agreement, the managers can adopt emergency regulations to use in a time of catastrophe that prevents members from assembling for a meeting, such as a hurricane or flood). [Section 608.423] Specific rules for amendment of articles were not found in the Act.

Admission of Members

Except as provided in the articles or operating agreement, new memberships must be issued with unanimous written consent of the members. [Section 608.4232] Unless otherwise stated in the articles, the admission of a transferee as a member must be approved by unanimous consent of the nontransferring members. [Section 608.433]

Withdrawal of Members

A member may withdraw from an LLC only in accordance with the articles of organization or operating agreement and only at the time or upon the occurrence of an event specified in those documents. Notwithstanding anything to the contrary under applicable law, unless the articles of organization or operating agreement provide otherwise, a member may not resign from an LLC prior to its dissolution and winding up. Notwithstanding anything to the contrary under applicable law, the articles of organization or operating agreement may provide that an LLC interest may not be assigned prior to the LLC's dissolution and winding up. Upon withdrawal, a withdrawing member is entitled to receive any distribution to which he is entitled under the articles of organization or operating agreement, and, if not otherwise provided in the articles of organization and operating agreement, the withdrawing member is entitled to receive, within a reasonable time after withdrawal, the fair value of his interest in the LLC as of his date of resignation based upon his right to share in distributions. [Section 608.427]

Continuation of the LLC

Except as may be provided in the articles, a vote to continue the LLC after dissociation of a member (cessation or termination of a membership interest) is not required. [Section 608.441]

Special Statutory Rules

Voluntary dissolution of the LLC must be approved by unanimous consent of voting members. [Section 608.441]

GEORGIA

LLC Filing Office

Secretary of State
Corporations Division
Suite 315, West Tower
2 Martin Luther King Jr. Drive
Atlanta, GA 30334

Telephone: 404-656-2817

www.sos.state.ga.us/corporations

State LLC Act

The Georgia LLC Act starts with Section 14-11-100 of the Georgia Code, and is browseable from the following Web page. Go to the following URL, then select "GA Code" in the left panel. Select Title "14" in the top Titles grid, then select Chapter "14-11" in the Chapters column, then select sections in the right Sections column to browse the LLC Act:

www.legis.state.ga.us/

State Tax Office

Department of Revenue, Atlanta

www2.state.ga.us/departments/dor

LLC Management

An LLC is managed by its members unless the articles or operating agreement state that the LLC is to be managed by one or more managers. [Section 14-11-304]

Manager Election

Unless otherwise provided in the articles or operating agreement, managers must be elected and removed by more than one-half the number of members. Managers are elected for an indefinite term unless otherwise stated in the articles or operating agreement. [Section 14-11-304]

Meeting Requirements

Except as provided in the articles or operating agreement, members and managers have one vote each in reaching membership decisions, and, except for special voting rules specified in the LLC Act for special decisions, the approval of a majority of members is required to take membership or manager action. Except as provided in the articles or operating agreement, members or managers may take action by unanimous written consent, or, if allowed by the articles or operating agreement, by the minimum number of votes that would be necessary to approve the action. If not otherwise fixed under the articles or operating agreement, the record date for determining members or managers entitled to

take action by written consent is the date the first member or manager signs a consent. If action is taken by members or managers by written consent, unless otherwise provided in the articles or operating agreement, all voting members or managers who did not sign the consent must be given written notice of the action taken by written consent not more than ten days after the date of written consent. [Section 14-11-309]

Except as otherwise provided in the articles or operating agreement, meetings of members and managers shall abide by the following rules. [Section 14-11-310]:

- Membership meetings must be called by at least 25% of the members; manager meetings may be called by any manager.

- The members or managers calling a meeting shall give at least two days' notice of the meeting to the other members or managers.

- A majority of the members or managers constitutes a quorum for membership or manager meetings.

- Members and managers act at a meeting by the approval of a majority of the members or managers present at a meeting at which a quorum has been reached.

- Notice of a meeting should be in writing unless oral notice is reasonable under the circumstances. [Section 14-11-311]

- Members and managers may waive notice by signing a waiver before or after the date of the meeting. [Section 14-11-312]

Amendments

Unless otherwise provided in the articles or operating agreement, the approval of all members is required to amend the LLC's articles or the operating agreement. [Section 14-11-308]

Admission of Members

Unless otherwise provided in the articles or operating agreement, new memberships must be issued with unanimous approval of members. [Section 14-11-308]

Except as otherwise stated in the articles or operating agreement, the admission of a transferee as a member must be approved by unanimous consent of the nontransferring members. [Section 14-11-503]

Withdrawal of Members

For LLCs formed on or after July 1, 1999, specific approval by other members is not required for a member to withdraw. [Section 14-11-601.1]. Unless otherwise provided in the articles or operating agreement, the approval of all members is required to approve distributions to members prior to the dissolution of the LLC, to sell all LLC assets, and to voluntarily dissolve the LLC. [Section 14-11-308]

Continuation of the LLC

Except as may be provided in the articles, a vote to continue the LLC after dissociation of a member (cessation or termination of a membership interest) is not required (for LLCs formed on or after July 1, 1999). [Section 14-11-602]

Special Statutory Rules

If LLC articles that contain a limitation on the power of members or managers to convey real property are filed with the clerk of the superior court in a county, they will be effective against a purported grantee of real property owned by the LLC in that county. [Section 14-11-302]

Unless otherwise provided in the LLC articles or operating agreement, a contract or transaction that personally benefits a manager or managing member can be approved by members or managers without a personal interest in the contract or transaction after disclosure of the interest of the member or manager in the contract or transaction. [Section 14-11-307]

HAWAII

LLC Filing Office

Department of Commerce and Consumer Affairs
Business Registration Division
P.O. Box 40
Honolulu, HI 96810
Telephone: 808-586-2744
www.businessregistrations.com

State LLC Act

The Hawaii LLC Act is contained in Chapter 428 of the Hawaii Statutes, starting with Section 428-101, and is browseable from the following Web page.Select Legal Info at the left of the page, click Statutes, then select Uniform Limited Liability Company Act:

www.businessregistrations.com

State Tax Office

Hawaii Tax Department, Honolulu
www.state.hi.us/tax/tax.html

LLC Management

An LLC is managed by its members unless the articles state that the LLC is to be managed by one or more managers. [Section 428-203]

Manager Election

Unless otherwise provided in the articles or operating agreement, managers must be elected and removed by a majority of the members for an indefinite term. [Section 428-404]

Meeting Requirements

Unless otherwise provided in the articles or operating agreement [Sections 428-103 and 428-404]:

- Members and managers have equal voting rights (for example, one vote per member or manager).

- Members and managers approve action by a majority vote.
- Members and managers may take action by unanimous written consent.

Rules for notice, time, place, and quorum for membership and manager meetings were not found in the Act, and presumably may be specified in the LLC's articles or operating agreement.

Amendments

Unless otherwise provided in the articles or operating agreement, all LLC members must approve amendments to its articles and operating agreement. [Section 428-404]

Admission of Members

Unless otherwise provided in the articles or operating agreement, new memberships must be issued with unanimous approval of the members. [Section 428-404] Except as otherwise stated in the operating agreement, the admission of a transferee as a member must be approved by unanimous consent of the nontransferring members. [Section 428-503]

Withdrawal of Members

A member has the power to dissociate (withdraw) from the LLC at any time. If the withdrawal is a breach of the operating agreement or happens before the end of the term of the LLC (if a definite term is set for the existence of the LLC), the LLC may offset the amount paid to the withdrawing member by the amount of damages to the LLC and other members caused by the withdrawal. [Section 428-602]

Unless otherwise provided in the LLC operating agreement, a withdrawing member, generally, is entitled to receive the fair value of his membership interest. The LLC must present an offer to purchase the withdrawing member's interest to the member no later than 30 days from the date of withdrawal (but, if the LLC has a specified term, the purchase apparently need not occur until the expiration of the term). Financial statements must be included with the offer. [Section 429-701] The LLC

Act also contains provisions allowing a withdrawn member to institute a court action to determine the fair value of a withdrawing member's interest. [Section 428-702]

Continuation of the LLC

A vote to continue the LLC after dissociation (withdrawal or loss) of a member is not required [Section 428-801]

Special Statutory Rules

Unless otherwise provided in the articles or operating agreement, the approval of all members is required to approve distributions to members prior to the dissolution of the LLC, to sell all LLC assets, or to voluntarily dissolve the LLC. [Section 428-404]

IDAHO

LLC Filing Office

Idaho Secretary of State
Corporations Division
700 West Jefferson
P.O. Box 83720
Boise, ID 83720-0080

Telephone: 208-334-2301

www.idsos.state.id.us/corp/corindex.htm

State LLC Act

The Idaho LLC Act is contained in Title 53 (Partnership), Chapter 6 of the Idaho Statutes, starting with Section 53-601, and is browseable from the following Web page:

www3.state.id.us/idstat/TOC/53006KTOC.html

State Tax Office

State Tax Commission, Boise

www2.state.id.us/tax/forms.htm

LLC Management

An LLC is managed by its members unless its operating agreement states that the LLC is to be managed by one or more managers. [Section 53-621]

Manager Election

Unless otherwise provided in the operating agreement, managers must be elected, removed, and replaced by a vote of more than one-half the members, and serve for an indefinite term. [Section 53-621]

Meeting Requirements

Unless otherwise provided in the operating agreement, members and managers have one vote each, and the approval of more than one-half of the members or managers is necessary to take action. [Section 53-623] Rules for notice, time, place, quorum, and other aspects of membership and manager meetings or actions by written consent of the members and managers were not found in the Act, and presumably may be specified in the LLC's operating agreement.

Amendments

Unless otherwise provided in a written operating agreement, the approval of all members is required to amend the operating agreement (no statutory rule was found for amendments to articles). [Section 53-623]

Admission of Members

Unless otherwise provided in the articles or operating agreement, new memberships must be issued with the written consent of all members. [Section 53-640] Unless otherwise stated in the operating agreement, the admission of a transferee as a member must be approved by unanimous written consent of the nontransferring members. [Section 53-638]

Withdrawal of Members

Unless the operating agreement prohibits a member from withdrawing, a member may withdraw upon 30 days' notice to the other members. If the withdrawal is a breach of the operating agreement or a result of a member's wrongful conduct, the LLC may offset the amount paid to the withdrawing member by the amount of damages caused by the breach or wrongful conduct, including the cost of obtaining replacement services owed by the member. Unless otherwise provided in the operating agreement, a withdrawal by a member prior to the end of the term of an LLC organized for a specific term is a breach of the agreement. [Section 53-641c]

Unless otherwise provided in the operating agreement, a withdrawing member is treated as an assignee of a membership interest. Generally, this means that the member is only entitled to receive ongoing distributions of LLC profits until the LLC is dissolved, unless the other members unanimously agree otherwise. A member who is removed, however, has a right to receive the fair value of her interest within a reasonable time after removal. [Section 53-630]

Continuation of the LLC

Unless otherwise stated in the operating agreement, the dissociation (loss of membership rights) of a member automatically causes the LLC to dissolve unless all its remaining members vote to continue the LLC within 90 days of the dissociation. [Section 53-642]

Special Statutory Rules

If an LLC is member-managed, transfers of LLC property may be transferred by a document signed by a member on behalf of the LLC; if manager-managed, only a manager can execute such a transfer document on behalf of the LLC. [Section 53-634]

In addition to any provision in the operating agreement, all members can vote to voluntarily dissolve the LLC. [Section 53-642]

ILLINOIS

LLC Filing Office

Illinois Secretary of State
Department of Business Services
Limited Liability Company Division
Room 359, Howlett Building
Springfield, IL 62756

Telephone: 800-252-8980

Branch office in Chicago: 312-793-3380 (for questions and info only; not LLC filing).

www.sos.state.il.us/departments/business_services/business.html

State LLC Act

The Illinois LLC Act is contained in Chapter 805 (Business Organizations), starting with Section 180/1-1, and is browseable from the following Web page (scroll down to the Business heading, then click "CHAPTER 805 Business Organizations," then scroll down and select the 805 ILCS 180/ Limited Liability Company Act link):

www.legis.state.il.us/legislation/ilcs/chapterlist.html

State Tax Office

For annual tax information, contact the Department of Business Services, Springfield

www.sos.state.il.us/departments/business_services/business.html

For other tax information, contact the Department of Revenue, Springfield

www.revenue.state.il.us

LLC Management

An LLC is managed by its members unless the operating agreement states that it is to be managed by one or more managers. [Sections 180/5-5 and 180/15-1]

Manager Election

Managers are elected, removed, and replaced by consent of a majority of members, and hold office for an indefinite term. [Section 180/15-1]

Meeting Requirements

Unless otherwise provided in the articles or operating agreement [Section 180/15-1]:

- Members and managers have equal voting rights (for example, one vote per member or manager).
- Members and managers approve action by a majority vote.

Rules for notice, time, place, and quorum for membership and manager meetings and action by written consent of members and managers were not found in the Act, and presumably may be specified in the LLC's articles or operating agreement.

Amendments

Except as otherwise provided in the LLC's articles or operating agreement, managers may, by a majority vote, amend the articles to remove the name of an initial manager who is no longer a manager, remove the name of the initial registered agent of the LLC, or change the LLC name. Other amendments to the articles or operating agreement require the full membership's approval. [Sections 180/5-15 and 180/15-1]

Admission of Members

Unless otherwise provided in the articles or operating agreement, new memberships must be issued with the written consent of all members. [Section 180/10-1] Unless otherwise stated in the articles or operating agreement, the admission of a transferee as a member must be approved by unanimous consent of the nontransferring members. [Section 180/30-10]

Withdrawal of Members

A member has the power to dissociate (withdraw) at any time by giving the LLC notice of withdrawal, but the member may be liable for financial damages if the withdrawal is in violation of the LLC's operating agreement. The LLC can also offset any distribution owed to the withdrawing member by the amount of the damages. [Section 180/35-45 and -50]

Generally, unless the operating agreement provides otherwise, after a member's withdrawal, the member's interest must be purchased for its fair value by the LLC.

The LLC must also provide a purchase offer to the withdrawing member 30 days after the withdrawal, as well as financial statements of the LLC. If the LLC and member cannot agree on the value of the interest within 120 days after the member's withdrawal, the member can institute a court action to determine the fair value of the interest. [Section 180/35-60]

Continuation of the LLC

A vote to continue the LLC after the dissociation of a member (cessation or termination of a membership interest) is not required. Unless otherwise stated in the LLC operating agreement, an Illinois LLC continues despite the dissociation of a member. [Section 180/35-1]

Special Statutory Rules

Unless a member's or manager's authority to do so is limited in the articles, in a member-managed LLC, transfers of LLC property may be transferred by a document signed by any member on behalf of the LLC; in a manager-managed LLC, any manager can execute such a transfer document on behalf of the LLC. [Section 180/13-5]

Unless otherwise provided in the articles or operating agreement, the approval of all members is required to approve distributions to members prior to the dissolution of the LLC, to sell all LLC assets, or to voluntarily dissolve the LLC. [Section 180/15-1]

INDIANA

LLC Filing Office

Indiana Secretary of State
Corporations Division
302 W. Washington, Room E018
Indianapolis, IN 46204

Telephone: 317-232-6576

www.in.gov/sos/business/index.html

State LLC Act

The Indiana LLC Act (also called the Indiana Business Flexibility Act) is contained in Title 23 (Business and Other Associations), Article 18 of the Indiana Code, starting with Section 23-18-1-1, and is browseable from the following Web page (select Title 23, then Article 18):

www.in.gov/legislative/ic/code

State Tax Office

Department of Revenue, Indianapolis

www.state.in.us/dor

LLC Management

An LLC is managed by its members unless the operating agreement states that it is to be managed by one or more managers. [Sections 23-18-2-4 and 23-18-4-1]

Manager Election

Unless provided otherwise in the articles or operating agreement, managers are elected, removed, and replaced by a majority in interest of members (this means members who have contributed more than 50% of the current capital of the LLC), and serve for an indefinite term. [Sections 23-18-4-1 and 23-18-1-13]

Meeting Requirements

Except as provided in the articles or operating agreement, members must take action by the vote or consent of a majority in interest; managers act by a majority vote of the number of managers. [Section 23-18-4-3]

Rules for notice, time, place, and quorum for membership and manager meetings and action by written consent of members and managers were not found in the Act, and presumably may be specified in the LLC's articles or operating agreement.

Amendments

Except as otherwise provided in the articles or operating agreement, amendments to the operating agreement require the approval of all members (no rule was found for amendments to the articles). [Section 23-18-4-3] Also, the initial operating agreement must be signed by all the LLC's current members. [Section 23-18-4-6]

Admission of Members

Unless otherwise provided in the articles or operating agreement, new memberships must be issued with the written consent of all members. [Section 23-18-6-1] Unless otherwise stated in the operating agreement, the admission of a transferee as a member must be approved by unanimous written consent of the nontransferring members. [Section 23-18-6-4]

Withdrawal of Members

Unless the operating agreement prohibits a member from withdrawing, a member may withdraw upon 30 days' notice to the other members. If the withdrawal is a breach of the operating agreement or a result of a member's wrongful conduct, the LLC may offset the amount paid to the withdrawing member by the amount of damages caused by the breach or wrongful conduct, including the cost of obtaining replacement services owed by the member. Unless otherwise provided in the operating agreement, a withdrawal by a member prior to the end of the term of an LLC organized for a specific term is a breach of the agreement. [Section 23-18-6-6]

Generally, unless otherwise provided in the operating agreement, a withdrawing member is entitled to receive the fair value of the member's interest within a reasonable period after withdrawal. [Section 23-15-5-5]

Continuation of the LLC

For LLCs formed after June 30, 1999, a membership vote to continue the LLC after dissociation of a member (cessation or termination of a membership interest) is not required. [Section 23-18-9-1.1]

IOWA

LLC Filing Office

Iowa Secretary of State
Corporations Division
Lucas Building, 1st Floor
Des Moines, IA 50319

Telephone: 515-281-5204

www.sos.state.ia.us/business/index.html

State LLC Act

The Iowa LLC Act is contained in Title XII (Business Entities), Chapter 490A of the Iowa Code, starting with Section 490A.100, and is browseable from the following Web page (click "Iowa Law" in the left panel, select the latest version of the code, then insert "490A" in the chapter search box. then press enter to see a browseable list of all sections in the Iowa LLC Act):

www.legis.state.ia.us/

State Tax Office

Department of Revenue and Finance, Des Moines

www.state.ia.us/government/drf/index.html

LLC Management

An LLC is managed by its members unless the articles or operating agreement state that the LLC is to be managed by one or more managers. [Section 490A.702]

Manager Election

Unless otherwise provided in the articles or operating agreement, managers are elected or removed and manager vacancies are filled by a majority vote of the members (membership voting is according to capital account balances unless otherwise provided in the articles or operating agreement). [Sections 490A.705 and 490A.701]

Meeting Requirements

Unless otherwise provided in the articles or operating agreement, members vote according to the current balance in their capital accounts. [Section 490A.701] Rules for notice, time, place, and quorum for membership meetings and action by written consent of the members depend on the LLC's operating agreement. [Section 490A.307]

Unless otherwise provided in the articles or operating agreement, a quorum for managers' meetings is a majority of managers, and managers, approvals must be made by a majority vote. [Section 490A.705] Rules for notice, time, and place for managers' meetings and actions by written consent of the managers were not found in the LLC Act, and presumably may be set forth in the LLC's operating agreement.

Amendments

Unless otherwise provided in the articles or operating agreement, a unanimous vote of members is required to amend the articles or operating agreement. [Section 490A.701]

Admission of Members

Unless otherwise provided in the operating agreement, new memberships must be issued with the written consent of all members. [Section 490A.306] Unless otherwise stated in the articles or operating agreement, the admission of a transferee as a member must be approved by unanimous written consent or a vote at a meeting of nontransferring members. [Section 490A.903]

Withdrawal of Members

Generally, unless otherwise stated in the articles or operating agreement, a member may not withdraw from the LLC prior to its dissolution (but the Act allows a member to resign if certain types of amendments to the articles or operating agreement adversely affect the member). [Section 490A.704A]

Generally, unless otherwise provided in the operating agreement, a withdrawing member is entitled to re-

ceive the fair value of the member's interest within a reasonable period after withdrawal. [Section 490A.805]

Continuation of the LLC

A vote to continue the LLC after the termination of a membership is not required.

Special Statutory Rules

Unless otherwise provided in the articles or operating agreement, a majority vote of members (voting is according to capital account balances unless otherwise provided in the articles or operating agreement) is required to dissolve the LLC or sell all its assets. [Section 490A.701]

A contract or transaction that personally benefits a manager can be approved by a majority of managers who have no personal interest in the contract or transaction after disclosure of the interest of the affected member or manager. [Section 490A.708]

The written consent of all members is required to voluntarily dissolve the LLC. [Section 490A.1301]

KANSAS

LLC Filing Office

Kansas Secretary of State
Corporation Division
First Floor, Memorial Hall
120 S.W. 10th Ave.
Topeka, KS 66612

Telephone: 785-296-4564

www.kssos.org

State LLC Act

The Kansas LLC Act is contained in Chapter 17 of the Kansas Statutes, Article 76, starting with Section 17-7662 (Ignore Sections 17-7601 to 17-7661; this is the prior LLC Act), and is browseable from the Web page listed below. Use the arrow keys to highlight Chapter 17, Corporations, in the center box, then press Get Articles in Chapter. Then use the arrow keys to highlight Article 76, Limited Liability Companies, and press List Statutes in Article to see a list of the LLC Act statutes.

www.kslegislature.org/cgi-bin/statutes/index.cgi

State Tax Office

Department of Revenue, Topeka

www.ksrevenue.org/

LLC Management

An LLC is managed by its members unless the articles or operating agreement state that the LLC is to be managed by one or more managers. [Sections 17-7607 and 17-7612]

Manager Election

Managers are elected by members as set out in the articles or operating agreement. [Section 17-7612]

Meeting Requirements

Unless otherwise provided in the articles or operating agreement, members have one vote each (presumably, managers also have one vote each in a manager-managed LLC). Regular meetings of managers and members are held at times stated in the operating agreement or, if not stated, upon at least ten days' written notice; other meetings of members or managers may be called at any time by members or managers, respectively, who hold at least 1/5 the voting power of the LLC, upon at least ten and not more than 60 days' written notice. Members can take action by written consent by consent of all members. A quorum for LLC meetings is a majority of the voting power. [Section 17-7613] Rules for notice, time, and place for managers' meetings and action by written consent of managers were not found in the LLC Act, and presumably may be provided in the LLC operating agreement.

Amendments

Rules for membership approval of amendments to the articles and operating agreement were not found in the LLC Act.

Admission of Members

Unless otherwise provided in the operating agreement, new memberships must be issued with written consent of all members. Unless otherwise provided in the operating agreement, the admission of a transferee as a member must be approved by majority of the nontransferring members. [Section 17-7618]

Withdrawal of Members

We found no specific provisions on withdrawal of a member; Section 17-7616 says that a member may demand a return of capital (which is, generally, the minimum amount requested by a member upon withdrawal) only on dissolution of the LLC or on a date specified in the articles. [Section 17-7616]

Continuation of the LLC

A vote to continue the LLC after the dissociation of a member (cessation or termination of a membership interest) is not required (but members can vote to dissolve the LLC, if they wish, within 90 days of the dissociation of a member). However, the LLC automatically dissolves if there are no remaining members. [Section 17-7622]

Special Statutory Rules

The written consent of all members is required to voluntarily dissolve the LLC. [Section 17-7622]

KENTUCKY

LLC Filing Office

Kentucky Secretary of State
Business Filings
P.O. Box 718
Frankfort, KY 40602
Telephone: 502-564-2848
www.kysos.com/BUSSER/BUSFIL/forms.asp

State LLC Act

The Kentucky LLC Act is contained in Title XXIII (Private Corporations and Associations), Chapter 275 of the Kentucky Statutes, starting with Section 275.001, and is browseable from the following Web page:

http://162.114.4.13/krs/275-00/CHAPTER.HTM

State Tax Office

Kentucky Revenue Cabinet, Frankfort

http://revenue.state.ky.us/

LLC Management

An LLC is managed by its members unless the articles or operating agreement states that the LLC is to be managed by one or more managers. [Sections 275.025 and 275.165]

Manager Election

Unless otherwise provided in the articles or operating agreement, managers are to be elected for an indefinite term, and removed or replaced by a majority in interest of members (unless otherwise provided in the operating agreement, this means members who have contributed a majority of the capital to the LLC). [Sections 275.165, 275.015, and 275.175]

Meeting Requirements

Unless otherwise provided in the articles or operating agreement, members vote in proportion to their contributions to the LLC, with a majority vote necessary to take membership action. In other words, the vote of members who have contributed a majority of the capital to the LLC is normally necessary to take membership action. [Section 275.175] Rules for notice, time, place, and quorum for members' and managers' meetings and action by written consent by members and managers were not found in the LLC Act, and presumably may be provided in the LLC operating agreement.

Amendments

Unless otherwise provided in the articles or operating agreement, a majority in interest is required to amend the articles to change management of the LLC from member- to manager-management, or vice versa, or to amend the operating agreement. [Section 275.175]

Admission of Members

Unless otherwise provided in the operating agreement, new memberships must be issued with written consent of all members. [Section 275.275] Unless otherwise provided in the operating agreement, the admission of a transferee as a member must be approved by written consent of a majority in interest of members (this normally means members who have contributed a majority of the capital to the LLC). [Section 275.265]

Withdrawal of Members

Unless the operating agreement says otherwise, a member can withdraw from the LLC only by obtaining the consent of all other members. [Section 275.280] No specific provision was found in the LLC Act that says how much the member is entitled to receive upon withdrawal in the absence of a provision in the operating agreement.

Continuation of the LLC

A vote to continue the LLC after termination of a membership is not required.

Special Statutory Rules

Unless otherwise provided in the operating agreement, the approval of a majority in interest of members is required to amend the operating agreement or to amend the articles to switch from member- to manager-management (or vice versa). [Section 275.175]

A promise by a member to make contributions to capital is not enforceable unless in writing. [Section 275.200]

In a member-managed LLC, transfers of LLC property may be transferred by a document signed by an authorized member on behalf of the LLC; in a manager-managed LLC, any authorized manager can execute such a transfer document on behalf of the LLC. [Section 275.245]

Unless otherwise provided in the operating agreement, the written consent of a majority in interest of members is required to voluntarily dissolve the LLC. [Section 275.285]

LOUISIANA

LLC Filing Office

Louisiana Secretary of State
Commercial Division
P.O. Box 94125
Baton Rouge, LA 70804

Telephone: 225-925-4704

www.sec.state.la.us/comm/corp-index.htm

State LLC Act

The Louisiana LLC Law is contained in Chapter 22, Title 12 of the Louisiana Statutes, starting with Section 12:1301. See the following Web page to browse the Law (click Louisiana Laws in the left panel, then select the RS check box to search the Revised Statutes, then insert in the search box the section number you wish to view—currently, the law must be browsed section by section):

www.legis.state.la.us

State Tax Office

Department of Revenue and Taxation, Baton Rouge

www.rev.state.la.us

LLC Management

An LLC is managed by its members unless the articles or operating agreement states that the LLC is to be managed by one or more managers. [Title 12, Sections 1305 and 1311]

Manager Election

Unless otherwise provided in the articles or operating agreement, vacancies in manager positions must be filled by a plurality vote of the members. Managers can be removed only by a majority of members at a meeting called for that purpose. [Section 1313] Apparently, managers are elected as provided in the operating agreement, and serve for an indefinite term.

Meeting Requirements

Unless otherwise provided in the articles or operating agreement, members and managers each have one vote, and members and manager decisions must be made by a majority of managers. [Sections 1316 and 1318] Rules for notice, time, place, and quorum for members' and managers' meetings and action by written consent by members and managers were not found in the LLC Act, and presumably may be provided in the LLC operating agreement.

Amendments

Unless otherwise provided in the articles or operating agreement, amendments to the articles or operating agreement require the approval of a majority of members. [Section 1318]

Admission of Members

No statutory rule was found for membership approval of the issuance of new memberships in the LLC. Unless otherwise stated in the articles or operating agreement, the admission of a transferee as a member must be approved by unanimous written consent of the nontransferring members. [Section 1332]

Withdrawal of Members

A member of an LLC organized for a specific term may withdraw from the LLC only for just cause arising out of the failure of another member to perform an obligation. Unless otherwise provided in the operating agreement, a member of an LLC with an indefinite duration may withdraw upon 30 days' prior written notice to each member and manager (notice must also be given to the LLC's registered office). Unless otherwise provided in the operating agreement (and except as provided in the LLC Act), a withdrawing member is entitled to be paid the fair market value of the member's interest within a reasonable time after withdrawal. [Section 1325]

Continuation of the LLC

A vote to continue the LLC after the termination of a membership is not required. [Section 1334]

Special Statutory Rules

Unless otherwise provided in the articles or operating agreement, the approval of a majority of members is required to voluntarily dissolve the LLC, sell all its assets, or approve a loan not in the ordinary course of business. [Section 1318]

To validate a contract or transaction between the LLC and a member or manager with a personal financial interest in the contract or transaction, approval of a majority of disinterested members after full disclosure should be obtained. [Section 1318]

MAINE

LLC Filing Office

Secretary of State
Bureau of Corporations, Elections and Commissions
101 State House Station
Augusta, ME 04333-0101
ATTN: Corporate Examining Section
Telephone: 207-624-7740
www.state.me.us/sos/cec/cec.htm

State LLC Act

The Maine LLC Act is contained in Title 31 (Partnerships and Associations), Chapter 13 of the Maine Statutes, starting with Section 601, and is browseable from the following Web page:

http://janus.state.me.us/legis/statutes/31/
title31sec601.html

State Tax Office

Maine Revenue Services, Augusta
www.state.me.us/revenue

LLC Management

An LLC is managed by its members unless the articles or operating agreement states that the LLC is to be managed by one or more managers. [31 Maine Revised Statutes, Sections 623 and 651]

Manager Election

Unless otherwise provided in the articles or operating agreement, managers are to be elected for an indefinite term and removed and replaced by a majority (per capita) vote of the members. [Section 651]

Meeting Requirements

Except as provided in the articles or operating agreement, members and managers must make decisions through approval by more than one-half of the members or managers on a per capita basis (one vote per member or manager). [Section 653]

Rules for notice, time, place, and quorum for managers' and members' meetings and action by written consent by managers and members may presumably be provided in the LLC articles or operating agreement. [Section 651]

Amendments

Amendments to articles must be made by a majority in interest of the members (a definition was not found in the LLC Act but, presumably, this means the vote of members owning a majority of the profits and capital interests in the LLC). [Section 623] Note that an amendment to the articles must be filed with the state LLC filing office within 90 days of a:

- change of LLC name
- change in management of the LLC from member-managed to manager-managed, or vice versa, or
- a change in the minimum or maximum number of managers (in a manager-managed LLC).

Except as provided in the articles or operating agreement, amendments to the operating agreement can be made only after approval by all the LLC members. [Section 653]

Admission of Members

Unless otherwise provided in the operating agreement, new memberships must be issued with written consent of all members. [Section 691] Admission of transferee as a member must be approved by unanimous consent of the nontransferring members and the transferee, and as otherwise provided in the articles or operating agreement. [Section 687]

Withdrawal of Members

Unless otherwise provided in the articles or operating agreement, a member of an LLC may withdraw upon 30 days' prior written notice to the other members. [Section 692(3)]

Upon withdrawal of a member, the member is not entitled to receive a distribution except as may be required under the LLC operating agreement. [Section 672]

Continuation of the LLC

A vote to continue the LLC after withdrawal of a member is not required. [Section 701]

Special Statutory Rules

An LLC may file a statement of authority with the Secretary of State, listing the names of managers or members authorized or not authorized to enter into transactions on behalf of the LLC, including the transfer of real estate. This statement also may be recorded in the county where the real property is located. Outside persons dealing with the LLC may rely on filed statements of authority and the LLC may hold outsiders bound with knowledge of the information contained in these filed statements. See statute for more information. [Section 626]

An LLC must file, upon the request of a third party, a list of the names and addresses of its members with the Secretary of State. [Section 647]

In a member-managed LLC, LLC property may be transferred by a document signed by a member on behalf of the LLC; in a manager-managed LLC, any manager can execute such a transfer document. [Section 683]

Written consent of all members is required to voluntarily dissolve the LLC. [Section 701]

MARYLAND

LLC Filing Office

Maryland Department of Assessments and Taxation
Corporate Charter Division
Room 801
301 West Preston Street
Baltimore, MD 21201-2395

Telephone: 410-767-1340

Toll-free: 888-246-5941

www.dat.state.md.us/sdatweb/charter.html

State LLC Act

The Maryland LLC Act is contained in the Corporations and Associations heading, Title 4A, starting with Section 4A-101, and is browseable from the following Web page (currently, sections of the Act must be browsed one at a time from this page—click the Statutes box, enter the section number in the search box, then click the Search button):

http://mgasearch.state.md.us/verity.asp

State Tax Office

Comptroller of Maryland, Revenue Administration Division, Annapolis

www.comp.state.md.us/default.asp

LLC Management

Unless otherwise provided in the operating agreement, members manage the LLC. [Section 4A-403] The LLC Act does not mention managers or manager-management, but allows the operating agreement to delegate management to persons who are not members. In effect, this allows LLCs to elect manager-management, and to assign management to one or more persons (who may or may not be members). [Section 4A-402]

Manager Election

No rules were found in the LLC Act, but the operating agreement is allowed to specify all aspects of LLC management—presumably this includes the manner of election and term for managers in a manager-managed LLC. [Section 4A-402]

Meeting Requirements

Unless otherwise provided in the articles or operating agreement, members must vote in proportion to their relative interests in the profits of the LLC. The approval of members owning a majority of such profits interests is required for membership action. [Section 4A-403] Rules for the notice, time, place, and quorum for managers' and members' meetings, and for action by written consent by managers and members, were not found in Act. Presumably, these may be provided in the LLC articles or operating agreement.

Amendments

Amendments to articles require unanimous consent of LLC members. [Section 4A-204] Except as otherwise stated in the operating agreement, the operating agreement must be amended by consent of all LLC members. If, as authorized in the operating agreement, the agreement is amended without full membership approval, a copy of the amendments to the agreement must be delivered to each nonconsenting member. [Section 4A-402]

Admission of Members

Unless otherwise provided in the operating agreement, new memberships must be issued with the written consent of all LLC members. [Section 4A-601] Admission of a transferee as a member must be approved by unanimous written consent of the nontransferring members, and as otherwise specified in the operating agreement. [Section 4A-604] Also, unless otherwise provided in the

operating agreement, if the LLC has no members (that is, the remaining member or members has/have assigned their membership interests), the assignee(s) can elect to become members. [Section 4A-604]

Withdrawal of Members

Unless otherwise provided in the operating agreement, a member can withdraw from the LLC by giving the other members no fewer than six months' prior written notice at the members' addresses shown on the LLC records. [Section 4A-605]

An LLC may elect to pay a withdrawing member or the member's successor in interest the fair value of the member's interest within a reasonable period after withdrawal (payment does not seem to be required; if a liquidating payment is not made, the withdrawing member is treated as an assignee—that is, is entitled to receive a continuing share of profits and other LLC distributions made to all members). [Section 4A.606.1]

Continuation of the LLC

A vote to continue the LLC after termination of a membership interest is not required. But, except as may otherwise be provided in the operating agreement, a Maryland LLC automatically dissolves if it has no members for a period of 90 consecutive days. [Section 4A-902]

MASSACHUSETTS

LLC Filing Office

Commonwealth of Massachusetts
Corporations Division
One Ashburton Place, 17th Floor
Boston, MA 02108

Telephone: 617-727-9640

www.state.ma.us/sec/cor

State LLC Act

The Massachusetts LLC Act is contained in Title XXII (Corporations), Chapter 156C of the Massachusetts

General Laws, starting with Section 1, and is browseable from the following Web page:

www.state.ma.us/legis/laws/mgl/gl-156C-toc.htm

State Tax Office

Department of Revenue, Boston

www.dor.state.ma.us/Dorpg.htm

LLC Management

An LLC is managed by its members unless the operating agreement states that the LLC is to be managed by one or more managers. [Chapter 156C, Sections 1 and 24]

Manager Election

Managers may be designated, elected, replaced, and removed for a term as provided in the LLC operating agreement. [Sections 2, 23, and 24]

Meeting Requirements

Unless otherwise provided in the operating agreement, the vote of members who own more than 50% of unreturned capital contributions to the LLC is required in order to make decisions. [Section 20] Unless stated in the operating agreement, managers must approve actions by a majority vote (one vote each). [Section 26] Rules for notice, time, place, and quorum for members' and managers' meetings and action by written consent by members and managers may be provided in the LLC operating agreement. [Sections 20 and 26]

Amendments

No voting rules for amendments to the Certificate of Organization or operating agreement were found in the LLC Act (presumably, these may be specified in the operating agreement).

Admission of Members

Unless otherwise provided in the operating agreement, new memberships must be issued with the written consent of all members. [Section 19] Admission of a trans-feree as a member must be approved by unanimous consent of the nontransferring members or as provided in the operating agreement. [Sections 39 and 41]

Withdrawal of Members

A member may resign from an LLC upon at least six months' prior written notice to the LLC and to each member and manager (at their addresses listed in the LLC records). If the resignation is in violation of the operating agreement, the LLC can recover damages for this breach, and can offset such damages against any amounts owed by the LLC to the resigning member. [Section 36]

A manager may resign from the LLC at any time upon prior notice to each member and manager. As noted just above, if the resignation is in violation of the operating agreement, the LLC can recover and offset against payouts owed to the manager any damages for breach of the agreement. [Section 37]

If not otherwise specified in an operating agreement, a resigning member is entitled to receive the fair value of the member's interest within a reasonable time after withdrawal. [Section 32]

Continuation of the LLC

For LLCs formed on or after January 1, 1997, a vote to continue the LLC after termination of a membership interest is not required. [Section 43]

Special Statutory Rules

The certificate of organization may list the names of one or more persons authorized to execute and record title documents for real estate. [Section 12]

An LLC manager who votes for or assents to the making of a distribution to members in violation of the LLC operating agreement is personally liable to the LLC for the amount of the unwarranted distribution. [Section 35]

In addition to any event specified in the operating agreement, the approval of all members may voluntarily dissolve the LLC. [Section 43]

MICHIGAN

LLC Filing Office

Michigan Department of Consumer and Industry Services
Corporation & Securities and Land Development Bureau
Corporation Division
P.O. Box 30054
Lansing, MI 48909-7554

Telephone: 517-241-9223

www.michigan.gov/cis

State LLC Act

The Michigan LLC Act is contained in Chapter 450
(Corporations) of the Michigan Compiled laws, Act 23
of 1993, starting with Section 450.4101, and is
browseable from the following Web page (select Chapter Index under Michigan Compiled Laws Information,
then select Chapter 450, then select Act 23 of 1993 at
the bottom of the page, which is the LLC Act):

www.michiganlegislature.org

State Tax Office

Michigan Department of Treasury, Lansing

www.michigan.gov/treasury

LLC Management

An LLC is managed by its members unless the articles or
operating agreement states that the LLC is to be managed by one or more managers. [Sections 450.4102,
450.4203, and 450.4401]

Manager Election

A vote of a majority in interest of the members entitled
to vote in accordance with section 502(1) is required to
select managers to fill initial positions or vacancies. The
members may remove one or more managers with or
without cause unless an operating agreement provides
that managers may be removed only for cause. The
members may remove a manager for cause only at a
meeting called expressly for that purpose, and that manager shall have reasonable advance notice of the allegations against him or her and an opportunity to be heard
at the meeting. [Section 450.4403]

Meeting Requirements

Except as provided in the articles or operating agreement, the vote of a majority of managers is required for
manager action, with managers given one vote each.
[Section 450.4405] Except as provided in the articles or
operating agreement, members take action by approval
of a majority of all members, with each member having
one vote. [Section 450.4502] Rules for notice, time,
place, and quorum for members' and managers' meetings, and for action by written consent by members and
managers, presumably may be provided in the LLC operating agreement.

Amendments

Only members may amend the articles. [Section
450.4502] Unless the articles or operating agreement allow amendment of articles by majority membership
vote, amendments of articles must be approved by all
voting members. [Section 450.4603] No statutory rule
was found for amending the operating agreement. Presumably these rules may be provided in the operating
agreement.

Admission of Members

Unless otherwise provided in the operating agreement,
new memberships must be issued with the consent of
all voting members. [Section 450.4501] Unless otherwise provided in the operating agreement, in an LLC
with more than one member, the admission of a transferee as a member must be approved by unanimous
consent of the voting members. An assignee of an LLC
with one member may become a member if allowed under the terms of the agreement between the selling
member and the assignee. [Section 450.4506]

Withdrawal of Members

A member may withdraw from the LLC only as provided in the LLC's operating agreement. [Section

450.4509] If the LLC operating agreement permits withdrawal, but is silent on the issue of payments to a withdrawing member, a withdrawing member is entitled to receive the fair value of the member's interest within a reasonable time after withdrawal. [Section 450.4305]

Continuation of the LLC

A vote to continue the LLC after termination of a membership is not required.

Special Statutory Rules

Only members may vote to voluntarily dissolve the LLC or, unless otherwise provided in an operating agreement, sell all its assets (presumably by the normal majority voting rule). [Section 450.4502]. Unless authorized in advance by an operating agreement, a majority of disinterested members must approve a contract or transaction that personally benefits a manager of the LLC after full disclosure of the facts surrounding the transaction. [Section 450.4502]

MINNESOTA

LLC Filing Office

Minnesota Secretary of State
Business Services Division
180 State Office Building
100 Rev. Dr. Martin Luther King Jr. Blvd.
St. Paul, MN 55155-1299

Telephone: 651-296-2803

Toll-free: 877-551-6767

www.sos.state.mn.us/business/index.html

State LLC Act

The Minnesota LLC Act is contained in Chapter 322B of the Minnesota Statutes, starting with Section 322B.01, and is browseable from the following Web page:

www.revisor.leg.state.mn.us/stats/322B

State Tax Office

Department of Revenue, St. Paul

www.taxes.state.mn.us

LLC Management

The Minnesota LLC Act presupposes management by a board of governors (management by governors is similar to the vesting of management power in a corporate board of directors). The law specifies that LLCs must have one or more governors, elected by the members, who serve for an indefinite term of office. Section 322B.606, however, recognizes that LLCs may wish to adopt membership management. That section says that the LLC members may act in the place of the governors as long as they make management decisions by unanimous vote; this is usually easy to achieve in smaller LLCs and we assume most smaller Minnesota LLCs will opt for membership management, rather than management by a board of governors (governor management is subject to many corporate type rules and procedures specified in the LLC Act). To reinforce this member-management election, the LLC operating agreement should require a unanimous membership vote for management decisions.

If you decide to go along with the statutory scheme and opt for management by governors, see Sections 322B.60 and following of the LLC Act to learn more about the default statutory management scheme, and special rules that apply to board of governor action.

To make matters more confusing, Minnesota law requires the appointment or election of two persons who function as the LLC president and treasurer, but who are called managers (one is called the chief manager, the other is called the treasurer). [Section 322B.67] Don't be confused by this nonstandard nomenclature. Simply decide which of your members (or managers, in a manager-managed LLC) will be chief manager and function as the LLC president, and also pick a member or manager to serve as treasurer.

Manager Election

Board of governors' election procedures are as specified in the articles or operating agreement. [Section

322B.613] Unless a fixed term is provided in the articles or operating agreement, governors serve an indefinite term until the next regular meeting of members; if a fixed term is specified, it cannot exceed five years. [Section 322B.616] Unless otherwise provided in the articles, members vote for governors by cumulative voting (similar to how shareholders vote for directors in larger corporations). [Section 322B.63] Unless otherwise provided in the articles or operating agreement, removal of governors requires the same membership vote as a vote to elect them. [Section 322B. 636] Unless otherwise provided in the articles or operating agreement, vacancies on the board of governors may be filled by persons approved by a majority of the remaining governors. [Section 322B.64]

These governor-management rules are complex, and riddled with exceptions. If you wish to follow them, see the LLC Act sections noted above. We expect most LLCs will allow management by unanimous vote of members instead. [Section 322B.606]

Meeting Requirements

Unless otherwise provided in the articles, members vote in proportion to the value reflected in the LLC records of each member's capital contribution to the LLC. [Section 322B.356] Unless otherwise provided in the articles, the approval of a majority of the membership voting power present at a meeting is required for membership action. [Section 322B.35] But remember, when members act as managers of the LLC (as is usually the case when members are asked to take action in a smaller LLC that wishes to avoid the governor-management rules), members must act by unanimous approval. [Section 322B.606] Members may take action by unanimous written consent without a meeting (articles may lower this written consent requirement to written consent of the members required to take action at a meeting at which all members were present). [Section 322B.35] Unless otherwise specified in the articles or operating agreement, regular meetings of members need not be held, unless demanded by a member under certain conditions. [Section 322B.333] Special members' meetings may be called by the chief manager (president), trea-

surer, two or more governors, or members owning 10% or more of the membership voting power. [Section 322B.336] Unless otherwise stated in articles, the operating agreement, or a special LLC Act provision, at least ten days' and no more than 60 days' notice must be given of a members' meeting. [Section 322B.34] Unless otherwise stated in the articles or operating agreement, a quorum for members' meetings is a majority of the membership voting power. [Section 322B. 353]

Board of governors' meetings may be held as provided in the articles or operating agreement. [Section 322B.643] Unless otherwise stated in the articles or operating agreement, governors' meetings can be held only after at least ten days' notice. [Section 322B.643] A quorum for governors' meetings is a majority of the number of governors unless otherwise stated in the articles or operating agreement. [Section 322B.65] Generally, governors take action by a majority of those present at a governors' meeting. [Section 322B.653] Unless otherwise provided in the articles, governors may take action by written consent of all governors. [Section 322B.656]

Again, these governor-management rules are complex, and riddled with exceptions. If you wish to follow them, see the LLC Act sections noted above. We expect most LLCs will allow management by unanimous vote of members instead. [Section 322B.606]

Amendments

Amendments to articles must be approved by the majority vote of LLC members. Section 322B.15 of the LLC Act has specific rules for calling, noticing, and holding a meeting of members to amend the articles. As an alternative, all members can approve the amendments by written consent. [Section 322B.35]

Amendments to the operating agreement are normally reserved to the governors, but governors are not allowed to make certain decisions (changing qualifications, terms of office, and decreasing number of governors, for example). [Section 322B.603] Again, we assume smaller LLCs will wish to avoid governor-management rules and, instead, will approve amendments to operating agreement by unanimous consent of members. [Section 322B.606]

Admission of Members

No statutory rule was found regarding issuance of new memberships. Unless otherwise stated in the articles, the admission of a transferee as a member must be approved by unanimous written consent of the nontransferring members. [Section 322B.313]

Withdrawal of Members

A member has the legal power to withdraw at any time from a Minnesota LLC. Also, a member cannot be expelled from the LLC except as provided in the articles of organization. If a member's resignation violates the operating agreement, the member is liable to the LLC for damages caused by the resignation. [Section 322B.306] No specific provision was found in the LLC Act that says how much the member is entitled to receive upon withdrawal in the absence of a provision in the operating agreement. Section 322B.51 simply says that a member is entitled to receive distributions prior to the termination of the LLC only as specified in the LLC operating agreement or by the act of the board of governors (managers) of the LLC.

Continuation of the LLC

For LLCs formed on or after August 1, 1999, the LLC automatically dissolves upon the occurrence of an event that terminates the continued membership of a member, but only if: (A) the articles of organization or a member control agreement specifically provide that the termination causes dissolution and in that event only as provided in the articles or member control agreement; or (B) if the membership of the last or sole member terminates and the legal representative of that last or sole member does not cause the LLC to admit at least one member within 180 days after the termination. [Section 322B.80]

Special Statutory Rules

The chief manager of the LLC shall:

1) have general active management of the business of the LLC

2) sign and deliver in the name of the LLC documents related to LLC business, including deeds, mortgages, bonds, and contracts

3) maintain records and certify all proceedings of the board of governors and the members, and

4) preside at meetings of the board of governors, and see that all orders of the board of governors are carried out. [Section 322B.673]

Again, we see the chief manager as the CEO of the LLC. If you have all members make management decisions in place of the board (as we expect most smaller LLCs will do to avoid cumbersome statutory rules) the chief manager's primary responsibilities will be acting as first-in-command in running the LLC, and performing the ministerial functions listed in the second and third items above.

MISSISSIPPI

LLC Filing Office

Mississippi Secretary of State
Corporate Division
P.O. Box 136
Jackson, MS 39205-0136

Telephone: 601-359-1633

Toll-free: 800-256-3494

www.sos.state.ms.us

State LLC Act

The Mississippi LLC Act is contained in Title 79 (Corporations, Associations, and Partnerships) of the Mississippi Code, Chapter 29, starting with Section 79-29-101, and is browseable from the following Web page (click Mississippi, select Mississippi Code in the left pane, select Title 79, then Chapter 29):

www.michie.com/resources1.html

State Tax Office

Mississippi State Tax Commission, Jackson

www.mstc.state.ms.us

LLC Management

An LLC is managed by its members unless the certificate of formation or operating agreement states that the LLC is to be managed by one or more managers. [Sections 79-29-103, -201, -302, and -401]

Manager Election

Unless otherwise provided by the certificate of formation or operating agreement, managers are elected or removed and manager vacancies are filled by members (presumably, by normal membership voting rules). [Section 79-29-401]

Meeting Requirements

Unless otherwise stated in the certificate of formation or operating agreement, members are given one vote each, with a majority vote required to take membership action. Rules for notice, time, place, and quorum for members' meetings and action by written consent by members may be provided in the certificate of formation or the LLC operating agreement. [Section 79-29-304] Managers take action by a majority vote of the managers unless otherwise provided in the certificate of formation or operating agreement. [Section 79-29-401] Rules for notice, time, place, and quorum for managers' meetings, and for action by written consent of the managers, were not found in the Act. Presumably, these may be provided in the certificate of formation or the LLC operating agreement.

Amendments

Unless otherwise provided in the certificate of formation or operating agreement, all members must agree to amend the certificate. [Section 79-29-202] Amendments to the operating agreement must be by approval of all members. [Section 79-29-306]

Admission of Members

Unless otherwise provided in the certificate of formation or operating agreement, new memberships must be is-sued with the written consent of all members. [Section 79-29-301] Admission of a transferee as a member must be approved by the unanimous consent of all nontransferring members, or as provided in the certificate of formation or operating agreement. [Section 79-29-704]

Withdrawal of Members

For LLCs formed on or after July 1, 1998, unless the certificate of formation or LLC agreement provides that a member has the power to do so, a member has no power to withdraw from an LLC. [Section 79-29-307(3)]

Unless otherwise provided in the operating agreement, a dissociating (withdrawing) member is entitled to receive the fair value of the member's interest within a reasonable time after withdrawal. [Section 79-29-602]

Continuation of the LLC

For LLCs formed on or after July 1, 1998, a membership vote to continue the LLC after the dissociation of a member (cessation or termination of a membership interest) is not required. [Section 79-29-801]

Special Statutory Rules

Unless a lesser vote is specified in the certificate of formation or operating agreement, approval of all members is required to voluntarily dissolve the LLC. [Section 79-29-801]

MISSOURI

LLC Filing Office

Secretary of State
Corporation Division
P.O. Box 778
Jefferson City, MO 65102

Telephone: 573-751-4153

www.sos.mo.gov/business/corporations/Default.asp

State LLC Act

The Missouri LLC Act is contained in Title XXIII (Corporations, Associations, and Partnerships) of the Missouri Statutes, Chapter 347, starting with Section 347.010, and is browseable from the following Web page:

www.moga.state.mo.us/STATUTES/C347.HTM

State Tax Office

Department of Revenue, Jefferson City

http://dor.state.mo.us/tax

LLC Management

An LLC is managed by its members unless the certificate of formation or operating agreement states that the LLC is to be managed by one or more managers. [Sections 347.039 and.079]

Manager Election

Unless otherwise stated in the articles or operating agreement, managers are elected for an indefinite term, and are removed and replaced by a majority vote of the members (with members given one vote each). [Section 347.079]

Meeting Requirements

Rules for voting by members and managers, and notice, time, place, and quorum for members' and managers' meetings, are as may be provided in the LLC operating agreement. [Section 347-081] Unless otherwise provided in the articles or operating agreement, action may be taken by unanimous written consent by members or managers in lieu of a meeting. [Section 347-083]

Amendments

Unless otherwise provided in the articles or operating agreement, all members shall approve amendments to the operating agreement or to the articles to change from member-management to manager-management, or vice versa. [Section 347.079]

Admission of Members

Unless otherwise provided in the articles or operating agreement, new memberships must be issued with the approval of all members. [Section 347.079] The admission of a transferee as a member is governed by the operating agreement. [Section 347.113]

Withdrawal of Members

Unless otherwise provided in the articles or operating agreement, a member can withdraw from the LLC at any time upon 90 days' written notice to other members. If the withdrawal is not prohibited by the operating agreement, but is otherwise in violation of the operating agreement, the member can be held personally liable for financial damages caused by the withdrawal. [Section 347.121]

Unless otherwise provided in the operating agreement, generally, a resigned member (except one who assigns his interest to another person in violation of the operating agreement or without the consent of all other members) has a right to receive the fair value of the membership interest (the member must demand payment within 180 days of withdrawal). If the withdrawal is a breach of the operating agreement, the value of the goodwill of the business is excluded from the computation of the value of the LLC used to value the resigning member's interest, and the LLC can offset any amount payable to the member by damages caused by the member's withdrawal. [Section 347.103]

Continuation of the LLC

A vote to continue the LLC after the dissociation (cessation or termination of a membership interest) of a member is not required. But, except as provided in the operating agreement, a majority (in number) of the remaining members are allowed to vote to dissolve the LLC within 90 days of the dissociation. [Section 347.137]

Special Statutory Rules

A promise by a member to make a contribution to the LLC must be in writing to be enforceable. [Section 347.099]

The written consent of all members is required to voluntarily dissolve the LLC. [Section 347-137]

MONTANA

LLC Filing Office

Montana Secretary of State
Corporation Bureau
P.O. Box 202801
Helena, MT 59620-2801

Telephone: 406-444-3665

http://sos.state.mt.us/

State LLC Act

The Montana LLC Act is contained in Title 35 (Corporations, Partnerships, and Associations) of the Montana Code, Chapter 8, starting with Section 35-8-101, and is browseable from the following Web page (select Title 35, then Chapter 8):

http://data.opi.state.mt.us/bills/mca_toc/index.htm

State Tax Office

Department of Revenue, Helena

http://discoveringmontana.com/revenue/css/default.asp

LLC Management

An LLC is managed by its members unless the articles or operating agreement states that the LLC is to be managed by one or more managers. [Sections 35-8-202 and 35-8-401]

Manager Election

Unless otherwise provided in the articles or operating agreement, managers are elected for an indefinite term and removed and replaced by the consent of more than one-half the members. [Section 35-8-402]

Meeting Requirements

Unless otherwise provided in the articles or operating agreement, the approval of more than one-half the members (or managers, in a manager-managed LLC) is required for member (or manager) decisions. Presumably, members and managers are given one vote each unless otherwise stated in the articles or operating agreement. [Section 35-8-403] Rules for notice, time, place, and quorum for members' and managers' meetings and action by written consent by members and managers were not found in the LLC Act. We assume these may be provided in the LLC articles or operating agreement.

Amendments

Unless otherwise stated in the articles or operating agreement, approval of all LLC members is required to amend the articles or the operating agreement. [Section 35-8-403]

Admission of Members

Unless otherwise provided in the articles or operating agreement, new memberships must be issued with the written consent of all members. [Section 35-8-801] Unless otherwise stated in the articles or operating agreement, the admission of a transferee as a member must be approved by unanimous consent of the nontransferring members. [Section 35-8-706]

Withdrawal of Members

Unless otherwise provided in the operating agreement, a member has the power to dissociate from an LLC at any time, rightfully or wrongfully, pursuant to Section 35-8-803(1). A member that wrongfully dissociates is liable to the LLC and the other members for damages caused by the dissociation. The liability is in addition to any other obligation of the member to the LLC or to the other members. If an LLC does not dissolve and wind up its business as a result of a member's wrongful dissociation, damages sustained by the company for the wrongful dissociation must be offset against distributions otherwise due the member after the dissociation. [Section 35-8-804]

Continuation of the LLC

A membership vote to continue the LLC after the dissociation of a member (cessation or termination of a membership interest) is not required. [Section 35-8-901]

Special Statutory Rules

In a member-managed LLC, LLC property may be transferred by a document signed by a member on behalf of the LLC. In a manager-managed LLC, any manager can execute such a transfer document. [Section 35-8-702]

Except as provided in the articles or an operating agreement, the written consent of all members is required to voluntarily dissolve the LLC. [Section 35-8-901]

NEBRASKA

LLC Filing Office

Nebraska Secretary of State
Corporate Division
P.O. Box 94608
Lincoln, NE 68509

Telephone: 402-471-4079

www.sos.state.ne.us/htm/corpmenu.htm

State LLC Act

The Nebraska LLC Act is contained in Chapter 21 (Corporations and Other Companies) of the Nebraska Statutes, starting with Section 21-2601, and is browseable from the Web page listed below (click on Laws of Nebraska, Statutes and Constitution, click the Statutes folder, open the Chapter 21 folder, then click the View Chapter link under the search box and scroll down to Section 21-2601 to begin browsing the LLC Act):

www.unicam.state.ne.us/index.htm

State Tax Office

Department of Revenue, Lincoln

www.revenue.state.ne.us/index.html

LLC Management

An LLC is managed by its members unless the articles or operating agreement states that the LLC is to be managed by one or more managers. [Sections 21-2606 and 21-2615]

Manager Election

Managers are elected by members for terms according to rules set out in the LLC operating agreement. [Section 21-2615]

Meeting Requirements

Unless otherwise stated in the articles or operating agreement, management power (voting power) of the members is according to each member's capital account balance in the LLC. [Section 21-2615] No rule is stated for management power of managers (presumably, each manager gets one vote in a manager-managed LLC unless otherwise stated in the articles or operating agreement). Rules for the notice, time, place, and quorum for members' and managers' meetings, and for action by written consent by members and managers, were not found in the LLC Act. Presumably, these may be provided in the LLC articles or operating agreement.

Amendments

No statutory rules were found for amendments to the articles or operating agreement (presumably, voting for amendments is according to provisions in the operating agreement).

Admission of Members

No statutory rule was found for issuance of new memberships (presumably, this can be done according to the operating agreement). Unless otherwise provided in the articles or operating agreement, the admission of a transferee as a member must be approved by written consent of two-thirds of a majority in interest (presumably, a majority of capital and profits interests in the LLC) of nontransferring members. [Section 21-2621]

Withdrawal of Members

In the absence of a contrary provision in the articles or operating agreement, unless all members agree otherwise, a withdrawing member has no right to a return of capital upon withdrawal, but is granted the status of a transferee of an interest (has a right to a share of continuing profits and distributions made to all members). [Section 21-2619]

Continuation of the LLC

A vote to continue the LLC after the termination of a membership is not required.

Special Statutory Rules

The members (or managers in a manager-managed LLC) of the LLC are liable to the same extent as corporate officers for the LLC's unpaid taxes. [Section 21-2612]

Only members (or managers in a manager-managed LLC) may contract debts or transfer property on behalf of the LLC. [Sections 21-2616 and 21-2617]

Except as otherwise provided in the articles or operating agreement, the written consent of all members is required to voluntarily dissolve the LLC. [Section 21-2622]

NEVADA

LLC Filing Office

Secretary of State
New Filings Section
202 North Carson Street
Carson City, NV 89701

Telephone: 775-684-5708

Filings may also be made at the Secretary of State Satellite Office in Las Vegas: 702-486-2880

http://sos.state.nv.us/comm_rec/index.htm

State LLC Act

The Nevada LLC Act is contained in Title 7 (Business Associations; Securities; Commodities), Chapter 86 of the Nevada Statutes, starting with Section 86.011, and is browseable from the following Web page (select the Table of Contents to the Nevada Revised Statutes from the submenu that appears from the Law Library item in the left panel, then select Title 7, Chapter 86):

www.leg.state.nv.us

State Tax Office

Department of Taxation, Carson City

http://tax.state.nv.us

LLC Management

An LLC is managed by its members unless the articles or operating agreement states that the LLC is to be managed by one or more managers. [Sections 86.161 and 86.291]

Manager Election

Managers are elected by members for terms according to rules set out in the LLC operating agreement. [Section 86.291]

Meeting Requirements

Unless otherwise provided in the articles or operating agreement, management power (voting power) is vested in members according to their current capital account balances. No rule is stated for manager voting. [Section 86.291] Rules for the notice, time, place, and quorum for members' and managers' meetings, and for action by written consent by members and managers, were not found in the LLC Act. Presumably, these may be provided in the LLC articles or operating agreement.

Amendments

Unless otherwise provided in the articles or operating agreement, amendments to the operating agreement must be approved by all members. [Section 86.286]

Admission of Members

No statutory rule was found for issuance of new memberships in the LLC (presumably, according to rules stated in the operating agreement). Unless otherwise provided in the articles or operating agreement, the admission of a transferee as a member must be approved by a majority in interest of the nontransferring members (by nontransferring members owning a majority of the rights to LLC profits). [Sections 86.351 and 86.065]

Withdrawal of Members

Generally, a member may not withdraw until the dissolution of the LLC, unless as otherwise provided by law, the articles, or the operating agreement. Upon withdrawal, unless provided otherwise by law, the articles, or the operating agreement, a member is entitled to receive the fair value of the membership interest within a reasonable time after withdrawal. [Section 86.331]

Continuation of the LLC

A vote to continue the LLC after termination of a membership is not required.

Special Statutory Rules

Only members (or managers in a manager-managed LLC) may contract debts on behalf of the LLC. One or more managers may transfer title to property in a manager-managed LLC. In a member-managed LLC, title to LLC property may be transferred by any member. [Sections 86.301 and 86.311]

Except as otherwise provided in the articles or operating agreement, the written consent of all members is required to voluntarily dissolve the LLC. [Section 86.491]

NEW HAMPSHIRE

LLC Filing Office

New Hampshire Secretary of State
State House, Room 204
107 North Main Street
Concord, NH 03301

Telephone: 603-271-3244

www.state.nh.us/sos/corporate/index.htm

State LLC Act

The New Hampshire LLC Act is contained in Title XXVIII (Partnerships), Chapter 304C of the New Hampshire Statutes, starting with Section 304-C:1, and is browseable from the Web page listed below (choose "Forms & Laws" in the left margin, then select "Limited Liability Companys," then click "Limited Liability Companies (Chapter 304-C)").

www.state.nh.us/sos/corporate/index.htm

State Tax Office

Department of Revenue Administration, Concord

http://webster.state.nh.us/revenue/index.htm

LLC Management

An LLC is managed by its members unless the certificate of formation or operating agreement states that the LLC is to be managed by one or more managers. [Sections 304-C:12, 304-C:1, and 304-C:31]

Manager Election

Election, removal, replacement, and terms of office of managers are as may be provided in the operating agreement. [Section 304-C:31]

Meeting Requirements

Unless otherwise provided in the operating agreement, consent of more than one-half the number of members (or managers in a manager-managed LLC) is required for membership (or manager) action. Rules for notice, time, place, and quorum for members' and managers' meetings and action by written consent by members or managers may be provided in the LLC certificate of formation or operating agreement. Unless otherwise provided in the certificate of formation, members and managers may take action without a meeting (presumably, by normal voting rules specified in the agreement or under default membership voting rule noted above). [Sections 304-C:24 and 304-C:31]

If a member-managed LLC is managed by less than all its members (if one or more members are issued a nonvoting membership interest), and if a meeting of members has not been held during the past 240 days, any member may demand a meeting to be held within 30 days of the demand. Unless otherwise provided in the certificate of formation or operating agreement, notice must be given of the meeting. A quorum for this meeting is one more than one half the number of all members, unless otherwise provided in the operating agreement or certificate. At the meeting, the members having management of the LLC must report on LLC affairs. [Section 304-C:24]

Amendments

Unless otherwise stated in the certificate of formation or operating agreement, the approval of all members is required to amend the operating agreement. [Section 304-C:24] No statutory voting rule was found for amendment of the certificate of formation.

Admission of Members

New memberships are issued according to provisions in the operating agreement. If the operating agreement does not provide a procedure, the admission of a new member occurs after the consent of all members and when reflected on LLC records. [Section 304-C:23] Unless otherwise stated in the operating agreement, the admission of a transferee must be approved by unanimous consent of the nontransferring members. [Section 304-C:48]

Withdrawal of Members

If not prohibited by the operating agreement, a member can withdraw from the LLC at any time upon 30 days' written notice to the other members. Unless otherwise provided in the operating agreement, if the LLC has a limited term or is formed for a particular undertaking (project), the withdrawal of a member before the end of the term or the accomplishment of the undertaking is a breach of the certificate or operating agreement. If the withdrawal is a breach of the operating agreement or is based upon wrongful conduct of the member, the LLC may offset the amount paid to the withdrawing member by the amount of damages caused by the breach or wrongful conduct, including the cost of obtaining replacement services owed by the member. [Section 304-C:27(III)]

Unless otherwise provided in the operating agreement, a dissociating (withdrawing) member is not entitled to be paid for the value of the membership interest, but has the status of an assignee of an interest, and is entitled only to the continuing payments of profits and other distributions made to all members. [Section 304-C:41]

Continuation of the LLC

A vote to continue the LLC after the termination of a membership is not required.

Special Statutory Rules

Except as otherwise provided in the certificate of formation or operating agreement, the approval of a majority of members is required to voluntarily dissolve the LLC. [Section 304-C:50]

NEW JERSEY

LLC Filing Office

New Jersey Department of Treasury
Division of Revenue/Corporate Filing Unit
P.O. Box 308
Trenton, NJ 08625-0308

Telephone: 609-292-9292

www.state.nj.us/njbgs/

State LLC Act

The New Jersey LLC Act is contained in Title 42 (Partnerships and Partnership Associations), Chapter 2B of the New Jersey Statutes, starting with Section 42:2B-1, and is browseable from the following Web page (select Statutes in the left pane, then select Browse by Table of Contents, then expand Title 42, and scroll to Section 42:2B-1):

www.njleg.state.nj.us

State Tax Office

Division of Taxation, Trenton

www.state.nj.us/treasury/taxation

LLC Management

An LLC is managed by its members unless the operating agreement states that the LLC is to be managed by one or more managers. [Sections 42:2B-2 and 42:2B-27]

Manager Election

Managers are chosen as provided in the operating agreement. [Section 42:2B-27]

Meeting Requirements

Rules for voting, notice, time, place, and quorum for members' and managers' meetings and actions by written consent by members or managers may be provided in the operating agreement. Unless otherwise provided in the operating agreement, members vote in proportion to their current ownership of the profits interests in the LLC, with the approval of members owning more than 50% of profits interests necessary to take membership action. [Sections 42:2B-22, 42:2B-27, and 42:2B-29]

Amendments

Amendments to operating agreements are approved as provided in the operating agreement. [Section 42:2B-22] No statutory rule was found for approval of amendments to the certificate of formation.

Admission of Members

New memberships are issued according to provisions in the operating agreement; if the operating agreement does not provide procedure, admission of a new member occurs after consent of all members and when reflected on LLC records. [Section 42:2B-21] Except as provided in the operating agreement, the admission of a transferee must be approved by all the nontransferring members. [Section 42:2B-46]

Withdrawal of Members

The operating agreement may prohibit a member from resigning from the LLC. If the operating agreement is silent on the issue, a member may resign after a minimum of six months' notice to the LLC and each other member and manager. [Section 42:2B-38] Unless provided otherwise in the operating agreement, a member is entitled to receive the fair value of the membership interest, based upon the net present value of his right to share in LLC distributions, less all applicable valuation discounts (due to lack of liquidity, relative size of holding, absence of trading market, and comparable factors), within a reasonable time after resignation. If the resignation is a breach of the agreement, the LLC may offset the amount due to the member by the amount of damages caused by the breach. [Section 42:2B-39]

Continuation of the LLC

A vote to continue the LLC after the termination of a membership is not required. But note that the LLC automatically dissolves 90 days after the date on which the LLC has no remaining members unless a member is admitted within the 90 days. [Section 42:2B-48]

Special Statutory Rules

Except as otherwise provided in the operating agreement, the written consent of all members is required to voluntarily dissolve the LLC. [Section 42:2B-48

NEW MEXICO

LLC Filing Office

Public Regulation Commission
Corporations Bureau
Chartered Documents Division
P.O. Box 1269
Santa Fe, NM 87504

Telephone: 505-827-4508

Toll-free: 800-947-4722

www.nmprc.state.nm.us/corporations/corpshome.htm

State LLC Act

The New Mexico LLC Act is contained in Chapter 53 (Corporations), Article 19 of the New Mexico Statutes, starting with Section 53-19-1. You can browse it from the following Web page (first select "New Mexico Statues" in the left panel, then click the HTML tab at the top of the page; in the left panel select the folder titled "Statutory Chapters in New Mexico Statutes Annotated 1978," then scroll down in the left panel and select the Chapter 53 folder, then use the right panel to scroll down to select Article 19 to browse the sections of the Act):

http://legis.state.nm.us/

State Tax Office

Taxation and Revenue Department, Santa Fe

www.state.nm.us/tax

LLC Management

An LLC is managed by its members unless the operating agreement states that the LLC is to be managed by one or more managers. [Sections 53-19-8 and 53-19-15]

Manager Election

Unless otherwise provided in the articles or operating agreement, managers must be elected for an indefinite term and can be removed only by a majority of the voting power of LLC members. [Section 53-19-15]

Meeting Requirements

Except as provided in the articles or operating agreement, members must vote in proportion to their capital account balances in the LLC, with a majority of the voting power necessary to take membership action. Managers can take action by a majority vote of the managers. [Section 53-19-17] Rules for the notice, time, place, and quorum for members' and managers' meetings, and for actions by written consent of the members or managers, were not found in the LLC Act. Presumably, these may be provided in the LLC articles or operating agreement.

Amendments

Unless otherwise provided in the articles or operating agreement, the approval of a majority of the voting power of members is required to amend articles or the operating agreement. [Section 53-19-17]

Admission of Members

Unless otherwise provided in the articles or operating agreement, new memberships must be issued with the written consent of all members. [Section 53-19-36] Unless otherwise stated in the articles or operating agreement, the admission of a transferee as a member must be approved by unanimous consent of the nontransferring members. [Section 53-19-33]

Withdrawal of Members

A member may withdraw from an LLC with a perpetual existence if withdrawal is not prohibited by the articles or operating agreement. A member may withdraw from an LLC with a limited term if allowed to do so in the articles or operating agreement. [Section 53-19-38]

Upon withdrawal, if the articles and operating agreement do not provide for a distribution to a withdrawing member, the member is entitled to receive the fair market value of the interest within a reasonable period after withdrawal. [Section 53-19-24]

Continuation of the LLC

A vote to continue the LLC after the termination of a membership is not required.

Special Statutory Rules

Unless otherwise provided in the articles or operating agreement, a member must be removed by approval of all other members. [Section 53-19-17]

Unless otherwise provided in the articles or operating agreement, the approval of a majority of the voting power of members is required to sell all LLC assets or voluntarily dissolve the LLC. [Sections 53-19-17 and 53-19-39]

In a member-managed LLC, LLC property may be transferred by a document signed by any member on behalf of the LLC. In a manager-managed LLC, any manager can execute such a transfer document. [Section 53-19-30]

NEW YORK

LLC Filing Office

Department of State
Division of Corporations, State Records and Uniform Commercial Code
41 State Street
Albany, NY 12231

Telephone: 518-473-2492

www.dos.state.ny.us/corp/corpwww.html

State LLC Act

The New York LLC Law is contained in Chapter 34 of the New York Consolidated Laws, starting with Section 101, and is browseable from the following Web page (click New York State Laws, then New York State Consolidated Laws, then Limited Liability Company Law, then select Article headings to view each part of the law):

http://assembly.state.ny.us/leg

State Tax Office

Taxation and Finance Department, Albany

www.tax.state.ny.us

LLC Management

An LLC is managed by its members unless the operating agreement states that the LLC is to be managed by one or more managers. [Limited Liability Company Law Sections 102, 206, and 401]

Manager Election

Unless otherwise provided in the operating agreement, managers are elected annually by the members. [Section 413] Unless otherwise provided in the operating agreement, managers may be removed or replaced and manager vacancies filled by a vote of members owning a majority of the profits interests in the LLC. [Section 414]

Meeting Requirements

The operating agreement may set rules for notice, time, place, and quorum for members' and managers' meetings and action by written consent by members or managers. [Sections 418 and 419]

Unless otherwise stated in the operating agreement, members vote in proportion to their share in the current profits of the LLC, and the approval of members owning a majority of the profits interests is necessary to take membership action. [Section 402]

Unless otherwise provided in the operating agreement, the following membership rules apply to the LLC:

- Members are required to hold meetings annually at the LLC office; one of the items of business is to elect managers of the LLC. [Sections 403 and 413]

- Members owning a majority of the profits interests in the LLC constitute a quorum for membership meetings. [Section 404]

- Notice of meetings must be given to members no fewer than ten nor more than 60 days prior to the meeting (for a special meeting, it must state the purpose of the meeting). [Section 405]

- Members may sign a waiver of notice prior to or after the date of a membership meeting. [Section 406]

- Members can take action by written consent if the number of members signing would have been sufficient to approve the action at a meeting at which all members were present and voted (generally, this means members owning a majority of the profits interests must sign a written consent to take action). Notice of action by written consent must be sent to members who did not sign the consent form. [Section 407]

Unless otherwise provided in the operating agreement, managers take action by approval of a majority of the managers or by the written consent of all managers.

[Section 408] Quorum, notice, and frequency rules for manager meetings were not found in the Act. Presumably, these may be provided in the operating agreement.

Amendments

Unless otherwise provided in the operating agreement or under the LLC Act for special amendments (see below), amendments to the articles or operating agreement require the approval of at least a majority in interest (that is, a majority of the profits interests in the LLC) of the members. But a majority of the managers of a manager-managed LLC may adopt the following amendments to the articles without membership approval:

1) change of the registered agent name or address

2) change of LLC address for service of process, and

3) correction of an error in the articles. [Sections 213 and 402]

Amendments to the articles or operating agreement that accomplish any of the following purposes must be approved by all members adversely affected by the amendment:

- a change in contributions made by members
- a change in the allocation of tax items, such as allocations of profits or losses, or
- a change in the manner of computing distributions made to members.

Admission of Members

Unless otherwise provided in the operating agreement, new memberships must be issued with the approval of members owning at least a majority of the interests in LLC profits. [Sections 402 and 602] Except as provided in the operating agreement, the admission of a transferee as a member must be approved by the vote or written consent of a majority in interest of nontransferring members (nontransferring members owning more than 50% of the interests in LLC profits). [Section 604]

Notwithstanding anything to the contrary under applicable law, an operating agreement may provide that a membership interest may not be assigned prior to the dissolution and winding up of the LLC. [Section 606]

Withdrawal of Members

A member may withdraw as a member of an LLC only in accordance with the operating agreement, at the time or upon the happening of events specified in the operating agreement. Notwithstanding anything to the contrary under applicable law, unless an operating agreement provides otherwise, a member may not withdraw from an LLC prior to its dissolution and winding up. [Section 606]

If not otherwise provided in the operating agreement, a member is entitled to receive the fair value of the interest within a reasonable period after withdrawing. [Section 509]

Continuation of the LLC

A membership vote to continue the LLC after the dissociation of a member (cessation or termination of a membership interest) is not required. [Section 701]

Special Statutory Rules

Unless otherwise provided in the articles or operating agreement, the approval of members owning at least two-thirds of the interests in the profits of the LLC is required to sell all LLC assets or to voluntarily dissolve the LLC. [Sections 402 and 701]

NORTH CAROLINA

LLC Filing Office

North Carolina Department of the Secretary of State
Corporations Division
P.O. Box 29622
Raleigh, NC 27626-0622

Telephone: 919-807-2225

Toll-free 888-246-7636

www.secretary.state.nc.us/corporations

State LLC Act

The North Carolina LLC Act is contained in Chapter 57C of the North Carolina Statutes, starting with Section 57C-1-01, and is browseable from the following Web page (click NC General Statutes at the bottom of the page, then click Table of Contents in the right-hand box, then select Chapter 57C, North Carolina Limited Liability Company Act):

www.secstate.state.nc.us

State Tax Office

Department of Revenue, Raleigh

www.dor.state.nc.us

LLC Management

An LLC is managed by its members unless the articles and operating agreement state otherwise. [Sections 57C-2-21 and 57C-3-20]

Manager Election

Managers are designated for an indefinite term as provided in the operating agreement. [Section 57C-3-21]

Meeting Requirements

Except as provided in the articles or operating agreement, members and managers have equal voting rights (presumably, one vote each), and member or manager action requires approval of a majority of the members or managers. [Section 57C-3-21] Rules for the notice, time, place, and quorum for members' and managers' meetings, and for actions by written consent by members or managers, were not found in the LLC Act. Presumably, these may be provided in the articles or operating agreement.

Amendments

Unless the articles or operating agreement state otherwise, amendments to the articles or operating agreement require the approval of all members. [Sections 57C-2-22 and 57C-3-03]

Admission of Members

Unless otherwise provided in the articles or operating agreement, new memberships must be issued with the approval of all members. [Section 57C-3-01] Except as provided in the articles or operating agreement, the admission of a transferee as a member must be approved by the unanimous approval of nontransferring members. [Section 57C-5-04]

Withdrawal of Members

A member may withdraw only at the time or upon the happening of the events specified in the articles of organization or a written operating agreement. [Section 57C-5-06] If not otherwise provided in the operating agreement, a member is entitled to receive the fair value of the interest within a reasonable period after withdrawal. [Section 57C-5-07]

Continuation of the LLC

A membership vote to continue the LLC after the dissociation of a member (cessation or termination of a membership interest) is not required. [Section 57C-6-01]

Special Statutory Rules

Unless otherwise provided in the articles or operating agreement, the approval of all members is required to sell all LLC assets or to voluntarily dissolve the LLC. [Sections 57C-3-03 and 57C-6-01]

The LLC must indemnify (pay back) managers for payments and personal liabilities incurred in carrying out authorized business for the LLC. Unless limited by the articles or operating agreement, a member or manager must be indemnified for expenses (lawyer's fees) incurred in defending any proceeding (lawsuit) based upon the member's or manager's status as a member or manager. [Section 57C-3-31]

NORTH DAKOTA

LLC Filing Office

North Dakota Secretary of State

Corporations Division

600 East Boulevard Avenue, Dept. 108

Bismarck, ND 58505-0500

Telephone: 701-328-4284

Toll free: 800-352-0867 ext. 4284

www.state.nd.us/sec/Business/businessinforegmnu.htm

State LLC Act

The North Dakota LLC Act is contained in Title 10-32 of the North Dakota Century Code, starting with Section 10-32-01, and is browseable from the Web page listed below (select State Laws, Select ND Century Code in the left pane, then scroll down and click 10 Corporations, then select Chapter 10-32 in the left-panel table of contents):

www.state.nd.us/lr

State Tax Office

Office of State Tax Commission, Bismarck

www.state.nd.us/taxdpt

LLC Management

The North Dakota LLC Act presupposes management by a board of governors (management by governors is similar to the vesting of management power in a corporate board of directors). The law specifies that LLCs must have one or more governors, elected by the members, who serve until re-election at the next regular meeting of members, or for an indefinite term if no such meeting is scheduled in the operating agreement (alternatively, a fixed term for governors of up to five years may be specified in the operating agreement). [Section 10-32-72] The LLC Act has a slew of corporate-like rules and procedures that divide action and authority between the governors and the members of the LLC, which we believe most smaller LLCs will find unwieldy. Section 10-32-69(2), fortunately, recognizes that LLCs may wish to adopt membership management. That section says that the LLC members may act in the place of the governors as long as they make management decisions by unanimous vote; this is usually easy to achieve in smaller LLCs and we assume most smaller North Dakota LLCs will opt for membership management under this Section of the Act. To reinforce this member-management election, the LLC operating agreement should require a unanimous membership vote for management decisions by members pursuant to Section 10-32-69(2).

If you decide to go along with the statutory scheme and opt for management by governors, see sections 10-32-69 and following of the LLC Act to learn more about the default statutory governor-management scheme, and special rules that apply to board of governor action.

To make matters more complicated, North Dakota law requires the appointment or election of two persons who function as the LLC president and treasurer, but who are called managers. [Section 10-32-88] Don't be confused by this nonstandard nomenclature; the real managers of your LLC are your governors (in a governor-managed LLC) or your members (in a member-managed LLC where members take action by unanimous agreement as explained above).

Manager Election

Board of governors' election procedures are as specified in the articles or operating agreement. [Section 10-32-71] Unless a fixed term is provided in the articles or operating agreement, governors serve an indefinite term until the next regular meeting of members. If a fixed term is specified, it cannot exceed five years. [Section 10-32-72] Unless otherwise provided in the articles, membership voting for governors is by cumulative voting (similar to how shareholders vote for directors in larger corporations). [Section 10-32-76] Unless otherwise provided in the articles or operating agreement, removal of governors requires the same membership vote as in a vote to elect them. [Section 10-32-78] Unless otherwise provided in the articles or operating agreement, vacancies on board of governors may be filled by a person approved by a majority of remaining governors. [Section 10-32-79]

These governor-management rules are complex, and riddled with exceptions. If you wish to follow them, see the LLC Act sections noted above. We expect most LLCs will allow management by unanimous vote of members instead. [Section 10-32-69(2)]

Meeting Requirements

Unless otherwise provided in the articles, members vote in proportion to the value reflected in the LLC records of each member's capital contribution to the LLC. [Section 10-32-40.1] Unless otherwise provided in the articles, the approval of a majority of the membership voting power present at a meeting (or a majority of a quorum, whichever is greater) is required for membership action. [Section 10-32-42] But remember, when members act as managers (governors) of the LLC (this is usually the case when members are asked to take action in a smaller LLC that wishes to avoid the governor-management rules), members must act by unanimous approval. [Section 10-32-69(2)] Members may take action by unanimous written consent without a meeting (the articles may lower this written consent requirement to written consent of members required to take action at a meeting at which all members were present). [Section 10-32-43] Unless otherwise specified in the articles or operating agreement, regular meetings of members need not be held, unless demanded by a member under certain conditions. [Section 10-32-38] Special members' meetings may be called by the LLC president, two or more governors, or members owning 10% or more of the membership voting power. [Section 10-32-39] Unless otherwise stated in the articles, the operating agreement, or a special LLC Act provision, at least ten days' and no more than 50 days' notice must be given of a members' meeting. [Section 10-32-40] Unless otherwise stated in the articles or operating agreement, a quorum for members' meetings is a majority of the membership voting power. [Section 10-32-44]

Board of governors' meetings are to be held as provided in the LLC articles or operating agreement. Unless these state otherwise, governors' meetings are to be held on at least ten days' notice. [Section 10-32-80] A quorum for governors' meetings is a majority of the number of governors unless otherwise stated in the articles or operating agreement. [Section 10-32-82] Generally, governors take action by a majority of those present at a governors' meeting (or a majority of a quorum if greater). [Section 10-32-83] Unless otherwise provided in the articles, governors may take action by the written consent of all governors. [Section 10-32-84]

Again, these governor-management rules are complex. If you wish to follow them, see the LLC Act Sections noted above. We expect most LLCs will allow management by unanimous vote of members instead. [Section 10-32-69(2)]

Amendments

Amendments to articles must be approved by a majority vote of the members present at the meeting (at which a quorum is present). Section 10-32-16 of the LLC Act has specific rules for calling, noticing, and holding a meeting of the members to amend the articles. As an alternative, have all members approve amendments by written consent. [Section 10-32-43]

Amendments to the operating agreement are normally reserved to the governors, but governors are not allowed to make certain decisions (changing qualifications, terms of office, and decreasing number of governors for example). [Section 10-32-68] Again, we assume smaller LLCs will wish to avoid governor-management rules and, instead, will approve amendments to operating agreement by unanimous consent of members. [Section 10-32-69(2)]

Admission of Members

No statutory rule was found regarding issuance of new memberships. Unless otherwise stated in the LLC's articles, the admission of a transferee as a member must be approved by the unanimous written consent of nontransferring members (but a member may assign full membership rights to another member without the consent of remaining members). [Section 10-32-32]

Withdrawal of Members

A member has the power, though not necessarily the right, to withdraw from the LLC at any time. The withdrawn member is given the status of an assignee of an interest, with the right to receive ongoing profits and other distributions along with the other members (presumably, unless the operating agreement provides otherwise—for example, the operating agreement may specify that the member shall be paid the value of his membership interest upon withdrawal). [Section 10-32-30] If a member withdraws in violation of the articles or operating agreement, the LLC may deduct damages caused by the wrongful withdrawal from the amount paid the member for the interest (this payment occurs on dissolution of the LLC unless provided otherwise in the articles or operating agreement). [Section 10-32-131]

Continuation of the LLC

Except as otherwise provided in the articles, a vote to continue the LLC after termination of a membership is not required. [Section 10-32-109] Note: This section requires dissolution when the LLC has no remaining members unless the last member or her legal representation admits a member within 180 days after the last member's termination.

Special Statutory Rules

The LLC president shall:

1) have general active management of the business of the LLC

2) sign and deliver in the name of the LLC documents related to the business of the LLC, including deeds, mortgages, bonds, and contracts

3) maintain records and certify all proceedings of the board of governors and the members, and

4) preside at meetings of the board of governors, and see that all orders of the board of governors are carried out. [Section 10-32-89]

If you have all members make management decisions in place of the board (as we expect most smaller LLCs will to avoid statutory rules for implementing governor management), the president's primary responsibilities will be acting as first-in-command in running the LLC, and performing the ministerial functions listed in the second and third items above.

Members can vote to voluntarily dissolve the LLC at a meeting called for that purpose by approval of a majority of members. [Section 10-32-111]

OHIO

LLC Filing Office

Ohio Secretary of State
Business Services Division
P.O. Box 670
Columbus, OH 43216

Telephone: 614-466-3910

Toll-free: 1-877-SOS-FILE (1-877-767-3453)

www.sos.state.oh.us/sos/busiserv/index.html

State LLC Act

The Ohio LLC Act is contained in Title XVII (Corporations-Partnerships), Chapter 1705 of the Ohio Statutes, starting with Section 1705.01, and is browseable from the following Web page (click Revised Code, select Title 17 in the left pane, click Chapter 1705, then select each Section of the Act you wish to view):

http://onlinedocs.andersonpublishing.com

State Tax Office

Taxation Department, Columbus

www.state.oh.us/tax

LLC Management

An LLC is managed by its members unless the operating agreement states otherwise. [Section 1705.24]

Manager Election

No statutory rules were found (presumably, managers may be elected, removed, and replaced, and their terms set, according to the LLC articles or operating agreement).

Meeting Requirements

Unless otherwise stated in the LLC operating agreement, membership voting is according to the current capital account balances of each member. [Section 1705.24] Rules for notice, time, place, and quorum for members' and managers' meetings and action by written consent by members or managers were not found in the LLC Act. The Act allows members or managers to adopt bylaws to regulate LLC affairs, including rules for members' and managers' meetings (as long as the bylaws are consistent with the articles and operating agreement). [Section 1705.27] We expect most LLCs to adopt these rules as part of their operating agreement, rather than to adopt a separate set of bylaws.

Amendments

No statutory rules for approving amendments were found in the LLC Act. Presumably, articles and operating agreement may be amended as provided in the articles or operating agreement.

Admission of Members

Unless otherwise provided in the operating agreement, new memberships must be issued with the written consent of all members. [Section 1705.14] Admission of a transferee as a member must be approved by unanimous consent of the nontransferring members, and as may be provided in the LLC operating agreement. [Section 1705.20]

Withdrawal of Members

For LLCs formed on or after 11-21-97, a member may withdraw only only at the time or upon the occurrence of an event specified in the LLC articles or operating agreement. [Section 1705.16]

Continuation of the LLC

For LLCs formed on or after 12-3-99, a vote to continue the LLC after withdrawal of a membership is not required. [Section 1705.43]

Special Statutory Rules

Unanimous written consent of members is required to voluntarily dissolve the LLC. [Section 1705.43]

OKLAHOMA

LLC Filing Office

Oklahoma Secretary of State
2300 N. Lincoln Blvd.
Room 101
State Capitol Building
Oklahoma City, OK 73105-4897

Telephone: 405-521-3912

www.sos.state.ok.us/business/business_filing.htm

State LLC Act

The Oklahoma LLC Act is contained in Title 18 (Corporations) Oklahoma Statutes, Chapter 32, starting with Section 2000, and is browseable from the Web page listed below.

First, click "Links to Statutes" in the left margin. Then click the "Expand" link for "Title 18, Corporations." Finally, scroll down the chapter index to Chapter 32 and click on section 2000, which marks the beginning of Chapter 32 and the Oklahoma LLC Act.

www.sos.state.ok.us/exec_legis/exec_leg_home.htmState Tax Office

State Tax Office

Tax Commission, Oklahoma City

www.oktax.state.ok.us

LLC Management

An LLC is managed by its managers unless the articles or operating agreement vest management in its members. [18 Okla. St. 2013] Also, if the articles or operating agreement say that the LLC will be managed without designated managers, members are considered managers under the LLC Act. [Section 2015] Note that this scheme is the reverse of most states, where member-management, rather than manager-management, is the default management scheme. We expect the articles or operating agreement of most smaller LLCs to specifically vest management in the members of the LLC.

Manager Election

Unless otherwise provided in the articles or operating agreement, managers are elected by a majority vote (presumably one vote each) of members, and managers are removed by written consent of (presumably all) the members. [Section 2014]

Meeting Requirements

Unless otherwise stated in the articles or operating agreement, members vote in proportion to their capital interests in the LLC, with the approval of members owning a majority of the capital interests necessary in order to take membership action. Membership approval by majority voting may be at a meeting or through signed written consents. [Section 2020] Unless otherwise stated in the articles or operating agreement, managers must take action by majority vote. [Section 2018] Rules for notice, time, place, and quorum for members' and managers' meetings were not found in the LLC Act. Presumably, these may be provided in the LLC articles or operating agreement.

Amendments

Unless otherwise provided in the articles or operating agreement, amendments to the articles or operating agreement require approval by a majority vote of the members (presumably, with each member being given one vote). [Section 2020] But note that all members must approve amendments to the articles or operating agreement that:

- reduce the LLC's term of existence
- reduce the vote necessary to dissolve the LLC or sell all its assets
- permit a member to voluntarily withdraw from the LLC, or
- reduce the vote required to amend the articles or operating agreement. [Section 2020]

Admission of Members

No statutory rule was found regarding issuance of new memberships in an LLC. Admission of a transferee as a member must be approved either as stated in the LLC operating agreement or by written consent of the members who hold a majority of capital interests in the LLC (not counting the capital interests being transferred to the new member). [Section 2035]

Withdrawal of Members

Unless specifically permitted by operating agreement, a member may not voluntarily withdraw from the LLC. If the withdrawal is a breach of the operating agreement or is based upon wrongful conduct of the member, the LLC may offset the amount paid to the withdrawing member by the amount of damages caused by the breach or wrongful conduct, including the cost of obtaining replacement services owed by the member. [Section 2036]

If not otherwise provided in the operating agreement, a member is entitled to receive the fair market value of the interest within a reasonable period after withdrawal. Fair market value is defined along standard legal lines as the amount which a willing buyer would pay a willing seller, neither being under a compulsion to buy or sell, and both being cognizant of all relevant facts concerning the value of the dissociating (withdrawing) member's interest. [Section 2027]

Continuation of the LLC

A vote to continue the LLC after the termination of a membership is not required. [Section 2037]

Special Statutory Rules

Unanimous written consent of the members is required to voluntarily dissolve the LLC. [Sections 2020 and 2037]

OREGON

LLC Filing Office

Oregon Secretary of State
Corporation Division
Business Registry Section
Public Service Building, Suite 151
255 Capitol Street NE
Salem, OR 97310-1327

Telephone: 503-986-2200

www.filinginoregon.com

State LLC Act

The Oregon LLC Act is contained in Chapter 63 of the Oregon Statutes, starting with Section 63.001, and is browseable from the following Web page (scroll down the left panel, then select Chapter 59-113, then select Chapter 63):

www.leg.state.or.us/ors/home.htm

State Tax Office

Department of Revenue, Salem

www.dor.state.or.us

LLC Management

An LLC is managed by its members unless the articles state that the LLC is to be managed by one or more managers. [Section 63.130]

Manager Election

Unless otherwise provided in the articles or operating agreement, the election and filling of manager positions and removal of managers is must be made by a majority vote of the members (with each member given one vote). [Sections 63.145 and 63.150]

Meeting Requirements

Unless otherwise provided in the articles or operating agreement, managers and members have one vote each, with a majority vote necessary to take action by mem-bers or managers. Members and managers may take action by unanimous written consent, unless the articles or operating agreement permit written consent approval by a lesser vote of managers or members. [Section 63.150] Rules for the notice, time, place and quorum for members' and managers' meetings were not found in the LLC Act. Presumably, these may be provided in the articles or operating agreement.

Amendments

Unless otherwise provided in the articles or operating agreement, these can only be amended by approval of all LLC members. [Section 63.444]. (But note that Section 63.150 allows amendments to the articles and operating agreement by just a majority of the members—we assume that the unanimous vote requirement, which is typical of many LLC Acts, is the intended requirement.) Managers may make nonsubstantive, technical changes to the articles, as allowed under Section 63.441, without membership approval.

Admission of Members

Unless otherwise provided in the operating agreement, new memberships must be issued with the consent of a majority of members. [Section 63.245] Unless otherwise provided in the articles or operating agreement, a transferee does not become a member until approved by a majority of the nontransferring members. Exception: The transferee of the last remaining membership interest in an Oregon LLC automatically becomes a member. [Section 63.245]

Withdrawal of Members

Unless the articles or operating agreement say that a member cannot withdraw or otherwise limit or restrict a member's power to do so, a member may withdraw upon six months' written notice to the LLC. The articles or operating agreement also may specify an alternate withdrawal procedure. If the withdrawal is a breach of the articles or operating agreement, the LLC may offset the amount paid to the withdrawing member by the amount of damages caused by the breach. Unless otherwise provided in the articles or operating agreement, if the LLC has a limited term or is formed for a particular undertaking (project), the withdrawal of a member before the end of the term or the accomplishment of the undertaking is a breach of the articles or operating agreement. [Section 63.205]

If not otherwise provided in the articles or operating agreement, a member is entitled to receive the fair value of the interest within a reasonable period after withdrawal. [Section 63.215]

Continuation of the LLC

A vote to continue the LLC after the termination of a membership is not required.

Special Statutory Rules

A majority vote of the members is required to sell all LLC assets or approve a transaction in which a member or manager has a personal financial interest. [Section 63.150]

Unless otherwise provided in the articles or operating agreement, all members must consent to a decision to voluntarily dissolve the LLC. [Section 63.621]

PENNSYLVANIA

LLC Filing Office

Commonwealth of Pennsylvania
Department of State
Corporation Bureau
P.O. Box 8722
Harrisburg, PA 17105-8722

Telephone: 717-787-1057

www.dos.state.pa.us/corps/site/default.asp

State LLC Act

The Pennsylvania LLC Act is contained in Title 15 (Corporations and Unincorporated Associations), Chapter 89 of the Pennsylvania Statutes, starting with Section 8901. Chapter 89 (the LLC Act) is not available online.

State Tax Office

Department of Revenue, Harrisburg
www.revenue.state.pa.us

LLC Management

An LLC is managed by its members unless the certificate of organization states that the LLC is to be managed by one or more managers. [15 Pa.C.S. 8904]

Manager Election

Managers are elected as provided in the operating agreement, and, except as provided in the operating agreement, serve for one-year terms (or until a successor is elected). [Sections 8941 and 8903]

Meeting Requirements

Except as provided in the operating agreement, the approval by a majority of the members or managers is necessary to take action on any matter submitted to the members or managers for approval. Rules for the notice, time, place, and quorum for members' and managers' meetings and actions by written consent of the members or managers may be provided in the operating agreement. [Section 8942] Presumably, in a manager-managed LLC, members will meet at least once each year to elect managers, unless the operating agreement makes managers' terms indefinite.

Amendments

Except as provided in the operating agreement, amendments to the articles or operating agreement require approval of all LLC members. [Section 8942]

Admission of Members

No statutory rule was found regarding the issuance of new LLC memberships. Unless otherwise stated in the operating agreement, the admission of a transferee as a member must be approved by unanimous written consent of the nontransferring members. [Section 8924]

Withdrawal of Members

An operating agreement may prohibit a member from withdrawing prior to the dissolution of the LLC; if it does and a member attempts to withdraw, the withdrawal is ineffective. [Section 8948]

A member who withdraws is entitled to receive the fair value of the interest within a reasonable period after withdrawal. [Section 8933]

Continuation of the LLC

Except as otherwise provided in the operating agreement, the LLC automatically dissolves after the dissociation of a member (cessation or termination of a membership interest) unless all remaining members vote to continue the LLC within 90 days of dissociation event. [Section 8971]

Special Statutory Rules

Unless otherwise provided in the articles or operating agreement, all members must consent to a decision to voluntarily dissolve the LLC. [Section 8971]

RHODE ISLAND

LLC Filing Office

Rhode Island Secretary of State
Corporations Division
100 North Main Street
Providence, RI 02903-1335

Telephone: 401-222-3040

http://155.212.254.78/corporations.htm

State LLC Act

The Rhode Island LLC Act is contained in Title 7 (Corporations, Associations, and Partnerships), Chapter 7-16 of the Rhode Island General Laws, starting with Section 7-16-1, and is browseable from the following Web page:

www.rilin.state.ri.us/Statutes/TITLE7/7-16/INDEX.HTM

State Tax Office

Division of Taxation, Providence
www.tax.state.ri.us

LLC Management

An LLC is managed by its members unless the articles state that the LLC is to be managed by one or more managers. [Section 7-16-14]

Manager Election

Unless otherwise provided in the articles or operating agreement, managers are to be elected and removed by a majority vote of LLC members. [Section 7-16-16]

Meeting Requirements

Unless otherwise provided in the articles or operating agreement, members must vote in proportion to the value of capital each has contributed to the LLC. A default voting rule for membership action at a meeting is not given (presumably, as specified in the operating agreement), but the Act specifically requires approval of a majority of capital interests of all members to approve certain substantial actions, such as the dissolution of the LLC. Members and managers may take action by unanimous written consent, and, if not provided otherwise in the articles or operating agreement, members can take action by written consent of the number of members who would be necessary to approve action at a meeting at which all members were present; all nonconsenting members must be given notice of the approval by less than unanimous written consent of members. [Section 7-16-21]

Unless otherwise stated in the articles or operating agreement, managers take action by majority vote, with each manager given one vote. [Section 7-16-19]

Rules for notice, time, place, and quorum for members' and managers' meetings were not found in the LLC Act. Presumably, these may be provided in the articles or operating agreement.

Amendments

Unless otherwise provided in the articles or operating agreement, members owning a majority of the value of capital contributions made to the LLC must approve amendments to the articles or operating agreement. [Section 7-16-21]

Admission of Members

No statutory rule was found regarding issuance of new memberships in an LLC. Unless otherwise stated in the operating agreement, the admission of a transferee as a member must be approved by unanimous written consent of nontransferring members. [Section 7-16-36]

Withdrawal of Members

A member may withdraw upon six months' written notice to the LLC and to each member and manager. If the withdrawal is a breach of the operating agreement, the LLC may offset the amount paid to the withdrawing member by the amount of damages caused by the breach. [Section 7-16-28.1]

Except as otherwise provided in the operating agreement, the withdrawal of a member does not entitle the member to payment for her interest; instead, the member is treated as an assignee of an interest, with the right to share ongoing profits and distributions along with the other members. [Section 7-16-29]

Continuation of the LLC

A vote to continue the LLC after the termination of a membership is not required. But unless otherwise provided in the articles or operating agreement, the LLC automatically dissolves when the last remaining member loses her interest unless the successor(s) or assignee(s) of the last member or members agree(s) in writing within 90 days to admit a new member into the LLC to continue its business. And note: Unless otherwise provided in the articles or the operating agreement, a majority of the capital interests of remaining members of an LLC may vote to dissolve the LLC after any membership is terminated. [Section 7-16-39]

Special Statutory Rules

Unless otherwise provided in the articles or operating agreement, members owning a majority of the value of capital contributions made to the LLC must approve a decision to voluntarily dissolve the LLC, sell all its assets, or approve a transaction in which a manager has a personal financial interest. [Section 7-16-21]

SOUTH CAROLINA

LLC Filing Office

South Carolina Secretary of State
Corporations Department
P.O. Box 11350
Columbia, SC 29211
Telephone: 803-734-2158
www.scsos.com/Corporations.htm

State LLC Act

The South Carolina LLC Act is contained in Title 33 (Corporations, Partnerships, and Associations), Chapter 44 of the South Carolina Code, starting with Section 33-44-101, and is browseable from the following Web page:
www.lpitr.state.sc.us/code/t33c044.htm

State Tax Office

Department of Revenue, Columbia
www.sctax.org

LLC Management

An LLC is managed by its members unless the articles state that the LLC is to be managed by one or more managers. [Section 33-44-203]

Manager Election

Unless otherwise stated in the articles or operating agreement, managers must be elected, removed, and replaced by the consent of a majority of members. Managers hold office for an indefinite term. [Section 33-44-404]

Meeting Requirements

Unless otherwise stated in the LLC articles or operating agreement, members and managers must approve action by a majority vote. Members and managers may take action by written consent (presumably, by normal voting rules). [Section 33-44-404] Rules for the notice, time, place, and quorum for members' and managers' meetings were not found in the LLC Act. Presumably, these may be provided in the LLC articles or operating agreement.

Amendments

Unless otherwise provided in the articles or operating agreement, consent of all members is required to amend the articles or operating agreement. [Section 33-44-404]

Admission of Members

Unless otherwise provided in the articles or operating agreement, new memberships must be issued with the consent of all members. [Section 33-44-404] Admission of transferee as a member must be approved by unanimous consent of the nontransferring members. [Section 33-44-503]

Withdrawal of Members

A member may withdraw upon notice to the LLC. If the withdrawal violates the operating agreement or is prior to the end of a specified term established for the LLC, the LLC may offset the amount paid the withdrawing member by the amount of damages caused by the breach or early withdrawal. [Sections 33-44-601 and 33-44-602]

Generally, a member is entitled to the fair value of the member's interest (different valuation dates are used, depending on whether the LLC has a specified term or a perpetual existence). The LLC must deliver an offer to purchase the interest of the withdrawing member and financial statements to the member within 30 days of the date of withdrawal. The member has a right to bring a court action to determine the fair value of the member's interest if the member and the LLC cannot agree. [Section 33-44-701]

Continuation of the LLC

A membership vote to continue the LLC after the dissociation of a member (cessation or termination of a membership interest) is not required. [Section 33-44-801]

Special Statutory Rules

Unless otherwise provided in the articles or operating agreement, consent of all members is required to authorize transactions that personally benefit managers of the LLC, make interim distributions to members (prior to departure of a member or winding up of the LLC), sell all LLC assets, or voluntarily dissolve the LLC. [Section 33-44-404]

SOUTH DAKOTA

LLC Filing Office

South Dakota Secretary of State
State Capitol
500 East Capitol Ave.
Pierre, SD 57501-5070

Telephone: 605-773-4845

www.state.sd.us/sos/corporations

State LLC Act

The South Dakota LLC Act is contained in Title 47 (Corporations), Chapter 34 of the South Dakota Codified Laws, starting with Section 47-34-1, and is browseable from the following Web page (click South Dakota, drill down through the links in the left pane, as follows: South Dakota Codified Laws, Title 47, Chapter 47-34):

www.michie.com

State Tax Office

Department of Revenue, Pierre

www.state.sd.us/revenue/revenue.html

LLC Management

An LLC is managed by its members unless the articles state that the LLC is to be managed by one or more managers. [Sections 47-34A-203 and 404.1]

Manager Election

Managers are elected for an indefinite term by a majority of members, unless the operating agreement provides otherwise. [Sections 47-34A-103 and 47-34A-404.1]

Meeting Requirements

Generally, unless the operating agreement provides otherwise, each member (and in a manager-managed LLC, each manager) has equal voting and management rights, and a majority of members, (or managers) must vote to approve an act or decision. But special matters, such as the amendment of the articles or operating agreement, the admission of new members, or the dissolution of the LLC, must be approved by all members. Managers and members may take action by written consent without a meeting. [Section 47-34A-404.1] Rules for notice, time, place, and quorum for members' and managers' meetings were not found in the LLC Act. Presumably, these may be provided in the LLC articles or operating agreement.

Amendments

Unless otherwise provided in the operating agreement, amendments of the articles or operating agreement must be approved by all members. [Section 47-34A-404.1]

Admission of Members

Unless otherwise provided in the operating agreement, the admission of a new member must be approved by all members. [47-34A-404.1]

Withdrawal of Members

A member may withdraw upon notice to the LLC. If the withdrawal violates the operating agreement or is prior to the end of a specified term established for the LLC, the member is liable to the LLC and the other members for the amount of damages caused by the breach or early withdrawal. [Sections 47-34A-601(1) and 602]

Apparently, unless the operating agreement provides otherwise, a member who withdraws is treated as a transferee, with the right to share ongoing profits and distributions along with the other members prior to the dissolution of the LLC. [Section 47-34A-603]

Continuation of the LLC

A vote to continue the LLC after the termination of a membership is not required. [Section 47-34A-801]

Special Statutory Rules

Consent of all members is required to voluntarily dissolve the LLC. [Section 47-34A-404.1]

TENNESSEE

LLC Filing Office

Tennessee Department of State
Division of Business Services
Corporations Section
312 Eighth Avenue North
6th Floor, William R. Snodgrass Tower
Nashville, TN 37243

Telephone: 615-741-2286

www.state.tn.us/sos/service.htm#corporations

State LLC Act

The Tennessee LLC Act is contained in Title 48 (Corporations and Associations), Chapters 201-248 of the Tennessee Code, starting with Section 48-201-101, and is browseable from the following Web page (click Tennessee, drill down through the links in the left pane, as follows: Tennessee Code, Title 48, Chapter 201 to view the first chapter of the LLC Act—select other chapters to continue browsing the remaining Sections of the Act):

www.michie.com/resources1.html

State Tax Office

Department of Revenue, Nashville

www.state.tn.us/revenue

LLC Management

An LLC is either managed by its members or by a board of governors (managers), as stated in the articles of organization. [Section 48-205-101] Note that the LLC Act refers to the people normally considered managers of the LLC as governors, and refers to the two chief officers of the LLC as managers. We use standard terminology in our list of the rules (that is, our manager-management rules are taken from the Act's rules for governor-management).

Manager Election

Unless otherwise provided in the articles or operating agreement, managers must be elected by a plurality vote of the voting power at a members' meeting at which a quorum is present. [Section 48-239-107] Unless otherwise provided in the articles or operating agreement, the managers' terms are indefinite and last until the next regular meeting of members, if any. If a manager is elected for a fixed term, it may not exceed three years. [Section 48-239-103] Removal of managers must be made at a members' meeting (or a managers' meeting if this is allowed by the LLC articles or operating agreement) called for that purpose. [Section 48-239-109] Unless otherwise provided in the articles or operating agreement, members or managers may fill a vacancy in a manager position. [Section 48-239-110]

Meeting Requirements

If the LLC is member-managed, any actions that would require the approval of governors (managers) under the Act are made by the members. Unless otherwise provided in the articles or operating agreement, each mem-

ber has equal per capita voting power (for example, one vote each). [Section 48-224-101] Members' meetings are to be held as required in the articles or operating agreement, but if the LLC is manager-managed, an annual members' meeting must be held for the election of managers. Unless otherwise provided in the articles or operating agreement, the president, secretary, and, in a manager-managed LLC, a manager, may call a meeting of members. Notice must be given to all members (no notice period specified) that includes the purpose of the meeting. [Sections 48-222-101 and 48-222-102] Except as otherwise provided in the articles or operating agreement, a quorum for members' meetings is a majority of the voting power. [Section 48-224-102] Unless the articles or operating agreement requires otherwise, the approval of a majority of members at a meeting at which a quorum is present is necessary to take membership action. [Section 48-240-101] Members may take action by the written consent of all members (but the articles or operating agreement may lower the written consent requirement to as little as a majority of the membership voting power). [Sections 48-223-101 and 48-223-102]

Unless the articles or operating agreement provides otherwise, managers must take action by a vote of a majority of the managers at a meeting at which a quorum is present. A quorum consists of a majority of the number of managers, but the articles or operating agreement may lower the quorum requirement to no less than one-third the number of managers. [Section 48-239-112] Unless otherwise provided in the articles or operating agreement, managers may take action by the written consent of the number of managers necessary to take action at a meeting. Manager meetings may be held at the times and places specified in the articles or operating agreement. Unless otherwise provided in the articles or operating agreement, managers' meetings may be called by the chief manager (president) or the lesser of a majority of managers or two managers by the giving of at least two days' notice to all managers. [Section 48-239-111]

Amendments

Unless otherwise provided in the articles or operating agreement, an amendment of the articles or operating agreement requires the approval of a majority of members (in a manager-managed LLC, article amendments are proposed by the managers, and managers may make certain amendments on their own, such as deletions or technical corrections to articles). [Sections 48-209-102, 48-209-103, and 48-206-102]

Admission of Members

Unless otherwise provided in the articles or operating agreement, new memberships must be issued with the consent of all members. [Section 48-232-102] Unless the articles allow transfers by a majority of the voting power of the LLC, the admission of a transferee as a member must be approved by unanimous written consent of the nontransferring members. Managers (who also are members) also can approve the admission of transferees into the LLC if allowed by the articles or operating agreement, and a member can transfer a membership to another member without approval unless otherwise provided in the articles or operating agreement. [Section 48-218-102] But note, Section 48-232-102 says that the articles and operating agreement cannot lower the vote to approve a new member to less than a per capita majority of the nontransferring members, a majority of the profits interests of the nontransferring members, a majority of the capital interests of the nontransferring members, or a majority in interest (a majority of the capital and profits interests) of the nontransferring members.

Withdrawal of Members

A member has the power to withdraw at any time. [Section 48-216-101] Generally, a withdrawing member is entitled to receive the lesser of the fair market value of the interest determined on a going concern basis or the fair market value of the interest determined on a liquidation basis. Generally, payments for the interest to the member must be made within six months of the determination of the value of the interest. If the member's withdrawal is contrary to the LLC Act, the articles, or the operating agreement, the damages caused by the wrongful withdrawal may be offset against the amount paid to the withdrawing member. Instead of assessing damages, a majority of the remaining members can vote

to reduce the value of the withdrawing member's interest by the value of the LLC's goodwill and going concern value attributable to the member's interest. The articles or operating agreement may modify any of these statutory provisions and procedures. [Section 48-216-101]

Continuation of the LLC

For LLCs formed on or after for LLCs July 1, 1999, a vote to continue the LLC after the dissociation of a member (cessation of membership) is not required (but may be required according to the provisions of the articles or operating agreement). [Section 48-245-101]

Special Statutory Rules

The Tennessee LLC Act is one of the longest, most comprehensive series of LLC statutes on the books. To understand the various default rules that apply to all areas of LLC operations in the absence of contrary provisions in your articles or operating agreement, we recommend you browse the law.

TEXAS

LLC Filing Office

Texas Secretary of State
Statutory Filings Division
Corporations Section
P.O. Box 13697
Austin, TX 78711
Telephone: 512-463-5583
www.sos.state.tx.us/corp/index.shtml

State LLC Act

The Texas LLC Act is contained in Title 32 (Corporations), Part 3 of the Vernon's Texas Civil Statutes, starting with Article 1.01, and is browseable from the following Web page (click Vernon's Texas Civil Statutes at the bottom of the page, then under Title 32-Corporations select Chapter 18-Miscellaneous, then at the bottom of the list select Article 1528n-Texas Limited Liability Company Act):

www.capitol.state.tx.us/statutes/statutes.html

State Tax Office

Comptroller of Public Accounts, Austin

www.window.state.tx.us

LLC Management

An LLC is managed by its members unless the articles state that the LLC is to be managed by one or more managers. [Art. 1528n, Sections 3.02 and 2.12]

Manager Election

Unless stated otherwise in the operating agreement, the number of managers in a manager-managed LLC is the number of initial managers named in its articles. The operating agreement governs how managers are elected by members, the length of their terms, and their removal. [Section 2.13] Unless otherwise provided in the articles or operating agreement, vacancies may be filled by majority of remaining managers, unless caused by an increase in the number of managers, which must be filled by members at a meeting called for that purpose. [Section 2.15]

Meeting Requirements

Except as provided in the articles or operating agreement, members' meetings in a manager-managed LLC must be held upon no fewer than ten nor more than 60 days' notice to each member. Except as provided in the articles or operating agreement, a majority of members or managers constitutes a quorum for a members' or managers' meeting, respectively, with the approval of a majority of those present at a meeting at which a quorum is reached necessary to take member or manager action. Unless otherwise provided in the articles or operating agreement, members and managers may take action by the written consent of the number of members or managers that would be necessary to approve the action at a meeting at which all members or managers were present and voted. [Section 2.23]

Amendments

Unless otherwise stated in the articles or operating agreement, the approval of a majority of all members is necessary to amend the articles or operating agreement to change the management of the LLC from member- to manager-management, and vice versa. [Section 2.23]

Note: The Texas LLC Act refers to operating provisions adopted by an LLC as its regulations. [Section 2.09] In other words, references in the Texas LLC Act to regulations mean the provisions contained in the LLC operating agreement.

Admission of Members

Unless otherwise provided in the articles or operating agreement, new memberships must be issued with the approval of a majority of members. [Sections 2.23 and 4.01] Admission of a transferee as a member must be approved by the unanimous consent of the nontransferring members, or as the operating agreement may provide. [Section 4.07]

Withdrawal of Members

A member may withdraw from the LLC at the time or on the occurrence of events specified in the regulations (LLC operating agreement). [Section 5.05]

Except as otherwise provided under the LLC Act, the articles, or the operating agreement, a withdrawing member is entitled to receive the fair value of the member's interest within a reasonable time after withdrawal. [Section 5.06]

Continuation of the LLC

Unless otherwise provided in the operating agreement, the LLC automatically dissolves upon the dissociation of a member (cessation of membership) unless all remaining members vote to continue the LLC within 90 days of the dissociation event. [Section 6.01]

Special Statutory Rules

Disinterested managers or members may approve transactions that benefit a manager of the LLC, after disclosure of the material facts of the transaction. [Section 2.17]

Unless otherwise provided in the articles or operating agreement, voluntary dissolution of the LLC must be approved by a majority of all members. [Section 2.23]

UTAH

LLC Filing Office

Utah Division of Corporations and Commercial Code
160 East 300 South, 2nd Floor
Box 146705
Salt Lake City, UT 84114-6705

Telephone: 801-530-4849

Toll-free: 877-526-3994

www.commerce.state.ut.us/corporat/corpcoc.htm

State LLC Act

The Utah Revised LLC Act is contained in Title 48 (Partnership), Chapter 2c of the Utah Code, starting with Section 48-2c-101, and is browseable from the Web page listed below (select search by Keyword, then expand the left pane folder to select Title 48, Chapter 2c):

www.le.state.ut.us/Documents/code_const.htm

State Tax Office

Utah State Tax Commission, Salt Lake City

www.tax.ex.state.ut.us

LLC Management

An LLC is managed by its members unless the articles state that the LLC is to be managed by one or more managers. [Section 48-2b-125]

Manager Election

Managers are to be elected and removed, and serve terms, as specified in the operating agreement. [Section 48-2b-125]

Meeting Requirements

Members vote in proportion to their profits interests in the LLC unless otherwise provided in the articles. [Section 48-2b-125] Rules for notice, time, place, and quorum for members' and managers' meetings and action by written consent by members and managers were not found in the LLC Act. Presumably, these may be provided in the articles or operating agreement.

Amendments

The LLC's operating agreement can be amended as provided in its operating agreement. [Section 48-2b-126] No statutory rule was found regarding amendment of the articles.

Admission of Members

New memberships can be issued with the written consent of all members or as provided in the operating agreement. [Section 48-2b-122] Except as otherwise provided in the operating agreement, the admission of a transferee as a member must be approved by consent of a majority of the nontransferred profits interests in the LLC of nontransferring members. [Section 48-2b-131]

Withdrawal of Members

No specific provisions were found in the LLC Act regarding withdrawal of members. Section 48-2b-132 generally provides that a member may demand a return of capital when the LLC dissolves or as specified in the LLC operating agreement.

Continuation of the LLC

A vote to continue the LLC after the termination of a membership is not required. Note: A Utah LLC automatically dissolves when it fails to maintain at least one member. [Section 48-2b-137]

Special Statutory Rules

LLC property can be transferred on behalf of the LLC by one or more members (in a member-managed LLC) or by one or more managers (in a manager-managed LLC). [Section 48-2b-127]

Unless otherwise provided in the operating agreement, a majority of the profits interests in the LLC can consent to dissolve the LLC. [Section 48-2b-137]

VERMONT

LLC Filing Office

Vermont Secretary of State
Corporations Division
81 River Street, Drawer 09
Montpelier, VT 05609-1104

Telephone: 802-828-2386

www.sec.state.vt.us/corps/corpindex.htm

State LLC Act

The Vermont LLC Act is contained in Title 11 (Corporations, Partnerships, and Associations), Chapter 21 of the Vermont Statutes, starting with Section 3001, and is browseable from the following Web page (select Vermont Statutes Online in the left panel, then scroll down to select Title 11, then Chapter 21):

www.leg.state.vt.us

State Tax Office

Vermont Department of Taxes, Montpelier

www.state.vt.us/tax

LLC Management

An LLC is to be managed by its members unless its articles state that the LLC is to be managed by one or more managers. [11 V.S.A. 3023]

Manager Election

Except as provided in the operating agreement, managers are elected for an indefinite term, and can be replaced and removed with the approval of a majority of members. [Section 3054]

Meeting Requirements

Unless otherwise provided in the operating agreement:

- Members have equal voting power (presumably, one vote each), and must take action by majority vote.

- Managers can approve decisions by majority vote. [Section 3054]

Rules for the notice, time, place, and quorum for members' and managers' meetings, and for actions by written consent by members and managers, were not found in the LLC Act. Presumably, these may be provided in the articles or operating agreement.

Amendments

Unless otherwise stated in the operating agreement, the articles and operating agreement can be amended with the consent of all members. [Section 3054]

Admission of Members

Unless otherwise provided in the operating agreement, new memberships must be issued with the approval of all members. [Section 3054] Admission of transferee as a member must be approved by unanimous consent of the nontransferring members, and as may also be provided in the LLC operating agreement. [Section 3073]

Withdrawal of Members

A member may withdraw upon notice to the LLC (in an LLC with a perpetual duration, notice must be in writing to the LLC and other members, and be given 90 days in advance of the withdrawal). If the withdrawal violates the articles or operating agreement or is prior to the end of a specified term established for the LLC, the member is liable to the LLC and the other members for the amount of damages caused by the breach or early withdrawal. [Sections 3081(1) and 3082]

Generally, a member is entitled to the fair value of the member's interest (different valuation dates are used, depending on whether the LLC has a specified term or a perpetual existence). The LLC must deliver an offer to purchase the interest of the withdrawing member and financial statements to the member within 30 days of the date of the withdrawal. The member has a right to bring a court action to determine the fair value of the member's interest if the member and the LLC cannot agree. [Section 3091]

Continuation of the LLC

Unless otherwise provided in the operating agreement, the LLC automatically dissolves upon the dissociation (cessation of membership rights) of a member (or a member-manager in a manager-managed LLC) unless a majority in interest of the remaining members (presumably, remaining members holding a majority of both the capital and profits interests in the LLC) consent to the continuance of the LLC within 90 days of the dissociation event. [Section 3101]

Note: The dissociation events that trigger dissolution (or a vote to avoid dissolution) differ for at-will and term LLCs (a term LLC is one whose articles specify a date for dissolution of the LLC; an at-will LLC is one that continues perpetually until dissolved). For an at-will LLC, the normal dissociation events apply: that is, the expulsion, withdrawal, death, bankruptcy, and so on, of a member. For a term LLC, only death, bankruptcy, or certain other events that occur prior to the date of dissolution of the term LLC as stated in the articles apply. For additional information see Sections 3101(3) and 3081 of the LLC Act.

Special Statutory Rules

The operating agreement may vary any provision of the LLC Act, except certain nonwaivable provisions listed in Section 3003 (mostly dealing with duties of care and loyalty owed by members and managers, rights to inspect records, the right of member to withdraw, and the right of the members to dissolve the LLC in special cases).

LLC property can be transferred on behalf of the LLC by any member (in a member-managed LLC) or by any manager (in a manager-managed LLC). [Section 3041]

Unless otherwise provided in the operating agreement, all members must consent to making distributions prior to the departure of a member or the winding up of the LLC, selling all its assets and voluntarily dissolving the LLC. [Section 3054]

VIRGINIA

LLC Filing Office

Clerk of the State Corporation Commission
P.O. Box 1197
First Floor
Richmond, VA 23218

Telephone: 804-371-9733

Toll-free 866-SCC-CLK1

www.state.va.us/scc/division/clk/index.htm

State LLC Act

The Virginia LLC Act is contained in Title 13.1 (Corporations) of the Virginia Code, Chapter 12, starting with Section 13.1-1000, and is browseable from the following Web page (click Code of Virginia, then click Table of Contents on the search page; then select the Title 13.1 heading, then click Chapter 12, Virginia Limited Liability Company Act to see a list of the sections in the LLC Act):

http://legis.state.va.us/codecomm/codehome.htm

State Tax Office

Department of Taxation, Richmond

www.tax.state.va.us

LLC Management

An LLC is managed by its members unless the articles or operating agreement states that the LLC is to be managed by one or more managers. [Section 13.1-1022]

Manager Election

Unless otherwise provided in the articles or operating agreement, managers are to be elected by the members, and managers can be removed and vacancies filled by a majority vote of the members (members vote according to their capital account balances with the LLC). [Section 13.1-1024]

Meeting Requirements

Unless otherwise provided in the articles or operating agreement, members must vote in proportion to their capital account balances with the LLC, with the approval of members holding a majority share of capital account balances necessary to take membership action. Unless otherwise provided in the articles or operating agreement, managers can take action by a majority vote (presumably, with each manager entitled to one vote). Members and managers may take action by written consent without a meeting by obtaining signatures from the members or managers who would be sufficient to approve the matter at a meeting of members or managers. [Sections 13.1-1022 and 13.1-1024] Rules for the notice, time, place, and quorum for members' and managers' meetings were not found in the LLC Act. Presumably, these may be provided in the articles or operating agreement.

Amendments

Unless the articles provide for a greater vote, amendments to the articles require the approval of a majority of the members (who vote according to capital account balances with LLC). [Sections 13.1-1014 and 13.1-1022] Unless otherwise provided in the articles or operating agreement, amendments to the operating agreement must be approved by all members. [Section 13.1-1023]

Admission of Members

Unless otherwise provided in the operating agreement, new memberships must be issued with the consent of all members. [Section 13.1-1038.1] Except as provided in the articles or LLC operating agreement, the admission of a transferee as a member must be approved by consent of a majority in interest (majority of profits and capital interests in the LLC) of the nontransferring members. [Sections 13.1-1040 and 13.1-1002]

Withdrawal of Members

A member may resign from the LLC only if and as provided in the articles or operating agreement. [Section 13.1-1032] No specific provision for distributions to resigning member was found in the Act; Section 13.1-1031 generally provides that distributions prior to the dissolution of the LLC are to be made according to the articles or operating agreement.

Continuation of the LLC

A membership vote to continue the LLC after the dissociation of a member (cessation or termination of a membership interest) is not required. [Section 13.1-1046]

Special Statutory Rules

All members must consent in writing in order to voluntarily dissolve the LLC. [Section 13.1-1046]

WASHINGTON

LLC Filing Office

Washington Secretary of State
Corporations Division
P.O. Box 40234
Olympia, WA 98504-0234

Telephone: 360-753-7115

www.secstate.wa.gov/corps

State LLC Act

The Washington LLC Act is contained in Title 25.15 (Partnerships) of the Washington Code, starting with Section 25.15.005, and is browseable from the following Web page:

http://search.leg.wa.gov/wslrcw/
RCW%20%2025%20%20TITLE/
RCW%20%2025%20.%2015%20%20CHAPTER/
RCW%20%2025%20.%2015%20%20chapter.htm

State Tax Office

Department of Revenue, Olympia

http://dor.wa.gov

LLC Management

An LLC is managed by its members unless the certificate of formation states that the LLC is to be managed by one or more managers. [Section 25.15.150]

Manager Election

Except as provided in the operating agreement, the approval of members who contribute more than 50% of the value of capital to the LLC is necessary to elect, remove, and replace managers. Managers hold office for an indefinite term unless otherwise provided in the operating agreement. [Section 25.15.150]

Meeting Requirements

Except as provided in the operating agreement, the approval of members who contribute more than 50% of the value of the LLC's capital is necessary for membership action. Rules for the notice, time, place, and quorum for members' meetings, or for actions by written consent of members without a meeting, may be provided in the operating agreement. [Section 25.15.120] Unless otherwise provided in the operating agreement, managers can take action by approval of more than one-half the number of managers. Rules for the notice, time, place, and quorum for managers' meetings, or for actions by written consent of managers without a meeting, may be provided in the operating agreement. [Section 25.15.165]

Amendments

Unless otherwise provided in the operating agreement, approval of all members is required in order to amend the operating agreement. [Section 25.15.120] No statutory rule was found for voting to amend the certificate of formation.

Admission of Members

Unless otherwise provided in the operating agreement, new memberships must be issued with the consent of all members. [Section 25.15.115] Admission of a transferee as a member must be approved by unanimous consent of the nontransferring members, and as may be provided in the LLC operating agreement. [Section 25.15.250]

Withdrawal of Members

A member may withdraw from an LLC at the time or upon the happening of events specified in and in accordance with the LLC agreement. If the agreement does not specify when a member may withdraw, a member may not withdraw prior to the time for the LLC's dissolution and commencement of its winding up, unless the member obtains the written consent of all other members at the time. [Section 25.15.130(3)]

Continuation of the LLC

A membership vote to continue the LLC after the dissociation of a member (cessation or termination of a membership interest) is not required. [Section 25.15.270]

Special Statutory Rules

All members must consent in writing to voluntarily dissolve the LLC. [Section 25.15.270]

WEST VIRGINIA

LLC Filing Office

West Virginia Secretary of State
Corporations Division
Bldg. 1, Suite 157-K
1900 Kanawha Blvd. East
Charleston, WV 25305-0770

Telephone: 304-558-8000

www.state.wv.us/sos/corp/startup.htm

State LLC Act

The West Virginia LLC Act is contained in Chapter 31B of the West Virginia Code, starting with Section 31B-1-101, and is browseable from the following Web page (select State Code from the WV Code folder in the left pane, then select the right arrow in the top drop-down box and scroll down until you select Chapter 31B, then press Go and select sections of the LLC Act from the left panel):

www.legis.state.wv.us/legishp.html

State Tax Office

Department of Tax and Revenue, Charleston

www.state.wv.us/taxdiv

LLC Management

An LLC is managed by its members unless the articles state that the LLC is to be managed by one or more managers. [Sections 31B-1-101 and 31B-2-203]

Manager Election

Except as may be provided in the operating agreement, managers are to be elected, removed, and replaced by a majority of members and hold office for an indefinite term. [Section 31B-4-404]

Meeting Requirements

Except as otherwise provided in the operating agreement, members and managers have equal management rights (presumably, this means equal voting power, such as one vote per member or manager), with a majority vote necessary to take membership or manager action. Members and managers make take action by written consent without a meeting (presumably, by normal member or manager voting rules). [Section 31B-4-404] Rules for the notice, time, place, and quorum for members' and managers' meetings, and for actions by written consent of members or managers without a meeting, were not found in the Act. Presumably, these may be provided in the operating agreement.

Amendments

Unless otherwise provided in the operating agreement, approval of all members is required in order to amend operating agreement. [Section 31B-4-404] No statutory rule was found for amendment of articles.

Admission of Members

No statutory rule was found regarding issuance of new memberships in an LLC. Except as may be provided in the operating agreement, the admission of a transferee as a member must be approved by unanimous consent of the nontransferring members. [Section 31B-5-503]

Withdrawal of Members

A member may withdraw upon notice to the LLC. If the withdrawal violates the operating agreement or is prior to the end of a specified term established for the LLC, the member is liable to the LLC and the other members for the amount of damages caused by the breach or early withdrawal, and the LLC must offset any amount paid to the withdrawing member by the amount of the damages. [Sections 31B-6-601(1) and 602]

Generally, a member is entitled to the fair value of the member's interest (different valuation dates are used, depending on whether the LLC has a specified term or has a perpetual existence). The LLC must deliver an offer to purchase the interest of the withdrawing member and financial statements to the member within 30 days of the date of withdrawal. The member has a right to bring a court action to determine the fair value of the member's interest if the member and the LLC cannot agree. [Section 31B-7-701]

Continuation of the LLC

Except as otherwise provided in the operating agreement, the LLC automatically dissolves upon the dissociation of a member (cessation of membership) unless the members who are entitled to receive a majority of current or future distributions vote to continue the LLC within 90 days of the dissociation event. Note: This statutory majority-of-distributions voting rule to continue the LLC applies in manager-managed LLCs only when a member who is also a manager is dissociated—a vote to avoid dissolution is not required when a nonmanaging member's interest is terminated in a manager-managed LLC (of course, the operating agreement can provide otherwise). [Section 31B-8-801]

Also note: The dissociation events that trigger dissolution (or a vote to avoid dissolution) differ for at-will and term LLCs (a term LLC is one whose articles specify a date for dissolution of the LLC; an at-will LLC is one that continues perpetually until dissolved). For an at-will LLC, the normal dissociation events apply: that is, the expulsion, withdrawal, death, bankruptcy, and so on, of a member. For a term LLC, only death, bankruptcy, or certain other events that occur prior to the date of dissolution of the term LLC as stated in the articles apply. For additional information see Sections 31B-8-801(b)(3) and 31B-6-601.

Special Statutory Rules

The operating agreement may vary any provision of the LLC Act, except certain nonwaivable provisions listed in Section 31B-1-103 (mostly dealing with duties of care and loyalty owed by members and managers, rights to inspect records, right of member to withdraw, and right of members to dissolve the LLC in special cases).

Unless otherwise provided in the operating agreement, approval of all members is required to make distributions prior to the departure of a member or the winding up of the LLC, sell all LLC assets, and voluntarily dissolve the LLC. [Section 31B-4-404]

WISCONSIN

LLC Filing Office

Department of Financial Institutions
Division of Corporate and Consumer Services
Corporations Section, 3rd Floor
P.O. Box 7846
Madison, WI 53707-7846

Telephone: 608-261-7577

www.wdfi.org/corporations/

State LLC Act

The Wisconsin LLC Act is contained in Chapter 183 of the Wisconsin Statutes, starting with Section 183.0102, and is browseable from the following Web page (scroll down the left panel and select Chapter 183):

http://folio.legis.state.wi.us/cgi-bin/om_isapi.dll?
clientID=80155&infobase=stats.nfo&jump=
ch.%20180&softpage=Browse_Frame_Pg

State Tax Office

Department of Revenue, Madison

www.dor.state.wi.us

LLC Management

An LLC is managed by its members unless the articles state that the LLC is to be managed by one or more managers. [Section 183.0401]

Manager Election

Except as provided in the operating agreement, the approval of members who contribute more than 50% of the value of capital to the LLC is necessary to elect, remove, and replace a manager. Managers hold office for an indefinite term unless otherwise provided in the operating agreement. [Section 183.0401]

Meeting Requirements

Except as provided in the operating agreement, the approval of members who contribute more than 50% of the value of capital to the LLC is necessary for membership action. Unless otherwise provided in the operating agreement, managers take action by approval of more than one-half the number of managers. [Section 183.0404] Rules for the notice, time, place, and quorum for members' and managers' meetings, and for action by written consent of the members and managers without a meeting, were not found in the Act. Presumably, these may be provided in the operating agreement.

Amendments

Unless otherwise provided in the operating agreement, the approval of all members is required to amend the articles or operating agreement. [Section 183.0404]

Admission of Members

Unless otherwise provided in the operating agreement, new memberships must be issued with the consent of all members. [Sections 183.0404 and 183.0801] Unless otherwise stated in the operating agreement, the admission of a transferee as a member must be approved by unanimous written consent of the nontransferring members. [Section 183.0706]

Withdrawal of Members

Unless the operating agreement prohibits withdrawals, a member may withdraw by giving written notice to the other members. If the withdrawal is a breach of the operating agreement or is otherwise based upon wrongful conduct, the LLC may offset the amount paid to the withdrawing member by the amount of damages caused by the breach or wrongful conduct. Unless otherwise provided in the operating agreement, if the LLC has a limited term or is formed for a particular undertaking (project), the withdrawal of a member before the end of the term or the accomplishment of the undertaking is a breach of the operating agreement. [Section 183.0802(3)]

If not otherwise provided in the operating agreement, a retiring member is entitled to receive the fair value of her interest within a reasonable time after resignation. [Section 183.0604]

Continuation of the LLC

For LLCs formed on or after October 1, 2002, a membership vote to continue the LLC after the dissociation of a member (cessation or termination of membership) is not required.   [Section 183.0901]

Special Statutory Rules

LLC property may be transferred on behalf of the LLC by any member (in a member-managed LLC) or by any manager (in a manager-managed LLC). [Section 183.0702]

Approval of all members is required to voluntarily dissolve the LLC. [Section 183.0901]

WYOMING

LLC Filing Office

Secretary of State's Office
Corporations Division
The State Capitol Building, Room 110
Cheyenne, WY 82002-0020

Telephone: 307-777-7311

soswy.state.wy.us/corporat/corporat.htm

State LLC Act

The Wyoming LLC Act is contained in Title 17 of the Wyoming Statutes, Chapter 15, starting with Section 17-15-101, and is browseable from the following Web page (click the link to the Limited Liability Company Act:

http://soswy.state.wy.us/corporat/statutes.htm

State Tax Office

Department of Revenue, Cheyenne

http://revenue.state.wy.us

LLC Management

An LLC is managed by its members unless the articles state that the LLC is to be managed by one or more managers. [Section 17-15-116]

Manager Election

Unless expressly dispensed with or overridden in the operating agreement, managers are to be elected annually by members in the manner specified in the operating agreement. [Section 17-15-117]

Meeting Requirements

Unless otherwise stated in the operating agreement, members vote in proportion to their capital account balances with the LLC. [Section 17-15-116] Rules for the notice, time, place, and quorum for members' and managers' meetings, and for actions by written consent of the members and managers without a meeting, were not found in the Act. Presumably, these may be provided in the operating agreement (but Section 17-15-131 says that members and managers can waive notice in writing if notice is required under the Act or the articles or operating agreement).

Amendments

No statutory rules for amendments to the articles or operating agreement were found in the Act.

Admission of Members

Admission of a transferee as a member must be approved by unanimous written consent of the nontransferring members (but an LLC that has elected flexible LLC status in its articles can state its own admission rule for transferees in the LLC operating agreement). [Sections 17-15-122 and 17-15-144]

Withdrawal of Members

Unless otherwise prohibited or restricted in the operating agreement, a member may withdraw and demand a return of her capital contribution upon six months' prior written notice to the other members. [Section 17-15-120(b)]

Continuation of the LLC

The LLC automatically dissolves upon the dissociation of a member (cessation of membership) unless the remaining members vote to continue the LLC by unanimous consent under a right to do so stated in the articles of organization (but an LLC that has elected flexible LLC status in its articles can state its continuance rule or procedure in the LLC operating agreement). [Sections 17-15-123 and 17-15-144]

Special Statutory Rules

Section 17-15-144 of the LLC Act allows the articles to contain a provision that elects flexible limited liability company status. In addition to allowing an LLC to have one member, rather than the default minimum of two members specified under the Act, this status allows the LLC to adopt its own operating agreement provisions for the approval of assignment of membership interests and for continuance of the LLC after a member is dissociated; without electing this status, the voting rules for admission of members and continuance of the LLC after the dissociation must be stated in the articles.

Only members, or managers in a manager-managed LLC, can contract debts, incur liabilities, or transfer property on behalf of the LLC. [Sections 17-15-117 and 17-15-118]

Unanimous written consent of the members is necessary to voluntarily dissolve the LLC. [Section 17-15-123]

2003 Federal Tax Act Summary

Every business owner's life is complicated by laws and regulations. While many laws stay the same from year to year, federal tax laws change at least a little bit every year, and have changed significantly in the past decade. Sometimes savvy business owners can turn new tax rules to their advantage. This is especially true of the 2003 federal tax act, known as the Jobs and Growth Tax Relief Reconciliation Act of 2003 (JGTRRA, pronounced "jigtra".)

WHAT JGTRRA GIVES, IT MAY ALSO TAKE AWAY

The tax breaks that JGTRRA gives business owners and others don't uniformly begin as of a certain date—nor are they perpetual.

- **When can you begin using JGTRRA?** Some provisions begin in 2003, but others won't kick in until later—as late as 2006, for example.

- **How long do the tax breaks in JGTRRA last?** The JGTRRA provisions lapse, or "sunset," at various times, but even the longest-lived will lapse at the end of 2010. For example, some will lapse as early as the end of 2004. While these sunset times are firm now, they're subject to change if Congress passes another tax bill to extend or change them (which it undoubtedly will). Keep in mind that you are reading about a shifting tax landscape.

Some of JGTRRA's provisions benefit all small businesses, no matter whether you're a sole proprietorship, partnership, LLC, or corporation. For example, you can now deduct up to $100,000 in one year for tangible personal property used in your business, up from $25,000. (Tangible personal property includes computers and off-the-shelf software.) This increased expensing provision applies through 2006, and will be a major incentive to upgrade or invest in new equipment.

Another generally applicable provision concerns "bonus" depreciation (the depreciation you can take against brand-new business property). It's increased from 30% to 50%, as long as you bought the property after May 5, 2003 and before January 1, 2005. This bonus depreciation will last through 2005.

Many of JGTRRA's provisions apply when a business takes a particular step, such as paying its owners who also work for the company or declaring a dividend. The rest of this appendix gives you a thumbnail sketch of JGTRRA's benefits for:

- sole proprietors, partners, or limited liability company owners (members) who pay taxes on business profits via their personal income tax returns (Section A)

- corporate owners (shareholders) who are salaried employees in their company (Section B)

- corporations who choose to keep earnings in the company (Section C)

- shareholders receiving dividends (whether from their own corporation or another corporation) (Section D)

- shareholders selling stock (lower capital gains) (Section E)

- "small" corporations selling stock (Section F), and

- married couples and parents (Section G).

Consult an accountant, tax planner, or tax lawyer before implementing new tax strategies in your business.
This appendix doesn't go into the details you'll need to consider before implementing a tax strategy based on JGTRRA—before taking that step, you'll need to consult an expert. It's also a good idea to meet with your tax planner before the end of your business's tax year to find out how tax laws will affect your business planning for the coming year.

A. BENEFITS FOR SOLE PROPRIETORS, PARTNERS, AND LLC OWNERS

If you own a small business organized as a sole proprietorship, a partnership, or an LLC, you know that business profits are taxed on your personal tax return. That's why sole proprietorships, partnerships, and LLCs are known as "pass-through" business entities (their profits and expenses "pass through" the business to their owners). Thanks to JGTTRA, starting in 2003 you'll pay less tax on your income—the top tax rates are lower and a little more income is taxed at the lowest rate. See "2003 Federal Individual Tax Rates," below, for a breakdown of these adjustments.

Lower rates for high income earners. The highest individual rate is lowered to 35% (down from 38.6%). Other upper brackets have also been lowered, by a couple of percentage points (35% to 33%, 30% to 28%, and 27% to 25%). This change sunsets at the end of 2010.

More income applies to low brackets. The 10% bracket now applies to more income than it did in the past (up from $6,000 to $7,000 for single returns, and from $12,000 to $14,000 for married filing jointly). This may help you pay less income tax if you are starting a business, don't expect much profit at first, and have no other income. This change sunsets in 2006, then comes back in 2007 under the terms of a prior tax bill.

2003 Federal Individual Tax Rates							
Single				**Head of Household**			
Taxable Income Over	But Not Over	The Tax is:	of the Amount Over	Taxable Income Over	But Not Over	The Tax is:	of the Amount Over
$0	$7,000	10%	$0	$0	$10,000	10%	$0
$7,000	$28,400	$700 + 15%	$7,000	$10,000	$38,050	$1,000 + 15%	$10,000
$28,400	$68,800	$3,910 + 25%	$28,400	$38,050	$98,250	$5,207.50 + 25%	$38,050
$68,800	$143,500	$14,010 + 28%	$68,800	$98,250	$159,100	$20,257.00 + 28%	$98,250
$143,500	$311,950	$34,926 + 33%	$143,500	$159,100	$311,950	$37,295.00 + 33%	$159,100
$311,950	∞	$90,514.50 + 35%	$311,950	$311,950	∞	$87,735.50 + 35%	$311,950
Married Filing Jointly				**Married Filing Separately**			
Taxable Income Over	But Not Over	The Tax is:	of the Amount Over	Taxable Income Over	But Not Over	The Tax is:	of the Amount Over
$0	$14,000	10%	$0	$0	$7,000	10%	$0
$14,000	$56,800	$1,400 + 15%	$14,000	$7,000	$28,400	$700 + 15%	$7,000
$56,800	$114,650	$7,820 + 25%	$56,800	$28,400	$57,325	$3,910 + 25%	$28,400
$114,650	$174,700	$22,282.50 + 28%	$114,650	$57,325	$87,350	$11,141.25 + 28%	$57,325
$174,700	$311,950	$39,096.50 + 33%	$174,700	$87,350	$155,975	$19,548.25 + 33%	$87,350
$311,950	∞	$84,389.0 + 35%	$311,950	$155,975	∞	$42,194.50 + 35%	$155,975

B. BENEFITS FOR SALARIED CORPORATE OWNERS

JGTTRA significantly affects the taxes owed by corporate owners who also work for and are paid by the company. It changes some of the calculations for determining the optimal amount of salaries and bonuses for tax purposes. Dividends are also more attractive—this is covered in Section D.

1. Income-Splitting Opportunities

The owners of a small corporation, who typically also work for the corporation as officers, pay individual income taxes on their salaries and bonuses, while the corporation pays corporate income taxes on the profits retained in the corporation (after it deducts the salaries and bonuses). A basic benefit of incorporating your business is your ability to determine, through your decisions to distribute or retain corporate profits, whether you want to pay taxes on your corporate profits at corporate rates or at individual rates. This tax strategy is called corporate "tax splitting" or "income splitting."

Let's take a closer look at income splitting. The goal of income splitting is to take advantage of any difference between individual and corporate tax brackets at the same level of taxable income. If you make distributions to yourselves as owners, you effectively split corporate profits between the corporation's taxable income and your taxable income. The result of spreading your income among both corporate and individual income tax brackets is that you can avoid having all business profits pile up into higher brackets on either the corporate or individual side. Even better, you get to choose whether you or the corporation pays taxes on the next piece of corporate income, based on which of you will be taxed at a lower rate on those dollars.

In effect, the real value of having a corporation with separate tax brackets is that you have two additional tax brackets—the lowest 15% and 25% corporate income tax brackets—into which you can pour business income. If these extra corporate tax rates are lower than the top individual rate that you'd pay if more business income were paid out to you, you'll save tax dollars by keeping the income in the corporation rather than paying it out to yourself at a higher "marginal" (top) rate.

Now let's return to the effect of JGTRRA on income splitting. As explained in Section A, JGTTRA lowered the individual tax rate, though corporate income tax rates have not changed. Consequently, you may decide to keep less profit in your corporation (and take out more as salaries or bonuses), and pay less tax on those payouts. JGTTRA doesn't change the basic benefit of income splitting. It just changes the calculations.

2. Using Income Splitting After JGTRRA

"2003 Income Tax Payments And Brackets," below, lists corporate and individual rates and tax payments side by side. Use the table to compare individual and corporate taxes on a set amount of taxable income. Each time a tax bracket changes, a new row starts, which calculates the total amount of tax paid by an individual or corporation up to that point. (An extra row has been added at the $30,000 income level for purposes of the discussion that follows the table.) For simplicity, the chart compares corporate tax rates with the rates of only two individual tax-filing categories: single, and married filing jointly.

What do these tax payment and bracket comparisons mean for the owner-employees of a small corporation? Can you conclude that single-owner corporations that earn between $30,000 to $100,000 will save taxes if they keep the profits in the corporation? Or, is it true that if corporate owners are married, the owners should always make sure to pay out all profits to themselves as deductible salaries so that they only pay individual income taxes on the profits? Or perhaps, should married business owners never incorporate their business?

Actually, none of the above conclusions is valid. In fact, the traditional one-to-one comparisons of individual versus corporate tax payments and brackets really miss the whole point of corporate income- and tax-splitting. Remember, the real value of having a corporation with separate tax brackets is that you have two additional corporate 15% and 25% tax brackets (or buckets) into which you can pour business income. If these extra corporate tax brackets are lower than the marginal (top) rate that would apply if a given amount of business income is paid out to you (which is often true for many single and married business owners), you will save tax dollars by keeping the income in the corporation rather than paying it out to yourself at a higher marginal rate.

> **EXAMPLE:** After taking your normal salary from your corporation, you expect to have $50,000 net income left in your corporation. If you keep the retained earnings in your corporation, it will pay a 15% corporate income rate on the $50,000. If you paid this extra $50,000 out to yourself as a salary increase or a bonus, it would be deducted from corporate income (the corporation would not pay income taxes on the $50,000). Instead, the extra $50,000 would be added to your regular salary on your individual income tax return and be taxed to you. If your regular salary puts you in an individual income tax bracket greater than 15%, you will pay more individual income taxes on the extra $50,000 than the amount of taxes your corporation would pay on it if the $50,00 were retained in the corporation. So, regardless of your marital status and despite the strict bracket-to-bracket comparison that seems to favor individuals, the lower corporate tax brackets let you shelter business income at rates that often are lower than the rates individuals pay on business income.

For a further discussion of corporate income splitting under the 2003 tax rates, see Nolo's 2003 Corporate Income Splitting E-Guide, available at www.nolo.com

C. BENEFITS FOR CORPORATIONS WITH RETAINED EARNINGS

The Internal Revenue Code lets most corporations accumulate earnings and profits of up to $250,000, no questions asked. Owners can keep amounts above this ceiling if they establish a valid business purpose for the extra accumulations (for example, to pay off debt or establish a corporate reserve for expected expenses). Corporations that hold onto excessive income without a valid business purpose are subject to an "accumulated earnings" penalty tax. This penalty used to be tied to the top individual tax rate (38.6%) before JGTTRA. The good news after JGTTRA is that these penalty rates are now tied to the tax rate that shareholders pay on dividends: 15%.

As the example above in Section B shows, you may want to keep corporate profits in the corporation for income tax reasons. But don't neglect to consider the accumulated earnings penalty—after all, though reduced, it's not zero.

There are additional potential tax reasons to retain profits in the corporation. Retained corporate earnings can eventually be "pulled out" of your corporation when you later sell your shares, at capital gains rates (which can be lower than individual tax rates; see Section E, below). Or they can be passed to your heirs after your death. Because your heirs will receive the shares with a basis "stepped up" to market value, they'll pay capital gains tax only on the appreciation in value that happens between the time they inherit and the time they sell the shares.

2003 Income Tax Payments And Brackets						
Taxable Income	Individual (Single)		Individual (Married Filing Jointly)		Corporate	
More Than	Tax Payment So Far	Bracket Rate	Tax Payment So Far	Bracket Rate	Tax Payment So Far	Bracket Rate
$0	$0	10%	$0	10%	$0	15%
$7,000	$700 +	15%	$700	15%	$1,050	15%
$14,000	$1,750	15%	$1,400	15%	$2,100	15%
$28,400	$3,910	25%	$3,560	15%	$4,260	15%
$30,000	$4,310	25%	$3,800	15%	$4,500	15%
$50,000	$9,310	25%	$6,800	15%	$7,500	25%
$56,800	$11,010	25%	$7,820	25%	$9,200	25%
$68,800	$14,010	28%	$10,820	25%	$12,200	25%
$75,000	$15,746	28%	$12,370	25%	$13,750	34%
$100,000	$22,746	28%	$18,620	25%	$22,250	39%
$114,650	$26,848	28%	$22,282	28%	$27,964	39%
$143,500	$34,926	33%	$30,361	28%	$39,215	39%
$174,700	$45,222	33%	$39,097	33%	$51,383	39%
$311,950	$90,515	35%	$84,389	35%	$104,911	39%
$335,000	$98,582	35%	$92,457	35%	$113,900	34%
$400,000	$121,332	35%	$115.207	35%	$136,000	34%
$500,000	$156,332	35%	$150,207	35%	$170,000	34%
$1,000,000	$331,332	35%	$325,207	35%	$340,000	34%

Let's look closely at how this table works, and what it tells you about how to handle corporate profits. To compare tax rates and taxes owed on $100,000 of taxable income, for example, find the $100,000 row in the table. The three columns in this row show that on this amount of taxable income:

- single individual taxpayers pay $22,746
- married taxpayers filing jointly pay $18,620, and
- corporations pay $22,250.

The row also shows the tax bracket that applies to each taxpayer on taxable incomes *above* $100,000. A single taxpayer will pay a tax rate of 28%, married filing jointly taxpayers 25% and corporate taxpayers 39% on taxable income *above* $100,000 (up to the next tax bracket).

If you use this table to compare tax brackets and payments for corporations and single taxpayers, you'll notice that a corporation pays less income tax than an individual on the same income between roughly $30,000 and $100,000. Above and below these thresholds, a single taxpayer pays less income tax than a corporation on the same income.

Now, let's compare the *married* and corporate tax payments and rates on the same levels of taxable income. You can see that married taxpayers filing jointly always pay less income tax than a corporation on the same levels of income. However, at $100,000, taxes paid by corporations and married taxpayers filing jointly are very close. Keep in mind that you don't always get a tax advantage by paying out corporate profit as salaries instead of keeping the earnings in the corporation.

D. BENEFITS FOR SHAREHOLDERS RECEIVING DIVIDENDS

JGTTRA reduces the taxes individuals pay on dividends, whether these dividends come from a corporation they own or not. Dividends are now a more desirable way to distribute corporate profits than they used to be, because:

- Individual recipients pay less tax. (Subsection 1.)

- Corporations are less tempted to structure payouts in ways that raise IRS suspicions. (Subsection 2),

- Owners who are salaried employees pay no FICA taxes on dividends, which saves them money, (Subsection 3.)

1. Lower Taxes on Dividends

A corporation can deduct salaries and bonuses, as we learned in discussing tax splitting in Section A, but it can't deduct the dividends it pays. This means the company must pay income tax on profits used as the source of dividend payments to shareholders, so both the corporation and the shareholders end up paying income taxes on dividends. Until 2003, dividends were taxed to shareholders at the top income tax rate of the shareholder, just like earned income (the top individual tax rate before JGTRRA was 38.6%). Understandably, owners were hesitant to declare dividends since they paid both corporate income and marginal (top-bracket) individual income taxes on the dividend payout, and also because it required a board meeting and the help of an accountant or lawyer to answer the financial and legal questions preliminary to declaring a dividend.

JGTRRA gives corporate owners a reason to reconsider this traditional reluctance. The 2003 tax law lowers the tax rate on dividends paid by most individuals to 15% (very low income taxpayers pay only 5%). In other words, dividends are taxed separately from other individual income, not added to your other income to be taxed at your top individual tax rate. This change will sunset in 2008.

2. Fewer Fights With the IRS

Lowering the tax rate on dividends will probably have a salutary effect on shareholder/IRS relations, too. Because dividends were taxed at the recipient's top individual rate, corporations were tempted to devise creative methods of paying money out to shareholders—without calling these payouts dividends (these methods included excessive salary payments, buy-backs of a portion of an owner's stock, and the like). The IRS frequently challenged these actions. Now that the dividend tax rate is so attractive, there's less need for creative maneuvers to avoid dividend treatment.

3. Save Money on FICA Taxes

FICA taxes support the Social Security and Medicare systems. Employees, whether salaried or wage earners, pay half the tax from their earnings; the employer pays the other half. If you're incorporated and work in your business, you're an employee and will ordinarily get a salary—and, just like any other employee, you'll pay FICA taxes on your salary (the corporation pays the other half). But think of what happens when you own the corporation—in effect, you pay both the corporate and the individual portion. The total FICA tax is 15.3%, or $13,833, on the first $87,000 and 2.9% on any salary over $87,000.

FICA applies only to earned income, and *dividends are not considered earned income*. Consequently, you don't pay FICA taxes on dividends, which means that dividends have a built-in potential 15.3% tax savings when they replace a portion of the owner's corporate salary. In other words, it can make sense for a small corporation to pay out some money to its owners as dividends rather than salaries. This little-recognized strategy can save some tax dollars in some situations, but understand that it makes sense only if the corporation's income tax on that money, plus the 15% individual tax on dividends, is less than the individual income tax and FICA taxes that would be paid on the same money if it were paid as additional salary (remember, the corporation deducts salaries paid out to employees, so the corporation does not pay corporate income tax on salaries).

SHAREHOLDERS THAT ARE CORPORATIONS

Corporations that own shares in other corporations have a dividend tax rate break under pre-JGTRRA tax law that stays in effect. They can exclude from 70% to 100% of dividend income from the corporate shareholder's taxable income. A corporation that pays a maximum 35% income tax on only 30% of its dividend income pays an effective corporate dividend tax rate of 10.5%, at most.

The rationale for this corporate tax break is that dividends should be taxed twice, not three times. The corporate shareholder may distribute its dividend income to its own shareholders, who will themselves pay income tax on it. And the corporation that distributed the original dividend already paid tax on that money as income.

⚠ Make sure your tax adviser does the math before you decide on a dividend.
The tax savings achieved by owners paying out a dividend on a small corporation's earnings may not be worth the hassle of calling a board meeting and making the necessary analysis before declaring the dividend. You'll also experience a long-term disadvantage if you underfund your Social Security and Medicare account.

EXAMPLE: Camilus and Patrick form a specialized flight instruction school for air-show acrobatic pilots, Blue Sky Barnstorming. They incorporate to limit their personal exposure to lawsuits and claims that might be made against their high-risk venture. The corporation earns $100,000 in net profits and pays out the entire amount as salary to the owners. Each owner is single, and each has no additional (noncorporate) taxable income to report for the year.

Here's the tax costs:

Corporate tax	$ 0
Patrick's individual income tax on $50,000 salary payout	$9,310
Camilus's individual income tax on $50,000 salary payout	$9,310
Total Social Security cost on salaries ($50,000 x 15.3 x 2)	$15,300
Total income and FICA taxes	$33,920

After talking to their tax adviser, they learn that they can save a few dollars by declaring and paying a dividend instead of paying the total $50,000 out to each owner as a salary. They decide to pay each owner a salary of $28,400 (the point at which the single individual tax bracket changes from 15% to 25%) and the balance of the payout ($50,000 - $28,400 = $21,600) as a dividend. This means the corporation will retain $43,200 to pay out as a dividend to both owners ($21,600 x 2 = $43,200).

Here are the re-computed tax costs:

Corporate tax on retained $43,200	$7,600
Patrick's individual income tax on $28,400 salary payout	$3,910
Camilus's individual income tax on $28,400 salary payout	$3,910
Patrick's and Camilus's income tax on the dividend ($21,600 dividend x .15 individual dividend tax rate x 2)	$6,480
Total social security cost on salaries ($28,400 x 15.3 x 2)	$8,691
Total income and FICA taxes	$30,591

This is a tax savings of $3,329 ($33,920 - 30,591) compared to the previous scenario. While not a mammoth tax cut, the $3,000+ may come in handy when, as here, the owners are only able to pull modest amounts of profits from their corporation.

APPENDIX D

Forms

Filename	Form Name (for Resolutions forms only)	Title of Form	Chapter	Section
MEETSUM		Meeting Summary Sheet	3	B2
CALL		Call of Meeting	3	B3b
MEETLIST		Meeting Participant List	3	B4
NOTICE		Notice of Meeting	3	B5d
ACKREC		Acknowledgment of Receipt of Notice of Meeting	3	B7
PROXY		Membership Voting Proxy	3	B8
MAILCERT		Certification of Mailing of Notice	3	D9b
LLCMTG		Minutes of LLC Meeting	5	B
WAIVER		Waiver of Notice of Meeting	6	B1
APPROVE		Approval of LLC Minutes	6	B3
PAPERLET		Cover Letter for Approval of Minutes of LLC Meeting	6	B4
CONSENT		Written Consent to Action Without Meeting	7	Step 2
CH08	CH08_01	Authorization of Treasurer to Open and Use LLC Accounts	8	B1
	CH08_02	Authorization of Treasurer to Open and Use Specific LLC Account(s)	8	B2
	CH08_03	Authorization of LLC Account and Designation of Authorized Signers	8	B3
	CH08_04	Authorization of Rental of Safe Deposit Box	8	B4
	CH08_05	Adoption of Assumed LLC Name	8	C
	CH08_06	Approval of Contract	8	D
	CH08_07	Approval of Lease of Premises by LLC	8	E1
	CH08_08	Purchase of Real Property by LLC	8	E2
	CH08_09	Authorization of Sale of Real Property by LLC	8	E3
	CH08_10	Delegation of LLC Authority	8	F1
	CH08_11	Ratification of Contract or Transaction	8	F2
	CH08_12	Rescission of Authority	8	F3
	CH08_13	Certification of LLC Resolution	8	G1
	CH08_14	Affidavit of LLC Resolution	8	G2
	CH08_15	Acknowledgment	8	G3
CH09	CH09_01	LLC Election of Corporate Tax Treatment	9	A
	CH09_02	Approval of Independent Audit of LLC Financial Records	9	B
	CH09_03	Approval of LLC Tax Year	9	C
CH10	CH10_01	Approval of Amendment to Articles of Organization	10	B1
	CH10_02	Approval of Restatement of Articles of Organization	10	B2
	CH10_03	Amendment of Articles Form	10	B3
	CH10_04	Amendment of LLC Operating Agreement	10	C1
CH11	CH11_01	Approval of LLC Distribution	11	A3
	CH11_02	Approval of Additional Contributions of Capital by Members	11	B3
	CH11_03	Admission of New Member	11	C1c
	CH11_04	Approval of Transfer of Membership	11	C2c
	CH11_05	Approval of LLC Purchase of Interest of Withdrawing Member	11	D3

MEETING SUMMARY SHEET

Name of LLC:

_____

Year of Meeting: _____

Type of Meeting: ☐ Regular or ☐ Special

Meeting of: ☐ Managers and/or ☐ Members

Date: _____ Time: _____:_____ _____.M.

Place: _____

Meeting Called by: _____

Purpose: _____

_____

Committee or Other Reports or Presentations: _____

Other Reminders or Notes: _____

Notice ☐ Written ☐ Verbal ☐ None

Notice Must Be Given by Date: _____

Notice of Meeting Given to:

Name	Type of Notice*	Date Notice Given	How and Where Communicated	Date of Acknowledgment
_____	_____	_____	_____	_____
_____	_____	_____	_____	_____
_____	_____	_____	_____	_____
_____	_____	_____	_____	_____
_____	_____	_____	_____	_____
_____	_____	_____	_____	_____

*Types of Notice: Written (mailed, hand-delivered); Verbal (in person, telephone conversation, answering machine, voice mail); Email; Fax.

CALL OF MEETING

Secretary: _____

Name of LLC: _____

LLC Address: _____

The following person(s):

Name	Title	Membership Interest (if any)
_____	_____	_____
_____	_____	_____
_____	_____	_____

authorized under provisions of the operating agreement of the LLC and/or provisions of state law, hereby make(s) a call and request to hold a meeting of _____ of the LLC for the purpose(s) of:_____ _____.

The requested date and time of the meeting is:_____ .

The requested location for the meeting is:_____

_____ .

The following LLC officers and other Individuals are expected to attend to present reports or otherwise contribute to the meeting, and, in addition to managers and/or members, should be included in those who receive notice of the meeting:

Name	Address
_____	_____
_____	_____
_____	_____

The secretary is requested to provide all proper notices as required by the operating agreement of the LLC and state law to all persons entitled or asked to attend the meeting, and to include with the notice any other materials necessary or helpful to the holding of the upcoming meeting. If possible, the secretary is requested to provide at least _____ notice of the meeting to all meeting participants.

Date: _____

Signed:_____

Signed:_____

MEETING PARTICIPANT LIST

Name of LLC:_____

Type of Meeting: ☐ Regular (_____) or ☐ Special

Meeting of: ☐ Managers and/or   ☐ Members

Date: _____ Time: _____:_____ __.M.

Meeting Participants (list names in alphabetical order):

Name:_____

Address: _____

_____ Telephone: _____

☐ Manager _____

☐ Member: Number or Percentage of Voting Power (per capita or according to percentage of capital,

profits, or capital and profits interests as specified in operating agreement):

_____

_____

☐ Officer: Title _____

☐ Other (position and reason for attendance): _____

Name: _____

Address: _____

_____ Telephone: _____

☐ Manager _____

☐ Member: Number or Percentage of Voting Power (per capita or according to percentage of capital,

profits, or capital and profits interests as specified in operating agreement):

_____

_____

☐ Officer: Title _____

☐ Other (position and reason for attendance): _____

NOTICE OF MEETING

Name of LLC: _____

A meeting of _____ of the LLC will be held

at _____,

on _____ at _____.

The purpose(s) of the meeting is/are as follows:

_____

_____

_____.

_____, LLC Secretary

Signature of Secretary

ACKNOWLEDGMENT OF RECEIPT OF NOTICE OF MEETING

LLC Name:_____

(Recipient of Notice: In paragraph 1, please fill in the date on which you received notice of the meeting; in paragraph 2, review for accuracy the type of notice checked, making and initialing corrections as appropriate; in paragraph 3, date and sign your name; and mail or deliver a completed copy to the LLC officer listed in paragraph 4.)

1. I received notice of a meeting of the _____ of the LLC on _____. The notice of meeting stated the date, time, place, and purpose of the upcoming _____ meeting.

2. The notice of meeting was:

    ☐   received by fax, telephone number _____

    ☐   delivered verbally to me in person at _____

    ☐   delivered verbally to me by phone call, telephone number _____

    ☐   left verbally in a message on an answering machine or on voice mail, telephone number _____

    ☐   delivered by mail to _____

    ☐   delivered via e-mail, e-mail address _____

    ☐   other: _____

3. Date: _____

    Signed: _____

    Printed Name: _____

4. Please return to:

    Name of LLC Officer: _____

    Name of LLC: _____

    Address: _____

    Phone: _____

    Fax: _____

MEMBERSHIP VOTING PROXY

(Member: Insert name of proxyholder—the person you are authorizing to vote in your place—in first paragraph, then date, sign, and return by the date indicated to LLC officer at address listed below.)

The undersigned member of _____, a limited liability company, authorizes _____ to act as his or her proxy and to represent and vote his/her LLC membership at a meeting of:

(Check one or both boxes)

☐ managers

☐ members

to be held on _____.

This proxy is effective for all items of business brought before the meeting.

Date: _____

Signature of Member: _____

Printed Name of Member: _____

Please return proxy by _____ to:

Name of LLC Officer: _____

Name of LLC: _____

Address: _____

Phone: _____ Fax: _____

CERTIFICATION OF MAILING OF NOTICE

I, the undersigned acting secretary of _____,

a limited liability company, certify that I caused notice of the meeting of the

_____ of the LLC to be held on _____

to be deposited in the United States mail, postage prepaid, on _____,

addressed to the following persons at their most recent addresses as shown on the books of this LLC

as follows:

_____

_____

_____

A true and correct copy of the notice is attached to this certificate.

Date: _____

Signed: _____, Secretary

Printed Name: _____

MINUTES OF LLC MEETING

LLC Name: _____

1. A meeting of the _____ of the LLC was held on _____ `
   at _____ at _____,
   for the transaction of all business that may properly be brought by participants before the meeting,
   including any of the special purposes listed below:

   (If applicable, check one or more boxes below, and supply additional information as appropriate.)

   ☐   Election of LLC manager(s) by LLC members

   ☐   Review of past LLC business and discussion of future operations

   ☐   The approval of one or more resolutions as follows:

                  [If this box is checked, insert summaries of resolutions.]

2. _____ acted as chairperson, and
   _____ acted as secretary of the meeting.

3. The chairperson called the meeting to order.

4. The secretary announced that the meeting was:

   [Check one of the boxes below and supply additional information.]

   ☐   a regular meeting scheduled to be held _____ under provisions
       in the LLC operating agreement

   (or)

   ☐   a special meeting called by the following person(s):

   _____   ☐ Manager   ☐ Member   ☐ Other: _____

   _____   ☐ Manager   ☐ Member   ☐ Other: _____

   _____   ☐ Manager   ☐ Member   ☐ Other: _____

5. The secretary announced that the meeting was held pursuant to notice, if required and as required under the operating agreement of this LLC, or that notice had been waived by all participants entitled to receive notice under the operating agreement. Copies of any certificates of mailing of notice prepared by the secretary of the LLC and any written waivers signed by participants entitled to receive notice of this meeting were attached to these minutes by the secretary.

6. ☐ **Members Voting.** (Check if members will vote at the meeting, and supply information below.)

   The secretary announced that an alphabetical list of the names and interests held by all members of the LLC was available and open to inspection by any person in attendance at the meeting. The secretary announced that there were present, in person or by proxy, the following voting power of the members of the LLC, representing a quorum of the members. (The secretary attached written proxy statements, executed by the appropriate members, to these minutes for any membership voting power listed below as held by a proxyholder.)

   Name of Member   Member's Voting Power

   _____   _____

   _____   _____

   _____   _____

   _____   _____

7. ☐ **Managers Voting.** (Check if managers will vote at the meeting, and supply information below.)

   The secretary announced that an alphabetical list of the names of the managers of the LLC was available and open to inspection by any person in attendance at the meeting. The secretary announced that the following managers of the LLC were present, representing a quorum of the managers:

   Name of Manager

   _____

   _____

   _____

   _____

8. The secretary announced that the following persons were also present at the meeting in the following capacities:

Name   Title

_____   _____

_____   _____

_____   _____

_____   _____

9. ☐ **Previous Meeting Minutes.** (Check if previous meeting minutes will be approved at this meeting, and supply information, checking one or both additional boxes below.)

The secretary announced that the minutes of the LLC meeting held on _____

☐ had been distributed prior to the meeting, and the secretary was in receipt of any written approval of minutes forms signed and returned by persons who had read and approved the minutes.

☐ were distributed at the meeting, then read by the secretary.

After counting any written approvals, and, if necessary, taking the voice vote of _____ at the meeting, the secretary announced that the minutes as distributed, read, and corrected, as appropriate, were approved. The secretary attached a copy of the approved minutes together with any signed approvals of minutes forms to these minutes.

10. The following reports were presented at the meeting by the following persons:

_____

_____

_____

11. ☐ **Election of Managers.** (Check if managers will be elected, and supply information below.)

The chairperson announced that the next item of business was the nomination and election of the managers for another _____ term. The following nominations were made and seconded:

Names of Manager Nominee(s):

_____

_____

_____

The secretary next took the votes of members entitled to vote for the election of managers at the meeting, and, after counting the votes, announced that the following persons were elected to serve as managers of this LLC:

Names of Elected Manager(s):

_____

_____

_____

☐ **Managers' Acceptance.** (Check if managers accepted positions.)

The above managers, having been elected, accepted their management positions. The secretary announced that the presence of current managers of the LLC at the meeting represented a quorum of managers of the LLC.

12. ☐ **Resolutions.** (Check if resolutions will be passed, and supply information below.)

After discussion, on motion duly made and carried by the affirmative vote of (check one or more boxes and supply any required information):

☐ a majority of the membership voting power in attendance

☐ a majority of the managers in attendance

☐ other, as follows:

_____

_____

_____

The following resolution(s) was(were) approved at the meeting:

_____

_____

_____

☐ **Additional Resolutions.** (Check if additional resolutions will be passed, and supply information below.)

After discussion, on motion duly made and carried by the affirmative vote of (check one or more boxes and supply any required information):

☐ a majority of the membership voting power in attendance

☐ a majority of the managers in attendance

☐ other, as follows:

_____

_____

_____

The following resolution(s) was(were) approved at the meeting:

_____

_____

_____

There being no further business to come before the meeting, it was adjourned on motion duly made and carried.

The above minutes were completed in final form on the date shown below by the undersigned secretary of the meeting:

Date: _____

Signature: _____

Title: _____

WAIVER OF NOTICE OF MEETING

Name of LLC: _____

The undersigned waive(s) notice of and consent to the holding of the meeting of the LLC held at

_____ on _____

at _____. The purposes of the meeting are as follows:

_____

_____

_____

_____

_____

_____

Dated: _____

Signature   Printed Name

_____   _____

_____   _____

_____   _____

_____   _____

_____   _____

APPROVAL OF LLC MINUTES

Name of LLC: _____

The undersigned consent(s) to the minutes of the LLC meeting held at _____

_____ on _____

at _____, and attached to this form, and accept(s) the resolutions passed and the

decisions made at such meeting as valid and binding.

Dated: _____

Signature   Printed Name

_____   _____

_____   _____

_____   _____

_____   _____

_____   _____

_____   _____

_____   _____

_____   _____

COVER LETTER FOR APPROVAL OF MINUTES OF LLC MEETING

Date: _____

Name: _____

Mailing Address: _____

City, State, Zip: _____

Re: Approval of LLC Minutes

Dear _____:

I am enclosing minutes of a meeting of _____ that show

approval of one or more specific resolutions.

Since these items were agreeable to the members and/or managers entitled to vote on them, we did not

hold a formal meeting to approve these decisions. We are now finalizing our LLC records and preparing

formal minutes that reflect these prior LLC decisions.

To confirm that these minutes accurately reflect past decisions of the LLC and to formally signify your

agreement to them, please date and sign the enclosed Approval of LLC Minutes form and mail it to me at

the address below. If you have corrections or additions to suggest, please contact me so we can hold a

meeting or make other arrangements to finalize and document these changes.

Sincerely,

_____,

Title: _____

enclosures: Minutes & Approval of LLC Minutes form

Please return to:

Name: _____

LLC: _____

Mailing Address: _____

City, State, Zip: _____

Phone: _____   Fax: _____

WRITTEN CONSENT TO ACTION WITHOUT MEETING

Name of LLC: _____

The undersigned hereby consent(s) as follows:

_____

_____

_____

_____

_____

_____

_____

Dated: _____

Signature   Printed Name

_____   _____

_____   _____

_____   _____

_____   _____

AUTHORIZATION OF TREASURER TO OPEN AND USE LLC ACCOUNTS

The treasurer of the LLC is authorized to select one or more banks, trust companies, brokerage companies, or other depositories, and to establish financial accounts in the name of this LLC. The treasurer and other persons designated by the treasurer are authorized to deposit LLC funds in these accounts. However, only the treasurer is authorized to sign checks and withdraw funds from these accounts on behalf of the LLC.

The treasurer is further authorized to sign appropriate account authorization forms as may be required by financial institutions to establish and maintain LLC accounts. The treasurer shall submit a copy of any completed account authorization forms to the secretary of the LLC, who shall attach the forms to this resolution and place them in the LLC records binder.

AUTHORIZATION OF TREASURER TO OPEN
AND USE SPECIFIC LLC ACCOUNT(S)

The treasurer of this LLC is authorized to open the following account(s), in the name of the LLC, with the following depositories:

Type of account: _____

Name, branch, and address of financial institution:

_____

_____

_____

Type of account: _____

Name, branch, and address of financial institution:

_____

_____

_____

The treasurer and other persons authorized by the treasurer must deposit the funds of the LLC in this account. Funds may be withdrawn from this account only on the signature of the treasurer.

The treasurer is authorized to complete and sign standard authorization forms for the purpose of establishing the account(s) according to the terms of this resolution. A copy of any completed account authorization form(s) must be submitted by the treasurer to the secretary of the LLC, who will attach the form(s) to this resolution and place them in the LLC records binder.

AUTHORIZATION OF LLC ACCOUNT AND DESIGNATION
OF AUTHORIZED SIGNERS

The treasurer of this LLC is authorized to open a _____ account in

the name of the LLC with _____ .

    Any officer, employee, or agent of this LLC is authorized to endorse checks, drafts, or other

evidences of indebtedness made payable to this LLC, but only for the purpose of deposit.

    All checks, drafts, and other instruments obligating this LLC to pay money must be signed on

behalf of this LLC by _____ of the following:_____

_____ .

    The above institution is authorized to honor and pay any and all checks and drafts of this LLC

signed as provided in this authorization.

    The persons designated above are authorized to complete and sign standard account

authorization forms for the purpose of establishing the account(s), provided that the forms do not vary

materially from the terms of this resolution. The treasurer must submit a copy of any completed account

authorization forms to the secretary of the LLC, who will attach the forms to this resolution and place

them in the LLC records binder.

AUTHORIZATION OF RENTAL OF SAFE DEPOSIT BOX

The treasurer of the LLC is authorized to rent a safe deposit box in the name of the LLC with an appropriate bank, trust company, or other suitable financial institution, and to deposit in this box any securities, books, records, reports, or other material or property of the LLC that he or she decides is appropriate for storage and safekeeping in this box.

ADOPTION OF ASSUMED LLC NAME

It was decided that the LLC will do business under a name that is different from the formal name of the LLC stated in its articles of organization (or similar organizational document that was filed with the state to commence the legal existence of the LLC). The assumed name selected for the LLC is

_____.

The secretary of the LLC was instructed to register the assumed LLC name as required by law.

APPROVAL OF CONTRACT

The _____ were presented a proposed contract to be entered into

between the LLC and _____ for the purpose of

_____, together with the following attachments:

_____.

Next, a report on the proposed contract was given by _____,

who made the following major points and concluded with the following recommendation: _____

_____ .

After discussion, _____

_____, it was decided that the transaction of the

business covered by the contract was in the best interests of the LLC, and the proposed contract and

attachments were approved.

The _____ was instructed to execute the contract

submitted to the meeting in the name of and on behalf of the LLC, and to see to it that a copy of the

contract executed by all parties, together with all attachments, be placed in the records of the LLC.

NOLO
www.nolo.com

APPROVAL OF LEASE OF PREMISES BY LLC

A proposed lease agreement between _____

and _____ for the premises

known as _____

was presented for approval. The lease covered a period of _____, with

_____ rent payments payable by the LLC of _____.

    After discussion, it was decided that the lease terms were commercially reasonable and fair to the LLC and that it was in the best interests of the LLC to enter into the lease.

    The lease and all the terms contained in it were approved, and the secretary of the LLC was instructed to see to it that the appropriate officers of the LLC execute the lease on behalf of the LLC, and that a copy of the executed lease agreement be attached to this resolution and filed in the LLC records binder.

PURCHASE OF REAL PROPERTY BY LLC

The purchase by the LLC of real property commonly known as _____

_____ was discussed.

The president announced that the property had been offered to the LLC for sale by the owner at a

price of _____. After discussing the value of the property to the LLC and

comparable prices for similar properties, it was agreed that the LLC should _____

_____.

    It was also agreed that the LLC will seek financing for the purchase of the property on the

following terms:

_____

_____

_____.

    The president was instructed to see to it that the appropriate LLC officers prepare all financial and

legal documents necessary to submit the offer or counteroffer to the seller and to seek financing for the

purchase of the property according to the terms discussed and agreed to in this resolution.

NOLO
www.nolo.com
Purchase of Real Property by LLC

AUTHORIZATION OF SALE OF REAL PROPERTY BY LLC

After discussion, it was agreed that the president of this LLC is authorized to contract to sell real

property of the LLC commonly known as: _____

on the following conditions and terms: _____

_____

_____.

    The president of the LLC and any other officers of the LLC authorized by the president can execute

all instruments on behalf of the LLC necessary to make and record a sale of the above property

according to the above terms.

DELEGATION OF LLC AUTHORITY

After discussion, it was agreed that the following individual, whose LLC title is indicated below, is granted authority to perform the following tasks or transact the following business by and on behalf of the LLC, or to see to it that such tasks are performed for the LLC under his or her supervision as follows:

_____

_____.

    This person is also granted the power to perform any and all incidental tasks and transact incidental business necessary to accomplish the primary tasks and business described above.

RATIFICATION OF CONTRACT OR TRANSACTION

After discussion, it was agreed that the following contract or other business transaction undertaken on behalf of the LLC by the following individual whose title appears below is hereby adopted, ratified, and approved as the act of the LLC and is accepted as having been done by, on behalf of, and in the best interests of the LLC:

_____

_____

_____ .

RESCISSION OF AUTHORITY

After discussion, it was agreed that prior authority granted to _____

on _____ for the purpose of _____

_____

is no longer necessary to the interests of the LLC and that any and all authority granted under the prior

approval of authority is hereby rescinded and no longer in effect.

CERTIFICATION OF LLC RESOLUTION

The undersigned, duly elected and acting _____ of

_____, certifies that the attached resolution was

adopted by the _____

□ at a duly held meeting at which a quorum was present, held on _____

or,

□ by written consent(s) dated on or after _____,

and that it is a true and accurate copy of the resolution and that the resolution has not been rescinded

or modified as of the date of this certification.

Dated: _____

_____

_____, Secretary [or other title]

AFFIDAVIT OF LLC RESOLUTION

STATE OF _____

COUNTY OF _____

Before me, a Notary Public in and for the above state and county, personally appeared

_____ who, being duly sworn, says:

    1. That he/she is the duly elected and acting _____ of

_____ , a _____ LLC.

    2. That the following is a true and correct copy of a resolution duly approved by the

_____ of the LLC _____

_____ :

_____

_____

_____

    3. That the above resolution has not been rescinded or modified as of the date of this affidavit.

_____

_____ , Secretary

Sworn to and subscribed before me this _____ day of _____ .

_____

Notary Public

My commission expires: _____

Notary Public

NOLO
www.nolo.com

ACKNOWLEDGMENT

STATE OF _____

COUNTY OF _____

I hereby certify that on _____, before me, a Notary Public in and for

the above state and county, personally appeared _____, who

acknowledged himself/herself to be the _____ of

_____ _____ and that he/she, having been authorized

to do so, executed the above document for the purposes contained therein by signing his/her name as

_____ of _____ .

_____

Notary Public

My commission expires: _____

Notary Public

LLC ELECTION OF CORPORATE TAX TREATMENT

After consultation with the LLC's tax adviser, the LLC treasurer recommended that the LLC elect to be taxed as a corporation, starting _____. After discussion, all members agreed that this election should be made, and the treasurer was authorized by the members to complete IRS Form 8832, "Entity Classification Election," to accomplish this election, and to sign the form on behalf of each of the members of this LLC, and to file it with the IRS.

It was also agreed that, if applicable, the treasurer file any additional forms necessary to elect corporate tax treatment of the LLC for state income tax purposes.

APPROVAL OF INDEPENDENT AUDIT OF LLC FINANCIAL RECORDS

After discussion, it was agreed that the accounting firm of _____

was selected to perform an independent audit of the financial records of the LLC for the _____

fiscal year and to prepare all necessary financial statements for the LLC as part of its independent

audit.

The LLC treasurer was instructed to work with the auditors to provide all records of LLC finances

and transactions that may be requested by them, and to report to the LLC on the results of the audit on

its completion.

APPROVAL OF LLC TAX YEAR

After discussion and a report from the treasurer, which included advice obtained from the LLC's accountant, it was resolved that the tax year of the LLC will end on _____ of each year. The treasurer was appointed to file the necessary tax forms on behalf of the LLC to adopt or change the tax year of the LLC with the IRS [add, if applicable, "and the appropriate state tax agency"].

APPROVAL OF AMENDMENT TO ARTICLES OF ORGANIZATION

RESOLVED, that Article _____ of the articles of organization of this LLC be _____

as follows: _____

_____

_____

_____

_____.

APPROVAL OF RESTATEMENT OF ARTICLES OF ORGANIZATION

RESOLVED, that the articles of organization be amended and restated to read in full as follows:

_____

_____

_____

_____

_____

_____

_____

_____

_____

_____

_____ .

AMENDMENT OF ARTICLES FORM

To: _____

Articles of Amendment

of

_____

One: The name of the LLC is _____ _____ ,

Two: The following amendment to the articles of organization was approved by the members on _____ :

_____
_____
_____
_____
_____ .

Three: The number of members required to approve the amendment was _____ , and the number of members that voted to approve the amendment was _____ .

Date: _____

By:

_____

_____ , President

_____

_____ , Secretary

AMENDMENT OF LLC OPERATING AGREEMENT

RESOLVED, that _____ of the operating agreement of the LLC is

_____ as follows:

_____

_____

_____

_____

_____.

APPROVAL OF LLC DISTRIBUTION

The LLC resolves that the LLC will make the following distribution of profits of the LLC to the following members:

Name of Member   Amount

_____ $_____

_____ $_____

_____ $_____

_____ $_____

_____ $_____

It was announced that the above distribution of LLC profits was in accordance with the requirements for the allocation of distributions to members as set out in the LLC operating agreement, or as required under state law. The treasurer presented a current balance sheet of the LLC at the meeting for review by the attendees, and announced that he/she had consulted the LLC's tax adviser. It was agreed that, after giving effect to the distribution, the LLC would continue to be able to pay its obligations as they become due in the normal course of its operations, and that the LLC would meet any applicable financial and legal tests under state law for making distribution to members. The treasurer was instructed to attach a copy of the balance sheet to this resolution for inclusion in the LLC's records binder.

The treasurer of the LLC is instructed to prepare and deliver or mail a check drawn on the LLC's account in the appropriate amount to each member entitled to the distribution no later than

_____.

APPROVAL OF ADDITIONAL CONTRIBUTIONS
OF CAPITAL BY MEMBERS

It was agreed that the following members will make the following contributions of capital to the LLC,

on or by _____:

Name of Member	Amount
_____	$_____
_____	$_____
_____	$_____
_____	$_____
_____	$_____

☐ It was agreed that the operating agreement of the LLC will be amended, if necessary, to reflect the capital, profits, voting, and other interests of all members of the LLC as a result of the making of the above capital contributions.

☐ It was agreed that the LLC will pay interest at the rate of _____% per year on the above capital contributions, subject to the following terms: _____ _____

_____.

ADMISSION OF NEW MEMBER

After discussion, it was agreed that the LLC will issue the following membership interest to the following person for the following payment or transfer of property to the LLC:

Name   Payment

_____   _____

It was agreed that the operating agreement of the LLC will be amended, if necessary, to reflect the capital, profits, voting, and other interests of all members of the LLC as a result of the admission of the person named above. It was also agreed that, as a condition to being formally accepted as a member of this LLC, the new member agrees to the rights and responsibilities associated with membership by signing the most current LLC operating agreement or by signing a statement, attached to the most current LLC operating agreement, in which the new member agrees to be bound by the terms of the agreement.

APPROVAL OF TRANSFER OF MEMBERSHIP

After discussion, it was agreed that the LLC approves the transfer of the membership interest of

_____, "former member," to _____,

"new member." The new member is admitted as a full member of this LLC, with all economic,

management, voting, and any other rights associated with the membership interest of the former

member.

It was agreed that the books of this LLC will be adjusted to show the termination of membership

rights of the departing member and the establishment of membership rights of the new member.

The operating agreement of the LLC will be amended, if necessary, to reflect the capital, profits,

voting, and other interests of all members of the LLC as a result of the admission of the new member

named above. It was also agreed that, as a condition to being formally accepted as a member of this

LLC, the new member must agree to the rights and responsibilities associated with membership by

signing the most current LLC operating agreement or by signing a statement, which will be attached to

the most current LLC operating agreement, agreeing to be bound by the terms of the agreement.

It was further resolved that the nontransferring members of the LLC, whose signatures appear

below, consent to the continuance of the business and legal existence of the LLC following the

withdrawal of the former member and the admission of the new member.

Date: _____

Signature: _____

Signature: _____

Signature: _____

Signature: _____

APPROVAL OF LLC PURCHASE OF INTEREST
OF WITHDRAWING MEMBER

The LLC resolves that the LLC will purchase the entire membership interest of

_____ , a member of this LLC, on the terms

specified below. It was agreed that the purchase of the membership interest will terminate all capital,

profits, loss, and, voting, and all other management, ownership, and economic interests of the

member in this LLC.

The date of purchase is: _____.

The terms of the purchase are as follows: _____

_____.

After a report of the treasurer, which included an analysis of the most recently prepared balance

sheet of the LLC and LLC operations since its preparation, it was agreed that the LLC was able

financially and in accordance with any applicable state legal requirements to purchase the

withdrawing member's interest according to the terms set out above.

The treasurer was instructed to prepare a balance sheet of the LLC as of the date set for purchase

of the withdrawing member's interest, and to see to it that a copy of the balance sheet, plus any

additional supporting documentation, be given to the member prior to the date of purchase for the

member's review and, if appropriate, signature. A copy of the balance sheet and any supporting

documentation, signed by the withdrawing member if appropriate, will be attached to this resolution

and placed in the LLC records binder.

On completion of the necessary paperwork, the treasurer will pay, or make appropriate

arrangements for payment, on behalf of the LLC to purchase the withdrawing member's interest on the

terms specified above.

It was further resolved that the remaining members of the LLC, whose signatures appear below,

consent to the continuance of the business and legal existence of the LLC following the withdrawal of

the member named above.

Date: _____

Signature: _____

Signature: _____

Signature: _____

Signature:_____

APPROVAL OF LLC HIRING

After discussion, the hiring of _____ to the position of

_____ was approved.

    It was agreed that the duties of this position and compensation for performing these services will

be as follows: _____

_____.

APPROVAL OF BONUSES AND SALARY INCREASES

The LLC considered the question of salary increases and bonuses to persons who performed compensated services for the LLC. After discussion, the LLC approved the following salary increases and bonuses, to be paid to the following persons:

Name and Title	Amount	Type	
_____	$ _____	☐ Salary Increase	☐ Bonus
_____	$ _____	☐ Salary Increase	☐ Bonus
_____	$ _____	☐ Salary Increase	☐ Bonus
_____	$ _____	☐ Salary Increase	☐ Bonus
_____	$ _____	☐ Salary Increase	☐ Bonus
_____	$ _____	☐ Salary Increase	☐ Bonus
_____	$ _____	☐ Salary Increase	☐ Bonus

The above salary amounts or bonuses will be paid as follows: _____

_____

_____.

APPROVAL OF INDEPENDENT CONTRACTOR SERVICES

After discussion, the following independent contractor services were approved to be performed by

_____ :

_____

_____

_____

_____

APPOINTMENT OF LLC OFFICERS

After discussion, the following individuals were appointed to serve in the following LLC officer positions. Any annual salary to be paid to any officer and approved is shown below next to the name of the officer:

Title of Officer	Name	Compensation, if any
_____:	_____	$_____
_____:	_____	$_____
_____:	_____	$_____
_____:	_____	$_____

Each officer has the duties that are specified in the operating agreement of the LLC and as may be designated from time to time by the LLC management. An officer serves until his or her successor is elected and is qualified to replace the officer.

AUTHORIZATION OF PAYMENT FOR ATTENDING LLC MEETINGS

After discussion, it was agreed that all of the following persons will be paid the following amounts for each day, or fraction of a day, during which they attend a meeting of the LLC.

Name and Title   Per Diem Amount

_____ $_____

_____ $_____

_____ $_____

_____ $_____

It was also discussed and agreed that the following persons will be _____ the following reasonable and necessary travel expenses incurred to attend meetings of the managers and/or members of the LLC:

Name and Title   Per Meeting Travel Allotment

_____ $_____

_____ $_____

_____ $_____

_____ $_____

ANNUAL STIPEND FOR ATTENDANCE AT LLC MEETINGS

After discussion, it was agreed that, on or by _____ of each year, the

following persons will be paid the following annual amounts, which comprise a yearly travel allotment

for traveling to and attending regular and special meetings of the LLC:

Name and Title   Annual Stipend and Travel Allotment

_____ $ _____

_____ $ _____

_____ $ _____

_____ $ _____

LLC INDEMNIFICATION AND INSURANCE

The LLC will indemnify its current and former _____ to the fullest extent permitted under the laws of this state. Such indemnification is not deemed to be exclusive of any other rights to which the indemnified person is entitled, consistent with law, under any provision of the LLC Articles of Organization (or similar organizing document of this LLC) or the LLC operating agreement; as a result of any general or specific action of the members or managers of this LLC; under the terms of any contract; or as may be permitted or required by law.

The LLC may purchase and maintain insurance or provide another arrangement on behalf of any person who is or was a _____ of this LLC against any liability asserted against him or her and incurred in such a capacity or arising out of his or her official capacity with this LLC, whether or not the LLC would have the power to indemnify him or her against that liability under the laws of this state.

AUTHORIZATION OF LOAN TO LLC AT SPECIFIC TERMS

It was announced that the officers of the LLC have received a loan commitment from the following bank, trust company, or other financial institution on the following terms:

Name of Lender: _____

Loan Amount: _____

Terms of the Loan:_____

_____

_____

It was resolved that the proposed terms of the loan are fair and reasonable to the LLC and that it is in the best interests of the LLC to borrow the funds on the terms stated above.

It was further resolved that the following member, manager, or officer is authorized to execute the notes and documents necessary to make the above loan on behalf of the LLC:

Name   Title

_____   _____

_____   _____

AUTHORIZATION OF MAXIMUM LOAN AMOUNT TO LLC

It was resolved that it is in the best interests of the LLC to borrow up to the following amount from the following bank, trust company, or other financial institution:

Name of Lender: _____

Loan Amount:_____

On behalf of the LLC, the following member, manager, or officer is authorized to sign the appropriate notes and documents necessary to borrow an amount that does not exceed the amount noted above, on terms commercially reasonable to the LLC:

Name   Title

_____   _____

_____   _____

AUTHORIZATION OF LLC REPRESENTATIVE TO BORROW FUNDS
ON BEHALF OF LLC AS NEEDED

It was resolved that the following member, manager, or officer of the LLC is authorized to borrow funds on behalf of the LLC from one or more banks or other financial institutions in the amounts he or she decides are reasonably necessary to meet the business needs of the LLC:

Name   Title

_____   _____

_____   _____

AUTHORIZATION OF LOAN TERMS SECURED BY LLC PROPERTY

It was resolved that the following LLC member, manager, or officer is authorized to borrow the sum of

_____ on behalf of the LLC from _____:

Name   Title

_____   _____

_____   _____

The person named above is authorized to execute a promissory note for the principal amount

shown above, together with a mortgage, deed of trust, or security agreement and any other

documents necessary to secure payment of the note with the pledge of the following LLC property:

Property Used as Security for Note: _____

The terms for repayment of the note will be as follows:

Terms of Note: _____.

AUTHORIZATION OF LINE OF CREDIT

It was resolved that it is in the best interests of the LLC to obtain a line of credit for borrowing funds from _____ .

    The following LLC member, manager, or officer is authorized to complete all necessary forms, documents, and notes and to pledge as security for the loan any LLC assets necessary to obtain and use the line of credit:

Name   Title

_____   _____

_____   _____

    It was further decided that the authority granted by this resolution be limited and that the person named above not be allowed to establish a line of credit that exceeds _____ .

AUTHORIZATION OF LINE OF CREDIT WITH CAP
ON EACH TRANSACTION

It was resolved that it is in the best interests of the LLC to obtain a line of credit from

_____.

    The following LLC member, manager, or officer was authorized to complete all necessary forms, documents, and notes necessary to obtain and utilize the line of credit to allow borrowing by the LLC in an aggregate amount that does not exceed _____.

Name

_____

_____

Title

_____

_____

    It was further resolved that the amount borrowed under the line of credit in one transaction will not exceed _____ unless any excess amount is specifically approved by further resolution of the LLC.

AUTHORIZATION OF LINE OF CREDIT
SECURED BY LLC PROPERTY

It was resolved that it is in the best interests of the LLC to obtain a line of credit for borrowing funds

from _____.

The following LLC member, manager, or officer is authorized to complete all necessary forms, documents, and notes and to pledge as security for the loan any LLC assets necessary to obtain and utilize the line of credit:

Name   Title

_____   _____

_____   _____

The person named above is authorized to execute a promissory note for the line of credit amount shown above, together with a mortgage, deed of trust, or security agreement and any other documents necessary to secure payment of the note with the pledge of the following LLC property:

Property Used as Security for Note: _____

The terms for repayment of the note will be as follows:

Terms of Note: _____.

APPROVAL OF LOAN TO THE LLC

It was resolved that it is in the best interests of the LLC to borrow the following amount(s) from the following individuals:

Name of Lender   Amount

_____ $_____

_____ $_____

The terms of each loan were included in a proposed promissory note presented for approval at the meeting. The LLC determined that these terms were commercially reasonable. The LLC also determined that LLC earnings should be sufficient to pay back the loan(s) to the lender(s) according to the terms in the note(s), and that such repayment would not jeopardize the financial status of the LLC.

Therefore, the LLC approved the terms of each note and directed the treasurer to sign each note on behalf of the LLC. The secretary was directed to attach a copy of each note, signed by the treasurer, to this resolution and to place the resolution and the attachment(s) in the LLC records binder.

NOLO
www.nolo.com

LLC PROMISSORY NOTE:
INSTALLMENT PAYMENTS OF PRINCIPAL AND INTEREST
(AMORTIZED LOAN)

For value received, _____, the borrower, promises to pay to

the order of _____, the noteholder, the principal amount of

_____, together with simple interest on the unpaid principal balance from the date

of this note until the date this note is paid in full, at the annual rate of _____%. Payments will be made

at _____.

    Principal and interest will be paid in equal installments of _____, be-

ginning on _____, and continuing on _____ until

the principal and interest are paid in full. Each payment made by the borrower shall be applied first to ac-

crued but unpaid interest, and the remainder will be applied to unpaid principal.

    This note may be prepaid by the borrower in whole or in part at any time without penalty. This note is

not assumable without the written consent of the noteholder. Consent will not be unreasonably withheld.

This note is nontransferable by the noteholder.

    If any installment payment due under this note is not received by the noteholder within _____

of its due date, the entire amount of unpaid principal and accrued but unpaid interest due under this note

will, at the option of the noteholder, become immediately due and payable without prior notice by the

noteholder to the borrower. In the event of a default, the borrower is responsible for the costs of collection,

including, in the event of a lawsuit to collect on this note, the noteholder's reasonable attorney fees as de-

termined by a court hearing the lawsuit.

    Date of Signing: _____

    Name of Borrower: _____

    Address of Borrower:_____

    City, or County, and State Where Signed _____

    Signature of Borrower: _____, Treasurer

    on behalf of _____

LLC PROMISSORY NOTE:
INSTALLMENT PAYMENTS OF PRINCIPAL AND INTEREST
(AMORTIZED LOAN) SECURED BY LLC PROPERTY

For value received, _____, the borrower, promises to

pay to the order of _____, the noteholder, the principal

amount of _____, together with simple interest on the unpaid principal balance from

the date of this note until the date this note is paid in full, at the annual rate of _____. Payments will

be made at _____.

    Principal and interest will be paid in equal installments of _____ , beginning on

_____ , and continuing on _____

until the principal and interest are paid in full. Each payment made by the borrower will be applied first to

accrued but unpaid interest, and the remainder will be applied to unpaid principal.

    This note may be prepaid by the borrower in whole or in part at any time without penalty. This note is

not assumable without the written consent of the noteholder. Consent will not be unreasonably withheld.

This note is nontransferable by the noteholder.

    If any installment payment due under this note is not received by the noteholder within

_____ of its due date, the entire amount of unpaid principal and accrued but un-

paid interest due under this note will, at the option of the noteholder, become immediately due and pay-

able without prior notice from the noteholder to the borrower. In the event of a default, the borrower is re-

sponsible for the costs of collection, including, in the event of a lawsuit to collect on this note, the

noteholder's reasonable attorney fees as determined by a court hearing the lawsuit.

    Borrower agrees that until the principal and interest owed under this note are paid in full, the note is

secured by the following described mortgage, deed of trust, or security agreement:

_____.

Date of Signing: _____

Name of Borrower: _____

Address of Borrower: _____

City, or County, and State Where Signed _____

Signature of Borrower: _____, Treasurer

on behalf of _____

LLC PROMISSORY NOTE:
INSTALLMENT PAYMENTS OF PRINCIPAL AND INTEREST
(AMORTIZED LOAN) WITH BALLOON PAYMENT

For value received, _____, the borrower, promises to pay

to the order of _____, the noteholder, the principal

amount of _____, together with simple interest on the unpaid principal balance

from the date of this note until the date this note is paid in full, at the annual rate of _____.

Payments will be made at _____.

Principal and interest will be paid in equal installments of _____, begin-

ning on _____, and continuing on _____.

On the installment payment date on _____, a balloon payment of

_____ will be added to the installment amount paid by the borrower in order to pay off

this note in its entirety on this final installment payment date. Each payment made by the borrower will be

applied first to accrued but unpaid interest, and the remainder will be applied to unpaid principal.

This note may be prepaid by the borrower in whole or in part at any time without penalty. This note is

not assumable without the written consent of the noteholder. Consent will not be unreasonably withheld.

This note is nontransferable by the noteholder.

If any installment payment due under this note is not received by the noteholder within _____ of

its due date, the entire amount of unpaid principal and accrued but unpaid interest due under this note will,

at the option of the noteholder, become immediately due and payable without prior notice from the

noteholder to the borrower. In the event of a default, the borrower is responsible for the costs of collection,

including, in the event of a lawsuit to collect on this note, the noteholder's reasonable attorney fees as de-

termined by a court hearing the lawsuit.

Date of Signing: _____

Name of Borrower: _____

Address of Borrower:_____

City, or County, and State Where Signed _____

Signature of Borrower: _____, Treasurer

on behalf of _____

LLC PROMISSORY NOTE:
PERIODIC PAYMENTS OF INTEREST
WITH LUMP-SUM PRINCIPAL PAYMENT

For value received, _____, the borrower, promises to pay

to the order of _____, the noteholder, the principal

amount of _____, together with simple interest on the unpaid principal balance

from the date of this note until the date this note is paid in full, at the annual rate of _____.

Payments will be made at _____.

Interest will be paid in equal installments of _____,

beginning on _____, and continuing on the _____

until _____, on which date the entire principal amount, together with total

accrued but unpaid interest, will be paid by the borrower.

This note may be prepaid by the borrower in whole or in part at any time without penalty. This note is

not assumable without the written consent of the noteholder. Consent will not be unreasonably withheld.

This note is nontransferable by the noteholder.

If any installment payment due under this note is not received by the noteholder within

_____ of its due date, the entire amount of unpaid principal and accrued but un-

paid interest due under this note will, at the option of the noteholder, become immediately due and pay-

able without prior notice from the noteholder to the borrower. In the event of a default, the borrower is

responsible for the costs of collection, including, in the event of a lawsuit to collect on this note, the

noteholder's reasonable attorney fees as determined by a court hearing the lawsuit.

Date of Signing: _____

Name of Borrower: _____

Address of Borrower:_____

City, or County, and State Where Signed _____

Signature of Borrower: _____, Treasurer

on behalf of _____

LLC PROMISSORY NOTE:
LUMP-SUM PAYMENT OF PRINCIPAL
AND INTEREST ON SPECIFIED DATE

For value received, _____, the borrower, promises to pay to

the order of _____, the noteholder, the principal amount of

_____, together with simple interest on the unpaid principal balance from the

date of this note until the date this note is paid in full, at the annual rate of _____. Payments

will be made at _____.

The entire principal amount of the loan, together with total accrued but unpaid interest, will be paid by

the borrower on _____. Any payment made by the borrower prior to the due

date specified above will be applied first to accrued but unpaid interest, and the remainder will be applied

to unpaid principal.

This note may be prepaid by the borrower in whole or in part at any time without penalty. This note is

not assumable without the written consent of the noteholder. Consent will not be unreasonably withheld.

This note is nontransferable by the noteholder.

In the event of a default, the borrower is responsible for the costs of collection, including, in the event

of a lawsuit to collect on this note, the noteholder's reasonable attorney fees as determined by a court hear-

ing the lawsuit.

Date of Signing: _____

Name of Borrower: _____

Address of Borrower:_____

City, or County, and State Where Signed _____

Signature of Borrower: _____, Treasurer

on behalf of _____

www.nolo.com   LLC Promissory Note:
                          Lump-Sum Payment of Principal
                          and Interest on Specified Date

LLC PROMISSORY NOTE:
LUMP-SUM PAYMENT OF PRINCIPAL
AND INTEREST ON DEMAND BY NOTEHOLDER

For value received, _____, the borrower, promises

to pay to the order of _____, the noteholder, the

principal amount of _____, together with simple interest on the unpaid

principal balance from the date of this note until the date this note is paid in full, at the annual rate of

_____. Payments will be made at _____.

The entire principal amount of the loan, together with total accrued but unpaid interest, will be paid

within _____ of receipt by the LLC of a demand

for repayment by the noteholder. A demand for repayment by the noteholder will be made in writing and

will be delivered or mailed to the borrower at the following address: _____

_____. If demand for repayment is mailed, it will

be considered received by the borrower on the third business day after the date when it was deposited in

the U.S. mail as registered or certified mail.

Any payment made by the borrower prior to the due date specified above will be applied first to ac-

crued but unpaid interest, and the remainder will be applied to unpaid principal.

This note may be prepaid by the borrower in whole or in part at any time without penalty. This note is

not assumable without the written consent of the noteholder. Consent will not be unreasonably withheld.

This note is nontransferable by the noteholder.

In the event of a default, the borrower is responsible for the costs of collection, including, in the event

of a lawsuit to collect on this note, the noteholder's reasonable attorney fees as determined by a court hear-

ing the lawsuit.

Date of Signing: _____

Name of Borrower: _____

Address of Borrower:_____

City, or County, and State Where Signed _____

Signature of Borrower: _____, Treasurer

on behalf of _____

LLC PROMISSORY NOTE:
SPECIAL SCHEDULE OF PAYMENTS
OF PRINCIPAL AND INTEREST

For value received, _____ , the borrower,

promises to pay to the order of _____ , the

noteholder, the principal amount of _____ , together with simple interest

on the unpaid principal balance from the date of this note until the date this note is paid in full, at the

annual rate of _____ . Payments will be made at _____

_____ .

Principal and interest will be paid as follows:

_____

_____

_____

This note may be prepaid by the borrower in whole or in part at any time without penalty. This note is

not assumable without the written consent of the noteholder. Consent will not be unreasonably withheld.

This note is nontransferable by the noteholder.

If any installment payment due under this note is not received by the noteholder within

_____ of its due date, the entire amount of unpaid principal and accrued but unpaid

interest of the loan will, at the option of the noteholder, become immediately due and payable without prior

notice by the noteholder to the borrower. In the event of a default, the borrower is responsible for the costs

of collection, including, in the event of a lawsuit to collect on this note, the noteholder's reasonable attorney

fees as determined by a court hearing the lawsuit.

Date of Signing: _____

Name of Borrower: _____

Address of Borrower:_____

City, or County, and State Where Signed _____

Signature of Borrower: _____ , Treasurer

on behalf of _____

APPROVAL OF LLC LOAN TO INSIDER

It was resolved it is in the best interests of the LLC to make the following loan to the following persons under the following terms:

Name and Title of Borrower: _____

Principal Amount of Loan: _____

Rate of Interest: _____

Term of Loan: _____

Payment Schedule: _____

    It was further resolved that the above loan could reasonably be expected to benefit the LLC and that the LLC would be able to make the loan without jeopardizing its financial position, including its ability to pay its bills as they become due.

    Therefore, the LLC approved the terms of the note and directed the borrower to sign the note. The secretary was directed to attach a copy of the note, signed by the borrower, to this resolution and to place the resolution and the attachment(s) in the LLC records binder.

NOLO
www.nolo.com
Approval of LLC Loan to Insider

INDIVIDUAL PROMISSORY NOTE:
INSTALLMENT PAYMENTS OF PRINCIPAL
AND INTEREST (AMORTIZED LOAN)

For value received, _____, the borrower(s),
promise(s) to pay to the order of _____, the
noteholder, the principal amount of _____, together with simple
interest on the unpaid principal balance from the date of this note until the date this note is paid in full, at
the annual rate of _____. Payments will be made at _____
_____.

    Principal and interest will be paid in equal installments of _____, beginning
on _____, and continuing on _____
_____ until the principal and interest are paid in full. Each
payment made by the borrower(s) will be applied first to accrued but unpaid interest, and the remainder
will be applied to unpaid principal.

    This note may be prepaid by the borrower(s) in whole or in part at any time without penalty. This note
is not assumable without the written consent of the noteholder. Consent will not be unreasonably withheld.
This note is nontransferable by the noteholder.

    If any installment payment due under this note is not received by the noteholder within
_____ of its due date, the entire amount of unpaid principal and accrued but
unpaid interest due under this note will, at the option of the noteholder, become immediately due and payable without prior notice by the noteholder to the borrower(s). In the event of a default, the borrower(s) is/
are responsible for the costs of collection, including, in the event of a lawsuit to collect on this note, the
noteholder's reasonable attorney fees as determined by a court hearing the lawsuit.

    If two persons sign below, each is jointly and severally liable for repayment of this note.

Name of Borrower #1: _____

Address: _____

City, or County, and State Where Signed: _____

Date of Signing: _____

Name of Borrower #2: _____

Address: _____

City, or County, and State Where Signed: _____

Date of Signing: _____

INDIVIDUAL PROMISSORY NOTE:
INSTALLMENT PAYMENTS OF PRINCIPAL AND INTEREST
(AMORTIZED LOAN) SECURED BY PROPERTY

For value received, _____, the borrower(s), promise(s) to pay to the order of _____, the noteholder, the principal amount of _____ , together with simple interest on the unpaid principal balance from the date of this note until the date this note is paid in full, at the annual rate of _____. Payments will be made at _____.

Principal and interest will be paid in equal installments of _____, beginning on _____, and continuing on _____ until the principal and interest are paid in full. Each payment made by the borrower(s) will be applied first to accrued but unpaid interest, and the remainder will be applied to unpaid principal.

This note may be prepaid by the borrower(s) in whole or in part at any time without penalty. This note is not assumable without the written consent of the noteholder. Consent will not be unreasonably withheld. This note is nontransferable by the noteholder.

If any installment payment due under this note is not received by the noteholder within _____ of its due date, the entire amount of unpaid principal and accrued but unpaid interest of the loan will, at the option of the noteholder, become immediately due and payable without prior notice by the noteholder to the borrower(s). In the event of a default, the borrower(s) is/are responsible for the costs of collection, including, in the event of a lawsuit to collect on this note, the noteholder's reasonable attorney fees as determined by a court hearing the lawsuit.

Borrower(s) agree(s) that until such time as the principal and interest owed under this note are paid in full, the note will be secured by the following described mortgage, deed of trust, or security agreement: _____.

If two persons sign below, each is jointly and severally liable for repayment of this note.

Name of Borrower #1: _____

Address: _____

City, or County, and State Where Signed: _____

Date of Signing: _____

Name of Borrower #2: _____

Address: _____

City, or County, and State Where Signed: _____

Date of Signing: _____

INDIVIDUAL PROMISSORY NOTE:
INSTALLMENT PAYMENTS OF PRINCIPAL AND INTEREST
(AMORTIZED LOAN) WITH BALLOON PAYMENT

For value received,_____, the borrower(s), promise(s) to pay to the order of _____, the noteholder, the principal amount of _____ , together with simple interest on the unpaid principal balance from the date of this note until the date this note is paid in full, at the annual rate of _____. Payments will be made at _____.

Principal and interest will be paid in equal installments of _____, beginning on _____, and continuing on _____. On the installment payment date on _____, a balloon payment of _____ will be added to the installment amount paid by the borrower in order to pay off this note in its entirety on this final installment payment date. Each payment made by the borrower(s) will be applied first to accrued but unpaid interest, and the remainder will be applied to unpaid principal.

This note may be prepaid by the borrower(s) in whole or in part at any time without penalty. This note is not assumable without the written consent of the noteholder. Consent will not be unreasonably withheld. This note is nontransferable by the noteholder.

If any installment payment due under this note is not received by the noteholder within _____ of its due date, the entire amount of unpaid principal and accrued but unpaid interest of the loan will, at the option of the noteholder, become immediately due and payable without prior notice by the noteholder to the borrower(s). In the event of a default, the borrower(s) is/are responsible for the costs of collection, including, in the event of a lawsuit to collect on this note, the noteholder's reasonable attorney fees as determined by a court hearing the lawsuit.

If two persons sign below, each is jointly and severally liable for repayment of this note.

Name of Borrower #1: _____

Address: _____

City, or County, and State Where Signed: _____

Date of Signing: _____

Name of Borrower #2: _____

Address: _____

City, or County, and State Where Signed: _____

Date of Signing: _____

INDIVIDUAL PROMISSORY NOTE:
PERIODIC PAYMENTS OF INTEREST
WITH LUMP-SUM PRINCIPAL PAYMENT

For value received,_____, the borrower(s), promise(s)

to pay to the order of _____, the noteholder, the

principal amount of _____, together with simple interest on the unpaid principal

balance from the date of this note until the date this note is paid in full, at the annual rate of_____.

Payments will be made at _____.

    Interest will be paid in equal installments of _____, beginning on

_____, and continuing on _____ until

_____, on which date the entire principal amount, together with total accrued but unpaid interest, will be paid by the borrower(s).

    This note may be prepaid by the borrower(s) in whole or in part at any time without penalty. This note is not assumable without the written consent of the noteholder. Consent will not be unreasonably withheld. This note is nontransferable by the noteholder.

    If any installment payment due under this note is not received by the noteholder within

_____ of its due date, the entire amount of unpaid principal and accrued but unpaid interest of the loan will, at the option of the noteholder, become immediately due and payable without prior notice by the noteholder to the borrower(s). In the event of a default, the borrower(s) is/are responsible for the costs of collection, including, in the event of a lawsuit to collect on this note, the noteholder's reasonable attorney fees as determined by a court hearing the lawsuit.

    If two persons sign below, each is jointly and severally liable for repayment of this note.

Name of Borrower #1: _____

Address: _____

City, or County, and State Where Signed: _____

Date of Signing: _____

Name of Borrower #2: _____

Address: _____

City, or County, and State Where Signed: _____

Date of Signing: _____

INDIVIDUAL PROMISSORY NOTE:
LUMP-SUM PAYMENT OF PRINCIPAL
AND INTEREST ON SPECIFIED DATE

For value received,_____, the borrower(s), promise(s)

to pay to the order of _____, the noteholder, the

principal amount of _____, together with simple interest on the unpaid principal

balance from the date of this note until the date this note is paid in full, at the annual rate of _____.

Payments will be made at _____.

The entire principal amount of the loan, together with total accrued but unpaid interest, will be paid by

the borrower(s) on _____. Any payment made by the borrower(s) prior to

the due date specified above will be applied first to accrued but unpaid interest, and the remainder will be

applied to unpaid principal.

This note may be prepaid by the borrower(s) in whole or in part at any time without penalty. This note

is not assumable without the written consent of the noteholder. Consent will not be unreasonably withheld.

This note is nontransferable by the noteholder.

In the event of a default, the borrower(s) is/are responsible for the costs of collection, including, in the

event of a lawsuit to collect on this note, the noteholder's reasonable attorney fees as determined by a court

hearing the lawsuit.

If two persons sign below, each is jointly and severally liable for repayment of this note.

Name of Borrower #1: _____

Address: _____

City, or County, and State Where Signed: _____

Date of Signing: _____

Name of Borrower #2: _____

Address: _____

City, or County, and State Where Signed: _____

Date of Signing: _____

INDIVIDUAL PROMISSORY NOTE:
LUMP-SUM PAYMENT OF PRINCIPAL AND INTEREST
ON DEMAND BY NOTEHOLDER

For value received, _____, the borrower(s),
promise(s) to pay to the order of _____, the noteholder, the
principal amount of _____, together with simple interest on the unpaid principal
balance from the date of this note until the date this note is paid in full, at the annual rate of _____.
Payments will be made at _____.

    The entire principal amount of the loan, together with total accrued but unpaid interest, will be paid
within _____ of receipt by the borrower(s) of a demand for repayment by
the noteholder. A demand for repayment by the noteholder will be made in writing and will be delivered or
mailed to the borrower(s) at the following address: _____
_____. If demand for repayment is mailed, it will be considered
received by the borrower(s) on the third business day after the date when it was deposited in the U.S. mail
as registered or certified mail.

    Any payment made by the borrower(s) prior to the due date specified above will be applied first to accrued but unpaid interest, and the remainder will be applied to unpaid principal.

    This note may be prepaid by the borrower(s) in whole or in part at any time without penalty. This note
is not assumable without the written consent of the noteholder. Consent will not be unreasonably withheld.
This note is nontransferable by the noteholder.

    In the event of a default, the borrower(s) is/are responsible for the costs of collection, including, in the
event of a lawsuit to collect on this note, the noteholder's reasonable attorney fees as determined by a court
hearing the lawsuit.

    If two persons sign below, each is jointly and severally liable for repayment of this note.

Name of Borrower #1: _____

Address: _____

City, or County, and State Where Signed: _____

Date of Signing: _____

Name of Borrower #2: _____

Address: _____

City, or County, and State Where Signed: _____

Date of Signing: _____

NOLO
www.nolo.com

Individual Promissory Note:
Lump-sum Payment of Principal and Interest
on Demand by Noteholder

INDIVIDUAL PROMISSORY NOTE:
SPECIAL SCHEDULE OF PAYMENTS
OF PRINCIPAL AND INTEREST

For value received,_____ ,
the borrower(s), promise(s) to pay to the order of _____ ,
the noteholder, the principal amount of _____ , together with simple interest on the
unpaid principal balance from the date of this note until the date this note is paid in full, at the annual rate
of _____ . Payments will be made at _____
_____ .

Principal and interest will be paid as follows:
_____
_____

This note may be prepaid by the borrower(s) in whole or in part at any time without penalty. This note
is not assumable without the written consent of the noteholder. Consent will not be unreasonably withheld.
This note is nontransferable by the noteholder.

If any installment payment due under this note is not received by the noteholder within
_____ of its due date, the entire amount of unpaid principal and accrued
but unpaid interest of the loan will, at the option of the noteholder, become immediately due and payable
without prior notice by the noteholder to the borrower(s). In the event of a default, the borrower(s) is/are responsible for the costs of collection, including, in the event of a lawsuit to collect on this note, the
noteholder's reasonable attorney fees as determined by a court hearing the lawsuit.

If two persons sign below, each is jointly and severally liable for repayment of this note.

Name of Borrower #1: _____

Address: _____

City, or County, and State Where Signed: _____

Date of Signing: _____

Name of Borrower #2: _____

Address: _____

City, or County, and State Where Signed: _____

Date of Signing: _____

RELEASE OF PROMISSORY NOTE

The undersigned noteholder, _____, in consideration

of full payment of the promissory note dated _____ in the principal

amount of _____, hereby releases and discharges the borrower(s),

_____,

_____,

from any claims or obligations on account of the note.

Dated: _____

Name of Noteholder: _____

Signature: _____

[If the LLC is the noteholder, use the following signature lines instead:]

Name of Noteholder: _____

By: _____, Treasurer

on behalf of _____

LLC APPROVAL OF TRANSACTION BENEFITING
A MEMBER OR MANAGER

The members and/or managers of the LLC have considered:_____

_____. It was understood that the following

persons have a material financial interest in this transaction or contract as follows: _____

_____

_____.

    After discussion, it was agreed that the approval of this business was fair to and in the best

interests of the LLC because _____

_____.

Therefore, it was approved by the votes of the members and/or managers as follows:

Name   Vote

_____   _____

_____   _____

Index

■

CATALOG

...more from Nolo

	PRICE	CODE
BUSINESS		
Buy-Sell Agreement Handbook:		
Plan Ahead for Changes in the Ownership of Your Business (Book w/CD-ROM)	$49.99	BSAG
The CA Nonprofit Corporation Kit (Binder w/CD-ROM)	$59.95	CNP
Consultant & Independent Contractor Agreements (Book w/CD-ROM)	$29.99	CICA
The Corporate Minutes Book (Book w/CD-ROM)	$69.99	CORMI
Create Your Own Employee Handbook	$49.99	EMHA
Dealing With Problem Employees	$44.99	PROBM
Drive a Modest Car & 16 Other Keys to Small Business Sucess	$24.99	DRIV
The Employer's Legal Handbook	$39.99	EMPL
Everyday Employment Law	$29.99	ELBA
Federal Employment Laws	$49.99	FELW
Form Your Own Limited Liability Company (Book w/CD-ROM)	$44.99	LIAB
Hiring Independent Contractors: The Employer's Legal Guide (Book w/CD-ROM)	$34.99	HICI
How to Create a Noncompete Agreement	$44.95	NOCMP
How to Form a California Professional Corporation (Book w/CD-ROM)	$59.95	PROF
How to Form a Nonprofit Corporation (Book w/CD-ROM)—National Edition	$44.99	NNP
How to Form a Nonprofit Corporation in California (Book w/CD-ROM)	$44.99	NON
How to Form Your Own California Corporation (Binder w/CD-ROM)	$59.99	CACI
How to Form Your Own California Corporation (Book w/CD-ROM)	$34.99	CCOR
How to Get Your Business on the Web	$29.99	WEBS
How to Write a Business Plan	$34.99	SBS
Incorporate Your Business	$49.95	NIBS
The Independent Paralegal's Handbook	$29.95	PARA
Leasing Space for Your Small Business	$34.95	LESP
Legal Guide for Starting & Running a Small Business	$34.99	RUNS
Legal Forms for Starting & Running a Small Business (Book w/CD-ROM)	$29.99	RUNS2
Marketing Without Advertising	$24.00	MWAD
Music Law (Book w/CD-ROM)	$34.99	ML
Nolo's Guide to Social Security Disability	$29.99	QSS
Nolo's Quick LLC	$24.99	LLCQ
Nondisclosure Agreements	$39.95	NAG
The Small Business Start-up Kit (Book w/CD-ROM)	$29.99	SMBU

Prices subject to change.

ORDER 24 HOURS A DAY @ www.nolo.com

Call 800-728-3555 • Mail or fax the order form in this book

	PRICE	CODE
The Small Business Start-up Kit for California (Book w/CD-ROM)	$34.99	OPEN
The Partnership Book: How to Write a Partnership Agreement (Book w/CD-ROM)	$39.99	PART
Sexual Harassment on the Job	$24.95	HARS
Starting & Running a Successful Newsletter or Magazine	$29.99	MAG
Take Charge of Your Workers' Compensation Claim	$34.99	WORK
Tax Savvy for Small Business	$36.99	SAVVY
Working for Yourself: Law & Taxes for the Self-Employed	$39.99	WAGE
Your Crafts Business: A Legal Guide	$26.99	VART
Your Limited Liability Company: An Operating Manual (Book w/CD-ROM)	$49.99	LOP
Your Rights in the Workplace	$29.99	YRW

CONSUMER

	PRICE	CODE
How to Win Your Personal Injury Claim	$29.99	PICL
Nolo's Encyclopedia of Everyday Law	$29.99	EVL
Nolo's Guide to California Law	$24.95	CLAW
Trouble-Free Travel...And What to Do When Things Go Wrong	$14.95	TRAV

ESTATE PLANNING & PROBATE

	PRICE	CODE
8 Ways to Avoid Probate	$19.99	PRO8
9 Ways to Avoid Estate Taxes	$29.95	ESTX
Estate Planning Basics	$21.99	ESPN
How to Probate an Estate in California	$49.99	PAE
Make Your Own Living Trust (Book w/CD-ROM)	$39.99	LITR
Nolo's Simple Will Book (Book w/CD-ROM)	$36.99	SWIL
Plan Your Estate	$44.99	NEST
Quick & Legal Will Book	$16.99	QUIC

FAMILY MATTERS

	PRICE	CODE
Child Custody: Building Parenting Agreements That Work	$29.99	CUST
The Complete IEP Guide	$24.99	IEP
Divorce & Money: How to Make the Best Financial Decisions During Divorce	$34.99	DIMO
Do Your Own California Adoption: Nolo's Guide for Stepparents and Domestic Partners (Book w/CD-ROM)	$34.99	ADOP
Get a Life: You Don't Need a Million to Retire Well	$24.99	LIFE
The Guardianship Book for California	$39.99	GB
A Legal Guide for Lesbian and Gay Couples	$29.99	LG
Living Together: A Legal Guide (Book w/CD-ROM)	$34.99	LTK
Medical Directives and Powers of Attorney in California	$19.99	CPOA
Using Divorce Mediation: Save Your Money & Your Sanity	$29.95	UDMD

	PRICE	CODE

GOING TO COURT

	PRICE	CODE
Beat Your Ticket: Go To Court and Win! (National Edition)	$19.99	BEYT
The Criminal Law Handbook: Know Your Rights, Survive the System	$34.99	KYR
Everybody's Guide to Small Claims Court (National Edition)	$26.99	NSCC
Everybody's Guide to Small Claims Court in California	$26.99	CSCC
Fight Your Ticket ... and Win! (California Edition)	$29.99	FYT
How to Change Your Name in California	$34.95	NAME
How to Collect When You Win a Lawsuit (California Edition)	$29.99	JUDG
How to Seal Your Juvenile & Criminal Records (California Edition)	$34.95	CRIM
The Lawsuit Survival Guide	$29.99	UNCL
Nolo's Deposition Handbook	$29.99	DEP
Represent Yourself in Court: How to Prepare & Try a Winning Case	$34.99	RYC
Sue in California Without a Lawyer	$34.99	SLWY

HOMEOWNERS, LANDLORDS & TENANTS

	PRICE	CODE
California Tenants' Rights	$27.99	CTEN
Deeds for California Real Estate	$24.99	DEED
Dog Law	$21.95	DOG
Every Landlord's Legal Guide (National Edition, Book w/CD-ROM)	$44.99	ELLI
Every Tenant's Legal Guide	$29.99	EVTEN
For Sale by Owner in California	$29.99	FSBO
How to Buy a House in California	$34.99	BHCA
The California Landlord's Law Book: Rights & Responsibilities (Book w/CD-ROM)	$44.99	LBRT
The California Landlord's Law Book: Evictions (Book w/CD-ROM)	$44.99	LBEV
Leases & Rental Agreements	$29.99	LEAR
Neighbor Law: Fences, Trees, Boundaries & Noise	$26.99	NEI
The New York Landlord's Law Book (Book w/CD-ROM)	$39.99	NYLL
New York Tenants' Rights	$27.99	NYTEN
Renters' Rights (National Edition)	$24.99	RENT
Stop Foreclosure Now in California	$29.95	CLOS

HUMOR

	PRICE	CODE
Poetic Justice	$9.95	PJ

IMMIGRATION

	PRICE	CODE
Becoming A U.S. Citizen: A Guide to the Law, Exam and Interview	$24.99	USCIT
Fiancé & Marriage Visas	$44.95	IMAR
How to Get a Green Card	$29.99	GRN

	PRICE	CODE
Student & Tourist Visas	$29.99	ISTU
U.S. Immigration Made Easy	$44.99	IMEZ

MONEY MATTERS

	PRICE	CODE
101 Law Forms for Personal Use (Book w/CD-ROM)	$29.99	SPOT
Bankruptcy: Is It the Right Solution to Your Debt Problems?	$19.99	BRS
Chapter 13 Bankruptcy: Repay Your Debts	$34.99	CH13
Creating Your Own Retirement Plan	$29.99	YROP
Credit Repair (Quick & Legal Series, Book w/CD-ROM)	$24.99	CREP
Getting Paid: How to Collect form Bankrupt Debtors	$29.99	CRBNK
How to File for Chapter 7 Bankruptcy	$34.99	HFB
IRAs, 401(k)s & Other Retirement Plans: Taking Your Money Out	$34.99	RET
Money Troubles: Legal Strategies to Cope With Your Debts	$29.99	MT
Stand Up to the IRS	$24.99	SIRS
Surviving an IRS Tax Audit	$24.95	SAUD
Take Control of Your Student Loan Debt	$26.95	SLOAN

PATENTS AND COPYRIGHTS

	PRICE	CODE
The Copyright Handbook: How to Protect and Use Written Works (Book w/CD-ROM)	$39.99	COHA
Copyright Your Software	$34.95	CYS
Domain Names	$26.95	DOM
Getting Permission: How to License and Clear Copyrighted Materials Online and Off (Book w/CD-ROM)	$34.99	RIPER
How to Make Patent Drawings Yourself	$29.99	DRAW
Inventor's Guide to Law, Business and Taxes	$34.99	ILAX
The Inventor's Notebook	$24.99	INOT
Nolo's Patents for Beginners	$29.99	QPAT
License Your Invention (Book w/CD-ROM)	$39.99	LICE
Patent, Copyright & Trademark	$39.99	PCTM
Patent It Yourself	$49.99	PAT
Patent Pending in 24 Hours	$29.99	PEND
Patent Searching Made Easy	$29.95	PATSE
The Public Domain	$34.95	PUBL
Trademark: Legal Care for Your Business and Product Name	$39.95	TRD
Web and Software Development: A Legal Guide (Book w/ CD-ROM)	$44.95	SFT

RESEARCH & REFERENCE

	PRICE	CODE
Legal Research: How to Find & Understand the Law	$39.99	LRES

ORDER 24 HOURS A DAY @ www.nolo.com
Call 800-728-3555 • Mail or fax the order form in this book

	PRICE	CODE

SENIORS

Choose the Right Long-Term Care: Home Care, Assisted Living & Nursing Homes	$21.99	ELD
The Conservatorship Book for California	$44.99	CNSV
Social Security, Medicare & Goverment Pensions	$29.99	SOA

SOFTWARE
**Call or check our website at www.nolo.com
for special discounts on Software!**

LeaseWriter CD—Windows	$129.95	LWD1
LLC Maker—Windows	$89.95	LLP1
PatentPro Plus—Windows	$399.99	PAPL
Personal RecordKeeper 5.0 CD—Windows	$59.95	RKD5
Quicken Legal Business Pro 2004—Windows	$79.95	SBQB4
Quicken WillMaker Plus 2004—Windows	$79.95	WQP4

Special Upgrade Offer

Save 35% on the latest edition of your Nolo book

Because laws and legal procedures change often, we update our books regularly. To help keep you up-to-date, we are extending this special upgrade offer. Cut out and mail the title portion of the cover of your old Nolo book and we'll give you **35% off** the retail price of the NEW EDITION of that book when you purchase directly from Nolo. This offer is to individuals only.

Call us today at 1-800-728-3555

Prices and offer subject to change without notice.

ORDER 24 HOURS A DAY @ www.nolo.com
Call 800-728-3555 • Mail or fax the order form in this book

Order Form

Name

Address

City

State, Zip

Daytime Phone

E-mail

Our "No-Hassle" Guarantee

Return anything you buy directly from Nolo for any reason and we'll cheerfully refund your purchase price. No ifs, ands or buts.

☐ Check here if you do not wish to receive mailings from other companies

Item Code	Quantity	Item	Unit Price	Total Price

Method of payment

☐ Check   ☐ VISA   ☐ MasterCard
☐ Discover Card   ☐ American Express

Subtotal	
Add your local sales tax (California only)	
Shipping: RUSH $9, Basic $5 (See below)	
"I bought 3, ship it to me FREE!"(Ground shipping only)	
TOTAL	

Account Number

Expiration Date

Signature

Shipping and Handling

Rush Delivery—Only $9

We'll ship any order to any street address in the U.S. by UPS 2nd Day Air* for only $9!

* Order by noon Pacific Time and get your order in 2 business days. Orders placed after noon Pacific Time will arrive in 3 business days. P.O. boxes and S.F. Bay Area use basic shipping. Alaska and Hawaii use 2nd Day Air or Priority Mail.

Basic Shipping—$5

Use for P.O. Boxes, Northern California and Ground Service.

Allow 1-2 weeks for delivery. U.S. addresses only.

For faster service, use your credit card and our toll-free numbers

**Call our customer service group
Monday thru Friday 7am to 7pm PST**

Phone	1-800-728-3555
Fax	1-800-645-0895
Mail	Nolo
950 Parker St.
Berkeley, CA 94710

**Order 24 hours a day @
www.nolo.com**

more from

N O L O
Law for All

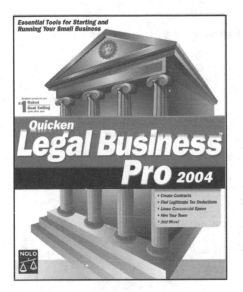

Quicken Legal Business Pro 2004
Windows CD-ROM

Software

SBQB4/$79.95

When starting and running a business, most of the legal work involved simply requires proper forms and reliable information—and with *Quicken Legal Business Pro*, you'll get everything you need to get the job done and save money on legal fees.

The software provides over 140 legal, business, tax and marketing documents—many of which you can complete onscreen with a simple step-by-step interview!

Quicken Legal Business Pro breaks it all down into six categories:

- Starting & Running a Small Business
- Tax Savvy for Small Business
- Everyday Employment Law. The Basics
- Leasing Space for Your Small Business
- Marketing Without Advertising
- Guide to Small Claims Court

Completely searchable, *Quicken Legal Business Pro* is the all-in-one legal resource that every businessperson needs. Give your business the advantage it needs to succeed—get it today!

PLUS

Protect your family, your property and yourself with **Quicken WillMaker Plus!** Create a will, authorizations, living trust, agreements and more on your desktop, quickly and easily.

Want a big discount on *Quicken Legal Software*?

ORDER IT ONLINE AT NOLO.COM

8 0 0 - 7 2 8 - 3 5 5 5 or w w w . n o l o . c o m

Better Business Books

Legal Guide for Starting & Running a Small Business
by Attorney Fred S. Steingold

Small business owners are regularly confronted by a bewildering array of legal questions and problems. Ignoring them can lead to disaster—but *Legal Guide for Starting & Running a Small Business* provides the practical and legal information you need!

$34.99/RUNS

The Small Business Start-Up Kit
A Step-by-Step Legal Guide
by Peri H. Pakroo, J.D.

Book with CD-ROM

Launch your new business quickly and efficiently with this book. User-friendly and loaded with tips, *The Small Business Start-Up* Kit will guide you through the process step by step. Includes all the forms you need both as tear-outs and on CD-ROM.

$29.99/SMBU

The Small Business Start-Up Kit for California
by Peri H. Pakroo, J.D.

Book with CD-ROM

Step-by-step, *The Small Business Start-Up Kit for California* outlines how to set up your enterprise in the Golden State quickly and easily, pointing out the hurdles, fees and forms along the way. Includes all the forms you need as tear-outs and on CD-ROM.

$34.99/OPEN

Form Your Own Limited Liability Company
by Attorney Anthony Mancuso

Book with CD-ROM

The LLC has become the business entity of choice for smaller, privately-held companies. *Form Your Own Limited Liability Company* provides the step-by-step instructions and forms you need to form one in your state, without the expense of hiring a lawyer.

$44.99/LIAB

Tax Savvy for Small Business
by Attorney Frederick W. Daily

Nearly every decision a business makes has tax consequences that affect its bottom line, and the IRS is always watching. Fortunately, it's possible to run an honest business, minimize taxes and stay out of trouble—and this book shows you how.

$34.99/SAVVY

8 0 0 - 7 2 8 - 3 5 5 5   o r   w w w . n o l o . c o m

Little publishers have big ears.
We really listen to you.

Take 2 Minutes & Give Us Your 2 cents

Your comments make a big difference in the development and revision of Nolo books and software. Please take a few minutes and register your Nolo product—and your comments—with us. Not only will your input make a difference, you'll receive special offers available only to registered owners of Nolo products on our newest books and software. Register now by:

PHONE	FAX	EMAIL	or **MAIL** us
1-800-728-3555	1-800-645-0895	cs@nolo.com	this registration card

fold here

- -

NOLO

Registration Card

NAME _____ DATE _____

ADDRESS _____

_____

CITY _____ STATE _____ ZIP _____

PHONE _____ E-MAIL _____

WHERE DID YOU HEAR ABOUT THIS PRODUCT? _____

WHERE DID YOU PURCHASE THIS PRODUCT? _____

DID YOU CONSULT A LAWYER? (PLEASE CIRCLE ONE)   YES   NO   NOT APPLICABLE

DID YOU FIND THIS BOOK HELPFUL?   (VERY)   5   4   3   2   1   (NOT AT ALL)

COMMENTS _____

_____

_____

WAS IT EASY TO USE?   (VERY EASY)   5   4   3   2   1   (VERY DIFFICULT)

We occasionally make our mailing list available to carefully selected companies whose products may be of interest to you.

❑ If you do not wish to receive mailings from these companies, please check this box.

❑ You can quote me in future Nolo promotional materials.
   Daytime phone number _____.

LOP 3.0

Nolo *in the* **NEWS**

"Nolo helps lay people perform legal tasks without the aid—or fees—of lawyers."

—USA TODAY

Nolo books are ..."written in plain language, free of legal mumbo jumbo, and spiced with witty personal observations."

—ASSOCIATED PRESS

"...Nolo publications...guide people simply through the how, when, where and why of law."

—WASHINGTON POST

"Increasingly, people who are not lawyers are performing tasks usually regarded as legal work... And consumers, using books like Nolo's, do routine legal work themselves."

—NEW YORK TIMES

"...All of [Nolo's] books are easy-to-understand, are updated regularly, provide pull-out forms...and are often quite moving in their sense of compassion for the struggles of the lay reader."

—SAN FRANCISCO CHRONICLE

fold here

- -

Place stamp here

Nolo
950 Parker Street
Berkeley, CA 94710-9867

Attn: LOP 3.0